EMBODYING
the Sacred

EMBODYING
the Sacred

WOMEN MYSTICS IN
SEVENTEENTH-CENTURY LIMA

Nancy E. van Deusen

...

Duke University Press   Durham and London   2018

Printed in the United States of America on acid-free paper ∞
Designed by Courtney Leigh Baker
Typeset in Garamond Premier Pro by Copperline Books

Library of Congress Cataloging-in-Publication Data
Names: Van Deusen, Nancy E., author.
Title: Embodying the sacred : women mystics in seventeenth-century Lima /
Nancy E. van Deusen.
Description: Durham : Duke University Press, 2017. |
Includes bibliographical references and index.
Identifiers: LCCN 2017024813 (print)
LCCN 2017042412 (ebook)
ISBN 9780822372288 (ebook)
ISBN 9780822369899 (hardcover : alk. paper)
ISBN 9780822369950 (pbk. : alk. paper)
Subjects: LCSH: Women mystics—Peru—Lima—History—17th century. |
Mysticism—Peru—Lima—History—17th century.
Classification: LCC BV5077.P4 (ebook) | LCC BV5077.P4 V36 2017 (print) |
DDC 282/.85255082—dc23
LC record available at https://lccn.loc.gov/2017024813

Cover art: Collage with details from Laureano Dávila, *Los árboles se inclinan ante Santa Rosa* (eighteenth century).

Contents

Acknowledgments

The cast of characters portrayed in this book has been with me for a long time, their stories simmering in the background as I worked on other projects. Along the road toward the book's completion, I have had the immense pleasure of meeting and engaging with very special individuals who have enriched my life and my historical thinking. They are Christopher Adamo, Kenneth Andrien, Laura Bass, Wendy Brooks, Sherwin Bryant, Kathryn Burns, James Carson, the members of Dance Gallery, Cecilia Danysk, Jason Dyck, Celes Alonso Espinoza Rúa, Javier Augusto Espinoza Ríos, Juan Carlos Estenssoro Fuchs, Javier Flores Espinosa, Lesley Fong, Robert Fong, Serena Fong, Alan Gallay, Luis Miguel Glave, Lori Ames Grant, Pedro Guibovich, Cheryl Gurnsey, Nora Jaffary, George Lovell, Kenneth Mills, Iris Montero, Ramón Mujica Pinilla, Rachel Sarah O'Toole, Ishita Pande, T. Y. Pang (in memoriam), Karen Powers, Joanne Rappaport, Amanda Rodríguez, Neil Safier, Susanne Seales, Tatiana Seijas, Serena Sprungl, Margarita Suárez, Tanya Tiffany, Efraín Trelles, Rafael Varón, Margarita Zegarra, and Ari Zighelboim.

At the various archival repositories and libraries to which I traveled over the decades, I would like to thank Laura Gutiérrez and Melecio Tineo Morón at the Archivo Arzobispal de Lima, Ana María Vega de Zárate (in memoriam) at the Archivo San Francisco de Lima, the staff at the Archivo General de la Nación–Perú, the archivists and staff at the Archivo Histórico Nacional (Madrid), the Archivo General de Indias (Seville), and the librarians at the Biblioteca Nacional del Perú, Lilly Library, the Newberry Library, the Nettie Lee Benson Latin American Collection, and the John Carter Brown Library. I would like to thank the Departments of History and Anthropology at Western Washington University for access to library privileges. In particular, I am grateful for the dedicated research efforts of Marcos Gildemaro Alarcón Olivos, Ilana Aragón Noriega, Patricia Díaz, and Giovanna Valencia. I thank the editors and staff of Duke University Press, including Lisa Bintrim; Mark Mastromarino, the indexer; Kim Miller, the copyeditor; and particularly Gisela Fosado for supporting the project. I would also like to thank the two anonymous readers for their penetrating and wonderful comments. I extend a special thanks to Maureen Garvie for her keen writer's eye. To my parents, Nancy G. and Edwin H. van Deusen, who are still with me and with whom I have been fortunate to share the joys of being a historian and a writer: an infinite "thank you." I would also like to express my deep appreciation for my husband, Preston Schiller, and for our wondrous journey through life together. Finally, I dedicate this book to the memory of my sister, Bonnie Jeanne van Deusen Lavric.

...

Chapter 2 is a slightly modified version of "Reading the Body: Mystical Theology and Spiritual Appropriation in Early Seventeenth-Century Lima," *Journal of Religious History* 33, no. 1 (2009): 1–27. Several paragraphs of chapter 3 appeared in "'In So Celestial a Language': Text as Body, Relics as Text," in *Women's Negotiations and Textual Agency in Latin America, 1500–1799*, edited by Mónica Díaz and Rocío Quispe-Agnoli, 62–81 (New York: Routledge, 2017). Chapter 4 is a modified version of "'The Lord Walks among the Pots and Pans': Religious Servants of Colonial Lima," in *Africans to Spanish America: Expanding the Diaspora*, edited by Sherwin Bryant, Rachel O'Toole, and Ben Vinson III, 136–60 (Urbana: University of Illinois Press, 2012).

Introduction

In his history of Lima, completed in 1639, the Jesuit Bernabé Cobo described the city as the "mystical body" of a "Christian republic." Other observers would have agreed with his characterization of a locale forever "caught up in an endless cycle of liturgical celebration."[1] Processions of statues of popular saints and other public rituals took place on a daily basis. Different religious orders were represented on every street in churches, schools, monasteries, and convents.[2] Some would argue that the gradual transformation of this metropolis into a "baroque theatre state" over the course of the seventeenth century only increased its spiritual and political power.[3] Each hour, the chiming church bells reminded *limeños*, the inhabitants of Lima, of the centrality of the sacred to their lives. Each evening, bells tolled on behalf of the dead during the *toque de animas*, and heads nodded in unison in prayer, uniting the living faithful and fleshless souls.[4] The exemplary religiosity displayed by its populace, Cobo suggested, was the city's principal ornament; it allowed Lima to live up to its reputation as the American epicenter of baroque Catholic culture.[5] In the greater scheme of things, the *urbs* (city) was an integral part of the supernatural and divine order. Like the Eucharist, the City of Kings was a consecrated space and a territorial container for the fully divine and fully human body of Christ.[6]

Lima was therefore seen as a *cuerpo místico*, itself part of a larger, organic soul, with each member contributing to the well-being of the two corporate republics of Spaniards and Indians.[7] Given the variety of people from Asia, America, Europe, and Africa migrating to and living in the lively viceregal capital, it is not surprising that distinct manifestations of Catholicism should make up the substance of daily life.

The purpose of this volume is to consider the variety and complexity of individual and collective spiritual pathways taken by renowned and lesser-known women religious figures—including nuns, laywomen, and beatas—in seventeenth-century Lima, many of whom knew one another. I explore the humanity of their acts of charity, their engagement with material objects, and the meanings of their interiorized visions, revelations, and mystical communion as expressed in narrative accounts of their lives. I argue that as women experienced moments of spiritual transformation, they engaged in innovative and powerful ways with the material and immaterial worlds of early modern Catholicism.[8]

In colonial Lima, Peru, one of the two viceregal capitals of the early modern Spanish Empire, women chose a spiritual vocation based on faith, often without knowing where their journeys would lead. Thousands of females lived lives of simple piety in a body politic that encompassed both church (*el cuerpo místico*) and state (*el cuerpo político*).[9] In their ongoing search for the sacred and in their actualization of their piety, they hoped that the pathways they followed, whether inside or outside a monastic setting, would ultimately lead to closer direct, mystical union with God and, perhaps, salvation.

In the stories of the lives of these mystics and deeply pious women we follow the plurality of human impulses that led to the metamorphosis of Catholicism in the "organic soul" of colonial Lima. This book focuses primarily on women and their life narratives, but, in doing so, it underscores the multifarious nature of early modern Iberian Catholicism as it was experienced by all colonial vassals, female or male, and European, African, or Native American.[10] The heterogeneous diffusion and transformation of key theological notions by women facing different kinds of constraints and possibilities was part of this monotheistic religion's richness, adaptability, and perseverance.[11] Women could work as servants in convents, beg for food on the streets, or live in a viceregal palace and still experience the transcendence of the divine.

Expressions of piety ranged from modest to grandiose. Catholics believed that through private acts of faith they could draw closer to God. They whispered supplications to any of the number of saintly individuals from Lima who were being promoted for beatification in Rome, hoping that, in exchange for their veneration, the saints would offer them protection. Maidens or long-married and elderly couples might opt to take formally sanctioned vows of celibacy, thus effectuating monastic-like vows within lay society.[12] Catholics also believed that they could access divinity through holy material objects, and nowhere was this more evident than in the microcosm of the home. Most households contained religious images; families read hagiographic texts and regularly discussed theological issues that departed from orthodox ideas of the supernatural. In their actions, limeños engaged continually with relics and images of saints—both local and European—in their supplications for health, wealth, and safety. If we consider, for example, the manner in which colonial vassals appropriated saints in their different incarnations—as relics, shrines, paintings, or statues—we see how the belief that sacred energy could manifest in material objects (that were intended to represent the original person) was embedded in praxis.[13]

In the seventeenth century, "sacred materialities" mattered a great deal. David Morgan defines this construct in terms of the features of physical objects, as well as the cultural spaces in which these objects were "produced, consumed, exchanged and displayed."[14] Sacred objects are mentioned in manifold ways in documents, but historians can easily overlook them or consider them only as a part of the mise-en-scène they are trying to depict. But sacred objects were important not only for their symbolic content but also for the ways in which they were actualized and appropriated by women who employed their senses to mediate what they deemed to be holy. Understanding how the sacred became "real" to women is key to understanding the gendered nature of female spiritual expression, which could occur in the most quotidian of ways. Limeñas embodied the sacred when they wore scapulars near their hearts and jeweled sacred images pinned to their cloaks. They embodied the sacred as they arranged freshly cut flowers on altars or cut their hair as a symbol of their complete rejection of the world. Expressions of devotion toward the divine could occur at a moment's notice or take the form of lavish, scripted gestures. Anyone could engage with the supernatural world—by gazing at a portrait of the Christ child, snipping a piece of a garment still gracing a holy corpse, or stitching birds and flowers on the banners to be carried in a procession by a venerated saint's confraternity. Divinity was present in the mundane.

Sacred acts and actions were also gendered. Pious women might take calculated risks, engaging in behaviors that would lead some to see them as conforming to orthodox Catholic tenets, but others to condemn them for excessive pride or self-aggrandizement. María Jacinta Montoya (1645–1710), one of the mystics considered in this volume, had to navigate the fine line between arrogance and respectability in how she represented herself before ecclesiastical authorities. She was an esteemed figure in Lima, the governess of a lay pious institution called a *beaterio*, and the wife of the saintly indigenous tailor Nicolás de Ayllón (1632–77), whose beatification hearings began soon after his death. Like other women, Montoya interpreted the tenets of Catholicism in creative ways. She was a writer, an advocate, and a mystic (someone chosen by God to channel divine knowledge). In her understanding, theology meant scrutinizing the soul's interior under the steady guidance of a confessor or experiencing a wordless comprehension of the divine alone in a spare monastic cell. Female mystics seeking an internal path toward God might express their beliefs in the ineffable by engaging with holy, venerated objects; by uttering prayers they knew by heart; or by entering a state of mystical rapture. That is not to say that men did not perform the same actions. But these women's cultural opportunities and constraints, ideas of self in relation to others and particularly to God, and venues for written and verbal expression were uniquely feminine.

This book focuses on female religiosity in part because, by 1700, Lima was indeed a city of women raising the hems of their skirts as they stepped into carriages or navigated the muddy streets. Fifty-eight percent of limeños were female. Accustomed to having their husbands, fathers, or brothers leave for the silver-rich city of Potosí in Bolivia, bounteous coastal estates, or faraway Atlantic and Pacific ports, they ran households and were often the de facto center of families. Many women operated small businesses selling slaves or merchandise, or earned income from renting properties or plots. In a metropolis with a wealthy Spanish aristocratic minority and a large plebeian majority, one-quarter of all women lived independently from men in their own dwellings. Dozens of unhappily married women sought annulments or divorces (legal separations) before the ecclesiastical court.[15]

Certain sacred spaces were uniquely female, however. In this viceregal capital, home to the royal court (the Audiencia, established in 1542), the seat of the archbishopric and the Inquisition tribunal, 20 percent of females lived in convents, *recogimientos* (institutions of enclosure and education for women and girls), *beaterios* (lay pious houses generally affiliated with a religious order), or smaller, informal establishments, as nuns, *donadas* (religious servants), boarders, schoolgirls, servants, or slaves.[16] Entering any one of the dozen convents for life or on a temporary basis a popular option. Even if a female did not spend time in a convent, she knew an aunt, sister, or daughter of a servant or slave who had. Girls and women entered the cloistered domain for different reasons and at different stages of their lives. Girls of Spanish heritage might enter at a tender age to be schooled, leaving years later with an institutional imprimatur that enhanced their chances of a favorable betrothal to the worthiest of suitors. Convents were also spaces that reinforced hierarchies of difference based on lineage, ethno-racial categories, or economic status. Only women of Spanish or mestiza heritage could become nuns of the black veil (the highest rank) or white veil (the second-highest rank). The only option available to women of African or indigenous descent was to take informal vows as *donadas* or to work as *criadas* (personal servants).

Devout women who preferred life in *el siglo* (the world) might become *beatas*, or lay pious women who were affiliated with the third rule of the regular clergy, which included the Franciscans, Dominicans, Mercedarians, and Augustinians. They might also seek the counsel of Jesuit priests. Some beatas lived alone or informally in a community with other women. To survive, they formed broadly based consanguine and fictive kinship ties with other families, including with women (married or single, elite or disenfranchised) who later took their vows as poor nuns in convents. Others worked as servants in the homes of wealthy benefactors. Facing poverty, unemployment, marital strife, or issues with child care or health, these women supported one another as they attempted to eke out meager livings: changing the bandages of the infirm in hospitals, requesting alms for the poor, or sewing mattresses for convents.[17] After 1660 the foundation of several formal institutions called *beaterios* allowed women of modest means to take vows as beatas; many of them were genuinely committed to social assistance and education efforts.[18] Life as a poor tertiary (a synonym for *beata*) was their only option, since the required large dowry prevented them from entering a convent.[19]

Others had different reasons for disavowing a monastic life. When Feliciana de Jesús (1600–64) came to Lima from the northern city of Trujillo, she feared that convent life would be too confining.[20] At the age of fifteen, she took her vows as a tertiary, while Isabel (Rosa) Flores de Oliva (1586–1617, canonized in 1671 as Santa Rosa) was still alive, and sought her advice. Like the hundreds of female migrants to Lima in the early seventeenth century, Feliciana sought gainful employment as one of the dozens of lay religious employed by the city's convents and monasteries.[21] She supported herself, her mother, and her sister by arranging flowers and gardening. She also gained a reputation as a skilled seamstress by stitching linens. Even then, she was barely able to pay for her small room in the humble neighborhood of San Lázaro; as curtains she used "paper (or cards) stamped with images of saints to whom she was devoted, and especially [those of] Our Lady."[22]

Despite the strict cloistering in convents and beaterios mandated by the Council of Trent (1545–63), beatas actively participated in the broader Lima community as prophets, mystics, healers, and teachers.[23] Because of their charitable efforts, several beatas were recognized by the Lima community as being living saints or worthy of sanctification.[24] The most celebrated, the aforementioned Rosa (Isabel Flores de Oliva), who died in 1617, set the *pri-*

mus inter pares example for a number of poor and wealthy women in Lima to emulate.[25] Even after several beatas were sentenced by the Inquisition for false sanctity in 1625, tertiaries continued to thrive in Lima. Most of these women were not recognized by the Lima community as worthy of sanctification, but documents such as wills, inventories, and divorce proceedings reveal them leading quiet, pious lives and engaging in charitable activities. These beatas were not the *alumbradas* (false mystics) or sorceresses demonized in Inquisition proceedings, sources on which scholars often rely too heavily to understand female devotional practices.[26] If we compare Inquisition-generated sources with other documents, a more balanced view of female experiences and concerns emerges.

Not only did pious women inhabit institutional spaces reserved for their gender, but many spent a great deal of time in each other's company, dressing statues about to be carried in procession, witnessing a moment of rapture in a friend's home, or kneading dough in convents. Clustered in private and public settings, women labored, bickered, and imparted their innermost thoughts.[27] Hierarchical differences based on *calidad* (categorizations based on physicality, occupation, and other criteria) distinguished the kinds of opportunities that women of Spanish or African descent, orphans, or women with aristocratic surnames had in those public and private spaces.[28] On outings to Mass or any of the religious festivities that occurred on a daily basis, for instance, elite women of Spanish descent would surround themselves with a retinue of female servants and slaves. Mistresses and servants alike, some adorned in "a thousand silks," covered their faces with lace veils and devotional scapulars and embellished their lavish apparel with jeweled medallions. Less affluent women, concerned with the mouths they had to feed, might wear a simple gold-lacquered cross inherited from their mothers, a coarser cloth shrouding their heads.

Females learned about the sacred from other women. Lay and religious women apprenticed with one another; they studied recondite secrets in each other's homes, in convent vestibules, or in the churches they frequented. From sermons they understood how sins received particular punishments, and why it was so necessary for souls to gain assistance. From visions they learned to "see" and "hear" the multitudes of needy souls. In churches they read the narrative details of paintings depicting naked souls caught in flames and reaching for redemption.[29] Learning about the lives of medieval female saints facilitated a sororial dialogue connecting past and present.

In gender-specific locations, and in shared company, women iterated their social positioning vis-à-vis other women in an exchange of material objects and theological ideas.[30] Women carried in processions crosses and banners they had sewn, or stood on the edge of a crowd hoping to get a glimpse of a passing statue, or collected grains of earth from the tomb of a recently deceased "saint." These public spaces were not exclusive to women; men could inhabit the same "physical" space: a church vestibule, the marketplace, or the streets where processions passed by. But they did not participate in the interactions and exchanges that occurred there in the same ways.[31] Women also created patterns of habitual movement as they traveled from their homes into public spaces—plazas, hospitals, and churches—and facilitated the everyday "performance of gender."[32] On their daily routines they would pass by one or more of the female institutions that distinguished each city block, thus enhancing their epistemological understandings of what it meant to be female in seventeenth-century Lima.[33]

How to Write a History of Female Catholic Religiosity

Scholars who study female Catholic religiosity in the late medieval and early modern periods often engage historian Joan Kelly's classic argument in her article "Did Women Have a Renaissance?" that women lost status in the Renaissance period and beyond.[34] Those who follow this line of argumentation argue that female mystics often experienced oppression under the Inquisition or other censorious ecclesiastical figures but that they also manifested gendered forms of authority in navigating patriarchal constraints.[35] This volume takes as a given that women continually faced specific, gendered limitations, some of them severe, and that they were sometimes perceived and treated as inferior beings.[36] Masculine biases against pious women were further complicated by perceived differences in European, African, or indigenous American heritage; the strength of family connections; and economic constraints, as well as physical appearance and dress. But feminine expressions of spirituality were generally not manifested to counter male oppression or subvert ideological constructs, since the ultimate goal for pious women was spiritual self-transformation on behalf of others. Spiritual self-transcendence involved submitting to God's will, but it was a process that empowered women and gave them spiritual authority in the eyes of others.[37] If transcendence involved women experiencing the divine beyond form or substance, it also meant conveying in language "what is there."[38]

Moreover, males and females were not opposite poles on a religious spectrum: they often collaborated and cooperated to produce new forms of Catholic expression.[39] Deeply pious, spiritual men also lived under the watchful gaze of Inquisition bureaucrats; they too risked adapting the complexities of Catholicism to their own conceptualizations of the divine, to their own palette of understanding. But a gendered study of masculine religiosity in Lima has yet to be written.[40]

Generally, considerations of how early modern women acquired theological knowledge emphasize the pivotal nature of the confessorial relationship and the dominant role confessors played in women's lives. Confessors were responsible for ensuring that their female protégées were following orthodox practices. They were also authorized to represent their pious confessees in hagiographic and other writings that described visions, supernatural healings, and prophecies. These accounts would determine how the women would be remembered and accessed in the centuries to come. But these unequal power-laden relationships could, as Jodi Bilinkoff and John Coakley have shown, be mutually constituting and filled with tenderness and affinity.[41] Furthermore, although "dominant male personalities" certainly played a key role in many women's lives, their influence needs to be seen in tandem with the intimate spiritual relations that developed among women. The "binomial relationship between confessor and holy woman" formed only one aspect of the circulation and expression of mystical knowledge.[42]

Men were continually present in women's lives, but at times they stood in the background. There were the confessors who loaned women books or offered them sage advice, or the authors of *vidas* who scripted the lives of some of the female subjects considered in this volume. Male ecclesiastical authorities regularly co-opted the words and experiences of women for their own glorification, and women had to gain or maintain their support. Pious women still referenced their deceased, saintly husbands, or how the women had defied formidable brothers and imposing archbishops. But this book is a history about women who were at the center of a small universe. It seeks to convey their individual and collective experiences of the sacred but does not take as a given that the categories of "female mystic" or "pious woman" were stable ontological categories. Rather, this book's exploration of the sacred— itself a complex array of practices—questions some of the universalizing representations of female piety in a new way. It takes as its foundation "the relentless interrogation of the taken-for-granted" and explores unspoken assumptions about femininity.[43] At the same time, it moves the lens away from dissecting patriarchal discourses or analyzing how women negotiated or resisted the strictures of the female pious self. Instead, it moves the discussion of piety into the realm of relationality with other women and objects and, with the exception of chapter 5, away from a consideration of the oppositional binary of "male" and "female." Moreover, the book's methodologies do not ask the reader to make a false choice between representation and discourse, on the one hand, and the lived experiences of women, on the other. Instead, it centers on female sensorial, linguistic, and relational resonances with the sacred at a particular historical place and time.

Admittedly, part of the problem of seeing pious "women" as continually navigating misogynist discourse (overcoming one's weak nature, for one) is in the nature of male-generated sources. A heavy reliance on Inquisition records has led to the general assumption that female expressions of piety threatened society more broadly. The presence of one of three Spanish-American Inquisition tribunals in Lima in 1570 determined the parameters of orthodox and unorthodox female religiosity and pursued disciplinary measures to ensure that women conformed to those guidelines. As the seventeenth century progressed, the tendril-like inquisitorial bureaucracy insinuated itself into the private domain of limeños, enabling authorities to determine whether Lima's Catholic subjects (excluding Indians) were abiding by the Catholic canon.[44] In the locus of Lima, female mystics and beatas were particularly susceptible to being scrutinized and discredited. Although men were tried more often than women for crimes of minor and major heresy, women were punished more severely if proven guilty. Thus, these records would have us believe that an increased criminalization of female piety corresponded to the Inquisition's active interventions to constrain and persecute women.[45]

It is important to keep in mind that Inquisition authorities, not the women placed on trial, drew the line in the sand that defined orthodox and deviant conduct.[46] One could accept at face value the assertion of one ecclesiastical authority who described the gathering of some lay pious women in 1622 as a "grangería de raptos"—a commercialization of ecstatic raptures.[47] Certainly this view came to predominate in a major sea change that occurred in the early 1620s among the upper echelon of the Jesuits and regular orders.[48] But beyond the disparaging portrayals of contemporary female spiritual practices, and beyond the valorizations that codified the experiences of pious women as "false" inventions (or what might later be characterized as Freudian hysteria), lies a wealth of information about the complex and contradictory gendered notions of spirituality in daily life.[49]

Despite the watchful presence of the Inquisition and a devaluation of female sanctity, a spiritual renaissance and a "feminization of piety" characterized by affective spirituality, visionary experiences, contemplation, penitential asceticism, and suffering in imitation of Christ was occurring in the vibrant urbs.[50] A broad constituency of devoted Catholics—from ecclesiastical superiors to mendicant widows to beatas—embraced the practice of *interioridad*, deep, internal spiritual contemplation.[51] Performing external manifestations of faith was also a key component of female piety; good works, including charity toward the dispossessed, were integral to female expressions of conformity to God's will.[52] Mystics might suffer bodily on behalf of the souls in purgatory, but they also took on the suffering of the infirm and the poor by begging for alms or sewing linens for hospitals.

In an urban environment where inward piety and external displays of charity were not only promoted but much admired, healers, nuns, beatas, and sorceresses developed personal contacts and fomented important spiritual networks.[53] One could argue that feminine knowledge of the sacred in this period was often based less on formal learning than on what was "spiritually experienced" (*experimentado*), which transpired both corporeally and through visions.[54] Learning about the sacred could occur through word of mouth, through personal tutoring, or through the *imitatio morum*—literally, the "imitation of ways" of pious authorities, both male and female. It could also occur in the process of imparting understandings of specific texts, religious icons, or a body in rapture. By being in each other's company and by sharing knowledge of the divine, women developed cognitive maps of the ineffable and feminine understandings of theological matters.[55] They shared religious ideas about the self in relation to God, sin, notions of the corporeal and immaterial body, and the power of the material to manifest the divine. They also imparted to other women the centrality of service to the infirm or poor, the meaning of monastic vows, and ideas about what constituted a saint.[56]

If an overreliance on Inquisition records has led to a false reading of how early modern women conceptualized unorthodox and orthodox conduct, so too we have tended to identify the spiritual practices of "sorceresses" as distinct from those of "nuns." Generally, we associate predictions and incantations with sorceresses, but nuns and beatas regarded by limeños as virtuous and saintly also invoked the spirit worlds through distinct means—spells, prayers, or self-flagellation—to alleviate poverty, illness, or marital strife.[57] That can be explained by the fact that, for limeños of all walks of life, the line between religion and the supernatural was opaque. "Magicality," or the belief that divinity was ubiquitous and readily accessible in material form, was integral to daily life.[58] Magicality could be made manifest by silently appealing to Jesus or Mary or by placing earth from the tomb of a venerated mystic on an afflicted area. Incantations to aid in healing the infirm or finding a lost object might mix orthodox, bona fide and magical practices.

Nuns commonly pleaded with the saints to intervene on behalf of distressed patrons, and they shared visions and prognostications with the members of the religious community or visitors in the *locutorio* (visitors' parlor).[59] In her Inquisition hearing in 1592, doña Isabel de Angulo, accused of sorcery, responded that she had learned "holy incantations" and rituals from nuns in Seville.[60] When Gerónima de San Francisco, a discalced nun of the Monasterio de las Descalzas de San José (or San Joseph), heard that a woman had not given birth to her stillborn child for three days, she located an old cord once worn by a friar, cleaned it, and prayed to Saint Francis for a miracle while the afflicted woman held the object against her swollen belly and successfully expelled the dead child.[61] Even Santa Rosa, known for performing major miracles, also participated in more mundane, "magical" spiritual practices. She once predicted that a fugitive slave would return to work the following day; she helped cure an *india* (female Indian or indigenous) servant working in a convent.[62] Secular and ecclesiastical authorities lauded the ability of Isabel de Porras Marmolejo (1551–1631), the former governess of the Colegio del Carmen, a school for elite girls, to heal the sick by making the sign of the cross over the afflicted area.[63] Just as female religious were involved in so-called esoteric practices, the activities of so-called sorceresses were generally not the result of megalomania or harmful intentions; on the contrary, they formed the economic and spiritual manna of daily life.[64] In spite of the wishes of Inquisition authorities, the desire to control the unknown operated along a continuum where the boundaries between life and death, the quotidian and the esoteric, were not readily distinguishable. In churches, markets, small apartments, and crowded convents, laywomen and nuns shared perceptions that combined the heretical and the fantastic with the theologically sound.[65]

Biography and Autobiography, Person and Object

As difficult as it is to discern how women established networks inside and outside institutional settings, or to gain an understanding of their shared experiences of orthodox and unorthodox beliefs from extant sources, it is also sometimes difficult to determine where the life of a pious woman began and ended. Thus, we turn to biographies and autobiographies to frame life events into narratives with beginnings and endings that create a believable "truth." As a genre, spiritual vidas (life writings) are like autobiographies and biographies in that they focus on key events and transitions in an individual's life, and emphasize the impact on others of the subject's actions, gestures, and words.[66] A vida might be published or unpublished, and its author might be the nun or mystic herself, a confessor, or some other religious authority.[67] In the medieval and early modern periods, dozens of autobiographic vidas were written by women in Spain and Spanish America at the bequest of their spiritual confessors. Dozens more spiritual biographies were written by male ecclesiastics (occasionally ones penned by nuns would remain in manuscript form) hoping to promote a female candidate for sainthood.[68]

Like biographies and autobiographies, vidas stress their subjects' major achievements but also emphasize their heroic virtues of charity, prudence, love, and fortitude.[69] They follow the canonical conventions of the period, conventions that were constrained by how the saintly characteristics of the candidate for beatification or canonization should be crafted, the construction of the timeline of the "life" from childhood to death and beyond, and the kinds of miracles that would attract attention in Rome. Vidas might be book length or only take up several folios in the larger histories of a given order (called *crónicas conventuales*).[70] The sources on which vidas were based included confessional narratives as well as the notes (*apuntamientos*) left by confessors or nuns.

That being said, vidas had their own methodological baggage distinguishing them from more conventional biographies and autobiographies. They were meant to demonstrate irrefutably that the female mystic had manifested extraordinary devotion to God and had been chosen by God to be a voice of divinity and to act on behalf of others. Although vidas provide important insights into popular religious beliefs and female spiritual practices, they must be used with caution, since they tend to reveal more about imagined, gendered notions of female sanctity than about women's creative interpretations of theology.[71] Moreover, contemporary notions of physical and cultural difference, including the relationship between whiteness and purity, also determined how archetypes of white saints and saints of color came into being.[72]

Produced in a specific context at a specific time, these texts and their conventions were shaped by local historical contingencies and intended for specific audiences.[73] Just as the mystic's exemplary life was scripted to conform to specific conventions related to heroic virtues, vidas were meant to convey a sense of spiritual truth *in time*.[74] Time in these texts could be a chronological simulation of the woman's life (*chronos*), or it could follow certain annual liturgical events in Christ's or a saint's life (*kairos*). The writings of or about female mystics shared a common discourse sometimes dating back to the medieval period as women mimicked the emplotment of one another's life stories.[75] Women's self-portrayals also engaged in sororial dialogue with the written accounts of their medieval and early modern predecessors, linking (and integrating) past and present lives *across* space and time.[76] This literary connection concatenated time and space in new ways. For example, the unpublished vida of Gerónima de San Francisco (written on the orders of her confessor in 1635) was at once deeply personal as well as highly scripted and predictable. Gerónima's conscious attempt to mimic the structure and contents of other female vidas, like that of the Spanish Carmelite nun and mystic Teresa de Ávila (1515–82), was by no means unusual. Because it closely followed contemporary canons of hagiographic writings and engaged with some of the ideas expressed by Teresa de Ávila, it was more than a simple biography. It was also a composite of "biographies" and intricately linked to a larger canon of writings by female mystics.[77] Teresa de Ávila in particular served as a model for seventeenth-century female writers. She was canonized in 1622, and her vida (or that written by her confessor), mystical treatises, and regulations for her Carmelite nuns provided written guidelines for seventeenth-century mystics in Spain and Latin America wishing to pursue similar paths.[78] Given the intersected nature of vidas, how, then, do we as readers navigate the temporal and structural parameters of life narratives and still gain a sense of both extemporaneity and authorship in them? What is their relationality?

Beatification hearings provide another rich source by which to study the gendered nature of female religious practices and beliefs. These *procesos* had two stages—the ordinary or diocesan stage and the apostolic one—which might lead to the beatification and, ultimately, canonization of the holy person in question. Initiated by the Vatican in Rome, the hearings were inquiries that followed an established set of questions about the virtues and miracles of the saintly candidate, which scores of witnesses were required to answer. Although the questions were somewhat formulaic, respondents' answers often included unrehearsed stories and vibrant particulars, especially during the first, diocesan phase.[79] This material would later be excerpted and recast or rescripted into published or unpublished vidas that fit canonical norms of virtuous conduct.[80]

The purpose of vidas, and, to a lesser extent, beatification *procesos*, was to demarcate a "life" within the ideal gendered parameters of sanctity. This contrasts with Inquisition trials meant to delineate which spiritual practices deviated from orthodox norms. Inquisition proceedings (or the summaries of them) present another kind of challenge in finding a woman's voice because of the structural nature of procedures to be followed, the line of questioning, and the time and manner in which they were produced.[81] Nevertheless, in the responses of female mystics answering charges that they were engaged in heretical or delusional practices, we can detect certain truths about how they negotiated sanctity and gendered practices.[82] There are fissures within their portrayals of constraint and conformity. There are glimmerings of the sacred in the mundane. Even within the rigid interrogation framework and structuring of narratives about unorthodox conduct, elements of spontaneity can be found, as Stacey Schlau argues. The devil is in the details.[83]

It is also possible to find the multivalent locations of female voice in other kinds of sacred materialities: texts that include petitions, the female body in ecstasy, or a list of relics.[84] These too were "readable" texts, as historian Roger Chartier argues. Texts, he posits, "did not necessarily come in book form: some were orally produced works, or visions which were then rendered into a narrative structure using language and symbols to invite interpretation and appropriation."[85] Descriptions of a female body in ecstasy and a list of relics of the living and dead were texts containing voice, plot, and a sense of change over time. Documentary fragments, including the rather formulaic, two-sentence *autos de ingreso* (entrance petitions) and *expedientes de profesión* (profession documents) of girls and women seeking to enter convents as donadas, contain biographical elements. When considered in the aggregate, they produce prosopographical narratives that enhance our understanding of the desires, constraints, and possibilities of spiritual expression for young women, many of them women of color. These bits and pieces representing human experience can be communicated, translated, and assimilated into story form.[86] In sum, the kind of text, its form of transmission (orally, in writing, or through a visual performance), and its reception (how the "language" of that text was received by means of the senses) help explain how sacred texts were created and how we might use them.

Each of the six chapters in this volume considers a variety of sources to re-create autobiographies and biographies in the broadest sense of the term. In general, our understanding of female saints comes from examining how they were appropriated and emplotted as characters into an already known story. We know the beginnings and endings of saints' lives because of the subjective renderings made by others in beatification and Inquisition procesos, and in unpublished or published hagiographies.[87] We know how renowned pious women were supposed to behave, because written accounts or oral testimonies (in beatification hearings, for example) recounted specific supernatural events that were then used to construct spiritual vidas or to promote the women's candidacy for beatification or canonization. As students, we are trained to distinguish between the narrating and the narrated self.[88] We pay attention to the selves in these texts, since there were the "I's" in the past (the observer and the observed in the past) and the "I's" in the present reflecting on the past while constituting a narrative in the present.[89]

But what if we look at the creation of the subject and the emplotment of events (who did what when) in the saint's life in another way? According to Michel de Certeau, mystical practices created new spaces (texts) from which spirit could speak and from which different *biographical* utterances were rendered knowable.[90] Thus, if we consider the objects with which Rosa de Lima interacted as narrative fragments, we can explain how she used them to teach theological principles to her disciples.[91] Exchanges of knowledge were taking place, even if they are scarcely visible in the written account. These objects are integral to Rosa's story and that of her disciples. If we step back and observe the observer observing the mystic do something with something or someone (the event fragment that will help unify the narrative thread), we can see the narrator recounting an event where learning and creating meaning vis-à-vis her engagement with objects and with each other occurred simultaneously.[92] Material objects were often the intermediaries between a mystic and her audience, and between the processes of communication and reception. The *interrelationality* of religious expression and the communication of ideas and meaning is, therefore, key to deepening our understanding of early modern female spirituality.

This book's first section, "Material and Immaterial Embodiment," consists of three chapters and argues that the biography of things is the story of their classifications, renderings, valuations, and performances.[93] Things have "thingness," but they also have a social life because of how they are perceived, adopted, and utilized. Sacred material objects like statues, cloth, and relics contain biographical elements, and stories about the relationality between humans and objects inform one another. Early modern individuals employed their somatic literacy to access what was divinely alive in these ever-changing sacred objects. Sacred objects or "holy matter" might include relics, contact relics (things that the saint or holy person had touched), and devotional images such as statues. But these things were also believed to have cultural meaning in themselves. Their thingness or capacity to convey divine ineffability was also what made limeñas covet and engage with them. They were believed to be loci where profound religious exploration might occur.[94] That being said, religious objects differed in how they were conceptualized and consumed.[95] There were differences, for instance, in how a mystic engaged with a statue of the baby Jesus, a deceased nun's finger bone, or a swatch from a garment once worn by a holy individual. Moreover, because Catholics believed they could also objectify the body of the mystic (not the flesh-

and-blood self), people interpreted and "read" bodies as mystical texts. Furthermore, relics, or holy body fragments of the living or the dead, could also convey biographical information about the fragmentary objects or about the mystic whose body parts were being circulated.

Chapter 1, "Rosa de Lima and the Imitatio Morum," considers Isabel Flores de Oliva (known as Santa Rosa de Lima or Rosa de Santa María), one of America's most revered saints, who was beatified in 1667 and canonized in 1671. I build on the vast literature on Santa Rosa to center on the small circle of devotees called *hijas espirituales*, laywomen and beatas who knew Rosa intimately. Several went on to found monastic institutions or become renowned spiritual leaders, or they were themselves the subjects of short biographical accounts. Their testimonials during the first, ordinary (1617–18) and second, apostolic stage (1630–32) of Rosa's beatification hearings contain information about how her companions gained a sensorial knowledge of prayer, ritual, and theological precepts of charity, fortitude, and humility by means of the imitatio morum, learning by imitation.[96] Rosa's disciples observed and listened to her give spiritual talks or teach them prayers, some of which she had written. But they also observed her engaging with material objects, most notably cloth and statues, which were thought to contain divine matter. Through their actions, words, and intentions, by dressing and praying to what Amy Whitehead calls "statue-persons," they invested them with divine personhood.[97] One of the statues mentioned frequently by respondents during the beatification hearings was that of Saint Catherine of Siena (1347–80), a spiritual model for Rosa with whom she regularly communicated.[98] Adorning religious statues and readying them for processions not only connected disciple and teacher, with the material objects as intermediaries, but enabled them to "think back through" (to adapt Virginia Woolf's term) their saintly predecessors and commune with the saints' divine essence and history.[99]

Chapter 2, "Reading the Body: Mystical Theology and Spiritual Actualization in Early Seventeenth-Century Lima," focuses on the stories that the bodies of female mystics could tell.[100] The body was composed of flesh, but it was also a site of pious expression and a divine vessel that facilitated spiritual ecstasy (*arrobamiento*), healing, protection, and salvation. Of course, flesh-and-blood women were involved in communicative supernatural processes, but their bodies were also objects that held meaning and could be appropriated and read. As illuminated women, their spiritual bodies served the higher purpose of facilitating spiritual communications. It was not their personhood but their communicative bond with the divine that mattered;

observers could access and then interpret the interior layers of these mystics' souls—their godness, if you will. Particular women mentioned in the chapter, including Isabel de Porras Marmolejo, Luisa Melgarejo de Sotomayor (1578–1651), Rosa de Lima, and Gerónima de San Francisco, were all considered to be conduits through whom God spoke.[101] As a result, others constituted narratives about the encounters these mystics had with the beyond. The ecstatic female body therefore had a particular kind of biography that tells us a great deal about how seventeenth-century readers and mystics experienced and conveyed their understandings of the divine in a gendered, somatic manner.

Early modern Iberian vassals also believed that the parts of the whole, and especially relics, could embody Christian materiality and that holy body parts were endowed with supernatural powers. Chapter 3, "Living in an (Im)Material World: Ángela de Carranza as a Reliquary," considers the biography of the living Augustine beata Ángela de Carranza (ca. 1642– after 1694). Ángela's history was more than a biography of a strong-willed, intelligent woman who developed her own theological notions, claimed to be illuminated, and questioned the male ecclesiastical power structure. As she gained recognition and authority as a mystic, theologian, and prophet among limeños, she dispensed (and sold) the products of her body, including her hair, nails, and urine, as well as objects which she came in contact with (i.e., contact relics) to her devout followers. The more these relic fragments of Ángela circulated, the more power and prestige she gained.[102] They told stories, stories that created multiple narratives and rendered Ángela both a relic and a reliquary, or dispensary of relics.

Whereas part 1 of the book explores how material objects helped compose the biographies of mystics, part 2, "The Relational Self," argues that the "lifelines [of female piety] came from and extended to others," whether at the individual or group level.[103] Each of the three chapters in the second half of the book considers how pious women constituted their spiritual, gendered selves in relation to others, male and female, kith and kin.[104] If we accept the liberating and limiting aspects of biographical and autobiographical writings and our reliance on these texts to understand female spirituality, it becomes essential to interrogate more closely the forms and elements that structure life narratives, whether in documentary or published form. What follows in this section of the book is an exploration of *relationality*, or the mutually constitutive self-constitution and constitution by other individuals, as key to understanding biographical and autobiographical portrayals. Relationality assumes that the "I" is predicated by relationships to other persons, and that the "I" in autobiographical writings is both subject and object. The framing of a spiritual self might occur as juxtaposition to someone else's behavior or through gendered mirroring. Spirituality in this period was also defined in a positional manner, vis-à-vis superiors or divine beings.

In 2004 the publication of *The Souls of Purgatory* made available the spiritual diary of Úrsula de Jesús (1604–66), an Afro-Peruvian donada, recorded at the request of her confessors. This source has a lot to say about Lima and the conventual culture within which the freed slave Úrsula lived, worked, and experienced mystical communications with divine beings and souls in purgatory. Her diary also contains heart-wrenching passages about how she suffered discrimination, fear, and bone-weary tiredness. It references the "little ones," or those servants and slaves ignored by the convent's nuns but considered blessed by God.[105] Apart from Úrsula's diary, we know little about the hundreds of other women of African and indigenous heritage who lived and labored in Lima's highly regimented convents and who, like Úrsula, were denied the right to be nuns because of their color or legal status. Instead, they chose the only available option and took vows as donadas. Chapter 4, "Carrying the Cross of Christ: Donadas in Seventeenth-Century Lima," creates a prosopographical assemblage of the biographies of over five hundred donadas based on the petitions and licenses associated with the legal process of entering a convent as a novice and taking one's vows a year later.[106]

Generally, prosopographies seek to unite the common characteristics of a particular group. However, to avoid essentializing the spiritual practices of disparate women who all happened to hold the same title and status as donadas in any number of Lima's convents, I tease out the *dimensionality* of donadas. By considering the heterogeneous motivations for wanting to take formal vows, and the different economic and family backgrounds of the aspirants, I illuminate what some would call the sociographic aspects of their collective biographies as well as their relationality to others living inside and outside the convent walls. Donadas lived in convents with hundreds of other religious women, and they expressed themselves as spiritual beings in a relational or positional manner to the nuns, their superiors, and other donadas, as well as the servants and slaves. As they polished floors and chopped wood, they maintained sororial dialogues about their intimate understandings of the divine with their peers, protégés, and superiors. They also related to those living in the siglo, especially their parents or other family members. That donadas were laborers did not make them less spiritual than the nuns.

Chapter 5, "María Jacinta Montoya, Nicolás de Ayllón, and the Unmaking of an Indian Saint in Late Seventeenth-Century Peru," follows the complex story of a wife's pursuit of her husband's beatification. In 1679 ecclesiastical authorities initiated proceedings to consecrate the Indian tailor Nicolás de Ayllón (1632–77), a popular "saint" known as the "Apostle of the Poor." Within twelve years, however, the *proceso* had stalled. The delay was blamed on Ayllón's wife, the mestiza María Jacinta Montoya (1645–1710), who was viewed as having an "arrogant nature" and accused of falsifying information related to Ayllón's miracles. An examination of the beatification hearings and Montoya's self-denunciation before the Inquisition in 1701 reveals how she created a "relational self." As she fashioned the symbolic identity of her husband as a humble, masculine, Christlike Indian saint in her writings and political activities, she also contrasted his positive qualities with her own negative ones. Through gender mirroring, she promoted her own Magdalene conversion, thus constructing herself symbolically as "what he is not, and therefore as an essential reminder of what he is."[107] At the same time, as she peered into a hall of mirrors, she acted on his behalf as a strong religious authority in her own right. Her writings express a double consciousness: a deep awareness of others' perceptions of her and her husband and also of the complex gender norms that reinforced her representations of herself as a female authority and mystic. Her relations with others also extended to the public. She encouraged indigenous authorities and the general populace to vocalize and record the heroic events of Ayllón's sacred life narrative that they had experienced, while simultaneously highlighting her own self-discovery of the sacred within.[108]

Chapter 6, *"Amparada de mi libertad*: Josefa Portocarrero Laso de la Vega and the Meaning of Free Will," concerns a mother's and daughter's struggles around the daughter's wish to establish and enter a convent. Following the death of the Count of Monclova (viceroy, 1689–1705), his daughter, the Spanish aristocrat doña Josefa, determined to invest her ample inheritance in founding a new monastery in Lima dedicated to the now-canonized Santa Rosa de Lima and to take her vows as a nun and remain there for life. This decision prompted her mother to file a legal suit against her, involving the archbishop of Lima, the king of Spain, and other secular and ecclesiastical authorities. This chapter examines the conflicting interpretations that lay at the heart of Josefa's power struggles: the meaning of freedom (*libertad*) and of being protected (*amparada*) by canon (and natural) law to choose a monastic vocation. Her self-characterization, predicated by her relationship to her self, to other family members, and to God, contrasted sharply with her mother's representation of Josefa as she attempted to foil her daughter's desires. Here is another kind of mirroring, pitting mother against daughter as each attempted to control the gendered message of who Josefa was.

On one level, this volume explores the possibilities of spiritual expression—opportunities, venues, ways of learning—that were effective for women. I show how pious women conveyed a knowledge of theology to others, how others created narratives about female mystics' spiritual practices, and how women gained power for themselves or for others through the written word and in relationship to nuns, masters, husbands, and mothers. I explore how ideas of the self were expressed in a relational manner.

On another level, the book is a study of the modal underpinnings of biographical and autobiographical representations of female Catholic spirituality in early modern Lima. My intention is to broaden our understanding of the range of possible texts that contain the elements of narrativity: whether in the piecemeal petitions that constituted the lives of donadas, or in the objectification and representation of body parts representing a blessed whole. Texts such as vidas, ecstatic bodies, and cloth were invested with meaning based on their ability to constitute stories about the interrelationship between divinity and humanity. Indeed, life narratives were always in dialogue with early modern understandings of sacred materiality and immateriality.

Each of the six chapters of this book reveals women searching for meaning, investigating who they were in relation to God, who they were in relation to others, and who they were in relation to the sacred objects that completed their lives. Such multivalent forms of self expression helped construct early modern Catholicism, writ large. A gendered consideration of women's mysticism and piety in seventeenth-century Lima contributes to our understanding of how the broad palette of Catholicism evolved in a colonial context and transcended restrictive assumptions about European versus other forms of spiritual expression. It helps to move us beyond stale paradigms that assume that Catholicism was both monolithic and oppositional to other religious practices.[109] Indeed, in the most basic of acts, in the smallest of gestures or touches, or in the carefully chosen words on a page, women engaged with the materiality and immateriality of early modern Catholicism in meaningful and multifarious ways.

PART I

Material and Immaterial Embodiment

I

ROSA DE LIMA
AND THE IMITATIO MORUM

. . .

Iridescent butterflies circling around her; fragrant flowers, plants, and trees blooming and bowing in her presence: this was Santa Rosa in God's garden, as depicted in visual portrayals and narrative accounts of her life.[1] In this particular painting, Rosa walks in the garden of her parents' home; beside her is a finely dressed lady who gestures toward the trees, which are inclining their branches toward Rosa in a sign of reverence. The lady wants to see firsthand how Rosa encouraged the plants, trees, and birds in her garden to praise God. She is not disappointed.[2]

In an insert at the top-left corner of the same painting, a less bucolic but equally important scene is portrayed in a more muted, enclosed balcony in a tall structure.[3] In Rosa's case, the tower is meant to signify, albeit allegorically, a small cell that Rosa had built in the corner of the garden depicted in the main section of the painting.[4] Rosa is seated with three modestly dressed

FIGURE 1.1. Laureano Dávila, *Los árboles se inclinan ante Santa Rosa* (eighteenth century).

young women; Rosa and one of her companions have embroidery pillows on their laps. Rosa gesticulates with one hand, her mouth open as though she is speaking. The woman to her left imitates the gesture. Behind them sit two young women, also engaged with what Rosa is saying. In the two scenes of garden and room, we see evidence of Rosa and her female companions engaged in the art of imitatio morum—learning from and imitating a wise elder's behavior. We see female communion, learning that takes place through speech and action, and a sharing of the wonders of God.

According to medievalist Anneke B. Mulder-Bakker, the instructional method of imitatio morum was an essential component of knowledge transmission in the late Middle Ages.[5] Learning involved a pupil focusing on the example being shown or explained and then attempting to imitate it through action or speech. The didactic process was considered complete once the student had internalized the knowledge.[6] Well into the early modern period, novices in monasteries and apprentices in workshops learned by emulating the physical actions of their teachers and the ideas these teachers articulated.[7] In different, gendered spaces, boys and girls listened, watched, and appropriated knowledge of crafts or theology, which was stored in the heart, the seat of memory. The insert of the painting shows Rosa speaking to her protégées about spiritual matters while the handwork on her lap awaits her attention.

During her brief life, Rosa de Santa María (Isabel Flores de Oliva, 1586–1617, canonized in 1671) was central to the education of a select group of protégées living in the viceregal capital.[8] For more than a decade, from 1606 to 1617, Rosa set the primus inter pares example for a number of women, both poor and wealthy, to emulate. Her guidance and personal tutelage persuaded some to abandon their licentious or ostentatious ways and draw closer to God.[9] For those girls and women who called Rosa "mother," she was a living book, a model of ascetic piety. Her spiritual trajectory—living as a beata in the secular world—followed the pattern of devout medieval mystics, including Angela of Foligno and Margaret of Cortona, both women who lived lives of charity, penitence, and contemplation outside of a monastic setting.[10] But for Rosa and her disciples, Catherine of Siena (1347–80) was their most esteemed model. They called Rosa "mother" based on what Catherine's followers had done centuries before. The medieval Italian tertiary had joined a small group of pious women (*mantellate*) in Siena, and her closest companions called her mother (*mamma*).[11] Catherine's writings also refer to a broader circle of female and male devotees as her *famiglia*, or family.[12]

We know from recent scholarship that pious women gained theological literacy by reading and discussing the contents of sacred texts, a topic that will be considered in more detail in chapter 2. Some of this knowledge was passed down orally from woman to woman. According to beatification records and vidas, Rosa's devotees listened to her give spiritual talks and discussed the contents of books that Rosa had read. From these works, they learned how to save souls in purgatory and engage in practices of mental prayer. They also gained practical skills. According to Rosa's hagiographer, Leonard Hansen, Rosa organized her weekly prayer regimen around the advice given in the works of the mystic theologian Luis de Granada.[13]

By any measure, Rosa had gained a deep knowledge of theology over the course of her short life. Her confessors note her prodigious memory: she could recall the contents of books she had read or sermons she had heard and discussed with her confessors long before.[14] No doubt Rosa shared this knowledge with her female companions, even if there is no direct evidence to support that claim.

We do know that Rosa afforded a spiritual education to her devotees by other means. Pious girls and women gained a nonliterate, somatic knowledge of how to discern what was holy and unholy by engaging their senses and interacting with material objects. This process of imitatio morum involved a three-way dialogue between the pupil, the teacher (in this case, Rosa), and the items that the pupils and Rosa touched, smelled, tasted, and heard.

In this opening chapter, I argue that an understanding of abstract theological precepts, including discerning what was divine and what was corrupt, gaining a sense of the ever-expanding relationship between self and God, and coming to understand that matter was alive, could be obtained through a sensorial engagement with material objects. Items such as sculptures, cloth, and relics were loci of profound spiritual exploration, since they were believed to be containers of both material and immaterial matter.[15] Pious Catholic women invested these items with meaning, and, in turn, the objects informed them how they could and should respond sensorially. Women then shared with others, by means of speech or by touching, holding, gazing, smelling, sensing them, the knowledge they had gained through their interactions with objects.[16]

To understand "Rosa" as she was constructed by the women who surrounded her, I consider the somewhat challenging testimonies given by Rosa's *hermanas* (sisters) and disciples in the diocesan (1617–18) and apostolic (1630–32) beatification hearings. They are challenging for scholars in the sense that the depositions, taken months after her death, were already in memory form and were circumscribed by the need to frame the events in Rosa's life in ways that would increase her chances for sainthood. Moreover,

Rosa's disciples who testified in the second beatification hearing in 1630–32 had other reasons to be concerned about how they portrayed their beloved "saint." The Inquisition had tried several beatas and nuns, some of whom had been part of Rosa's inner circle, for false mysticism. These trials, as scholars have argued, complicated but ultimately did not undermine efforts to canonize Rosa.[17]

Furthermore, the language that witnesses used to describe Rosa's activities, whether mundane or grand, often elides the materially, emotionally, and sensorially oriented experiences embedded in such descriptions. So, from a brief statement by Catalina de Santa María about the need to find flowers "to adorn the platform [carrying] the Glorious Saint Catherine," we have to imagine how Rosa and her disciples engaged their senses as they dug, cut, and arranged the carnations.[18] There are ways, however, to access some of the teachable moments reflected in these depositions. For instance, we learn that on one occasion Rosa had shared her sense of unease with the beata Catalina de Santa María and Catalina's sister. Rosa had misplaced a valuable item and believed that the devil was testing her resolve by playing a trick on her. To mitigate the inner turmoil she felt, she had asked her brother to paint the ugliest version possible of the *patón tiñoso* (club-footed one), as she liked to call the devil. Catalina watched as Rosa threw the image on the ground, stamping and spitting on it. Rosa then instructed Catalina and her sister to do the same.[19] Here a deeply experiential moment of the imitatio morum—learning from Rosa how to cast off what was unholy and corrupt—was captured in a deposition. Rosa was teaching Catalina and her sister that the physical object—in this case, a rendering of the devil—was more than a symbol. The stamped-on drawing embodied the qualities of evil and could be acted on by teacher and student with destructive physical force. Such actions could help to cleanse the mind of sinful thoughts, often attributed to darker forces. Catalina's deposition recounts a moment when bodily responses and interiorized notions worked in tandem to comprehend *fortaleza* (spiritual forbearance).

From Rosa, women learned that objects like cloth contained *virtus* (a term they used to refer to divine energy) and that the relationship between immateriality and materiality was fluid and interchangeable. Even mundane activities like sewing could serve as pathways to a deeper relationship with God. While doing embroidery and other handwork together, Rosa and her devotees engaged the senses of touch, sight, taste, and hearing. They prayed that their stitches would please God or Mary. But they also engaged with cloth in other ways. As they donned garb made of coarse fabric and mortified their flesh, they learned about the textured sensations of spiritual-corporeal pain and sorrow and the fragility of human nature. They learned viscerally through their senses, not intellectually, that mortification helped fight "the wars that the enemy [the devil] conducts, interiorly and exteriorly."[20] The counterpoint to their own tactile engagement with drab and bristly apparel was to fashion lush, soft robes and mantles for religious statues of the Virgin or Saint Catherine of Siena and then dress the statues. As they rendered these "statue-persons" into objects of great beauty, Rosa and her disciples listened to them "speak" and give council. Through their sense of touch, they learned to feel the sacred energy in the decorated cloth that adorned these beloved statues.[21]

Accessing holiness was, however, not limited to so-called inanimate objects. The relationship between Rosa and her disciples was also extremely tactile. Her hermanas kissed her feet and garments; they held her hand; they fingered the same scissors and thread as she. Sitting near their friend, Rosa's disciples could sense the virtus of the threadbare garments and mortification devices that touched the flesh of someone they deemed to be holy. They could hear her labored breath as she suffered pain. Later, as they handled the linen sheets that covered Rosa's dying body, they came to understand the fine line that separated flesh from spirit.

Rosa's spiritual biographers like to emphasize her hermeticism and solitary engagement with God. She shunned the world by retreating to the tiny cell in her parents' garden to achieve inner stillness.[22] But these accounts tend to minimize Rosa's engagement with people and objects in the world. Theologians and confessors advised women, and especially beatas, to remain recogida, enclosed and sheltered, as much as possible to avoid carnal temptations.[23] But the realities of life did not always match those expectations. Accompanied by her devotees, Rosa served God, the Virgin, and the saints in public places. Through her actions Rosa taught her disciples that the active and the contemplative aspects of communion with God were inseparable. This made sense: like other women living in early seventeenth-century Lima, Rosa labored intensively for hours each day doing handwork that she could sell to help support her parents and siblings.[24] Remunerated labor meant having food in the larder and curtains on the windows. Moreover, such toil could easily resonate with the heroic virtues of charity, poverty, and devotion to God. Rosa did not perform these activities alone; she often labored and prayed in the company of other women. Together, she and her hermanas would go to the homes of wealthy women to beg for alms or request that they donate their gems to decorate a statue of the Virgin. She and the other beatas would adorn church altars and kneel before images in private chapels.

As they engaged tenderly with objects they considered to be sacred, Rosa and her disciples formed a female epistemological community around a body of spiritual knowledge they had gained through their senses.[25]

That many of these women were living in the world (as opposed to a monastic setting) and expressing their devotion to God in public was not without controversy, and their depositions must be read with this in mind. Beatas had to be careful not to display arrogance or pride, nor to demonstrate too much theological learning. Moreover, they needed to craft a humble, extremely modest "Rosa" who assiduously avoided any display of her mortification practices, however esteemed they might be.[26] Aware of the gendered strictures that informed her testimony, the Dominican beata Luisa de Santa María stated that she had had a tremendous desire to "engage and communicate with [Rosa]" during the last year of Rosa's life. But Luisa claimed full responsibility for pressuring Rosa to reveal details about her fasting, abstinence, and penitence.[27] Everyone knew that Rosa was reticent to reveal such intimate habits. According to Luisa, Rosa relented when she realized that Luisa was a serious student.[28] Rosa also quietly shared her mortification "tricks" with others. The beata Feliciana de Jesús had learned from the sleep-deprived Rosa how to stave off the "enemy of sleepiness" by "attaching her [pulled-up] hair to a nail and then hanging from it." Such severe pain, she had learned, only intensified her vigilance (and alert state) while she endeavored to continue saying her prayers.[29]

Scholars who work on religious vidas (spiritual biographies or autobiographies) like to remind us that the life stories of female mystics are multivalent in their fashioning. They are created by many "I's," many voices, many perspectives.[30] Rosa's afterlife, which began at her death (some might argue that it began while she was alive), was thus constituted by how others thought they should represent her mystical and devotional practices. Her devotees, her confessors, and her subsequent hagiographers managed her holiness to fit prescriptive norms.[31] It was these self-conscious observers who created the prospective saint, bringing the world of the text (that of the mystic herself) into contact with the reader (for whom the narrator is a proxy).[32] If we pay attention to the observer (the female disciple; here, the reader might recall Catalina de Santa María watching Rosa stomp on the image of the devil) observing Rosa *do something* with something (cloth or a statue), we can "see" the narrator recounting an event in which learning and the creation of scripted meaning were occurring simultaneously. We may also note that, in the process of creating these narrative truths, material objects were often the tutorial "intermediaries" between Rosa and her intended audience.[33]

I consider cloth, clothing, and dressing as a way to understand how these sensorial learning processes transpired and how "Rosa" was constituted by means of these moments of imitatio morum. Cloth, as cultural anthropologist Jane Schneider argues, was a "transformative medium."[34] It could do so many things. It had depth and texture; it touched and penetrated the epidermis; it was seen as an extension of the body. Cloth could vibrate with color. It shielded and disguised. It kept the lascivious male eye from seeing wisps of hair that were trying to escape the veil, or glimpsing the curve of an ankle or the marble-like surface of the neck. Cloth fashioned into clothing was a visual representation of what was contained within. The design, shape, and color of the raiment were cultural codes that triggered in observers associations with wealth, religion, and status. They were meant to be read by the public eye.[35] Cloth interacted with the skin and with the tactile sensations of the body. A rough texture or binding shape could scrape the flesh or restrict the diaphragm—aiding in the mortification of the flesh, a practice considered essential to expressions of early modern Catholic devotion. Cloth could swathe a wound or still the throbbing blood, something Rosa's hermanas who attended to the sick in hospitals or infirmaries knew firsthand.

Finally, cloth was key to religious expression because it was thought to contain the virtus of the person wearing it. It was matter that also pulsated with immaterial energy. For that reason, contact relics, including the garments worn by the living and the dead, were prized possessions. Snippets of divinely infused fabric could be fingered or caressed while praying on behalf of the infirm. A soft, moist relic swatch could poultice and then cure an afflicted area. Tenderly caressing an ornately embroidered cloak while readying a statue of the Virgin for a procession was akin to touching *her*. A closer examination of how early modern subjects engaged with cloth provides clues to the relationship between the inner and outer senses and the ways one could access the divinity held within a material object.

For many, the story of Rosa de Lima's path toward sainthood is familiar. But we know little about the women who answered the carefully composed questions that helped to create the first American saint. We know little about how Rosa engaged with these women and helped them on their own spiritual journeys. Rosa was the epicenter of an inner circle of hijas espirituales (spiritual daughters) that then expanded outward to include a larger community of women.[36] Rosa met regularly with a small group of female confidantes in the tiny cell that she had built on her parents' property or, later, at the home of Gonzalo de la Maza, where she lived for the last three years of her life. Her contacts included wealthy and poor, widowed and unmarried girls, and women of African, indigenous, and Spanish descent. She attracted celebrated mystics like Luisa Melgarejo (1578–1651), who always greeted the future saint on her knees.[37] Other spiritual confidantes included the nun Inés de Ubitarte, who later transferred from the Monasterio de la Encarnación to the newly founded Monasterio de Santa Catalina when Rosa's predictions came to pass and it was established in 1624. Inés's written revelations received the initial approval of the abbess, Lucía de la Santíssima Trinidad (d. 1649, Daga), who had met Rosa at the home of one of her spiritual daughters, Isabel Mexía.[38] Lucía thought so highly of Rosa's close companion Luisa Melgarejo that she gave her a rare copy of Luis de Granada's *El perfecto cristiano*. María de Bustamante, a nun in the Monasterio de la Trinidad, also frequented Rosa's home and later testified during her beatification hearing. Rosa also met some of her closest companions through mutual confessors.[39]

Some of Rosa's friendships with girls-turned-nuns went back to childhood and to contacts her mother had developed with women whose daughters she had tutored. The aforementioned María de Bustamante had frequented Rosa's home for over ten years as she grew into adulthood.[40] On many occasions, María and her four sisters had communicated "very familiarly" with Rosa at evening dinners at her parents' home.[41] Rosa had even predicted, much to their surprise, that several family members, including María, would become nuns. Another companion, Catalina de Jesús, explained in her deposition that she had met Rosa when she was twelve years old and had learned from her how to renounce "the vanities of the world" long before she took her vows as a Trinitarian nun.[42] The young Rosa also communed regularly with a Franciscan beata named Juana de Jesús.[43]

When Rosa was about twenty-one years old, a number of young girls and widows whom she called her spiritual daughters began to gather formally at her home.[44] Under Rosa's direction, they would eventually take informal vows as Dominican tertiaries. Rubén Vargas Ugarte described the ceremony:

> Being now eight in total, and considering that they were ready to receive the habit of the Third Order, [Rosa] resolved to ask Friar Luis de Ojedo, the current sacristan of Santo Domingo [to perform the ceremony]. On Christmas Eve [the eight women] gathered in Rosa's home, and before an image of Saint Catherine they set about preparing the candles, palms, and floral arrangements they were going to carry. Then, [following] the instruction of their teacher [Rosa], each told the Christ child what was in her heart; each placed a veil over her head; and [then the group] set forth to the [Church of] Santo Domingo. There,

before the altar of Our Lady of the Rosary, they deposited their flowers and palms, and after confessing [their sins] and taking communion, received the blessed habit.[45]

Rosa's protégées also included servants and slaves who served some of the wealthier beatas and nuns in Rosa's inner circle. They, too, witnessed and participated in the delicate intimacies of Rosa's life, as evidenced by their value as corroborative witnesses in the beatification hearings.[46] The india Mariana, who had been raised by Rosa's parents and served Rosa as she grew into adulthood, had a tactile knowledge of Rosa's body unlike anybody else's. She was intimately familiar with Rosa's eating and mortification practices and reluctantly obeyed when Rosa asked to be whipped. She helped to heal Rosa's lacerated and bruised shoulders and washed her bloodied garments or the blood-spattered walls of her cell.[47] Servants who stood obediently in corners or hallways learned important lessons about the wonders of Catholicism by observing Rosa. For instance, Juana Criolla, the child servant of Rosa's godmother, Isabel Mejía, confessed to her mistress that she had once seen Rosa walking in the garden with a small resplendent boy dressed in blue and white.[48]

Finally, Rosa's disciples included elite secular women. The central figure in Rosa's life was doña María de Uzástegui, the wife of Gonzalo de la Maza. During the last three years of her life, Rosa lived in doña María's home, such was the confidence Rosa had in her.[49] Because of this proximity, doña María's two daughters, Micaela and Andrea, claimed to have benefited tremendously from the tutoring they received from Rosa.[50] Rosa's female world therefore included religious women and laywomen, the wealthy and the impoverished, members of the elite and servants. They spent time together discussing spiritual matters and, more important, doing the work that had to be done.

Las Manos *(Hands)*

Rosa and her disciples considered employing the hands "in heroic and valorous things" a reputable enterprise.[51] Sewing, as contemporary chroniclers noted, was one of the female activities most pleasing to God. Several seventeenth- and eighteenth-century depictions of Rosa show her stitching the initials "JHS" for Jesus or a sacred heart on pillows, or embroidering while in the company of the Christ child.[52] Even on a practical level, however, sewing was what women did during those few still moments when they sat by the lamplight. There were always piles of mending, darning, or embroidering awaiting their attention. Luisa de Santa María recalled that when she stayed in Rosa's cell, the two labored together, doing "the handwork at hand."[53]

Rosa's participation in these routine, essential activities was not unique. Two of the more well-known tertiaries in Lima supported the highly ritualistic economies of convents and monasteries. The mestiza Franciscan beata Isabel de Cano (d. 1638) and her companion, Estefanía de San Joseph (1561–1645; described as being the color *parda* [brown] and the daughter of a slave), collected alms on behalf of Franciscan nuns. Estefanía was named the perpetual sacristan (*sacristana*) of the Chapels of Nuestra Señora de la Candelaría and the Virgen de la Soledad.[54] For many years she also tenderly cleansed the feet and dressed the wounds of the infirm in Lima's hospitals.[55] Isabel de Cano served as a sacristan of three different altars, a labor-intensive position that involved washing and ironing the mantles and other cloths used on the altar, obtaining flowers, and setting out the host for the Mass. In addition to their efforts as sacristans, Isabel and Estefanía did the laundry and sewed mattresses for the infirmary of the Franciscan convent. The little money they earned went to buy soap to wash the altar cloths.

If we return for a moment to consider the inset of the painting described at the beginning of this chapter, we can see that Rosa is speaking to her female companions while her handwork rests on her lap. Rosa's heart and hands, as her companions observed, were rarely still, and the two were one.[56] While Rosa embroidered pillows or sewed garments for the Virgin in her cell, or assembled a statue in the chapel of a church, she listened and gave counsel. Yet gaining access to Rosa was not easy, and the Dominican chronicler Juan Meléndez cited an instance when a reputable lady made several efforts before finally succeeding in speaking to her about "spiritual matters."[57] To those who waited patiently to see her, she gave advice about lost objects, a sick family member, or a son's vocation for becoming a friar or a priest. More than one witness noted that after even a minimal introduction, they sensed that Rosa had penetrated into their souls to discern their true intentions.[58] She was also known to cure ailments or offer consolation to those facing abject poverty. But to her hermanas and others, she gave *plácticas*, talks that addressed spiritual matters, the contents of which were never revealed by those who testified at her beatification hearings. Her disciples would not have wished to ascribe too much power or authority to Rosa since they were well aware that any discussion of theology was reserved for confessors. Still, her words were known to move them deeply, sometimes inspiring what was called a spiritual *mudança*, a movement of the spirit. In general, the depositions state these matters simply, without adornment, but occasionally a female devotee would qualify Rosa's talks as "celestial."[59]

We tend to think of spiritual communion with God and manual labor as separate endeavors, but for Rosa they were one and the same. Confessors who scrutinized Rosa's conscience were astonished that her outward and inward senses were both always engaged: she could embroider, murmur her prayers, and communicate with God in internal union at the same time.[60] Even while engaged in "external exercises," María de Uzástegui noted, Rosa was always fingering the rosary beads she wore around her wrist.[61] For Luisa de Santa María, Rosa's life was one continual prayer on behalf of others.[62] Ritual gestures of piety like bowing the head, kneeling before an image, and placing the hands together in prayer were second nature to Rosa and her disciples.[63] *Doing* and *being* with God were therefore not mutually exclusive practices.

The Skin of the Soul

If busy hands were a sign of an industrious and pure spirit, cloth and clothing were like the skin of the soul, an entryway to the rich interior world where God's presence could be discerned. Rosa's contemporaries placed great emphasis on clothing because the types of garments worn provided clues to a woman's zeal and rendered God's presence visible. Clothing externally mirrored the inner spiritual domain and the spiritual transformation occurring from within. The type of garments worn was a measure of spiritual progress and the degree of commitment to a life of poverty and humility. Beatas who worked and performed charitable acts in public wore a habit specific to tertiaries, which, according to Meléndez, "edified [others] with their [modest] composure and moved [those with] the greatest lack of composure to sacred emulation."[64] Clothing therefore shaped the "in-habitant" in the eyes of the beholder and served as a model for others to imitate.[65]

Rejecting ornate, soft clothing was a common leitmotiv in medieval and early modern hagiographies and sermons and was considered part of the spiritual life cycle of early modern pious women. From childhood, girls were taught that adorning the body with lustrous silks of rich hues was evidence of corruption within. Limeñas, friars argued, were too obsessed with their gusseted skirts and matching shoe color. A transition from sumptuous to humble outerwear was a clear sign of a Magdalene spiritual conversion. This change of habit was like peeling off a layer of the soul to allow oneself to begin the process of nurturing an interior life. Such a change of disposition could only enhance the person's true, godly nature.[66] The more drab and threadbare the raiment, the deeper the commitment to a life of piety and humility.[67]

In colonial Lima there were many ways for lay and religious women to demonstrate a material commitment to the sacred path. For elite laywomen, discarding luxurious frocks for tattered, coarse garments was a sign of deep transformation, or *mundanza*, and a way of both living in the world and shunning it.[68] In a monastic setting, novitiates formally professed after one year of training by being invested with the habit of a particular order. At that transitional moment, the novice exchanged rich fabrics for coarse, irritating cloth, thus inviting in new sensorial experiences of the sacred.[69] Unlike nuns, however, beatas like Rosa still inhabited the world, which meant that it was even more imperative to demonstrate their rejection of the secular domain through their choice of dress. To the delight of the chroniclers who composed the *vidas* of exemplary beatas, taking on the habit of a tertiary was intended "to banish all trace of superfluous vanities with marvelous ingenuity and skill."[70] After taking informal vows of poverty, chastity, and obedience, beatas would walk the streets in old skirts, "capes with a thousand tears," or sackcloths fashioned roughly into blouses. They would tie up their hair with rags or cover it with a thick veil. Weather permitting, they would go barefoot or wear cheap, flat cotton shoes.

Although the linkage between morality and dress was certainly made before the Council of Trent (1545–63), it took on a greater didactic meaning after 1563.[71] Putting on a particular type of monastic garment, Italian philosopher Giorgio Agamben argues, was a way of inhabiting a set of practices and dispositions that were anchored in the body.[72] It also acted as a shield against evil. The Franciscan Diego de Córdova y Salinas noted the fortitude with which beatas like Estefanía de San Joseph suffered public derision. As she walked the streets of Lima in her threadbare garments, young boys would pelt her with stones.[73]

It should come as no surprise, then, that Rosa would choose to wear a religious habit reflecting her internal state of mind and her complete rejection of the vanities of the world. She understood that physical and spiritual clothing were not mutually exclusive, "for the physical could cross into the spiritual realm and vice versa."[74] Witnesses commented on the white Dominican mantle that Rosa had worn in public since taking her vows in 1606.[75] Underneath she wore a tunic made of pig bristles, until her confessor ordered her to substitute for it one of serge.[76] The layers worn closest to the skin, the entryway to the soul, were meant to be the coarsest. Rosa's companion Catalina de Santa María remarked in 1617 that Rosa always wore "an underskirt of very thick serge, of the kind they use to make sacks; and [Rosa] called it her bro-cade, because she esteemed it as such."[77] She believed that her spiritual body within was adorned with shimmering taffeta in eye-dazzling hues.

Rosa's engagement with cloth drew on what she had learned from reading vidas of Saint Catherine of Siena.[78] For Catherine, her choice of dress not only aided her own salvation but served as a model for others to emulate.[79] Outer garments could easily be given to the needy. Rosa was known to cut away extra pieces of fabric from her outer skirt and donate them to the poor, as Catherine had done centuries earlier.[80] Catherine, like Rosa, could sew clothing, give it away, and see it in visions. Christ had once bestowed on Catherine an invisible dress, a blood-red vestment drawn from the wound in his side that protected her from even the harshest cold.[81] Cloth was to be worn (physically and spiritually), but it could also teach much about divine gifts of grace, as well as the virtues of perseverance and long-suffering.

Rosa's disciples also learned these lessons as they watched the future saint engage with cloth on a daily basis. María de Uzástegui commented that Rosa had once shown her daughters a boar-bristle garment that covered her body from the shoulders to the knees, "to give them a good example and to attract them to an act so virtuous and meritorious." No doubt the girls would have wanted to touch the mortification objects, giving them a tactile understand-ing of Rosa's emulation of the suffering that Christ endured during his Pas-sion. Seeing and touching, perhaps even smelling, the rankling and abrasive garments would link mind and body and give the girls an ineffable under-standing of the connection between materiality and divine immateriality.[82] Those who reported sleeping next to Rosa in her tiny cell also experienced the interpenetrability of flesh and cloth; they were in proximity to her blood-ied garments, her *cilicios*, and her pig-bristle bedsheets.[83] In the dark, Catalina de Jesús would listen to Rosa's shallow breathing and sighs or note her fear as she lay down or rolled over on her bed covered with pottery shards.[84] Al-though they never said so, each hermana would have felt, firsthand, that she was touching holiness, since these objects had grazed, lacerated, and engaged Rosa's purpled flesh and radiant spirit on and below the cutaneous surface. The heart and the senses learned what the mind could not fathom.

Thus, flesh and cloth (which covered the material and spiritual bodies) were two sides of the same spiritual fabric. Rosa's hermanas learned this im-portant lesson as they watched Rosa mortify her body. Her disciples gained a tactile, olfactory, and visual understanding of the relationship between decay and sensory stimulation by seeing her flesh cut by a chain she had wrapped around her body.[85] They learned about the relationship between the surface of the skin and its interior, the exquisite nature of pain and the wisdom of spiritual suffering.[86] The textured nature of these objects—their coarseness and sharpness—engaged both the minds and the penetrable bodies of Rosa and her disciples. Cloth and clothlike garments had much to teach about "dying while living."[87] They had a great deal to teach about self-transformation and the practice of knowing God.

Dressing the Virgin

From an outsider's perspective, the threadbare tertiaries walking the streets of Lima looked disheveled and shabby. But those limeños who were rooted in the religious culture of the city could sense that the interior garb of the beatas was brimming with the light and color of God's grace. It is no coincidence, therefore, that the same beatas who lacerated their flesh and scorned frippery and finery adorned religious statues with the most sumptuous cloth and jewels available.[88] Rosa and her disciples spent hours meticulously and devotedly snipping threads and sewing gems and sequins onto the thick, velvety cloth that adorned sculptures that they believed to be saturated with divinity. Adorning these statue objects gave concrete form to the divine, making the sacred "available to the senses and facilitating spiritual as well as physical interaction."[89]

Representations of the sacred were everywhere to behold. Lima's dozens of ornate churches were filled with sculptures that were venerated, kissed, knelt before, and carried in a procession. They were representations of someone who had once been alive, but they were still considered to be matter, both potent and changeable. They did not have to resemble the saint or the Virgin but might only contain elements (books, palm leaves, etc.) that connected the sculpture or statue to its historical referent.[90] Moreover, they were believed to have tremendous power. Statues were known to demonstrate their aliveness by sweating, bleeding, or somehow transforming before the beholder's eye. Those beatas who frequented particular chapels and gazed at the same statues week after week would report seeing them move or weep.[91] They wanted the statues to perform the impossible. According to the beata Feliciana de Jesús's confessor, she had once asked the statue of an angel at Saint Gertrude's side to shoot a dart into her heart (this divine act was called *transverberation*) so she could feel the fire of God's presence there.[92]

Rosa and her small circle of devotees considered the statues of the Virgin of Rosario and Saint Catherine of Siena, which they regularly dressed in regal garb, to be divinely animated statue-persons.[93] According to Meléndez,

Rosa dressed and undressed the statue of Saint Catherine three times a year for many years.[94] For Rosa, Saint Catherine, "her mother and teacher," was alive in many ways.[95] Catherine's "hypercharged" power was based on Rosa and her disciples' understanding of Catherine's saintly attributes that they had read or heard about from published vidas.[96] Following the tradition of imitatio morum, they imagined the sacred events of Catherine's life and then reenacted them in their own lives. They learned, for instance, that Catherine spoke directly and continually to images of Christ and Mary Magdalene as clearly as she would to any living person.[97] Rosa imitated her "elder" mother by speaking directly to Saint Catherine and then shared some of her insights with her own spiritual daughters.

Just as Catherine of Siena had relied on her "mother," Mary Magdalene, for advice, Rosa communicated her own and others' deepest desires to the statue of Catherine in whispered prayers.[98] Catherine was at once a confidante, a granter of wishes (she would miraculously make money appear to buy fabric to dress her statue, for example), and someone who, with compassion and grace, watched over those inhabiting Rosa's world. "It was as though she were speaking to a close friend," was how disciple doña María Eufemia de Pareja described Rosa's exchanges with the statue.[99] At times Rosa would go and kneel before the image and then return to reassure her troubled companions that Catherine would intervene on their behalf.[100]

Dressing religious sculptures in fine regalia was the best way for Rosa and other beatas to show deep reverence. First and foremost, however, adorning a religious statue required funds.[101] Rosa sometimes relied on her mother's contacts with wealthy women who would donate money to buy the expensive cloth and accessories. She could also depend on those confraternity members who were dedicated to Saint Catherine of Siena's image to provide the necessary funds.[102] Once the money had been garnered, Rosa and her hermanas would then buy the sequins; the gold, silver, and colored threads; the pearl inlays; and long swaths of ornate cloth, which they would then spend months fashioning into embroidered and ornamented garments for their beloved Catherine.

Starting with a rudimentary, skeletal body made of wood (generally, for processional statues only the head and hands were carved with any detail), which had to be light enough to easily move, Rosa and her hermanas began the elaborate ritual of sewing garments and adorning the statue "from the crown to the shoe."[103] Sitting next to Rosa, the women would measure, cut, and stitch the velvet, taffeta, brocade, or damask cloth to be used for the robe or mantle.[104] Appliqués and embroidered patterns were also carefully designed and sewn onto the cloth. Part of the imitatio morum, in this instance, meant following Rosa's instructions: snip here, place the jewel here. On another level, however, it meant investing the meditative self into each action involved in creating the beautiful garments. Each object, each action, was singularly and collectively considered part of a larger sacred whole, imbued with meaning through the unity with spirit.

As Hansen wrote in his vida of Rosa, the future saint treated each step in the process of dressing a statue with such devotion, tears, kisses, and prayers that it was as though she were in the presence of the original.[105] Dressing the statues involved a union of the external and internal senses, which occurred through prayer and penitence. María Eufemia de Pareja learned this while she sat with Rosa as she readied the Virgin of Rosario's dress for an upcoming procession. María Eufemia had shared with Rosa her hope that because she had bought the richest brocade possible for the Virgin, the heavenly mother would reciprocate by granting María Eufemia's wish. But Rosa explained to María Eufemia that, in order to gain a divine favor, "the dress did not need to be of silk and [rich] cloths but rather of fasting and disciplines, mortifications and mental prayer."[106] This, indeed, was the truth, according to Rosa.

As Rosa dressed the Marian statues or that of Saint Catherine, she engaged her body in ritualistic fasting and prayer for a prescribed number of days.[107] In Meléndez's chronicle *Tesoros verdaderos*, there is a transcription of an account written in Rosa's hand entitled, "Account for the dress that I, Rosa de Santa María, unworthy slave of the Queen of the Angels, begin to make, with the blessing of the Lord, for the Virgin Mother of God."[108] It details the ritual prayers and penitential activities involved in crafting each garment, from inner to outer, for the queen of heaven. In honor of the Immaculate Conception, Rosa began by sewing the innermost tunic. As she did so, she said six hundred Hail Marys and other prayers and fasted for fifteen days. Next came the creation of the cape, while repeating the same number of prayers and days of abstinence. Third, she and her assistants prepared the adornment, trimmings, and embellishments that would go on the cape, which required the same number of prayers and meditation on the sacrifice made by God on behalf of his son. For the belt buckle, made of gold, Rosa said another six hundred Hail Marys and fasted for two weeks. This was followed by crafting the choker, or necklace, again with the requisite number of prayers and days of abstinence. Finally, Rosa picked and then arranged the bouquet of flowers to be placed in the statue's hands, all the while saying thirty-three Our Fathers and other prayers corresponding to the thirty-three years that Christ walked the earth. She ended the dressing process by praying to God, in Christ's honor, to forgive her defects and impudence.[109] Once the dressed statue had been placed on the processional platform, Rosa arranged fresh flowers and candles, incense, and embroidered cloth around it.

Such a prolonged, intense process was known to produce miracles. Felipa de Montoya, one of four sisters who engaged intimately with Rosa, reported a marvelous event that had occurred while the two were dressing the statue of Catherine of Siena. She recalled that Rosa was embroidering a scapulary for Catherine and asked Felipa to fetch a little skein of silk from the room adjacent to where the statue was located. Upon reentering the room, Felipa noticed that Catherine's face had changed color and was now resplendent. Rosa seemed not the least bit surprised to hear this: "Don't you see, *hermana*," Rosa responded, "that my sainted mother rejoices [in knowing] that we are finishing the scapulary?"[110] A later hagiographer, Antonio de Lorea, interpreted the information in Felipa's testimony as a teachable moment. For him, Rosa was letting her disciple know that the communion between Rosa and Catherine was not only profound but frequent and that Rosa was accustomed to seeing even greater things.[111]

Not only did Rosa teach her hermanas the sequence of rituals to follow and prayers to say while fashioning garments for the religious statues, but she also taught them about the kinetic potential of the unseen world, and the possibilities of communicating with the blessed ones living in the beyond. As they touched, kissed, and caressed the carved wooden face and hands or the garments draped over them, they learned how to access the virtus contained within the cloth and adornments. Through their continual tactile, emotional, and interactive relationships with these material-immaterial objects, they came to understand how to access the realm of the miraculous.

As Rosa's health deteriorated—the result of years of severe fasting and mortification practices—she could do less and less. A year before she died, she expressed a fervent desire to undress the statue of Saint Catherine that had been brought to the de la Maza home where Rosa was then living.[112] It was what she had done many times, for many years. Rosa longed to snip off the jewels and return them to their owner, but her inflamed hand impeded the use of scissors. So, as always, she turned to her spiritual mother for help. María de Uzástegui, who witnessed the event, stated that, after communing with Saint Catherine in the private oratory of Uzástegui's home, Rosa returned looking refreshed. She then took a small pair of scissors and "began to cut and unstitch brooches and collars that were on the glorious saint [Catherine]." When she had finished, Rosa said to Uzástegui, "This is now done, my mother." An astonished Uzástegui asked, "With what hands?" As Rosa showed Uzástegui her nearly normal hand, she explained that her mother, Catherine, had healed her.[113]

Imitatio Morum, Postmortem

As loci of spiritual exploration, cloth and clothing served as intermediaries between teacher and student. Through the five senses, pious women learned to feel divinity in the Virgin's mantle. They came to experience an intimacy with these statue-persons, in whom they could confide their deepest desires. They came to understand that rough cloth's chafing of the skin would serve as a continual reminder to renounce the vanities of the world. For cloth could mediate between internal and external sensations—experiences within and on the body's surface. It converted beauty into pain, and pain into beauty. In death—the transition from this world into the next—cloth signified yet another kind of transformation. Death was a moment of transcendence when the extremely vulnerable and still-clothed body was material, yet becoming immaterial. First there was the final touching of the cloth-flesh before Rosa left her body. Then came the undressing of the breathless corpse and the shedding of the cloth skin. Next, the women closest to Rosa washed her body and dressed her in a pristine Dominican habit, her burial garment. From this moment, Rosa was no longer human, no longer the intimate flesh-and-blood companion of many years from whom they had learned so much. Her corpse and outer garments now belonged to the cuerpo místico (mystical body) of Lima and would become highly sought-after curative relics.

Even as Rosa lay dying, she gave her final lessons to María de Uzástegui's daughters, her hermanas, as she called them, exhorting them to obey God and their parents and putting out her hand for them to kiss.[114] She gave her blessing to the other women in the room, asking God to watch over all the "ladies and the other female friends and ones I know who are present and absent." Then she asked the household servants and slaves to gather around her bedside and pleaded for their forgiveness for any sins she might have committed against them.[115]

To the very end, Rosa continued to mortify her flesh. When María de Uzástegui attempted to put a more comfortable nightgown on the mortally ill woman, she noted that a serge tunic Rosa wore beneath her outer garment was abrading her skin. Uzástegui notified Rosa's confessor, who immediately ordered that Rosa be dressed in softer fabric.[116] Several witnesses detailed her symptoms—the coloring of her face, her paralyzed side, her grimaces and arched back.[117] Luisa de Santa María and some of the other girls in the room began singing softly to Rosa to help ease her pain.[118] When her hermanas placed a "candle for a good death" in her hands—a symbol of her impending demise—María Antonia de Carrillo, a devotee who became intimate with Rosa near the end of her life, noticed how reserved and composed she looked.[119] But then one last material engagement with cloth took place between María Antonia and Rosa. María Antonia noted that Rosa, consumed by fever, had a shawl or habit—she couldn't remember exactly which—covering her ordinary nightgown. It seemed to be suffocating her, María Antonia thought, but she was quickly told that Rosa had insisted, with the greatest degree of modesty, in "cover[ing] over the different parts of her body that might be seen."[120] Even as she died, Rosa was virtuous to the bone.

Rosa had expressly asked that only María de Uzástegui be allowed to prepare her body for burial. But Uzástegui knew she could not do it alone and had asked Rosa whether she would allow María Antonia to help her.[121] One last time, the two women combed Rosa's cropped hair and gently cleansed her entire body. Once they had dressed her in her burial habit, they propped her against a cushion of scarlet taffeta.[122] In life, Rosa would never have allowed any part of her body to come in contact with such luxurious fabric. But she was no longer the same "Rosa": she had been transmogrified into a sacred object destined to be honored with fine silks and jewels. The shabby garments and severity with which she had treated her body were now being rewarded, "in similar currency," in the next.[123] Her bodily remains were now objects of consumption, full of sacred virtus. As the word of her death spread throughout the city, throngs of visitors soon appeared at the de la Maza home. They called her "saint." They kissed her hands, feet, and face; touched her rosaries; and cut off swatches of her religious habit (and, some say, her body parts).[124]

In the morning, the grieving beata Luisa de Santa María followed the corpse as it was removed from the de la Maza home. Walking behind Rosa, she saw the great commotion in the streets but refused to leave her friend until her body was safely deposited in the Iglesia de Santo Domingo. Once Rosa was placed in the casket, Luisa noted, she was covered with colorful brocaded cloth, "as a sign [that she was in] glory."[125] The crowds were so thick that Catalina de Santa María and her sisters could not get anywhere close to the casket. Catalina did, however, get a glimpse of Rosa's dazzling countenance: "As it was impossible to see her, the saint [Rosa] turned her face fully toward where this witness and her sisters [stood], [and] they could now see her very well; [from this Catalina and her sisters] experienced a singular joy and contentment to see that face so resplendent."[126]

This last physical contact with their beloved sister consoled the beatas. It was a moment of realization: the intimacy of touch, breath, and voice was now gone. Rosa was no longer their teacher, no longer part of a small nucleus of spiritual women. She was now larger than life, and death only intensified limeños' belief in her holiness. Her body and contact relics (including the dirt surrounding her tomb) were treasures for all of Lima, and beyond, to consume.[127] Over the decades, and throughout the Spanish Empire, Rosa's intercessory and healing powers would only continue to grow.[128] And with the passage of time, the miracles associated with Rosa's life (and afterlife) would be altered in the retelling. The stories told by the beatas would be embroidered in extravagant language by male writers and published in the dozens of hagiographies that would soon appear in print.[129]

Conclusions

In the decades following Rosa's death, her virtus continued to be appropriated in material form. Chroniclers recorded stories of young women expressing a fervent desire to imitate Rosa and become beatas or reform their lost and scandalous ways. Like Rosa's contemporaries, they changed their habits and donned plain garb.[130] They copied Rosa's penitential practices and learned about her life from published vidas and stories about her that continued to circulate in Lima. For many years, her childhood home and garden—considered to be sacred spaces—were accessible to those who wanted to seek solace and comfort or reach out to Rosa in prayer. Limeños came hoping to appropriate some of Rosa's healing energy and access her intercessory powers, which they believed were still present there. Lost women sat near the remnants of Rosa's tiny cell and were known to experience spiritual conversions.[131] Although by the 1660s there was much talk about the decaying state of the property, which had changed owners several times, poor Dominican beatas did their best to care for it. The garden was still being imagined by chroniclers as the site where flowers and trees had once bowed in Rosa's presence, but it was now weedy and overgrown and in a ruinous state.[132]

By 1669, the year Rosa was beatified, visitors could barely distinguish the doorways where Rosa had once come and gone. That may be because, just days after Rosa's passing and in the years to come, limeños had been chipping away pieces of the bloodstained walls of the cell and cutting off parts of the door latch, planks from the floor, and pieces of the tiny cupboard.[133] Much to their chagrin, the beatas who had once lived on the property, and who had hoped that a female convent would be erected on the site, were asked to vacate the premises as plans for a male-run sanctuary were put in place after 1669. The beatas were forced to move across the street from Rosa's childhood home and watched as the ramshackle building and water-soaked garden (due to runoff from the nearby hospital's irrigation ditch) were destroyed and a new Dominican sanctuary built.[134] They deeply lamented losing direct access to Rosa's virtus.

Despite the decay of Rosa's body and the destruction of her childhood home, pious women could access her virtus in yet another powerful way. Like her predecessor Saint Catherine of Siena, Rosa had now become a divinely animated statue-person dressed in glorious bejeweled garb and displayed for all to see. To great applause, a statue of Rosa, crafted in Rome, had arrived in the viceregal capital in 1669. That year, during a pageant meant to honor the newly beatified Rosa, the platform carrying her statue was processed next to that of her spiritual mother, Saint Catherine.[135] Meléndez wrote about the event as though it were a reunion of two old friends. He commented, "Rosa could also have let Catalina be free [of obligation] on the day of [Rosa's] festival, but Catherine did not want to leave Rosa alone. For having the daughter come out in public for all the World to see, it was [only] just [that] the Mother [Catherine] be in her proper place [next to Rosa]."[136] In front of the two statues, of mother and daughter, walked twelve young girls dressed in the habits of Dominican beatas. They wore crowns of roses and carried garlands in their hands. For those who observed them, these "devotees" were "insignias of our fragrant Rosa, the beauty of each of these [girls] painted better than in [Rosa's] Image."[137] The "painted" girls resembled Rosa's innocence and beauty more than any simulacrum ever could. In this instance, the material and immaterial bodies of the saint and her protégées were interconnected, spiritually and materially. As one would expect, Rosa followed behind them, as any mother would.

Michel de Certeau once wrote that "something essential is at work in this everyday historicity"—in this case, in the relationships among the belief in the divine nature of materiality, sensorial learning, and female interaction.[138] Indeed, it is in the descriptions of seemingly mundane actions that a deep vein of female spirituality lies. A consideration of the process of imitatio morum that occurred between Rosa and her disciples teaches us about how sensory transfers with and between bodies and objects mattered, how Rosa was remembered as a figure both absent and present at the moment of her death, and how her virtus was accessed decades later by young beatas who were thought to resemble her. Rosa's biography was therefore not simply found in vidas: it was constructed in the depositions of beatification hearings and in the everyday historicity of doing and being. In their testimonies, pious women described their observations of Rosa and in the process rendered the sensorial experiences they had had with their beloved spiritual mother into viable narratives. From these sources we therefore come to understand that these beatas could experience the perceptible form of things apart from their matter; they also understood that seeing or sensing Rosa's body was intricately linked with their own bodily and sensorial experiences and the material objects with which they engaged.

But what does this knowledge circulating among Rosa and her disciples tell us about the connections between the world of the mind and external actions in the world? It suggests a mobility for women in terms of how they might express their spirituality, their sense of social place in Lima, and their spatial pathways. It also suggests a deep undercurrent of sacred exchanges occurring almost unseen, yet visible in the most public of places. The existence of female circuits of knowledge does not presume a *conscious* network of female solidarity, friendship, or loyalty, especially given the climate of suspicion generated by inquisitorial scrutiny, nor did all pious women share the same perspectives or knowledge. Dressing statues and engaging with cloth were deeply gendered spiritual experiences that were integral to a feminine epistemological experience of the sacred, even if men also dressed sculptures and engaged sensorially with their material and immaterial properties. The mutable knowledge of the material-immaterial world was, then, passed on from woman to woman, generation after generation, creating a sororial dialogue that transcended time and space.

2

READING THE BODY
Mystical Theology and Spiritual Actualization
in Early Seventeenth-Century Lima

. . .

The first line of Genesis, "In the beginning was the Word and the Word was God," assumes that the "Word," or language, preceded "God." With his breath, or *spiritus*, God then created flesh and all other forms of signification in the world. Because of this belief in the origin of life, most seventeenth-century Catholics were convinced that there *must be* a "speech of God" and that a concord between the infinite and language must exist.[1] Given that God's word (or spiritus) was the object to be read, Catholics also believed that sacred language (which was both spirit and matter) could be accessed in specific loci. Books were one of the vehicles by which one could access the word of God, or eternal wisdom.[2] To capture the essence (the -*ness*) contained in language, humans merely needed to employ any of their five senses.[3]

The previous chapter argued that Rosa de Lima's disciples learned through the senses and through an engagement with material objects such as cloth and religious statues, which they believed to be alive. As they communicated by means of these immaterial-material objects, they conveyed knowledge to one another through spoken and written language. Their bodies, both physical and spiritual, were also actively involved in acts of divine transmission. Through their senses they learned to "read" what was divine in Rosa and then conveyed that in narrative, biographical form. Like a book, Rosa was a readable text.

This chapter continues to explore the relationship between materiality and immateriality by considering how the biographies of pious women were constructed through a reading of their bodies while they were in an altered state of consciousness called *arrobamiento*, communicating with divine beings. Just as early modern subjects employed their senses to appropriate the content of books, they could also *read* the bodies of mystics. The ecstatic body therefore had a particular kind of biography, which tells us a great deal about how seventeenth-century readers and mystics accessed and communicated their understandings of divinity. To understand this more fully, however, an exploration of reading and of what was considered a readable text is required.

Reading mystical discourse in books involved different senses. In 1635 Gerónima de San Francisco wrote in her vida that her contemplative years began when she discovered books on prayer and interioridad, which, she claimed, impelled her movement toward God.[4] Her confessor, the well-respected Juan Pérez Menacho, directed her to read Teresa de Ávila (1515–82). Her reaction to that text was powerful:

> He greatly encouraged me to read from the book of Saint Theresa, and that afterward I should tell him what I thought. I then looked for the book, and read from it. I did not even notice the time when I finished it, because of the great consolation and satisfaction I felt from that great teacher who had been taught by the Holy Spirit. . . . Reading it [brought] a thousand tastes of pleasure, and joy to see the tremendous benefits I had received from the hand of God, without deserving or impeding them. . . . I became so devoted to this saint and her book and her image, that I always have her with me, and will have her [with me] until I die.[5]

For Gerónima, it was a tremendous consolation to verify her own experiences through Teresa, probably the most influential authority for pious female visionaries in seventeenth-century Latin America.[6] Even more notable is that Gerónima literally carried Teresa within her, by constantly reading her images and her writings and by filling herself with the *spiritus* of God projected through each of Teresa's words.

Like visual images or objects, a book was thought to contain both the real content and a likeness of that content. A reader like Gerónima could imprint the real contents of the text and the simulacrum within her imagination. The internalized imprint of the book could then act as both a stimulus and a mnemonic device as one read or listened to other spiritual literature. But as experts on the history of reading and communication, including Roger Chartier, Fernando Bouza, and others, have emphasized, seventeenth-century forms of reading were not divided systematically into a typology associated with the *object* to be read (the *literality*), whether it be a book, a painting, or the body itself.[7] According to Michel de Certeau, readers had two expectations: "that there be a *readable* space (a literality)" and that a means exist "for the *actualization* of the work (a reading)."[8] What constituted readable texts varied because they "did not necessarily come in book form: some were orally produced works, or visions which were then rendered into a narrative structure using language and symbols to invite interpretation and appropriation."[9] For readers, "what was oral, visual or iconic, and written (in both printed and manuscript texts) all fulfilled the same expressive, communicative, and recollective functions."[10]

This broad definition of what constituted a readable text had a dramatic effect on reading habits in colonial Lima, the viceregal capital of the Spanish Empire.[11] By the first third of the seventeenth century, the availability of books in Lima had increased, thanks to an active printing press and a vigorous transatlantic market. Reading, or the actualization of a work, however, continued to involve both aural and oral transmission of the language contained in a printed text. In fact, one form was not privileged over the other.[12] Books and manuscripts were read aloud and listened to, not merely captured by the eye scanning the page.

The way that individuals read and then comprehended religious doctrine was directly related to early modern notions of sense perception, adapted from Galenic and Aristotelian notions. Most theologians and scientists believed that the body contained three souls—in order from lower to higher, the vegetative, the sensitive (which contained the perceptual faculties of the external and internal senses), and the intellective—and that each successively higher layer of the soul contained the lower form(s).[13] Employing the five external senses of sight, hearing, smell, taste, and touch and the five internal senses of cognition, memory, fantasy, imagination, and common sense within the sensitive soul, an individual could perceive absent sense objects, including language. Thus, when Gerónima read Teresa de Ávila, she experienced God through her senses, which were equipped to receive the sensible forms of images of material objects—to be distinguished from their substantial or specific forms—without the associated matter.[14] An aerated fluid called *spiritus* (known as the "first instrument of the soul") was believed to carry the perceived sensation contained within the object (in this case, God's spiritus on the page) to the fantasy or imagination, which then sent the image to the heart, which could accept or reject it.[15] In Spanish this action of perceiving objects through sensory mechanisms was called *sentimiento*, or feeling.[16]

Likewise, reading God's divine essence required sensory perception. Although a reader might initially not grasp the divine content (God's spiritus held within the words on the page) in scripture or other religious texts, many Catholics believed that the continued actualization of the text would eventually lead to God. Reading spiritual texts stimulated the spiritual faculties to locate or sense the material and immaterial referents (*sentir*, "to perceive"), and this process eventually opened up the possibility of deeper and more intimate personal communication with God.[17] The goal (which might take decades to accomplish) was to perceive God from within the intellective soul, considered by the renowned Spanish theologian Luis de Granada (1504–88) to hold "some of God's imprints or footprints." Granada argued, "Because what [God] blew [i.e., his breath] came from within himself, He wanted us to understand that the soul was something divine, and that it came from God's breast."[18]

Achieving what mystics such as Teresa de Ávila and John of the Cross (1542–91) called mystical union with God was a profound experience that took years of preparation. But this communication at the deepest level of the soul did not occur through the mind. For mystics, the body was indispensable to achieving union with God. Most Christians knew that in the beginning, God (the Word) wrote his first book when he created the world and the first humans. They also knew that later, to "write the word conceived in his breast, the concept of his heart, [and] the verb of his understanding," God wrote his second, "very white and pure volume" of humankind, within the "divine book" of Mary. The incarnation of the Word in Mary's body became "the earthly generation of his son, Christ," embodied in human flesh.[19] Thus, the body was a locus through which one could potentially access God's divine imprint.

Just as Christ was both human and spirit, the body, according to Catholic theology, comprised both flesh and spirit. Most theologians and scientists of the seventeenth century agreed that (rather than consisting of the three divisions—body, soul, and mind—that we associate with modern thought) the "body" was composed of spheres of souls, ranging from the outer flesh (*carne*) to the innermost dwelling of the intellective soul, where the imprint of God's spiritus resided.[20] Mystical theologians of the sixteenth century, including John of the Cross and Teresa de Ávila, believed that one should endeavor to strip down through the layers of the soul to reach the innermost sanctum of the intellective soul, where mystical communication with God was possible.

However, gendered perceptions distinguished the male from the female body. By the beginning of the seventeenth century, the Aristotelian notion that women were imperfect males had begun to fade; most now believed the female body contained the vegetative, sensitive, and intellective souls.[21] However, theologians argued that females were more closely associated with the lower sensitive soul than with the higher intellective soul. Weaker powers of reason and intellect, a tendency toward flights of fantasy, a strong imagination, and more susceptibility to vice (women were considered subject to their passions) were seen as the psychological consequences of their physical shape and colder humors, "which [did] not possess sufficient energy to drive matter up towards the head." A woman's body was likened to wax, because "impressions can be registered easily and remain filed on cold and moist substances."[22]

Because of these deficiencies, women's spiritual formation required self-scrutiny, discernment, and a vigilant confessor. Yet, from the perspective of mysticism, their physical weaknesses, and in particular their impressionability and vulnerability, could also be strengths.[23] These qualities supported a propensity toward reading mystical experiences sent by God through the perceptual faculties of the external and internal senses. For that reason, a visionary could literally read her body (or the imprints received by the sensitive and intellective souls, which formed part of her body), because it was considered a space that could be read or actualized as a text. Once the spoken mystical experiences of the visionary were translated and embodied in language, they were often recorded and then transmitted and shared with others, by reading aloud or by silently drinking in the text through the eyes.

Reading therefore involved the parallel processes of aural and visual transmission of divine knowledge by means of books and the body. The bodies of female mystics told stories that were read by eager observers. To explore books and the body as readable texts, this chapter follows encounters between what Paul Ricoeur calls "the world of the text" and the "world of the reader" in the realm of mystical communications with God.[24] In Lima between 1600 and

1650, the world of the text included the bodies of distinguished (*esclarecidas*) and venerable mystics such as Isabel de Porras Marmolejo (1551–1631), a Spanish professed beata of the Third Order of Penitent Franciscans; Gerónima de San Francisco (1573–1643), a Spanish nun in the Monasterio de las Descalzas de San Joseph; Rosa de Lima (1586–1617), a Dominican beata canonized in 1671 (see chapter 1); Luisa Melgarejo de Sotomayor (1578–1651), a Franciscan beata; Úrsula de Jesús (1604–66), a black donada (religious servant) of the Order of Poor Clares; as well as several other visionaries tried by the Inquisition in 1623 and condemned as false mystics in an auto-da-fé in 1625. The world of the reader involved seeing, hearing, speaking, reading, and writing: all interrelated forms of actualization that could lead toward divine knowledge. It involved creating narratives, or biographies, from their observations of mystics, who could access both the materiality and the immateriality of divinity while in an altered state of consciousness.

Reading Practices in Seventeenth-Century Lima

By 1600 the proliferation of the printed word in Europe and Latin America in general, and in Lima in particular, meant that the lay population, which until that time had received its education through iconography, sermons, and the confessional, now learned visually and aurally through books.[25] In fact, these different but complementary practices of literacy formed the centerpiece of the Catholic Church's efforts to Christianize its subjects during the Counter-Reformation. Ecclesiastical authors insisted that it was the transmission of the word from an authority to a lay audience that mattered most, not the form by which the transmission occurred. Books were particularly treasured objects for church authorities living in a Counter-Reformation world, who now pressed for deeper and more widespread Catholic devotion by actively disseminating knowledge about the lives of saints and martyrs to inspire emulation.[26] As an anonymous Jesuit priest proclaimed in a sermon given in Chuquisaca (in modern-day Bolivia) in 1617, knowledge gained from books could serve as a weapon against ignorance, the nourishment of the devil: "Not only is wisdom better than weapons, but studying [the contents of] books also serves as a weapon . . . the written lines as pikes . . . the letters, the punctuation marks [and] the commas as balls and cannon shot used in warfare to defeat an enemy. God knows how to use books as weapons and commas as jewels to make men tremble."[27]

Religious texts acted as shields against ignorance and evil, but they could also allow access to the divine in myriad ways. Devotional works and books of hours could help regulate the pulse of daily spiritual life. Mystical works often contained descriptions of the development of a Christian life; they served as praxis manuals for mental prayer, and they provided an interpretive vocabulary for supernatural experiences. Hagiographies newly translated into Spanish enabled readers to access and imitate the virtues of medieval and early modern saints and mystics.[28] In fact, hagiographies, or the lives of saints, topped the best-seller lists, in part because, between 1480 and 1700, 443 of these works were published for the first time in Spanish.[29] The sheer volume of published vidas and their vigorous transatlantic circulation had the effect of inscribing reading and readers in entirely new ways. Laypersons incorporated the stories of saints long dead into their storytelling repertoires. More dramatically, dozens of pious visionaries and mystics throughout seventeenth-century Latin America began to emulate the conduct of the exemplary individuals they were reading about, sometimes for the first time. The imitation of the lives of European female saints, combined with the flowering of a new affective spirituality movement (dedication to and imitation of the life and Passion of Christ), led to the publication of dozens of vidas of exemplary nuns in the viceroyalties of New Spain and Peru.[30]

The Society of Jesus arrived in Lima in 1567, establishing a printing press there that helped to foster interest in Catholicism among colonial subjects. It also facilitated the circulation of inexpensive prayer books and books of hours among elite and nonelite limeños.[31] By the seventeenth century, both lay and religious persons, elites and nonelites, were reading and listening to religious texts in their homes, at Mass, or in the presence of their confessors.[32] As contemplative and mystical works became available to a wider public, limeños began to consider reading as integral to their spiritual growth and their daily lives. For some, the ability to access spiritual texts produced conversion experiences.

The increasing availability of mystical works in early seventeenth-century Lima also helped produce a mystical movement there. But this movement occurred in a Counter-Reformation Catholic world where standards of orthodoxy were fairly rigidly defined, although not always enforced. Just as Inquisition authorities sought to distinguish true mystics and visionaries from those who feigned sanctity, they also sought to censor and control the publication, sale, and distribution of books containing potentially heterodox ideas.[33] The first attempt to censor mystical works that promoted interioridad had come with the publication of the *Index Librorum Prohibitorum* in Spain in 1559. The church's initial ban on works by Luis de Granada and other mystics sent shock waves through the viceregal capital. However, Granada's writings were circulating freely there by 1600, suggesting that the enforcement of censorship was uneven and sporadic.[34] For instance, following on the heels of the increasing publication and distribution of books in Lima between 1601 and 1640 came orders from Madrid to the Lima Inquisition tribunal to search for questionable books.[35] The *calificadores* (assessors) and *comisarios* (commissioners) then examined those works deemed questionable to see whether the contents conformed to standards of orthodoxy.[36] The continuing concern is attested by the inquisitors' assessments of particular books in 1619 and then again in 1629.[37]

Not only were authorities concerned with the content of certain mystical texts, but they also expressed consternation that women should be savoring the contents. Given that females were thought to be unformed and incomplete males, subject to "breaches in boundaries, with lack of shape or definition, with openings and exudings and spillings forth," they were considered more vulnerable and more suspect to wayward and dangerous influences.[38] Because the feminine capacity for rational discernment was also regarded as limited, some theologians warned against women reading devotional texts, or even reading at all.[39] This misogynist discourse can be detected as early as 1583 in Lima, when Inquisition authorities condemned a small prayer book entitled *Consuelo y oratorio espiritual*, claiming that if copies circulated among "common people and women . . . these [people] would interpret them in their own way."[40] But opinions on whether women were imperfect beings and whether they should read religious texts were diverse and often contradictory. Popular writers like Juan Luis Vives (1492–1540) promoted female literacy and paid a great deal of attention to "those things that aide in cultivating the soul[s]" of young women.[41] In that regard, Vives suggested a list of appropriate spiritual books "composed by saintly men" to "shed light on the darkness and gloominess within which we walk in this life."[42]

The uneven but persistent sanctioning and censoring of devotional and theological texts, along with the wide-ranging opinions about the virtues of female literacy, was contradicted by the active circulation of these works, many of which had been translated into the vernacular for the first time. Yet, in the end, what mattered to confessors and to Inquisition authorities monitoring the conduct of pious women was not that they were reading religious texts but how they appropriated the content. Although confessors in Lima were responsible for ensuring that their confessees were reading appropriate texts and that their visions were not demonically influenced, their enforcement of orthodox standards was uneven and sporadic.[43] Most pious women were ignored; quite often it was only the most public individuals (whether considered to be living saints or part of a dangerous group) who were held under the microscope. As we know from the previous chapter, the sine qua non mystic Rosa de Lima was considered by many of Lima's key ecclesiastical authorities to be the model, *perfecta religiosa*, or the epitome of truly orthodox religious virtues.[44] Although she had read a great deal and, as several scholars have pointed out, her visions and texts were directly influenced by other mystical thinkers, she had to assure Inquisition authorities, when they scrutinized her in 1614, that her mystical knowledge had not been learned from books. Not only would this have been considered unorthodox, but for a potential saint it would also greatly diminish the argument that God had chosen to speak directly through her. To quote Rosa herself: "I confess in all truth and in the presence of God that all the favors I have written about in the notebooks as they are inscribed and portrayed on these two pieces of paper, I have not seen nor have I read in any book, but [the favors have only been] represented in this sinner by the powerful hand of God, in whose book I read what is Eternal Wisdom."[45]

While, in Rosa's case, interpreting mystical texts might have diminished the prospects of sainthood, the collective reading practices of the six false mystics called before the Inquisition tribunal in 1623 were automatically considered unorthodox. During the proceedings, several were questioned at length because they were thought to have misappropriated the content of the books they had read.[46] One of them, Inés de Velasco, maintained that "all women who try to serve Our Lord and to commend themselves to Him have many prayer books." Her statement indicated that reading spiritual texts was a common practice among women, but she then qualified it by adding, "[Having] so many books is unsuitable and [even] harmful for them."[47]

In the end, intermittent book censorship and the public trial of six beatas accused of false sanctity in 1623 did not hinder pious women in Lima from reading devotional and contemplative texts as a means of deepening their spiritual knowledge.[48] In fact, it was customary for confessors to recommend, give, or loan books in the vernacular to their confessees to help guide their spiritual progress. Moreover, after 1600 many hagiographies and behavior manuals were readily available for women in Lima to buy, loan, or borrow.[49]

The proliferation and availability of spiritual texts both inside and outside monastic settings illustrates the creation and expansion of "readable spaces," to use Certeau's term, in seventeenth-century Lima. These changes also affected the actualization of religious works, because the appropriation and internalization of the contents of such works (that is, reading) fostered new forms of sociability; they created new modes of theological thought, and they deepened understandings of the divine Word.[50]

During the actualization of texts, men and women continued to hear rather than see the narrative content of devotional texts or hagiographies, which were meant to be communicated or performed orally.[51] It was not at all uncommon for people to say that "they had heard [a certain text] being read and had read [it]."[52] The *prelection*, or reading aloud to one or more people, whether in convent refectories, the confessional, or the drawing rooms or oratories of private homes, involved the act of an individual orally conveying the information contained in the text to the listener, who was considered an aural reader.[53] The synchronicity of aural and visual forms of actualization stemmed from the belief that the external sense organs transmitted knowledge through the eyes or ears to the heart. Forms of communication involved the texture of the reader's voice—her gestures, intonations, timbre, and expressivity—as well as the listener's reception of the spiritus (color, texture, light) of words through the eyes and the ears.[54] Archival evidence shows that reading in public was not gender specific. Both men and women performed written works aloud and received the narrative content aurally.[55] Whether in the small garden where Santa Rosa gathered with individual women or small groups, or in the homes of Luisa Melgarejo de Sotomayor or Gonzalo de la Maza and his wife, María de Uzástegui, men and women read extracts of the immensely popular *Flos Sanctorum*, a collective hagiography detailing the picturesque and tragic lives of saints and martyrs and stimulating the imagination. Men and women also discussed the most profound mystical writings of Teresa of Ávila or Luis de Granada.[56]

As hagiographies and devotional texts were read silently or performed orally, their contents provoked different responses from readers and listeners. Individuals "speaking" the written language took on the exalted, authoritative role as the "mediator of a body of highly valued texts."[57] In verbalizing the content aloud, readers also fed their eyes and ears as they listened to themselves.[58] For persons listening to the text, the book's content could be actualized in distinct ways.[59] At the most basic level, reading scripture, a spiritual text, or a hagiography could convert nonbelievers or transform dilatory Christians; these texts were meant to "move hearts to God."[60]

The aural or visual appropriation of the divine content contained in books might also produce behavioral changes based on the desire to imitate a saint or Jesus Christ. Inés de Velasco reported that "when she *saw* books in Latin being read or sung in church, it raised her spirit toward God, [and it was] as though she could understand the content, because she felt they were speaking with God."[61] The content of recently translated hagiographies also facilitated discussions among women about the virtues and spiritual adventures of medieval and early modern saints such as Lutgarde, Gertrude, Catherine of Genoa, María de la Antigua, and Catherine of Siena.[62] Many female disciples viewed the lives of their forebears as "living books" that could structure their daily lives and set the course of their spiritual paths. They copied the behavioral attributes of these female saints and memorized the contents of their works or works about them, and then reflected the saints' lives against their own empty and inadequate lives "like a painted altar screen."[63]

Reading, as we have seen, was meant to impress an image on the soul of the reader. It also involved selecting a passage from a religious text, or scripture, and then committing it to memory in order to recall—in essence, to reread—the imprinted and internalized knowledge from the book again and again. The mnemonic image held within the imagination became a simulacrum of the original content of the book as well as a means of recognizing the meanings contained in other readings. Reading also allowed the listeners to recognize spiritual commonplaces (rather than learning them for the first time) by searching their memory (an affect in the soul) and then completing the meanings of the text already imprinted in their minds.[64] We see evidence of this process in Vives's *Instrucción de la mujer cristiana*, where he suggested that *doncellas* (unmarried females) select a pertinent passage from sacred scripture and copy it many times until "it is firmly imprinted in the memory."[65]

To read spiritual texts (or to see them being read) not only imparted information but also facilitated internal contemplation.[66] For instance, both Luis de Granada and Teresa of Ávila advocated reading such passages to help to still the senses and prepare for meditative practice.[67] Reading also served as a bridge toward the next stage of prayer, or imaginative meditation on a particular passage related to some aspect of Christ's or Mary's life. Here, the visual (the word on the page) and the internally produced visual image (or reading) fused. At this stage, the immaterial quality of divineness held in the page (spiritus) was carried to the beholder's eye or ear; the spiritus then "moved" a particular faculty or sensation. Some believed that the spiritus traveled to the heart, where passionate reactions were formed. This view helps explain why Gerónima de San Francisco described reading as a guide toward placing "a treasure house in her heart." As she read, she prayed for guidance to capture some essence of divinity held in the text itself: "After a little while I discovered some books and I chose one very small one about the twelve excellences of Our Lady and about the offering of her very blessed Rosary. When

I discovered and read it, it gave me such pleasures and solace and I told Him so in my prayers. [Oh] extremely Blessed Virgin Mary, if I have found some treasure in this little book for my soul, I will carry it with me."[68]

The act of reading a religious text filled with visually stimulating narratives could also act as a catalyst for the divine word to emerge on the blank page of the soul in the form of visions or ecstatic supernatural experiences. The reading eye or ear carried the images to the heart, which then stimulated the body to reproduce a particular kind of experience—for example, of Christ's suffering or, in the case of Gerónima, joy.[69] Some believed that after reading a descriptive passage, they could more easily taste, smell, hear, and see Christ's Passion.

Vidas and devotional texts also produced supernatural effects such as visions, alternate states of consciousness, and communication with celestial beings and the dead. Several of the six beatas tried by the Inquisition in Lima in 1623 reported that their supernatural experiences occurred as a result of ingesting and actualizing in an unsanctioned manner the divine content held in the writings of Luis de Granada and Saints Teresa of Ávila, Catherine of Siena, and Lutgarde.[70] Through their sensorial and physical bodies, these women claimed to experience the "delights" of God.[71] For some the experience was even more profound; while Teresa of Ávila was reading, she at times experienced sentimiento, or the indubitable presence of God.[72]

The Body as a Living Book

Reading religious texts opened up new possibilities of mystical communion for women, although, as many realized, it was considered essential to avoid dangerous misinterpretations. Before 1559 Teresa of Ávila could choose from any number of mystical texts to read before she engaged in mental prayer.[73] After vernacular translations of the Bible as well as works on prayer and devotion were placed on the list of prohibited books in 1559, Teresa de Ávila began to find recourse in direct communion with God, who, she claimed, would speak the "living book" to her.[74] Needless to say, church authorities wished to exert control over Teresa de Ávila's direct access to God; however, their antimystical efforts were thwarted by those theologians and practitioners who saw mysticism as an integral tradition of Western Christendom. Inadvertently, the prohibition of mystical texts produced a new kind of readable space, which also provided a safeguard for women facing intense scrutiny from confessors and other ecclesiastical authorities. Instead of reading a book, they could now claim to read God through their bodies.[75] Teresa de

Ávila's creative response produced a new form of literacy for the generations of female mystics who followed her in Spain and Latin America. Her reliance on the living book as a source of actualization resonated with dozens of mystics around the globe. Even decades after the publication of Teresa de Ávila's *Vida*, the limeña donada Úrsula de Jesús referred to the living book in several of her visions, including one where Christ appeared to her, showing her his feet and saying, *"This is the book from which you must learn."*[76]

The possibility that God's divine wisdom could be communicated through the body relates to scripture as well as the belief in the quintessential female, the Virgin Mary, as the "Book in which God wanted to write the word conceived in his breast, the concept of his heart, and the verb of his understanding."[77] The bodies of sensitive women blessed by God could serve as texts of "experiences of mystical transport that spoken or written language did not and could not articulate."[78] Many female visionaries received God's word (in language, images, or sensorial impressions) while experiencing rapture (arrobamiento), described in orthodox texts as a type of trance where a loss (*enajenación*) of the senses occurred. Through ecstatic rapture, mystics "became engaged with God in an act of inscription," as one scholar described it.[79] While in this state (which could occur only after years of careful preparation and mental prayer), they were able to access and then read the internal domain of their spiritual senses, which received and processed the information sent from the beyond. At the same time, observers could note (read) the subtle changes registering on the physical body as the divine exchange occurred.[80] Thus, as when one turns the pages of a book, the body served as a somatic vessel through which divine knowledge could be transmitted, written, and then read by the self and others through a system of signs registered both in and on the body.

In her writings Teresa of Ávila described arrobamiento (she preferred the term *suspensión*) as a tool toward spiritual development, which formed a "continuum" from prayer of union (*oración de unión*) to ecstasy and, finally, to union with God.[81] As an outgrowth of continued prayer and meditation, arrobamiento was a means by which the internal senses could be dulled and the spiritual senses could begin to stir.[82] Teresa wrote that "during the rapture itself, the body is very often like a corpse, unable to do anything of itself."[83] As the hands became cold, the faculties dulled, the ability to speak was lost, and, eventually, the self was "annihilated," the blank parchment of the soul was readied for God to speak to and write on.[84] Teresa proclaimed in the *Moradas* (Interior Castle), "Here is this soul which God has made, as it were, completely foolish in order the better *to impress upon it* true wisdom. For as long as such a soul is in this state, it can neither see nor hear nor understand."[85]

At first, a pious individual would use her exterior bodily senses to read what were called corporeal, supernatural visions. But as she stripped down through the sensitive and then intellective layers of the soul, God could begin to write (*imprimir*) his book directly on those interior realms. At this next level, what were called *imaginative visions* would enter directly into the imagination and the fantasy (both internal senses located in the sensitive soul) using the spiritual eyes (*ojos del alma*) or ears. God could then communicate with or without language.[86]

Eventually, through continual mental prayer, the soul's evolving knowledge of God, and God's awakening of the soul, the divine would become a reality lived within the self, "not an Otherness perceived from the outside."[87] At this point, the third and highest level of intellective visions (Teresa preferred the term *nonimaginative visions*) would be mediated directly through the spiritual faculties, bypassing the bodily senses altogether. God would then engrave (*esculpir*) the innermost region of the intellective soul without using images or language.[88]

Just as mystical experiences were varied and distinguished by degrees of profundity, entering a state of rapture, often considered a prelude to visions, could occur under different circumstances. Some visionaries became absorbed while reading or discussing a spiritual text or an aspect of the life of Christ, others while praying the rosary, after taking communion, or while quietly meditating in church or at home.[89] Merely engaging in spiritual parlance might propel a visionary into a trancelike state. At a spiritual conventicle held in Lima, witnesses described Luisa Melgarejo falling into a trance while discussing the Immaculate Conception. According to Inés de Velasco, who was present at the event, Luisa then spoke "many things of God."[90] Her ready ability to enter a meditative trance caused Diego de Córdova y Salinas to note that he and others were cautious not to inadvertently trigger such a state: "Those who desired her conversation tried not to speak about divine love because then she [Luisa] would [immediately] enter a state of rapture in whatever posture she was in at that moment. I am a witness to this. Many times when I visited her I would lose her conversation, leaving her enraptured and absorbed, outside her senses, with no small disconsolation on my part, when carelessly I spoke with her about God."[91] This suspension of the senses could go on for extended periods of time. Gerónima de San Francisco became renowned throughout Lima for attending Jubilee masses at the Iglesia del Hospital de la Caridad. On one occasion she spent over forty hours on her knees in an ecstatic trance.[92]

The state of rapture, which left the senses in abeyance, could produce differing results, depending on the individual's degree of spiritual development. Some women would remain in a trance resembling unconsciousness; others had visions involving the faculties of hearing or speech.[93] Sometimes the visions—such as witnessing a scene in purgatory unfolding—were an appropriation or reading of narrative content originally read in a book. A visionary could also hear or see messages sent by God or other celestial beings, or receive instructions on how to read and interpret a difficult theological passage. In his monumental *Crónica franciscana*, Córdova y Salinas recorded an experience that Diego Pérez, the provincial of the Order of Saint Augustine, once had with the visionary Isabel de Porras Marmolejo:

> After he had read a difficult passage of Sacred Scripture he went to visit her [Isabel de Porras Marmolejo] and [during] their conversation he told her about the difficulty of the material he was reading. Instantly she entered a state of rapture and remained [in that state] for three-quarters of an hour. Having waited until after she returned from her ecstatic state, she [then] responded to the difficult questions, and resolved them with terms and words so ponderable, and with such acuity and probity of celestial wisdom, that the Padre Maestro, confused and as though beside himself, publicized that if there were saints in this city of Lima, this blessed woman was one of them.[94]

Despite the Inquisition's continued suspicion that raptures (*arrobos*) were the province only of deranged and arrogant women, descriptions and sightings of raptures not only pervaded contemporary hagiographies but were common parlance among Lima's inhabitants.[95] Archival evidence also suggests that many limeños considered ecstatic trances to be orthodox, acceptable, and accessible public practices. Confessors charged with carefully observing the conduct of their protégées actually encouraged and praised their arrobamientos as a superior method of prayer and a sign of sanctity.[96]

Because mystical transport fell outside the range of conventional behavior, witnesses found it necessary to develop a descriptive vocabulary that would give further credence to these experiences.[97] In that sense, interpreting somatic signs revealed in the ecstatic state replicated reading practices (for example, interpreting a difficult passage or allegory, or a gloss) and required that witnesses employ a comprehensible terminology and interpretive framework.[98] For instance, describing someone as "a body without feeling, estranged from the senses as though [it were] made of marble," was understood to mean that God had graced the ecstatic individual with his presence.[99] In 1618 Catalina de Santa María, a companion of Rosa de Lima (discussed in chapter 1), reported in the first beatification hearing for Rosa that she had once accompanied the future saint to a church to pray. When she saw that Rosa had entered a trance, she edged closer. She first noticed that Rosa's body remained immobile and without sensation; later her cheeks changed in color from a deathly pale to flushed to resplendent like the rays of the sun.[100] Fire or natural heat was considered a natural property contained within the body, but supernatural heat, especially with purgative qualities, came from God. Apparently, Catalina de Santa María was reading the sign of supernatural heat emanating from within Rosa's soul and heart.[101]

Because arrobos were given by God's grace as a blessing or favor (*merced*), witnesses imprinted memories of such readings in their minds. For instance, in 1632 former students from the Colegio de Santa Teresa, one of the most prestigious and elite educational centers for girls in Lima, were called by inquisitors to answer questions about their teacher, Isabel de Porras Marmolejo, celebrated throughout Lima as a visionary. "[They were asked] if they knew that she [Porras Marmolejo] showed great signs of the blessings and favors that our Lord gave her with ecstasies, raptures and total suspension of the bodily faculties; showing, at various times, and on many occasions, to be absorbed and totally engulfed by [her] love for God, seeing her on different occasions or [even] witnessing her various times levitated above the ground or without the use of her exterior senses while awake, and speaking to God."[102] Just as they memorized the content of devotional texts, these impressionable girls witnessed the frequent raptures and levitations of their beloved teacher and learned to read and interpret divine signs manifested on her body (text). In fact, the opportunity to observe someone like Porras Marmolejo firsthand formed part of the didactic training (probably unconsciously exerted) of the privileged daughters of the elite. Three years after Porras Marmolejo's death, these same students still had vivid recall of her in an ecstatic trance—sighing and groaning, her eyes vacant and staring, breath shallow, mouth shaped as though releasing a silent moan.[103] Witnesses at her beatification hearing claimed that although their teacher's body lacked a strong pulse, her face maintained a look of complete serenity throughout the rapture.[104]

The Language of Mystical Narratives: Reading, Speaking, and Writing

Just as mystical literature could, as Certeau once wrote, "compose scripts of the body," the bodies of women who had experienced profound mystical journeys could serve as "cinematographic" objects from which narratives and holograms of mystical truth could be derived.[105] God could imprint or engrave messages on the physical body, which could then be read as a text and preserved as a mnemonic device or a talisman. This process was integral to creating spiritual biographies. The most dramatic representation of it occurred after Porras Marmolejo expired in 1631. When her former students María de los Angeles and Juana de Cea undressed the corpse to prepare it for the wake, they beheld a wound, "colored and inflamed," in the shape of a half-moon on her left side below the breast.[106] Years later, in 1651, Córdova y Salinas's *Crónica franciscana* immortalized this event (or reading) when he compared the mark on Porras Marmolejo's body to "the spear wound they gave Christ on the Cross." Even more interesting than his scriptural analogy was his description of how devotees had flocked to read God's imprint on the corpse. Wanting to preserve the language of God's text, someone made an etching (estampa) of the wound as Porras Marmolejo lay in state. During her funeral oration, her former confessor stood in the pulpit and "showed the engraving of the wound to the congregation."[107] Here, reading and appropriating knowledge inscribed on the body occurred in three consecutive ways. First, the students read her body and located a sign of sanctity; next, an artist read the wound and reproduced it on paper; and, finally, the congregation read the simulacrum of Porras Marmolejo's wound forever imprinted on vellum.

This story also illustrates the profound interconnection between reading and writing as a process of actualization in seventeenth-century society. As Bouza has argued, writing, as a sort of "painting," transmitted a "reflection of an absent image or an echo of an absent voice. . . . It was understood as a faithful copy of that which is oral or visual."[108] The visual and written reproduction of an "absent image" (Porras Marmolejo's Christlike wound) also occurred when artists, commissioned to create portraits of a saintly individual lying in state, attempted to capture some of the spiritus of their now-absent souls with their palettes. When the beato Juan Ruíz died, his corpse remained available for the public to view for four days. At that point, several artists "reproduced some portraits of his face," which "was so suave and composed that it did not seem as though the soul had left the body, but rather, that it had been reunited with it."[109]

Attempts to skillfully reproduce the traces of divine spiritus in a saintly countenance or inflamed stigmata paralleled the intentions of those whose quills recorded descriptions of arrobos meant to capture the voice of the divine in an ecstatic body. Córdova y Salinas's *Crónica franciscana* included an entire chapter on the prayers, raptures, and ecstasies of the *ecstática* (ecstatic) Porras Marmolejo. Córdova y Salinas copied and inscribed others' readings of Porras Marmolejo from the past into his text. In doing so, he not only validated an interpretive vocabulary and practice of reading the body of this venerable woman but permanently codified Porras Marmolejo's experiences of the prayer of union and imaginative visions as part of the literary canon to be read and experienced by future generations. He was writing a biography of a body in ecstatic union with God.

Priests and witnesses were not the only ones to read and write about their observations of women in ecstatic rapture. Visionaries and mystics, too, kept careful track of their altered states. But if, as we have seen, reading was considered a potentially dangerous activity for lay and religious women, writing was even more so.[110] When Teresa de Ávila was denied access to key mystical works, she began to realize her own vocation as a writer, "speak[ing] in writing, [and] writ[ing] in speaking."[111] Written language helped her to align what she was going to say with what she had already said.[112] She always insisted that the words she spoke and recorded were not hers but God's, because, in Certeau's words, she temporarily substituted her speaking "I" voice "for the inaccessible divine."[113] In order to write (like a man), she could speak her writing like a woman, allowing her to circumvent prescribed gender norms and, moreover, to register a previously pronounced discourse—a practice that resonated with contemporary understandings of the symbiotic relationship between speaking (orality) and writing.[114] Her published writings, which explained how to communicate with the divine, had a profound impact on devout women throughout the Catholic world. Mystics in Lima zealously followed the Teresian model of "textualizing" their corporeal experiences of mystical union by rendering, as much as possible, the ineffable into an orthodox and comprehensible narrative structure.[115]

Of course, writing required the sanction of a confessor, which meant that pious women like Rosa de Lima, Gerónima de San Francisco, Luisa Melgarejo, and numerous other visionaries in Lima became *escritoras por obediencia*, female authors following the orders of confessors. As these women began to inscribe their living-book experiences on paper, their writings were scrutinized carefully to exclude unorthodox content and to ensure that their intention was not to draw attention to themselves but to allow God to speak to others. Luisa Melgarejo, for example, claimed that the Lord had ordered her to write as an exemplum for listeners to soften their hearts.[116] Inés de Velasco affirmed during her Inquisition trial in 1623 that she had always asked her confessors to review the content of her diaries.[117] Rosa de Lima's confessors had even encouraged her to follow the example of Teresa de Ávila and to write her autobiography "and the secret revelations that God transmitted to her during her arrobos."[118] However, immediately following her death in 1617, when a campaign was mounted to promote her case for sainthood, her writings were confiscated and sent to the Inquisition in Madrid. Prohibited in 1625, her written work was carefully tucked away in a still-undisclosed location.[119]

Before the Inquisition began to sequester any suspiciously unorthodox writings in 1623, spiritual diaries circulated widely and often constituted the main attraction of spiritual conventicles.[120] Several visionaries were prolific. Luisa Melgarejo de Sotomayor composed a total of fifty-nine notebooks, while the nun Inés de Ubitarte noted down more than ninety-eight revelations she had over the course of six years, some of which were recorded by her scribe, Lucía de la Santíssima Trinidad (d. 1649), the foundress of the Monasterio de Santa Catalina.[121] The thirty-five-year-old beata Inés de Velasco, originally from Seville, was also a productive writer who shared her work with several influential priests.[122] Excerpts from the journals of Luisa Melgarejo circulated among her Jesuit confessors, and Melgarejo's husband, Juan de Soto, kept a copy under lock and key.[123] Finally, the recorded raptures experienced by the discalced nun Gerónima de San Francisco influenced the discussions of a group of lay pious women.[124]

The creation and circulation of new spiritual diaries in manuscript form in Lima supports historian Fernando Bouza's argument that the increasing availability of printed theological works did not mark the disappearance of manuscripts.[125] On the contrary, as Roger Chartier has stated in his forward to Bouza's book, manuscript composition "constituted the essential instrument for the intellectual technique of the commonplace, which, in literate settings, governed both reading and writing."[126] Four reasons support this argument. By recording their "commonplace" visions in manuscript form, women translated their internal dialogues with God in a particular and legitimate manner. Second, their writings were read in an interactive way: not only were they appropriated and discussed in both public and intimate exchanges between confessors and confessees, but when the original notebooks were recopied, they were often modified and editorialized. Third, the informal recording of mystical experiences related profoundly to the domain of orality, because it reproduced an internally heard utterance.[127] Finally, as manuscripts circulated among Lima's circle of women mystics, they not only reproduced current mystical thought but generated new interpretations.[128]

The development and use of a comprehensible interpretive vocabulary derived from the Spanish mystics' struggle to find a language of God to describe the ineffable. Key in this regard were the writings of Teresa de Ávila and John of the Cross, serving as guideposts in interpreting visions and moving toward the deepest dwelling (*morada*) of the intellective soul.[129] To read their bodily sensations (as a site where discourse occurred) and then interpret and translate the visions and sensations they had experienced into an understandable rhetoric, visionaries often employed a language of "spiritual sensation."[130] The somatic senses of smell, touch or feelings (*tocados*), and *gustos* (tastes) served as metaphors and tropes to describe the soul's progressive union with God—felt and tasted, as Teresa de Ávila once described it, in delightful conjunctions.[131] For instance, Rosa de Lima once explained in somatic terms to the medical doctor and theologian Juan del Castillo that after she had experienced a terrifying vision of hell and purgatory, "a very subtle supernatural heat, along with a fragrance of the rays of glory came to the soul, and to the sensitive interior of the soul, and that, each time this happened, [she knew] she had united with God."[132]

Yet, try as they might, for these visionaries it was sometimes a matter of not knowing *how* to infuse experience into language.[133] Here the role of the confessor became essential to translate and provide theological explanations for the ineffable. During Rosa's first beatification hearing in 1618, Juan del Castillo explained that from the time she was twelve or thirteen years of age, Rosa had experienced frequent states of prayer of union (oración de unión). Because, he continued, "God gives this knowledge without the operation of the senses or the conversion to the fantasy," it became necessary for Rosa to find ways "to explain herself to individuals who would understand her, because she lacked the appropriate explanatory terminology."[134] Luisa Melgarejo, who claimed to have accomplished "close union with God," was encouraged by her confessors to pay close attention to her bodily functions and to record the sensations she experienced while in a state of arrobamiento.[135] Even though in 1623 inquisitors censored Melgarejo's description "of how one loses [some of] the senses during rapture," the fact that she attempted to explain scientifically what occurred during this bodily state shows how much weight raptures were given. She wrote, "During the state of rapture the least necessary senses of touch, sight and taste are lost completely, and the amount of sensation that is lost is relative to the abundance of glory that one receives. The two senses of hearing and smell are not completely lost, although at times they are not completely there."[136]

As individuals progressed toward deeper union with God, it became even more difficult for them to explain those experiences in language. Teresa of Ávila maintained that intellectual visions occurred in the deepest dwellings of the soul. There God made the "image" known in the soul "without images or words," in "so celestial a language." She explained further:

> The soul now seems to have other ears to hear with, and He makes it listen, preventing its attention from wandering. It is like someone with good hearing whose friends will not allow him to stop his ears, but talk to him altogether and loudly, so that he cannot help attending. He, however, plays a part, since he takes in what they are saying. But here the soul plays none; it is relieved now even of the minor activity of listening, which it performed in the past. It finds everything cooked and eaten for it; it has only to enjoy its nourishment. It is like a man who has had no schooling, and has never even taken the trouble to learn to read, yet who finds himself, without any study, in possession of all living knowledge. He does not know how or whence it came, since he has never done even so much work as would be necessary for learning the alphabet.[137]

In this state, the soul no longer listens for words and does not use the "other ears" (*otros oídos*) required in imaginative locutions.[138] Still, there is something more to experience.[139] Very few mystics reached this level, but, according to one of her male confidants, the saintly Rosa de Lima once reported speaking to Christ face to face without language.[140]

Among the most vivid and beautiful examples we have of a mystic "alluding to her own mission as a translator of these divine mysteries" is Rosa de Lima's "The Favors," a series of drawings reproduced and analyzed in the studies of Luis G. Alonso Getino and Ramón Mujica Pinilla.[141] The visual text produced by Rosa combined word and image—"like a topography of her interior landscape"—detailing her gradual illumination.[142] The third drawing, entitled "Flight toward God," symbolized a state of rapture, with a heart containing a cross in its center and surrounded by four wings, each inscribed "Fly toward God." Around the perimeter of the heart were the words "The center of the heart is filled with God's love, making a dwelling in it."[143] At this level, as Getino explained, "as a result of Christ's presence, the heart became transfigured and the Lord communicated to the soul ineffable secrets."[144] Drawn on a separate sheet, the fourth heart contained an image of the Holy Spirit at its center; a tiny hand held a large pen at the edge of the heart, which was encircled by the words, "Here the soul suffers a saintly impatience. Heart filled with love, writes outside itself."[145]

One final example demonstrates some of the main points in this chapter about the interconnectedness among reading, writing, and speaking divine knowledge. In 1618 Juan Costilla de Benavides testified during Rosa de Lima's beatification hearing that as people gathered around Rosa's deathbed, her intimate companion Luisa Melgarejo "became suspended and elevated in a state of ecstasy." In her trance Luisa began to speak of "the glory that the soul of the said blessed Rosa was enjoying." Members of the grieving but captivated audience, including Costilla, realized the import of what was being read, or said: "[They] garnered ink and paper and began writing all that the said doña Luisa Melgarejo was saying, including the inflections and pauses she made. Having written for about an hour, it seemed to the friar, Father Francisco Nieto of the Dominican Order that this witness [Costilla] was getting tired. . . . He [Nieto] [then] took the ink and paper, and in one hand continued [writing] until the said doña Luisa Melgarejo finished."[146] Melgarejo spoke for over three hours, and when she had finished, Nieto and Costilla compared and corrected their two versions. The manuscript (the spoken word in writing) was then included with other testimonies as evidence that Rosa had indeed ascended to heaven, a crucial sign of sanctity.[147] A fragment extracted from Melgarejo's lengthy testimony reads, "Wings of good works, enameled with the blood of Jesus Christ, they gave you to fly, and what flight, and what flight, and what flight, a flight in order to enjoy what the eye did not see, the ear did not hear, nor the heart was able to think. Who could comprehend it, who could understand, who will understand the incomprehensible God?"[148]

This example is important for several reasons. For one, the body of Luisa Melgarejo was involved in the production of Rosa's text, based on her sensations (sentimiento) and Melgarejo's ability to *speak* (that is, *read*) another's dictated text. Throughout the process, Melgarejo's body was never completely absent or eliminated. Even though she experienced a suspension of her external senses, which allowed Rosa's celestial voice to emerge, Melgarejo still had to receive the message and register a vocalized discourse that was pronounced. She then reproduced the disembodied voice in another form through her sensorial body.[149] Those present, included several of Rosa's *hermanas*, heard, saw, and felt (*sintieron*) the vocalized text as it entered their bodies through their eyes and ears. They then recorded the language of spiritual sensation as it spilled forth onto the page. Thus, writing involved embodying the transmission or reading of the absent voice of Rosa as first inscribed in Melgarejo (the previously pronounced discourse), then registering the discourse in the bodies of the listeners (readers), and then recopying the text onto vellum. Here was a spiritual biography in the making.

In the seventeenth century, one could still hear with the eyes and see with the ears in the souled layers of the body. With its internal dwellings, the world of the body produced a discursive space from which language and images could be read.[150] This form of actualization complemented both the oral and silent reading of books, which had become ever more prominent in limeños' daily lives. In the case of mystical discourse, however, reading practices both replicated and transcended the format of the book. The body was considered a readable text because it contained the possibilities of communication, transmission, and reception, all key components of reading. It was also a text that could constitute a biography, a linear narrative with a temporal trajectory.

The world of the reader in seventeenth-century Lima was also profound. The fact that female visionaries composed texts of their bodies, and that texts composed their bodies, can be explained in part by the belief that an individual could access and appropriate the mystical language of God in distinct ways. Readers knew that God's spiritus was a *readable* language—expressed in the divine and human presence of his son, Jesus Christ, but also legible in the whispered voice of an absent soul, understandable in a written description of a vision, tangible in a drawing of a stigmata, or palpable in a female body, still as marble.

3

LIVING IN AN (IM)MATERIAL WORLD
Ángela de Carranza as a Reliquary

...

By the time Ángela de Carranza (ca. 1642– after 1694) was apprehended by the Lima Inquisition in December 1688, she had developed a cult following of hundreds of well-heeled aristocrats, educated friars, and commoners.[1] It was a remarkable progress. Twenty-three years earlier, then around thirty years of age, she had arrived from Tucumán (in what is now western Argentina) in the viceregal capital with a lover. Soon realizing that marriage was not to be, she grappled with how to survive as a single woman in a large city.[2] When she heard a voice beckoning her to "follow me," she interpreted it as a clear sign that God wanted her to become a beata, or a lay pious woman, who called herself Ángela de Dios and followed the rules of the Augustinian order.

After several years of walking the streets, attending several masses a day, and preaching in the plaza, Ángela began to develop a reputation as a wise and saintlike visionary.[3] For nearly twenty years she earned her living by offering an array of services, including saving souls in purgatory and healing ill-nesses. She also sold objects, including rosary beads and her clothing, as well as her nail clippings, which she claimed had been endowed by God with par-ticular protective powers. Scribes recorded her visions each day. She handed out autographs guaranteeing salvation, and clients waited in long lines to request her favors and hear her prognostications about health and riches, safe voyages, lost items, and matters of the heart.[4] Often she was a key attraction at baptisms and weddings; she would sit at the head of the table and eagerly eat the rich food. At the conclusion of the meal, she would pull out a small pair of scissors and proceed to snip her nails and distribute them as party favors.[5]

Many of the bishops, viceroys, and prelates who observed Ángela closely admired her as a rare and unique saint in the making, one who might even rival Santa Rosa.[6] After all, she claimed in her writings that God had con-ceded to her the major prerogatives and favors of many of the holiest saints. To many, she was a female theologian.[7] With faith in her divine abilities, clients gave her gifts, fruit, and precious gems for the altar of the Virgin that she maintained in her private chapel.

Such unrestrained adoration was not universal, however. Even at the height of Ángela's popularity, from 1670 until 1688, some called her *Madre* ("Mother," a term used with female religious authorities), while others re-ferred to her as *La loca* ("Crazy Woman"). No matter what limeños thought of her, however, she was still a local phenomenon. After she was incarcerated in 1688, her trial proceeded at such a slow pace that when, in December 1694, she finally received the sentence *de levi* (having confessed her sins of heresy), the relief felt throughout the viceregal capital was palpable.[8]

This chapter continues to explore the relationship between materiality and immateriality and the way auto/biographies were constituted by looking at the period before the inquisitorial campaign against Ángela gained lever-age. I examine why Ángela's contemporaries, both famous and unassuming, listened intently to what she had to say and objectified her as a consecrated object of veneration. I ask what made her believable and, especially, effica-cious. I consider what drove the viceroy's brother-in-law to venerate a stool she had in her home, or the poor to stand for hours so that she might bless a basket or a sack of wood. I explore why they hung on her every word and sought out her portraits, her touch, her special rosary beads, and bits of her hair, fingernails, and the bodily fluids that she poured into ampoules of col-ored glass. No doubt some of her devotees utilized their visual, tactile, and auditory senses to consume Ángela in a voyeuristic and predatory manner, desiring parts of her for their own salvation. But the sensorial appropriation of Ángela—seeing, touching, tasting, smelling, and hearing her—in turn enhanced her power in Lima and in the celestial realms.[9] Ángela allowed, and in fact encouraged, others to find meaning in *her* body and thus own parts of it, while also objectifying, fetishizing, and fragmenting it. She was at once whole and dismembered, inside and outside her body, contained in glass and on paper. Just as she was a beata, preacher, and theologian, she was blood, urine, hair, nails, and vapors. The story of Ángela's life, therefore, can be found not only in her actions but in the very materiality of her body.

A Living Saint?

Little is known about Ángela's life before her arrival in Lima, except that she was of Spanish heritage, originally from Tucumán, and had a reputation for enjoying life. All that changed when she arrived in the City of Kings in 1665 and began to acquire a name as a holy woman. In 1673 her first confessor, the Augustinian Bartolomé de Ulloa, ordered Ángela to record her visions and even showed her notebooks to the archbishop and Inquisition authorities. Ever curious, Archbishop Melchor Liñán y Cisneros followed her case closely; he requested an audience with her, during which he scrutinized her conscience and grilled her on the spiritual exercises she practiced.[10] Later, when some of her most devoted clients—members of the nobility, secular authorities, ecclesiastical doctors, and theologians—were called in to testify during her six-year Inquisition trial (1688–94), they would claim to have been duped and misled. Some reported becoming squeamish when they heard that their names had been inscribed in Ángela's fifteen-volume manuscript entitled "Defamatory Charges against the Living and the Dead" ("Libelos infamatorios de vivos y muertos"), containing damning evidence about the defects, mortal sins, and condemnation to hell of key individuals.[11] In her work in progress, Ángela spared no one, not even the lawyers of the royal court, the viceroy, the ecclesiastical council, the king of Spain, or the members of Lima's Inquisition tribunal.[12] But even those who had escaped appearing in her notebooks felt insulted by her loose, sardonic tongue. They sympathized with those she accused of being drunks or robbers, arguing that their only crime might have been to imbibe water or "steal" air.[13]

It may be that the negative sentiments against Ángela grew in direct proportion to the expanding list of names in her "libelous" notebooks. Clearly, fear of her powers and dismay at her (perceived) arrogant conduct eventually gained a strong foothold among members of the ecclesiastical hierarchy, especially among those who wished to restrain a group of Augustinians all too eager to promote Ángela as their order's saint.[14] Her arrest in December 1688 would not have been a complete surprise to her because she had already received several warnings from ecclesiastical authorities demanding that she cease some of her more defamatory activities.[15]

During her trial, and until she was condemned in a public auto-da-fé in 1694 to silence and enclosure for a four-year period, Ángela was objectified and vilified. But it is important to point out that attacks against her occurred in a social and political climate rife with tension. Lima was no longer experiencing the economic boom that had benefited the growing aristocracy and merchant elite earlier in the century. Many interpreted the epidemics, the poor wheat harvests, and the various earthquakes, including a devastating one in 1687, as God's punishment for the city's continued degeneracy. Priests in their weekly homilies from the pulpit chastised limeños for immorality and blamed them for bringing the wrath of God on them all. The earthquake of 1687, some said, had unleashed a moment of "hell" when even criminals managed to escape their forced enclosure.[16] The priests recommended acts of contrition such as more frequent communion and mindful prayer as remedies against the "Babylon of their guilt" and the rampant immorality that pervaded the viceregal capital.[17] A sermon delivered in 1693 by the head of the Inquisition, Nicolás Antonio Diez de San Miguel y Solier, following an auto-da-fé, pointedly placed the blame for Lima's endemic corruption squarely on the shoulders of particular heretical individuals, including Ángela, whose trial, he sermonized, seemed never to end. Lima, of course, had long had its share of earthquakes, tsunamis, pirate attacks, and corruption, evidenced in the writings of Bernabé Cobo earlier in the century. But now, as the century drew to a close, Ángela symbolized all that was wrong with Lima. She was a hydra that spewed occult venom, and from her multiple heads emanated "an atrocious, harmful substance." Like the fork-tongued serpents in Paradise, who were "hidden among the gentle leaves of apparent goodness," she used sweet, seductive words and images to construct heretical fictions. Her copious writings were nothing but a dense assemblage of falsehoods, which had taken the Inquisition assessors (calificadores) an inordinate amount of time to work through.[18] José del Hoyo, the Inquisition's prosecuting attorney, who had witnessed and recorded the depositions and events that occurred throughout Ángela's six-year trial and imprisonment, published a work about her in 1695 that included excerpts from her trial proceedings, which were later mined by other authors.

The fascination with Ángela continued even after she disappeared forever into the confines of a beaterio. But in the nineteenth century, as interest in popular history (*costumbrismo*) grew, Ángela once again became a household name. Her story was reelaborated and inserted squarely into the canon of Lima lore.[19] Some authors emphasized the outrageous aspects of her case; others viewed her more as a curio. More recently, scholars who have pored carefully through the one hundred–folio summary by Francisco Valera, the head of Lima's Inquisition Council, have attempted to place her in a larger historical context. Other historians and literary scholars emphasize the narrative fragmentation within the text, the power embedded in its allegories, and Ángela's radical theological views, or they explore how and why she became an object of veneration among Augustinians eager to gain a saint.[20] For some, Ángela's trial and condemnation illustrate the Inquisition's attempts to exert control over heterodox beliefs.[21] For feminist critics, she was a controversial but powerful writer who brazenly crossed gender boundaries by preaching in a friar's robe and exposing her body at irrigation canals where she went to bathe. Most concur that she was a woman of authority who lived uncompromisingly on the edge.[22]

Inquisition authorities charged with judging her writings, like Hoyo, would have us believe that Ángela's arrogance oozed through every quill mark and that she purposefully overemphasized the fame and applause she continuously received. But we are reading these assertions through a filtered lens that frames her as a deranged woman driven by satanic forces to seek power and attention. Passages from her writings (comprising over seventy-five hundred folios) were qualified and categorized by eight judges who plucked them from their context, organized them thematically into propositions, and categorized errors that ranged from mildly suspicious to heretical.[23] Valera's summary report contains several of Ángela's circumscribed declarations, transcriptions from any number of her notebooks, and references to some of the 130 depositions made by witnesses called in to testify over the six-year period.[24] Two additional primary sources—Hoyo's work and a manuscript copy of the annotations made by the Franciscan Gregorio Quesada y Sotomayor (one of the eight calificadores)—provide additional insights into the unmaking of a popular holy woman.

Ángela de Carranza is a fascinating historical character whose rise and fall as a powerful visionary, theologian, and, for some, imposter has attracted important scholarly attention. But it is important to note that before 1688 she was also seen as a container of fragmented sacred body parts. Like many reliquaries, some of them sculpted to resemble the essential nature of the departed saint, Ángela "housed" the tissue and effluvium that would become sacred to those who consumed her.[25] The living, breathing woman who claimed to be a doctor of theology was both container and contents, a performing and perceiving body, and Lima's public made her so.[26] In her, the physical presence of the holy was made manifest in what was called *praesentia*.[27] She was a consecrated efficacious vessel who could access the incommensurable and ineffable mystical body and then transmit sacred virtus or *potentia* (energy or power) to others. Her relics were continually appropriated in different ways through the senses of sight, hearing, touch, taste, and smell. Her clients believed, for instance, that by touching, listening to (since they believed it could "speak"), or gazing at her portrait, they could possess the divine held within her and be psychically healed, protected, or cleansed. They could re-inscribe their own meanings into and project fantasies onto the disembodied or simulacrum parts of her—nails, blood, or bronze laminate depictions of her lovely face.[28]

To reassure her followers that she had been selected and consecrated by God to be a sacred vessel, Ángela relied heavily on her visions as supportive evidence. In a vision she had once seen God lift his finger, a sign she interpreted as having been chosen by God to help others. After that event, she claimed, anyone who gazed at her portrait, touched things that had been hers, looked at her face, or felt affection and devotion toward her would be saved.[29] But Ángela was not just the beneficiary of God's graces bestowed *on* her; she once asserted that while she was in a state of reverie her soul left her body and was received by the Virgin, who offered it to God while the Holy Spirit, accompanied by angels, entered her body. This was not only an offering but an exchange of spirit, an endowment, a substitution, and, one might even argue, a transubstantiation. As Ángela gained notoriety, she would rely on the tautological argument that the Host contained both Christ and Mary, that Ángela de Dios *was* Christ and Mary, and that Christ and Mary *were* Ángela; therefore, Ángela was also present in the Host.[30] The sacred authority that was vested in her somatically enabled her to claim that she was a mirror of Christ: "You are my mirror, and I am your mirror," she had once written. Each part of her body corresponded with each part of Christ's: "I am the mole on your face; you are the mole on my face."[31] Her physicality embodied the spiritual and material meeting of heaven and earth: a transubstantiation of the immaterial into a material object.[32]

Whether believably or not, Ángela engaged in affective and participatory spirituality that involved exchanges between corporeal and noncorporeal bodies as part of an ongoing, ever-evolving mystery.[33] In most exchanges of these sorts, mystics willingly and painstakingly replicated the torturous suffering of Christ by denying and gradually destroying their own flesh. Ángela chose instead to absorb divine power and mystery that enhanced rather than diminished her body. As a mirror and holder of divine power, Ángela-as-Christ had the authority to fragment her body and transform her body parts into relics that would provide redemption or protection for each recipient. Perhaps some, including Ángela, believed that the fragmentation and dispersal of her powers would eventually lead to her image being hung above altars, but things never reached that point.

Corpus Mysticum

For centuries Christians had believed that God could work miracles by means of the sapless bones, ashes, whitish pastes, and precious bodily unguents of saints. As early as the fourth century, Saint John Chrysostom, the golden-tongued archbishop of Constantinople, had sermonized about how body relics were God's gift to humankind and how God had dispersed sacred body parts and bones to help sinners achieve virtue.[34] Throughout the medieval period, the cult of relics continued to grow. Following the death of a renowned martyr or saintly individual, their corporeal relics and contact relics (including their clothing, objects used by them, and the soil surrounding their sepulchers) became cherished objects of veneration.[35] Their scraps of flesh and discarded bits of humanity—organic material that succumbed to the inevitable process of disintegration into particulates—were considered sacred. The late seventeenth-century Dominican Juan Meléndez iterated this point: "The disposable parts of the saints, that which is flung out onto the street, that which is stepped on by the foot, that which one cannot look at without feeling revulsion, these things make miracles. A cloth with the blood of our Saint Dominic, a piece of sackcloth used by the seraphic Saint Francis, some bandages [that wiped] the fistula of Saint Thomas Aquinas, a shoe of Saint Vincent Ferrer, the veil of Saint Mother Teresa of Jesús. The sackcloth without life gives life; blood without soul restores the soul; and the insensate aids consciousness, life and the soul."[36] That even the most mundane objects could provide such spiritual potentia is evident in the Second Council of Nicaea in 787, which declared that all consecrated altars must contain a relic. Just as an altar became blessed by the presence of a relic, the placement of fragments of a saintly person's remains helped codify that person as a potential saint.[37]

During Ángela's lifetime, bits and pieces of living history arrived in Lima from Rome and other parts of Europe to create a palpable, physical linkage between the viceregal capital and the Holy Roman Church.[38] The Iglesia de San Pedro, completed in 1641, contained the Altar of Relics, with neatly stacked cubicles of urns containing cheek and shin bones, putrid molars and teeth, and hands of identifiable saints, as well as the remains of unknown martyrs extracted from Roman catacombs. The altar with its miracle-producing array of life remnants became a popular place for the needy to pray. Even more impressive was a sliver of the cross of Jesus. Donated by the pope in 1649 and housed in the cathedral, it was considered the most precious relic of the city. Bits of Saint Faustus, a fourth-century martyr, arrived in 1670 and were carried with great fanfare from the cathedral to the Convento de Santo Domingo.[39]

Although the Catholic Church and Tridentine mandates clearly stated that corporeal and contact relics should be guarded in churches, Lima's populace and ecclesiastical hierarchy held a broader view.[40] In dozens of testimonies of miracles in beatification hearings, relics seemed to appear out of nowhere at critical moments; many secretly safeguarded them *just in case.* In emergencies a few privileged members of the church could rely on relics from the holiest of sites—Rome—but the city boasted its own reliquaries and relics that enhanced the power of the body politic. The bodies of blessed individuals, some never beatified or canonized, became part of the city. Lima in turn served as a consecrated vessel that held such saintly bodies.[41] For instance, the beneficial rays of light exuded by the future saints Francisco Solano and Rosa de Lima became more intensely powerful "when their soul[s], having cast off [their] bodily shell[s], returned to [their] celestial home."[42] Like the "limbs of Christ" described by Saint Thomas Aquinas, their bodies were viewed as "temples and organs of the Holy Spirit living and working in them and which, come the glorious Resurrection, [would] help to give its form to the body of Christ."[43] They had a reputation for sainthood while living, and their corpses were scrutinized by ecclesiastical authorities, doctors, and other witnesses to certify that they remained pliant and fragrant—clear signs of the miracle of incorruptibility.[44] Especially noteworthy was any sign of seepage of a clear, sweet-smelling liquor or blood fluid.[45] (While the body lay in state, ecclesiastical scribes conducted inventories of the contact items associated with the prospective saint.)[46] Not only were they deemed saints by virtue of the state of their bodies at the time of their death, but, additionally, according to Catholic tradition, once they were being considered for sainthood, popular belief held that the resting place of the mortal remains of the servants of God was where their power manifested most strongly.[47] The dirt closest to where their bodies lay in repose was believed to have more value "than even the richest garden of roses and violets."[48]

Corporeal and contact relics, collected, purchased, or inherited, were stored in silver vials and boxes, glass ampoules, or even "body-part reliquaries" shaped like a body part, which held contact relics such as bits of a habit, a rosary bead, or the heel of a shoe.[49] The sacred fragments were dispersed throughout the city (indeed, throughout the viceroyalty), expanding even further the locus of sanctification of these individuals and increasing the sacramentality of the urbs itself.[50] Throughout the seventeenth century, a veritable relic industry developed in the city, with individuals collecting these precious items in the hope of increasing their own protection and star power. Some convents and monasteries served as relic apothecaries in case of need, especially after all medical remedies had been exhausted. For many, the touch or smell of a relic from three of Lima's most famous saints—Francisco Solano, Martín de Porres, and Rosa de Lima—often made the difference between life and death.[51]

Miracles caused by saintly relics could occur immediately following the death of that person and might continue for years afterward. In 1607 witnesses noted that after having been disinterred a year after his death, the former archbishop Toribio de Mogrovejo had grown facial hair. As his remains were being transported to his new burial site, miracles were reported by people who touched the litter.[52] In the days and months following the death of Francisco Solano in 1610, scores of individuals, from poor and blind slaves and field-workers to the deathly ill wives of *oidores* (Audiencia judges), flocked to touch him or to lay moribund babies on top of the corpse, later reporting miraculous cures.[53] The healing powers of Solano's corporeal and contact relics seemed to expand exponentially as miracles were recounted and carefully recorded by the scribes charged with his beatification process. Twenty years after Solano's death, the Franciscan chronicler Diego de Córdova y Salinas attested to the heroic virtues of his relics: "The intercession of this apostolic man, his merits, his relics, the earth of his burial place, the oil of the lamps in his tombs calm the elements when there are storms at sea; they have the virtue of being able to quench fire, cheer the sorrowful, grant success in childbearing, heal the palsied, aid those suffering abscesses or bleeding; they give sight to the blind, hearing to the deaf, health to cripples and life to the dead."[54] In one dramatic case, bits of his bone placed in the mouth of a mother stopped her hemorrhaging after giving birth.[55]

Solano's corporeal relics were in such demand that he was disinterred multiple times to collect more bones, pastes (made from disintegrated bones and flesh), unguents, and blood. When Dominicans interested in promoting the beatification of Martín de Porres exhumed his body to check for signs of incorruptibility, they noted that his bones smelled faintly of roses and that "living flesh and blood" still clung to them. Hundreds accompanied his remains to their new burial site, and miracles were reported.[56] Any object that grazed Rosa de Lima's corpse gained curative powers. At her funeral in 1617 hundreds passed by to place rosaries, rings, ribbons, or holy medals on her body for a few seconds. They also touched and kissed her soft, pale hands and feet, fingered the dangling rosaries, and snipped pieces of her habit, which had to be replaced and carefully guarded so as not to leave her naked. When vigilance slipped, someone dared to cut off one of her fingers.[57]

But it was one thing to venerate the body fragments of the deceased reigning in the kingdom of Christ (as espoused by the Council of Trent [1545–63] and approved by ecclesiastical authorities) and quite another to create (and market) a cult of someone who was *alive*. Relics were supposed to help devotees remember an absent body (or experience "the presence of the absence"), but Ángela de Dios was still very much present.[58] Witnesses at the numerous beatification hearings that took place throughout the seventeenth century would not have dared to mention how they might have squirreled away a discarded garment, a work tool, or the hair or nails of their living companion. This would have been evidence of a cult existing before the person had died and would diminish the would-be saint's chances of beatification. In fact, evidence of a noncult (*non culto*) had to be shown—burial in a simple grave; no special images, candles, engravings, or medals nearby; and no mention of miracles—before testimonies were allowed to be gathered for the summary process and then for the follow-up apostolic process.[59]

So the question remains: how did Ángela transform herself into a living reliquary? In part, it was the context within which she operated. By the time of her arrival in 1665, Lima was already renowned as a holy site that held the sacredness of the invisible realm of heaven within its urban confines. As each saintly figure demonstrated miracles and signs of incorruptibility, Lima became holier and more venerated.[60] In April 1669 the entire city swelled with pride as it celebrated the arrival of the papal bull beatifying Rosa de Lima. The sacrosanct piece of paper was carried in a procession under a pallium to the cathedral.[61] By the time she was canonized in 1671 (six years after Ángela de Carranza had traversed the mountain passes from Tucumán to Lima), several generation of limeños had venerated her as a saint. Seventeen years later (in November 1686), people danced in the streets for days when word arrived that the apostolic process of Martín de Porres had been closed, the documents sealed and sent to the Sacred Congregation of Rites in Rome.[62] Two years after Ángela's friend Nicolás de Ayllón had died, the attorney general of Indians (procurador general de los indios) filed a petition before the archbishop to initiate the collection of information about his life and virtues.[63]

Ángela entered this urban corpus of sanctity, appropriated it, and expanded its circumference in her daily wanderings. Unlike Rosa de Lima, who spent much of her time in her garden and small cell adjacent to her parents' home; Isabel de Porras Marmolejo, who governed a school; or Martín de Porres, who swept the dusty corridors of the Dominican monastery each day, Ángela de Dios was extremely mobile and visible. Lima's inhabitants might see her slip into a church to hear bits of one sermon and then glimpse her rushing off to another church. She made the rounds of the homes of the elite and defied Saint Paul by standing on the steps of the cathedral and preaching.[64] As she wandered the streets and alleys of the city, people flocked to her, calling her "Madre" and whispering their supplications with bowed heads. To the chagrin (and perhaps pleasure) of close observers, Ángela bathed in the water tanks of some of the principal family residences of Lima. She also visited the flowing irrigation canals and other limpid pools of water where passersby came and went. (In her dreams she traveled to the River Jordan and bathed with the baby Jesus.)[65] By washing frequently (which most Christians did not do), she could cool her body of the tremendous heat of God's love that coursed through her heart and veins. Wherever Ángela's flesh touched the fluid essence of life, some of her virtus remained. Devotees could visit the spot where she had bathed and bow their heads in wishful prayer. They could dip their hands in the holy water; dab a little on their forehead, heart, and left and right shoulders, making the sign of the cross; and then collect a small amount in a vial.[66] Holy water, the essence of life, could cure a relentless fever; it could induce miraculous healings through the intervention of a holy person like Ángela.[67]

Hearing, Seeing, Tasting, Touching, and Smelling

As we know from the previous two chapters, the sacred could be perceived and absorbed through any of the five senses.[68] Writing was a means of rendering the invisible visible through the sensorial transmission from the object (the written word on the page) to the eyes and the ears and then to the heart and layered souls. The female body served as a type of text that could communicate divine language to others, which would then be recorded in writing. Although Ángela de Carranza appeared much later in the seventeenth century, her ways of speaking in writing and writing in speaking replicated the practices of Luisa Melgarejo and other beatas who wrote frequently. Like her deceased sisters, Ángela claimed to serve as an interlocutor of the voices of the Lord, Mary, angels, and saints. In some of her famously long trances and states of ecstasy, voices passed through her (she retained no memory of what had transpired), and she dictated the pictorial and verbal language to nearby scribes. Although crowned a doctor of doctors, she claimed to be a mere interlocutor between the three divine persons and the written word—only "pure language," as one historian has described her.[69] That she was destined to write was verified in a vision she had of the Holy Ghost transformed into a featherless dove who landed softly in her hands. God decoded the message by explaining to her that she was meant to be the feathered quill that would write his word.[70] She referred to these testimonials, visitations, and dialogues as her "lessons," which increased in frequency in her later years. On a given day she would enter a rapturous state before and after taking communion, and the messages, which came in bursts, were repeated several times, using both language and images.[71] A young indigenous man whom Ángela had raised would stand outside the door and wait until the lessons had begun and then escort guests into an interior room of Ángela's apartment to listen and watch. (Ángela also trained the boy to enter a trancelike state and respond to the questions she asked him.)[72]

Beginning in 1673, Ángela's confessor, Bartolomé de Ulloa, ordered her to record these phenomena. Over the course of the next fifteen years, her profuse and evocative visions filled 540 notebooks. Many of the early volumes she penned herself, but as time went on and her eyesight deteriorated (there were also complaints about her poor penmanship), she began dictating her otherworldly encounters, visions, and theological dialogues to amanuenses. The contents of these visions were of such import to ecclesiastical authorities (including, at one point, the archbishop) that many hovered over her every word.

Three of her scribes, all Augustinians, served as her confessors at different intervals. First there was Friar Ulloa, then Joseph de Prado and Augustín Coman. Ignacio de Híjar y Mendoza, the parish priest of San Marcelo, also guided her. Each confessor reviewed her work for doctrinal errors, which, she claimed in her Inquisition statement, allowed her to speak with a completely free conscience.[73] In addition to these men, an entire stable of copyists, assistants, and even her mother and sister (both living with her) provided support. They made certain to reproduce excerpts of her copious writings and distribute them to those eager to peruse and discuss their content.[74] Ángela's theological assertions were considered important, but the physical notebooks were also revered as relics.[75] While the spoken voice in writing was a way of affirming her corporeal presence while alive (as well as her connection with divinity), it also prepared limeños for Ángela's inevitable mortality, and thus these notebooks were seen as relics in the making. As they began to number in the hundreds, some had the foresight to think about how to preserve the different copies, but especially the originals, for posterity.[76] One wealthy limeño was willing to pay three thousand pesos for a copy of the notebooks, because he saw the future value of such extraordinarily unique texts.[77] But more than that, the written word of Ángela was believed to embody praesentia—God's presence. This is clearly demonstrated by the response of one of her devotees after the tremors of the devastating earthquake in October 1687 had subsided. Realizing that flooding was inevitable, Lima's inhabitants gathered all they could carry in their arms, on mules, or in carriages and ascended the nearby hills to safety. Some expressed concern that once the floodwaters reached the site where Ángela's notebooks were stored, they would become sodden and illegible. But the person in charge of guarding the trunk (*petaca*) reported that her sacred papers remained unperturbed. He told a worried bystander to step up onto the trunk, a veritable Noah's ark, saying that even if the city were deluged, not a drop of the surging waters would reach them.[78]

In a treatise published in 1623, the highly respected theologian and Spanish Jesuit Martín de Roa (1561–1637) wrote that painting and writing involve colors and words that produce and invoke the same response. Someone viewing a sacred painting could drink it in visually, whereas the written words of a blessed text would enter the soul through the sense of hearing.[79] Thus, it would have seemed logical, even natural, to Ángela and her confessors for God to order a painting of her surrounded by her confessors and lettered assistants as proof of the veracity of her writings.[80] A number of her more singular visions were reproduced on canvas, and some of these works entered the private collections of Lima's elite. They were meant to serve as relics of the event witnessed, transmitted to canvas and memorialized through color, line, and shape.[81] One painting confiscated by the Inquisition depicted the angel of the Apocalypse, who bore a remarkable resemblance to Ángela. Two of her wings extended heavenward; she held a bishop's staff (awarded to her by Saint Augustine); and at her feet lay the trampled and defeated dragon of original sin.[82]

Like contact relics, portraits of a saintly individual contained some of that person's virtus, which could connect the viewer with the departed one. The coexistence of relics and images, and the alliance between them, was crucial, because each object helped to fulfill the ritual function and veneration of the other.[83] Portraits or sculptures, for example, had limitless value in and of themselves, but they were also prized for their miracle-making abilities. In 1673 a fourteen-year-old Jesuit novice was cured of paralysis when an engraved portrait of Saint Stanislaus was placed on his crippled arms and legs.[84] When the saintly Indian tailor Nicolás de Ayllón died in 1677, indigenous people came from afar to kneel before his portrait and pray. Within a year, a nonofficial cult had developed around the miracles produced by his images (which were reproduced and distributed by his wife, María Jacinta Montoya), helping to pave the way for an official investigation into his life and virtues.[85]

To make the leap from venerating the images and contact relics of a dead saint to revering those of a living one would not have been difficult for most limeños. Many portraits and sketches of Ángela could be found in Lima, and some were decorated with bold insignia and banners.[86] Beholders who gazed at the simulacrum of her eyes appropriated the potency of the unseen into the realm of the visible. The familiar material landscape of flesh and bone transferred itself into color and image, and contact with Ángela in this form would assure that prayers would be answered. The same held true for objects that Ángela claimed had come in contact with God. She gave away and sold beads, rosaries, candles, the herb rosemary, and bells, all of which she claimed to have transported to heaven to be blessed. Clients also brought to Ángela chalices from home oratories, doubloons, rings, gold and silver coins, swords and daggers (meant to defend the faith), and small bells to be blessed in heaven, and then treasured them as relics for many years.[87] Nearly everyone in the city believed that her saintliness adhered to her belongings.

Her clients could finger or stroke a relic, but they could also simultaneously taste and ingest the fruit of heaven. The sense of taste (gusto) involved the sense of touch, because the tongue felt and perceived food.[88] Ángela often talked about how Jesus Christ had been transubstantiated into the pulp of the fruit of life, and how by eating this food one would be redeemed from sin. Such a proposition served to disassociate the sine qua non apple from original sin. The female vendors she encountered in the main plaza, or the generous devotees whose homes she visited, would lavish luscious fruit on her. Ángela then donated it to the poor and infirm, saying that God himself had blessed it. Fruit-filled bowls graced her home and her altar, and they appeared frequently in her visions. Those who came into her receiving room for a private session could readily pluck a piece brought directly from paradise by the angels or the saints.[89]

A ripened-to-perfection passion fruit, custard apple, persimmon, or lucuma could satisfy the palate and also the sense of smell, because the gustatory and olfactory senses were interconnected. Just as a sensitive nose could smell a rotten apple, it might detect a person's questionable moral characteristics—hence the popular saying, "I have a good nose."[90] Sin was known to give off a particularly putrid odor, and Ángela was renowned for being able to sniff out sinful conduct, which she recorded in her fat notebooks on libelous conduct. She once had a conversation with Mary Magdalene, who told her that she had used fragrances to cover up the foulness of her sins when she sought the Lord's company. Even so, the Lord (like Ángela) could discern the truth.[91]

Conversely, dying in the fragrance of sanctity distinguished a saintly body, which was deemed incorruptible because the decay of mortality could not disturb its pure essence. A corpse emitting a pleasant, flowery sweetness (of lilies, jasmine, or violets, in the case of Santa Teresa de Ávila) was a clear sign of God's presence; even the bones of exhumed saints were reported to smell like dried rose petals, more fragrant than balm.[92] The mere presence of a corporeal or contact relic could help eliminate the fetid odor of sin—as though its undetectable scent could transform a negative quality into a positive one. A relic on a brazier would waft purifying vapors over the infirm or dying person. This procedure saved the six-month-old daughter of Juana Micaela, who lived in Malambo (facing Lima across the Rímac River). The infant was near death, comatose and cold. In desperation, family members placed the fragments of two relics (they did not mention whether they were corporeal or contact relics) from Rosa de Lima on the coals of a small brazier. As the smoke passed over the tiny child's body and reached her face, she opened her eyes. All those present were convinced that the smoldering relics had miraculously brought her back from the dead.[93]

As we learned in chapter 1, the virtus in a holy cloth could be appropriated in multiple tactile ways. At funeral wakes it was quite acceptable for mourners shuffling by the saintly person's remains to snip off pieces of its coverings.[94] Such cloth or garment remnants, if placed directly on an injury, could give life or healing energy.[95] Gerónima de San Francisco's *Vida* related a particularly dramatic incident:

> An elite lady named doña Isabel Barreto had been carrying a dead child in her womb for three days. Doctors were determined to extract the unborn baby but she resisted. Someone came and asked me to send a relic and [explained] why it was needed. I had nothing to give her . . . [but] it was God's will that I would find a very old cord [worn about the waist] of Our Father Saint Francis in a corner [of the convent]. I cleaned and wrapped it in paper and then got down on my knees and said: "My Father Saint Francis, you are a great saint, and the one who

loved our Lord Jesus Christ so much. In His name I ask that you do this miracle on behalf of that lady who is experiencing such difficulty." All they did was place it around [the lady's] waist and God was served [because] the dead child was expelled.[96]

Items that had come in contact with Ángela's skin could relieve inflammation or pain. A mere touch of her bodice or dress (like the tassel from Jesus's garment) could work wonders.[97] Discarded shoes, padded slippers, undergarments, petticoats of coarse cloth, corsets, and even old tattered wool blankets were considered loci of corporeal and mystical commingling. Ángela's servants captured the fleas from her bedding and clothing and placed them in small containers. Her petticoats were in particular demand, as she told her clients that she frequently ascended to heaven in her undergarments—carefully rationalizing her eyebrow-raising conduct by stating that when she did so she was told to sit in the middle of the throne of the Blessed Trinity to receive her lesson. God once told her that her discarded dresses could serve as bandages for the infirm and that they should be applied directly to the injured parts. Especially sought after were the petticoats with which she had shrouded the Lord during one of her celestial visitations.[98] Ángela attributed the power of her shoes (available for purchase) to a vision in which she had loaned the barefoot Virgin a pair she was wearing. In return for her generosity, the Virgin determined that from then on Ángela's shoes would have the virtue of creating miracles.

Many of the venerated contact relics involved visitations between Ángela and her spiritual guides. Usually she traveled to heaven, but occasionally God and company paid their respects to her on earth. In one vision the Lord, accompanied by the Virgin, angels, and saints, entered Ángela's room. He looked around and then said, "Why don't you put a cushion on the bench where everyone sits: Are we not to sit? Do you not have any respect?" Once everyone was comfortably settled, the lesson proceeded. When word of the holy bench (and cushions) spread throughout Lima, these objects were in high demand. For a princely sum, the Audiencia judge Doctor D. Gaspar de la Cuba y Arce acquired the bench and its padding for himself and later bequeathed it to his son-in-law.[99]

Even in her earliest notebooks, Ángela discussed the special properties of her rosary beads. God had lifted his finger to say: "I will keep my word," meaning that his concession to bless her rosaries would hold true. Ángela would have known that Our Lady of the Rosary—named patroness and protector of Peru in 1643—was a particularly popular object of devotion in Lima, with her own basilica, altarpiece, and statue.[100] With the Virgin's blessing (in one vision she had placed prayer beads around Ángela's neck) and God's promise, a not-so-subtle linkage of Ángela to the Queen of the Rosary was created. This conferred on Ángela the power to answer the prayers of those who said the rosary (Ángela reported that she had healed Christ with them).[101]

Rosary beads were popular and ubiquitous; most families had them, and the beads could be simple or lavish, depending on the family's wealth. On Ángela's celestial travels she would take along beads and rosaries to "remit them to heaven."[102] Occasionally a few received a plenary indulgence from the pope and were carried by angels directly to Rome.[103] The rounded objects, made of stone, wood, semiprecious gemstones, and even pearls, emeralds, and gold, appeared on a holy altar stone with the assistance of a guardian angel holding an axe in flames. The Lord then blessed them. If the rosary belonged to a priest, Jesus might hang it around his neck or place it on his side near where he had once been wounded with the lance. At other times the Holy Ghost in the form of a dove hovered above the rosaries while tiny droplets (signifying grace) fell on each bead. But heaven had limits to its generosity. The demand for sanctified rosaries was so high that once when Ángela carried a large number to heaven to be blessed, an annoyed God complained that Ángela was turning it into a prosaic practice and more a matter for fruit sellers than for him.[104]

Once Ángela had returned to earth, she would distribute the blessed beads following God's orders, or on a particular saint's day. Those given out on the day of Saint Jerome were to help convert the unfaithful; Saint Joseph, to guard chastity; Saint Teresa, to enable prayer; Saint Ignatius of Loyola, to fight the devil; Saint Michael, to protect homes from robbery; Saint John, to protect against the plague, lightning, epilepsy, and heart trouble; Saint Peter Nolasco, to aid a woman in becoming pregnant or to protect a pregnancy; and Saint Mary Magdalene, to help guide a woman along the correct path.[105] Like David's sling, these beads and rosaries had the power to slay the giant and convert sinners, and on the most sacred days of the Christian calendar, they had even more power. On a Holy Thursday, God had told Ángela that any bead blessed on that day was equivalent to taking a consecrated host for those who were already in grace (in soul and in body). If any sinners were to take communion on Holy Thursday without receiving the sacrament of penance (a grave sin), angels would remove the host from their mouth and take it to the Virgin. Yet such offenders who possessed some of Ángela's beads could plead with God to restore them to grace at the hour of their death.[106] Like

Our Lady of the Rosary, Ángela's beads also had the power to convert, wipe away sin, and save sinners from damnation even in faraway places. Ángela recorded in one of her early notebooks a vision of a lady living far away who was dying and did not wish to confess. God ordered the devils (a heretical proposition) to carry Ángela to the lady, and when she laid her beads and rosaries on her, the lady confessed and was saved from damnation, without any resistance from the devils.[107]

Rosaries could multitask according to the days on which they were blessed and distributed, but Ángela's saving graces were also timely. In one vision the baby Jesus appeared showing her a sore on his little legs. He ordered Ángela to heal him with a rosary of San Roch, the patron saint of plagues, an indication that she could also heal some of the victims of the smallpox epidemic of 1686, especially the young children. Ángela's vision was very apt because the "black vomit" plague was on everyone's mind: sermons invoked Saint Roch, and a procession was held in his honor in December of that year.[108]

Inside: Flesh, Blood, Excrement, and Detritus

For many, Ángela was a mysterious and unfathomable character who helped render the unknown known and the unfamiliar familiar. The locus of this action was her body, considered a microcosmographic representation of the universe.[109] Body parts mapped something larger than mortal life, which included both the earthly and the transcendental. As part of the larger body politic—the corpus mysticum—of Lima, the parts of Ángela were metonymic, representing something bigger, but each part was also venerated for the saintly essence it possessed. Anyone who kissed her hands would remain chaste and free from lust.[110] Limeños swarmed to touch her habit, or her hair, but they wanted to appropriate more of her. Ángela was pressed (and was pleased) to relegate some of the more intimate parts of herself. What was inside became outside; the reliquary offered relics. Her extracted molars, as well as her fingernails stored in pear-shaped ampoules, were prized on earth and in heaven. It was said that, on one occasion, the Lord cut Ángela's hair and distributed it to the angels to retrieve souls in purgatory.[111]

Although defecation and urination—the natural elimination of superfluous matter resulting from eating and drinking—helped maintain the body's humoral balance, a *woman* relieving herself in public was considered somewhat scandalous. But Ángela did just that and, when an onlooker questioned her behavior, retorted, "What did God give me this for?"[112] The freedom with which she performed these functions reinforced her performative, otherworldly nature; she was not just *any* flesh-and-blood woman. Her urine, she claimed, had the power to penetrate the earth like a drill spiraling down to the center of hell—pungent, caustic "holy water" that would drip on the demons and scald them and make them jump about.[113] When she strolled about in public, people hovered about like flies, waiting to collect the precious specimens of urine or feces.

Blood was a more fragile relic, more easily subject to decay and corruption than bones or teeth.[114] But it was the most precious and holy substance on earth and readily associated with Christ's bleeding body. Blood possessed a different sort of virtus than fingernails, hair, urine, or feces. It was considered the most important of the body's four humors; Galenic medical philosophy insisted that the release of sometimes large quantities of excess blood would encourage a return to humoral balance.[115] Barbers and other blood letters targeted different veins and arteries that were associated with different organs like the liver or spleen. In the phlebotomies that Ángela occasionally received, she lay still as venal blood spurted and then dripped into a dish. Her clients lined up to dip handkerchiefs and small bandages into the scarlet substance. Ángela's assistants also distributed as relics the cloth used to collect her blood. Any bandage, handkerchief, or petticoat spattered with or bathed in her blood gained instant value. One of her confessors, Ignacio de Híjar y Mendoza, considered a handkerchief soaked in Ángela's blood to be his most precious relic.[116]

We can understand why the blood of Christ would be venerated, but why a saint's, to say nothing of a living woman's? "Fresh" blood, red and liquid, found in the marrow or joints of exhumed bones of a long-dead prospective saint was an important sign of immutability. A Dominican friar charged with transferring the skeletal remains of Martín de Porres found coagulated blood near the skull. At first it appeared to be a clump of soil, but it oozed red when the friar squeezed it. This find was an important sign of incorruptibility and was entered as evidence in Porres's beatification process in 1664.[117] Ángela, too, claimed to be incorruptible. She distributed the blood that coursed through her veins and arteries throughout the living, pulsing city to purge it of sin, illness, and moral decay.

This distribution—exposure—of Ángela's body parts to the public was like reading the plot of a known narrative about cosmography, sanctity, and the body.[118] As a relic in progress, she continually participated in the ongoing exchange among blood, flesh, and the divine. For many, this was an acceptable and natural practice. God had even conceded Ángela the greatest favor of all: to save (and, one would assume, distribute as relics) the holy hosts she placed on her tongue from one communion to the next. For Ángela was the "sacrament which could nourish all, and . . . in this manner they should seek her out to nourish themselves."[119] On one occasion the Lord asked Ángela for the host she had taken in communion the day before, saying he would give it to an angel to deliver to a man who was about to die. When Ángela would not allow this, the angel squeezed her ribs until the host popped out of her mouth, bloodied and covered in phlegm. The Lord said to her, "Look at what is affixed to your heart—the Holy Host—but I also want him to ingest your blood when he takes Communion."[120]

Corruptibility and Disintegration

Ángela, the incorruptible thaumaturge, entered the Inquisition prison on 22 December 1688 and would remain there for six years. While she was there, authorities left no stone unturned; they examined and prodded her multitudinous written records and collected over a hundred depositions. They also scrutinized her body, once the object of adoration and a prized reliquary. They spied on her as she ate or undressed; they tortured and overstretched her half-clothed limbs. They checked closely for signs of the wounds she said that Christ had impressed on her. They never materialized —another confirmation to the inquisitors of Ángela's false sanctity and arrogance. Her body, they argued, showed no signs of abstinence and mortification. A normal visionary would exhibit frailty or feebleness, pallid skin, a torso crisscrossed with whip lines. In contrast, Ángela had ruddy, ample flesh, supposedly nourished by her hearty appetite (although she complained about the meager portions in the prison).[121]

If she were not truly blessed by God, as she and her followers claimed, the inquisitors' job was then to demystify and humanize Ángela: to return her to the status of a mortal human brimming with defects and corruption. By the time she received her sentence of heresy in 1694, she had been humbled, contained, and silenced. After several torture sessions, she had confessed to her crimes. But the vehemence with which the Lima community reacted to the sentencing showed how far the tables had turned in the six-year trial period. Her public auto-da-fé took place on 20 December 1694 in the Iglesia de Santo Domingo. Tensions ran high as the wealthy vied for space to park their carriages and strained to catch a glimpse of the criminal leaving the Inquisition prison, surrounded by guards. Balconies near the Iglesia de Santo Domingo were at a premium. In the procession of the six penitents, Ángela was easy to distinguish: she was dressed in a bright yellow garment that fell to the knees; it was painted with red flames and demons. On her head she wore a tall, pointed cap decorated with serpents, devils, dragons, and other diabolical creatures. She carried a tall green candle to symbolize the three theological virtues—the wax, hope; and the flame, charity and faith.[122] After six hours of sermonizing, the ceremony ended, and Ángela's sentence was read aloud. Still, the authorities were reluctant to transport her to the beaterio where she would do penance for the next four years. They feared that the angry crowds would corral the carriage and set Ángela on fire. Some limeños had expressed such disappointment that the false mystic had not been burned at the stake that they took matters into their own hands and reduced several effigies of Ángela to smoldering ashes in the streets.[123] Instead, the inquisitors opted to wait several weeks until the fever had abated before relocating Ángela to the Beaterio de las Mercedarias, her new prison. To evade angry crowds, they left in the dark of night, the carriage windows covered so no one could see inside. But somehow word got out, and people gathered to hurl stones at her. That shadowy glimpse was the last that anyone ever saw of her.

Inquisition authorities then realized that there was more to Ángela than met the eye. Two days after the auto-da-fé, Inquisition authorities issued an edict that was publicized in the cathedral and nailed to the doors of churches throughout the city. All members of the Lima community and other cities within the district were to turn in any "beads, rosaries, medals, small and large bells, swords, daggers, handkerchiefs and bandages dipped in her blood, remnants from her petticoats, portraits, fingernails, hair, signatures, notebooks, either originals, copies, or transcripts [of her writings], and any other things that belong to her, or have [been] kept as her relics." Limeños were given nine days to come forward and present these objects to the Inquisition commission. Neighbors were encouraged to denounce neighbors who refused to comply with the order, and, if caught, the culprits would pay fines of five hundred pesos and suffer excommunication.[124] Images and relics revered and cherished for decades were now flung out like garbage; all these dismembered parts of Ángela were now condemned, much like when the land surrounding the razed home of a traitor is salted so it can never again sustain any life. Curled shoes, tattered threads, beads, portraits, liquid-filled vials, swords, and bells filled an entire room in the Inquisition tribunal, impressing even the hard-boiled inquisitor Hoyo, who was there to record the extraordinary event.[125] We are left to wonder, however, whether any unforthcoming individuals would have continued to worship some part of Ángela in secret.

For nearly two decades Ángela had "defended herself through fragmentation," by dispersing and selling bits of herself in Lima, Tucumán, Cuzco, and other provincial cities.[126] Devotees could gaze at her portraits or bits of nails or blood stored in vials or on a cloth—consuming Ángela's materiality. As part of the ritualistic pulse of life and death, limeños appropriated the potentia of Ángela's relics through their five senses. Her body parts provided a venue through which they could express their hopes and fears—and miracles did happen.

Blood, urine, teeth, nails, a chair, a petticoat that had shrouded Christ, shoes worn by the Virgin, bathwater, or a portrait—each relic contained different narratives consumed in different ways by Ángela's clients. Her voice included her bodily substances, her contact relics, her virtus, and the stories she relayed of her journeys to heaven. In turn, these objects that contained Ángela were the media by which spiritual knowledge was transmitted to her supporters. As Ángela's clients appropriated her through their senses, they employed a somatic literacy—knowledge of her immaterial-material body parts—to grasp the meanings they associated with each text. Although eventually some saw her stories as wildly fantastic and even dangerous, for many years she was revered as a spiritual authority, vested with divine power, and embraced as a text that could be both consumed and read. These objects created her biography, her story of divinity and fall from grace.

As a living reliquary Ángela was expected to work wonders, but clearly her powers to persuade and heal did not endure. She had made too many enemies and too many questionable theological assertions. By 1694 her hair, cloth remnants, blood, and images—bits of her that had once been sacred—had been discarded, burned, or left to disintegrate. All that was once Ángela disappeared. In the end she was proved all too human and was destined, like all corruptible beings, to become "ice with the warm blood mixing."[127]

PART II

The Relational Self

4

CARRYING THE CROSS OF CHRIST
Donadas in Seventeenth-Century Lima

. . .

The Lord walks among the pots and pans.
—Teresa de Ávila, *Foundations*, 5.8

In a sermon given in 1681 at the profession of a donada, José de Aguilar stood in the pulpit and emphasized that each nun was the señora of her own cross. But each servant, he added, whether a criada (servant) or a donada (religious servant who took informal vows), carried the cross of the señora "upon which they could not recline."

> To profess as a Nun and remain a Nun among the Señoras . . . is to carry the Cross of Christ, each with the honor of being the Señora of her Cross. But to profess as a Nun and not remain among the Señoras, but rather among the Servants of this Monastery [as a donada] is to carry the Cross of the Servants of this Monastery and to carry the Cross of Christ without it being her own. Those who profess as Servants carry everyone's Crosses because they have to serve them all, and help carry

those who are not as able. . . . The Nuns carry the Cross hoping to be chosen to do the honorable tasks of the Convent. The Servants [donadas] carry the cross without such expectations. Those [the nuns] are the Wives who hold the title of Señoras. These [the donadas] are the Wives who hold the title of Servants.[1]

One can imagine Aguilar gesturing from one side of the choir to the other as he explained how the different occupants of the convent, separated by rank, were meant to carry the cross of Christ. By virtue of having taken informal religious vows, donadas were more distinguished than the criadas; still, according to Aguilar, they could not rest, because the cross they carried was not their own. For free *parda*, *mulata*, and *morena* women of mixed African and European descent, or for indigenous females labeled as indias, becoming a donada was their best option to achieve religious status, because all religious orders prohibited them from professing as nuns of either the black veil or the lower-status white veil.[2]

The term *donada* literally meant that the candidate had been donated by someone to a monastery, or that she had donated herself, perpetually, to "engage in service to God and the community."[3] Generally, when adolescent girls entered the novitiate with the ultimate goal of becoming a donada, they agreed to perform certain tasks in exchange for a home (the convent), living quarters, and food. In Lima, where an African-descent population, both free and enslaved, was prevalent—and between one thousand and two thousand slaves of West African origin arrived at the nearby port of Callao each year—it makes sense that some five hundred free or freed women of African descent would decide to spend their lives in a cloistered setting over the course of the seventeenth century.[4] Indias also took their vows as donadas, some of them having traveled great distances from places such as Potosí, Huaylas, Huaura, Pisco, and even Panama.[5] Although the indigenous population of Lima did not surpass 8 percent in the seventeenth century, one has only to examine the census of indios of 1613 to gain a sense of the consistent flow of young children to Lima from highland and coastal cities.[6] Indeed, the migratory melting pot and multiethnic nature of the viceregal capital were mirrored in the places of origins of the servants and slaves in convents and also in urban households.

In chapter 1 I considered the intimate, tutorial relationship between Rosa de Lima and her disciples as expressed through material objects, including statues, cloth, and clothing. Rosa, I argued, was at the epicenter of a group of devout females who engaged in deep devotional practices outside the conventual setting. As beatas living in the siglo (the secular domain), they expressed their piety through quotidian actions like sewing and embroidering or dressing religious statues. In the monastic setting, girls and women enclosed together for decades developed social and intellectual networks and, like the pious women who sought Rosa's company, were drawn toward those more pious than themselves. They, too, expressed notions of spiritual kinship toward particularly blessed individuals, both living and deceased. They, too, engaged in innovative and powerful ways with the sacred materialities of early modern Catholicism. The questions I address in this chapter are twofold. I examine how spiritual kinship writ large remained imperative for donadas as they navigated their demanding labor obligations and moral responsibilities before God. I also explore how donadas engaged with the sacred while scrubbing and stirring and sweeping. For them, spiritual labor meant using their hands and their bodies to cultivate the spirit in service to others and to God.

Previous chapters have emphasized how individual women created sororial dialogues with others about knowledge of the body and ways to experience God in sacred objects. This chapter takes a prosopographical approach and considers the "groupness" of the hundreds of donadas living in Lima's convents. I base my study on an aggregate of the rather formulaic two-sentence autos de ingreso (entrance petitions) and expedientes or autos de profesión (profession documents) of girls and women seeking to enter convents as donadas. Taken together, the biographical elements found in these sources produce narratives that enhance our understanding of the dialogues taking place among women whose reality was the world of pots and pans. When combined with notarial and other sources, we can gain a sense of the constraints they faced and the spiritual solace they found in their sacred duties and intimate exchanges with others. Excerpts from the published diary of the black donada mystic Úrsula de Jesús (1604–66) give added insights into the quotidian, indeed material, nature of spiritual expression among women considered lesser beings by some of their superiors. Although exceptional because she was a mystic who was ordered by her confessor to record her spiritual visions, Úrsula's concerns with her positionality as a woman of color and her communion with divine beings echoed the concerns of the religious community in which she lived.

Generally, prosopographies connect the common characteristics of a particular group. However, to avoid essentializing the spiritual practices of disparate women who all happened to hold the same title and status as donadas in any number of Lima's convents, I consider the heterogeneous motivations for wanting to take formal vows, and the different economic and family backgrounds of the aspirants. Donadas expressed themselves as spiritual beings in a relational or positional manner to the nuns, who were their superiors, and to other donadas, as well as to the servants and slaves. They also continually engaged with God and other divine beings. The fact that donadas were laborers made them no less spiritual than the nuns. Their busy hands were signs of a pure and well-intentioned spirit.

In an attempt to explain the discriminatory barriers facing aspirants who wanted to become donadas, and the differences among them, the nuns, and the criadas, historians have often viewed their vocation as an "attractive alternative" to an insecure life in secular society. Both skilled and unskilled Afro-Peruvian and indigenous women, they argue, could find gainful employment, food, and shelter as religious domestics. Some might avoid rape or sexual torment by lascivious masters. Yet convent life was difficult, and categorical distinctions based on physical features and occupational hierarchies were more rigidly enforced in the governance of the convent than in the secular world; nuns and ecclesiastical authorities considered donadas as barely superior to criadas and slaves in rank.[7] While they were meant to serve the community first, and then the individual nuns, in fact, according to Luis Martín, donadas were viewed as nothing more than "exalted maids."[8] We only have to think of the words Úrsula de Jesús wrote in her spiritual diary—"they say the profession of the donada has no value"—to understand that some nuns did not even see them as "exalted."[9]

Sources generated by nuns and ecclesiastical authorities reiterate the position that donadas were laborers first and spiritual beings second. The documents imply that young women voluntarily submitted to the conditions and calidad (prestige, ranking) associated with this position because of inequality and poverty. In fact, the 237 extant autos de ingreso and expedientes de profesión for the largest convents—La Encarnación, La Concepción, and Santa Clara—rarely reveal the aspirants' motivations. Indeed, most of what we know about donadas comes from sources generated by individuals talking about them, not to or with them. When donadas do appear in the documents, they speak as litigants before an ecclesiastical notary to protest their physical and emotional abuse by previous owners or nuns, assert their hope that a testamentary legacy will be honored, or settle a property dispute.[10] Given these constraints inherent in the archival repository, and given that donadas are often depicted as shaping the lives of the elite women whom they served, how can we access their other, "unstoried" lives?[11] Perhaps, by repeating what the dominant discourse tells us, we are only reaffirming their subordination as the "tethered shadows" of those who portrayed them in that light.[12]

Gaining access to donadas' expressions of spirituality eludes our grasp in other ways. Scholars tend to focus on how the legal and religious discourse about people of African and indigenous descent marked them by excluding them from certain positions and spaces but including them in other, inferior ones.[13] Indeed, the historiography tends to cast men and women of color as being *apart* from rather than *a part* of monastic life, in particular, and colonial society, in general. This tendency is further reinforced when scholars pigeonhole and classify servants as "marginal peoples" and consider servitude as a total institution, just one notch above slavery.[14] The assumption is that someone could not be both a servant and a spiritual being.

More recent studies that focus on the intercultural religious exchanges and lived experiences of Africans in the Americas often use Inquisition records to discern how diverse African notions of the sacred were expressed in practices of daily life. However, when discussions of Christian practices arise, scholars tend to juxtapose African religious "traditions" with compliance with, strategic use of, or resistance to dominant Christian theological discourses.[15] But as recent scholarship has shown, Christianity was not always a "superficial veil," especially among the descendants of Central Africans long familiar with the basic tenets of Christianity.[16] Studies on confraternities as centers of Catholic spirituality, as well as a close reading of the wills of people of African descent, demonstrate that Catholicism was a centripetal rather than a marginal force in people's lives.[17] Perhaps this is evidence of the "sacred blackness" that Larissa Brewer-García has found in her investigation of Lima, where the majority of the populace had ancestral ties to West and Central Africa.[18] Indigenous people also tend to suffer from the "idols behind altars" approach to their participation in Catholic, colonial culture.[19] In contrast, archival repositories are replete with evidence of the active participation of indigenous people in confraternal and Christian charitable works.[20] In Lima, Christianity was a deeply lived experience for people of African and indigenous descent, whether they were living in their homes or in monastic settings.

Fortunately, even the rather skewed assemblage of testimonies from and about donadas enables the historian to reveal their discrete motivations and ways of dealing with the exigencies of life in the seventeenth century. While it is nearly impossible to get into the heads of these women, it is possible to speak about the *dimensionality* of donadas—and, especially, the external and internal pressures they faced; the matriarchal intimacies formed with their owners and patrons; and also the broader economic and religious climate in Lima that influenced their decisions. A prosopographical analysis of this religious category shows that donadas were not a homogeneous group and that their motivations for taking the veil varied. Most important, they made choices that did not always mimic those of the nuns. They emulated the behavior of servants with whom they worked and prayed on a daily basis. The fact that they were laborers made them no less spiritual than the nuns.

When considering donadas—whether as individuals or as a collectivity—we should be careful not to deemphasize the considerable constraints they faced. As Aguilar exclaimed in his sermon, donadas occupied themselves in the "humble ministries of the house" and, on a daily basis, had to strike a balance between communal tasks and the incessant requests of the pampered nuns whom they also served.[21] The demands placed on their time and their bodies caused resentment and enmity.

At any given time, the population of donadas in a convent might range from thirty to fifty, which for a smaller house such as the Monasterio de las Descalzas de San José, which had seventy nuns, could be significant.[22] Donada candidates were nearly always unmarried and of African or native Andean descent. According to canon law, at the time of entry and profession the candidate had to be free from bondage and over sixteen years of age. Most were between sixteen and twenty. Occasionally a married woman gained permission from her husband to take vows of celibacy and enter a convent.[23] The vast majority of donadas were demarcated as free *indias* or the African-descent *pardas, sambas, mulatas, negras,* or *quarteronas de mulata.*[24] Certainly these essentializing monikers, defined in the owners' terms, reinforced the "myth of [an] essential core" based on skin color or physical appearance.[25] These labels were important in the constitutions of each religious order, which specified the acceptability of candidates and the different subcategories of donadas.[26]

Yet, in convents and in secular society, these de jure "fixed orderings" were less crucial than the de facto positionality and valuations relative to economic and social status and the occupations held by women in the convent.[27] In determining the relationship of a donada self to others, these labels did not identify a racial parda essence but rather designated one of many figurative lines in the sand, eventually consumed by time and the prevailing winds of power. Nor did donadas have a fixed donada identity, because the relationships they established with others, including nuns, servants, and God, occurred positionally, in a manner defined internally within each convent. For instance, the nuns of Santa Clara, or *clarisas,* considered donadas to be third-tier nuns, but they were more lenient in accepting (and freeing) enslaved women candidates petitioning to become donadas than were other convents.[28] Distinctions were drawn between the white-veiled nuns, donadas, criadas, and slaves based on kinship associations as well as spiritual abilities and occupations held within the convent. There is no question that the title *donada* symbolized the hierarchical, unequal nature of social relations based on the extraction of labor for the benefit of others, but it also represented an opportunity to serve God and Christ honorably, which makes these women's positionality somewhat paradoxical.

Procedurally, an aspirant had to follow several time-consuming steps before becoming a donada. First, the candidate herself (if over the age of twenty-five), a nun, or a family member submitted an auto de ingreso formally requesting admittance to the religious community as a novice. A nun promoting a donada's candidacy to the community generally emphasized the young woman's occupational skills and any distinguishing spiritual virtues. The candidate (occasionally several applied at once) specified as some of her motivations her occupational talents, her motives based on piety, and the extent of her life spent in the convent, as well as her fear of living in the siglo. The candidate or the person nominating her also had to specify who would pay the required dowry of five hundred pesos.

If the community of nuns voted to approve the candidate's entry, the abbess would then request that the archbishop sign the auto de ingreso.[29] At that point, the novice entered the novitiate, technically for one year, during which time she was trained by teachers and kept under strict observance.[30] In the novitiate she learned to be obedient, charitable, and obsequious and to make gestures of humility; she studied the attributes of oral and mental prayer and the lives of the saints, and memorized the rules and constitutions of the order.[31] The most privileged learned to read designated spiritual texts. Once the candidate had completed her studies and training, a delegate of the archbishop oversaw her required examination (*examen de profesión*). Following the mandates established by the Council of Trent (1545–63) for all female religious, the novice answered several questions, after which she took simple vows (*votos simples*) of poverty, obedience, chastity, and enclosure. The vows were not formal (*votos solemnes*) in the juridical or canonical sense, but most convents and donadas took them very seriously, and the penalties for breaking them could be severe.[32] The solemn pledge voiced by the morena María de San Francisco before the community of nuns and the most important celestial beings expressed a deep connection with and commitment to the spiritual world, writ large:

I, María de San Francisco, out of love and service for Our Lord and Savior, Jesus Christ, and for the Blessed Virgin Mary, His mother, and for the devotion I have for the Immaculate Conception, without original sin, hereby vow and promise God and Mary and all the glorious apostles, Saints Peter and Paul, and the columns of the Church, and the Most Excellent and Reverend Archbishop don Bartolomé Lobo Guerrero and, thee, Abbess doña Aldonsa de Viveros, and all the female prelates who are and were of this convent, to live my entire life, in obedience and poverty, in chastity and perpetual enclosure under the Bull given by Pope Julius II (in living memory) and to our order, granted and confirmed. This I promise to uphold until I die.[33]

After reciting her vows, a donada like María de San Francisco was given a white shoulder-length veil to distinguish her from the nuns, and her life as a religious servant began.[34]

Establishing Parameters

Before the 1630s, entry procedures and the careful application of the order's constitutions may have been more the exception than the rule. Records for the first third of the century show nuns openly petitioning for a donada to enter first and foremost as a personal servant and secondarily as a servant of the community.[35] In fact, many young girls of African or indigenous descent entered convents as donadas to replace ill, deceased, or fugitive slaves; conversely, slaves replaced donadas when the latter's numbers plunged.[36] A few of the indias in convents had come to Lima as slaves captured in the wars that took place throughout much of the seventeenth century against the native population in Chile.[37]

Several convents failed to distinguish donadas who entered the novitiate from those women formally admitted as servants or slaves who never took vows and who served individual nuns.[38] The lenient dress code provides evidence of the slippage between servant and donada that could occur. Donadas might continue to wear the typical bodice, skirt, and shawl associated with criadas and then don a small scapulary and habit just before they went to Mass.[39] While these categorical distinctions provide clear evidence of their status as "exalted maids," as described by Martín, such inconsistencies and discrepancies changed somewhat after 1631, when Archbishop Fernando Arias de Ugarte (archbishop from 1618 to 1638) mandated that service to an individual nun should not in any way interfere with donadas' "obligations to perform designated tasks."[40] He also formalized the autos de ingreso to ensure that donadas would remain in the cloister and attempted to enforce the required ratio of one donada for every ten nuns.

If, as I have already argued, *positionality* involved establishing divisions between one category and another, were donadas really treated differently from, or considered superior to, the criadas? In some ways, yes. For one, donadas had tenure; they could not be expelled from convents, which became more significant after midcentury, as probing archbishops sought to curtail the excessive number of criadas, slaves, laywomen, and children in convents.[41] Faced with such exigencies, those nuns threatened with the loss of prized servants would scurry to promote the candidacy of specific criadas to the rank of donada. Even then, the acceptance of servants into the novitiate was not always guaranteed because the allotted slots for donadas were so limited.[42]

Ascending to the rank of donada certainly did not mean working less than the servants or slaves did, and those privileged enough to make the transition knew their lives would be labor intensive. To reinforce the subordination of their position, donadas taking their vows would be pointedly asked whether they knew that their profession was not meant to be a form of escape from a heavy workload.[43] However, ecclesiastical authorities tried to glorify the sacrifices involved in their labor. As Aguilar proclaimed in his sermon in 1678 at the Monasterio de la Encarnación's celebration of donadas, "the pardas donadas" could follow the example of the hard-working Marcela, the criada of Martha, in whose "castle and home" Christ resided.[44] Although preachers liked to point out that the humble Marcela was a hard worker, she was also a visionary who had intuitively recognized the incarnation of the Word of God in Mary.[45] This willingness to sacrifice one's life, so imbued in Christian thought and emphasized in weekly homilies, also permeated the words of young aspirants. The orphaned mulata Josefa de la Concepción y Meneses stated in her entrance petition, "It is my deepest desire to be the criada of the criadas in [the convent] and to do whatever is ordered in the infirmary and other offices."[46]

Unlike the criadas, donadas were listed on the registers of annually designated tasks (*tablas de oficios*) along with both black-veiled and white-veiled nuns. In this sense, the rotating positions they held served as differentiating occupational buffers between them and the nuns of the white veil, on the one hand, and between them and the servants and slaves, on the other.[47] For instance, the tablas de oficios frequently listed donadas as assistants to the nuns of the white veil, who oversaw the more mundane tasks of the convent. Yet, as they performed an array of duties in a largely self-sufficient community, they worked alongside their subordinates, the servants and slaves.[48] As assistants to the *silleras* (women in charge of the pantry), they ensured that the flour, wheat, barley, wine, oil, and legumes were properly protected against humidity. *Fuelleras* stoked and fanned with bellows the fires that heated the organ, and the *entonadoras* made sure it was properly tuned and ready to play. As well as aiding the laborers (*obreras*) and bakers (*panaderas*), donadas also served their teachers.[49] They ran to tell the nuns when visitors awaited them in the parlor, and the more senior donadas stood guard (as *celadoras*) over the others at public spaces such as the laundry.[50] In an environment where surveillance and attention to the actions of others were paramount, only the most responsible and trustworthy donadas were appointed as guardians of the donadas' dormitory.[51]

The tasks that donadas performed sometimes rotated on a monthly and even weekly basis.[52] Úrsula de Jesús noted in her spiritual diary that donadas cooked large pots of food, cleaned, and served the food in the kitchen and refectory; they also swept the offices, cleaned out the corrals and chicken coops, washed clothes, tilled the soil, pruned the trees, and collected the fruit in the orchard. In the infirmary they changed the linens; cooked for the ill nuns, servants, and other donadas; washed the clothing of the filthiest patients; carried out the orders given by the doctors who visited the convent; or spelled a black-veiled nun in charge of the infirmary.[53] They spent an enormous amount of their time and energy engaged in such monotonous activities, which meant that they had to find deeper spiritual meaning in them. Abiding chafed hands and aching backs, or holding one's tongue while waiting on demanding nuns, only strengthened and purified the spirit. Through their bodies, donadas could understand the suffering that Christ had endured.[54]

Their humble status was also reinforced in the deferential gestures they made to their superiors. After each midday meal in the Monasterio de la Trinidad, for instance, the donadas cleansed and dried the hands of the black-veiled nuns, beginning with the abbess, in preparation for their going to the choir.[55] In addition to the designated tasks and general communal duties required to feed the large convent population, donadas prepared stews and pastries for individual nuns, both robust and infirm, and attended to the beggars or regular clients who clamored for food and sweets through the *torno* (a small rotating door).[56]

No doubt Teresa de Ávila's proclamation that "the Lord walks among the pots and pans," which opened this chapter, resonated deeply with the convents' servants. Still, the words could not negate the fact that, more than anything else, the combination of communal duties (*la obediencia*) and service to individual nuns could lead to exhaustion and incite anger and frustration.[57] Although la obediencia meant following orders, being slotted into inferior positions and occupations produced infighting and rancor, because both nuns and servants used their own criteria to determine the value and prestige of specific tasks.[58] We know that these differentiations existed, but deciphering the rankings of certain spaces—the kitchen as superior to the laundry, or vice versa—and the tasks associated with them is extremely difficult. For Úrsula de Jesús, the kitchen in the Monasterio de Santa Clara was the last place she wanted to work, and she felt depressed and resentful when ordered to do so. Evidence suggests that donadas (and nuns) jealously guarded their "rights" to maintain the same post year after year; they could take "extraordinary measures" to prevent the abbess from properly executing her duties to assign coveted (or despised) positions.[59]

Finding a replacement to take on their more onerous tasks was an option that only a few privileged donadas had. Documents reveal that the occasional donada owned a slave, inherited as part of a testamentary legacy or donated or loaned by a family member or a pious individual.[60] Not only did slaves relieve the labor burden in the convent, but their work as *jornaleros* (wage earners) outside the convent allowed some donadas to garner additional income.[61] Ownership of a slave helped donadas gain additional status relative to the other donadas (some of the slave owners were referred to as *doñas* by the nuns) and to those nuns of the white veil who did not own slaves. It also lessened their dependency on their black-veiled nun patrons, because they could live more comfortably in their own cells or with a companion or relative.[62]

The internal rankings of specific tasks and spaces in the convent were most apparent in the designation of the most coveted occupations—those related to assistance in the Divine Office.[63] Although supervised by a nun of the white veil (called *sacristanas mayores*), some worked as sextons, cleaning religious objects and washing the linen for the altar in the sacristy.[64] They knew exactly where to place the incense and other sacred objects on the altar. But maintaining the daily rhythm of the Christian calendar involved other key posts. Donadas like Juana de Sejas rang the bell to specify the liturgical hours and to indicate when "sermons, processions, anniversaries, and religious commemorations" were about to occur (she held the position for several consecutive years in La Concepción).[65] An aptitude for a particular vocation also helped a candidate gain a slot in the novitiate, as noted by the twenty-six-year-old Lorensa de Mesa, who entered La Encarnación because she had been carrying the cross in processions for over ten years. She considered it to be her vocation.[66] It was also a great honor, desirable to many.

The prestige associated with particular tasks, particularly those related to the Divine Office, allowed donadas to position themselves favorably relative to other members of the religious community. On many different levels, however, matronage, or an association with a powerful female figure in the convent, was even more crucial in determining who would become donadas and when, and what their status would be in the years to come.[67] That was particularly true given that nearly 85 percent of the postulants had lived for years, if not decades, in the convent, serving a nun as a criada.[68] Some of these women were the daughters of slaves who had been freed by their owners. Others were in the situation of Catalina de San Joseph, who had grown up in the company of the nun María de San Cristóbal, who "wished only the best for [Catalina]" and donated five hundred pesos from a loan she had made to a widow to pay the dowry for Catalina to become a donada in the Monasterio de las Descalzas.[69] This pattern suggests an internal ranking among servants privileged enough to advance to the next level—from slave to criada to donada or from criada to donada—and also suggests that candidates whose patron was a well-known and powerful nun (or donada) stood a better chance of entering the novitiate.[70] Although the statistics reported in conventual chronicles are not always reliable, we might assume that in a given year (before 1670, when the numbers of servants increased dramatically) less than one-quarter of the total number of servants would be fortunate enough to ascend to the rank of donada or even enter the novitiate.[71] (Some donadas remained in the novitiate, as a type of holding area, for years.)[72] In fact, donadas rarely constituted more than one-third of the overall population of free servants of color in the convents of La Encarnación, Santa Clara, La Concepción, and Las Descalzas de San José (a smaller convent).[73]

The selective privileging of particular criadas as future donadas can be explained in several ways. As elite Spanish women entered the novitiate to become nuns of the black veil, they quickly insinuated themselves into the family clusterings of sisters, mothers, daughters, aunts, and nieces who resided, generation after generation, in the same cells.[74] Such privileged women brought with them young slaves and servants and then claimed to have raised their young protégées (*criandolas*) properly, which translated into feeding them, providing medical care, and protecting them.[75] Through this provision of services and meeting of obligations in exchange for child labor, unequal intimacies between nuns and children became naturalized.[76] The connection established between a powerful female family-cluster base and a future donada (sometimes without knowing this would eventuate) created distinct positionalities vis-à-vis other nuns and their servant girls.

An examination of the reproduction and maintenance of matrilineal households in convents helps us to see where donadas fit into the complex webs of social relations and obligations associated with convent households.[77] However, nonconsanguineous and power-based matriarchal networks were not exclusive to the elite mestiza and Spanish nuns. One can also trace inter-generational linkages among the slaves and servants entering with Spanish novices. The daughters, nieces, and granddaughters of these laborers would continue serving the next generation of nuns.[78] In the documentary corpus about life in convents, the *amas* (female masters) entering the novitiate jus-tified bringing in servants and slaves, whom they said they were raising (*cri-ando*) in exchange for their labor.[79]

Determining the degree of affective ties between servants and amas is dif-ficult, but female servants sometimes assumed the surnames of their amas and used the term *estrecha* (close) to characterize the relationship. The young mulata María Marchan, the legitimate daughter of the pardo sexton of La Concepción, Jerónimo Carrión, took the name of her matron, doña Maria Marchan, a nun of the black veil who supported her candidacy to become a donada in 1681 and with whom she claimed to have close ties.[80] Others passed down their matrons' surnames to their daughters.[81] Although the practice was more common before the 1630s, other *morenas conventuales* (African-descent servants) like Isabel Casanga, Ana Casanga (her sister?), Cecilia Bran, and Maria Fulupa maintained the "African" surnames of their mothers.[82]

Still, not all servant and slave girls had relatives in the convent to rely on for support and matronage. Given the intense migration to Lima, many young girls arrived in Lima at a tender age from various parts of the vice-royalty to serve a particular nun, often for life. Lacking contact with family members now far away, they were likely to develop ties within the cloister and particularly with nuns who could offer them financial support.[83] Orphans raised in other convents or hospitals who transferred to a new monastic set-ting had to create kinship ties with the new community.[84] But, again, this matronage was not the exclusive domain of the powerful and the elite. Just as nuns raised young servant girls to become donadas (but still remain their servants), donadas also raised young girls and provided for them financially as best they could.[85]

Wealthier donadas like María de San Joseph might leave a *celdita* (little cell) to a girl she had raised, hoping that she too would eventually take her vows.[86] In those little cells, which were sometimes the size of apartments, alternate kinship linkages and matriarchal intimacies were further reinforced by servants and even donadas who resided with their slaves and servants.[87] A codicil drawn up in 1670 by Catalina de Narvaez, a parda donada in La Concepción, shows "the love she had" for two sixteen-year-old pardas, Inés and Teresa de Narvaez. To them she donated her twenty-four-year-old slave named Felipa to meet their needs. It was also Catalina's desire that Inés and Teresa should become the new owners of her cell, where they would live the rest of their lives along with Ysabel de los Angeles and Zelda Lorensa Narvaez. To her thirty-year-old slave, Antonia, who had also adopted the surname Narvaez, Catalina promised freedom if she would continue working in the infirmary of La Concepción.[88] Thus, in the large tomes kept by a seventeenth-century notary, we find a document showing the intimate communion (sharing of a surname and an intimate space) among women who had spent years, if not decades, together. We will never know whether they were sisters, cousins, or nieces of Catalina. But even if blood did not link them, Catalina's concern for Inés, Teresa, Antonia, Ysabel, and Zelda shows a deeper, spiritual kinship and a concern for a secure future in her cell, whether sumptuous or modest (we can wonder). She was treating them as family members.

Although Catalina's codicil does not mention bequeathing sacred objects—small altar pieces, scapulars, images of the Virgin—to her protégées, no doubt they engaged with the intimate materiality of touch, sound, and taste on a daily basis. Occupying the same space would not have eliminated differential relations of power and position. But in this intimate familial context, nuns, servants, and slaves held, gazed on, or brushed against material objects such as linens, mattresses, candles, and furniture; they listened to the same scriptural passages being read; and, from youth to old age, they witnessed each others' lamentations and small victories.[89] Perhaps Catalina afforded these young girls a nonliterate education about how to discern what was holy and unholy by engaging their senses. We can also imagine the nun teaching them to read. Perhaps Antonia cured the elderly Catalina's aches and pains or consoled her by sharing a psalm she had once learned.

Donadas were relational selves who shared sacred knowledge in intricate and intimate webs of connection. However, access to economic capital, as historian Kathryn Burns has argued, also enhanced political, social, and spiritual clout.[90] Not only did some nuns of the black veil have the money to pay for dowries, but they also exercised their influence on behalf of controversial candidates.[91] Behind-the-scenes negotiations could result in an enslaved novice being declared free at the stroke of a pen.[92] Those donadas not so fortunate as to have a matron or to be a part of a convent household were financially and politically dependent on the good graces of the abbess.[93] In these instances, matronless donadas often expressed a willingness to take on the least desirable occupations, "to carry the cross of Christ" and donate their personal service to the convent for life.[94] Such was the case of Ventura de la Fuente, a free criada who dictated her own petition in 1687: "I was born a slave, and my master gave me a letter of freedom when I was still young. I am a mulata and young and in order to serve in religion with the merit of being a nun I desire to take the habit of donada. I have no money to give [as a dowry] because I am poor, but I am obligated to serve the community."[95] Below Ventura's petition, the abbess scribbled one line: "She is useful to the community."

Freedom from Bondage?

To carry the cross of Christ, one had to be free from legal bondage. Especially for young slaves, their destiny was often linked to the will of their owner. "Because I raised her from infancy in my home" was often cited as the reason for a charitable owner to grant freedom in his or her testament to a young girl who had once worked as a household servant (sometimes alongside her mother).[96] Other owners cited affection, piety, or Christian charity as their main motives, since benevolent works enabled one to prepare for the next life and lessen the time spent in purgatory.[97] Ana de Alvarado wanted to have some*thing* "to offer to the Mother of God," and so she donated her slave's daughter, Andrea, to two nuns in La Concepción.[98] Some of these deathbed gestures were decided on when the girl was extremely young.[99] In some cases, manumissions were granted because the girl's mother had served the owners well, or because the amas expressed having a strong attachment to the slave since infancy.[100] But freedom could be conditional on the girl taking her vows as a donada at a prescribed age and in a designated convent after years of service. Such charitable acts meant to redeem the soul of the owner might have positive consequences for a young woman freed from bondage before she entered a convent; however, sometimes the *carta de libertad* (declaration of freedom) contained labyrinthine clauses that specified that the girl would receive her freedom *only* if she became a donada.[101] For some young women, manumission came at too steep a price.

Although slave mothers were often happy to know that their daughters' future would be different from their own, not all girls viewed the position of donada as a salutary alternative to slavery, nor did they appreciate that their owners had made the decision for them—in some cases before they had the use of reason. Catalina Velásquez entrusted the four-year-old Isabel María, the daughter of her slave Constanza Terranova, to a black-veiled nun. Velásquez's will of 1641 included a clause stipulating that Isabel María would be free from bondage if she continued to serve in Santa Clara for her entire life. If she left the convent, however, she would remain a slave, but the convent would not be able to sell her. If she remained in the convent, she would be free to become a donada at the age of sixteen, and two hundred pesos from Velásquez's estate would pay for her dowry.[102] But becoming a donada under such conditions, even if refusing to do so meant continued bondage, did not appeal to Isabel María.[103] When she came of age, her aunt, the free black Ana de Mora, filed a complaint on behalf of Isabel María before the ecclesiastical notary stating that Isabel María had never wanted to become a donada. Knowing she was required to spend her life in the convent, she had fled, become pregnant, and—contrary to the legacy—was then sold by the convent to a new owner.[104] Isabel María expressed a willingness to pay the two hundred pesos she owed the convent, on the condition that the archbishop dispatch a license that would free her from "whatever rights the nuns claim to have against me."[105]

Just as Spanish families pressured girls to become nuns of the black veil or white veil, donadas were also occasionally coerced. Although she was unsuccessful in her attempt to nullify her vows, the petition of María de San Francisco illustrates the perceptions of a donada who felt constrained by her position. Her legal advocate explained that she had entered the convent as a servant of María de Retes, but then her uncle, Friar Manuel Franco, a lay brother (*lego*) in the Convento de San Agustín, threatened to cut her off economically if she did not become a donada; she expressed to the judge that she had acquiesced to his will only "out of respect and the reverential fear I had for him."[106] Her other arguments for annulling her vows were equally compelling. Delicate health meant she lacked the strength to do the tasks required of donadas; the convent did not provide her with proper clothing and other items; she felt that the nuns were holding her against her will; and she claimed that she had taken her vows before the legal age of sixteen. The nuns mistreated her because she was poor and miserable, she said. In spite of such forceful legally viable arguments, the judge denied her appeal to nullify her vows.[107]

As the cases of Isabel María, María de San Francisco, and others attest, some donadas resented being consigned to a convent, where they had to perform onerous tasks. The concept that "the obligations of religion are greater than those of the world" had little resonance, and they saw themselves as being treated unjustly.[108] For them, becoming a donada did not mean receiving better treatment. Nor did conditional manumission hold any appeal. However, such responses contrast sharply with the sentiments of other young women who cherished the thought of carrying the cross of Christ (and others) and who would tearfully entreat the abbess to let them profess.[109] The transition from criada to donada was a logical one, given that most applicants spent their lives serving a nun. But the 15 percent of postulants who had never before lived in a convent had different expectations. Some donadas were legitimate daughters whose families could afford to pay the five hundred–peso dowry.[110] Sisters and nieces from more well-to-do families might enter the novitiate together, sometimes with their own servants.[111] Other applicants came from humble economic backgrounds, and family members, including single mothers, had struggled earnestly for years as domestics or food sellers to garner the capital to secure their daughters' futures.[112] The adopted families of orphans also offered to pay their dowries.[113]

What might motivate a parent to place his or her child in a convent as a criada under the care of a nun? No doubt the reasons included a better future for their daughters through escape from poverty, protection from a ruthless master, and a rudimentary education in a convent.[114] For those benefits they were willing to part with their children.[115] Yet spiritual reasons also motivated them. In the seventeenth century, God opened his doors to everyone, including (and especially) people of African descent. As hundreds of colonial documents attest, Spaniards were not the only ones to fully embrace the multitudinous expressions of Catholicism that occurred on a daily, if not hourly, basis.

Many Afro-Peruvian limeños knew someone who served as a *mayorala* (female manager of a confraternity), hermana, or *cofrada* (member of the confraternity) in any one of the dozens of confraternities designated for African-descent people in a city overflowing with monasteries. Not only did these lay religious brotherhoods finance the ceremonious displays of religious devotion, but they also helped the sick, paid burial fees, and oversaw the establishment of chaplaincies for souls in purgatory.[116] They fostered new kinship relations based on a common organizational connection and, as we saw in chapter 1, on the religious ritual economy in which women participated. Although men generally held the most prestigious offices, it was grandmothers, mothers, and aunts who sewed the banners representing their particular confraternity. They maintained the cult of the Virgin by helping to dress her image for a particular procession; they traveled from house to house begging for alms to buy candles; and they cleaned and arranged sacred objects in their confraternity's chapel.[117]

It is also misguided to think that if a girl spent most of her young life working in the service of a nun, she would sever or relinquish family ties outside the convent. Even though they might be separated for lengthy periods of time, evidence shows that family members set aside the money to pay for girls' dowries to enter the novitiate.[118] Parents' voices also appear in autos de ingreso soliciting the acceptance of their daughters as novices.[119] For instance, Pablo de los Rios, a lieutenant, described his legitimate daughter Augustina as being "[endowed] with such virtue, that she never left the cloister, not even when the earthquakes occurred." He requested that she be given the opportunity to pursue her noble goal of taking the veil and serving Christ.[120]

It is important to remember that the convent was a sacred space where the possibility of living a deeply spiritual life was strong. God's presence could be perceived in every room, in every icon, and in every deferential gesture. Years and even decades of enclosure facilitated the development of characteristics and virtues that might lead to acceptance into the novitiate.[121] Many also believed that a life of enclosure was their destiny.[122] Indeed, because the convent was the only world many had ever known, some girls raised "in the Blessed Virgin's house" felt incapable of returning to el siglo, always portrayed to them as a lugubrious place where they might roam aimlessly.[123] As they made the transition from novice to professed donada, each vow of obedience, chastity, enclosure, and poverty was a step along the path to religious perfection.[124] Here their positionality of self to other related most profoundly to the most powerful force of life: God.

Donadas sometimes referred to their profession as a vocation and claimed to have received God's calling to the state of religious perfection. Following the example of the servant Marcela, "they pursued their devotion with ardor, until assured they were in a state of grace, a sure sign they would reach Glory."[125] Day after day, the rigorous conventual routines, divided methodically into component parts related to prayer, silence, and work, formed the quotidian expressions of spirituality for nuns and donadas alike. Those with access to capital invested in the religious culture of the convent. Melchora de los Reyes expressed her faith by borrowing eight hundred pesos to build an altar screen for Our Lady of the Incarnation.[126] Others took measures to care for their departed souls. Magdalena Choque, an india donada, established a chaplaincy to ensure that once she had passed, two weekly masses would be said on her behalf in La Encarnación.[127] Other donadas left bequests in their wills to maintain the cult of a particular saint, or to ensure a steady supply of wax for the candles placed at the foot of the statue of the Virgin.[128] In La Encarnación, parda servants even established their own confraternity.[129]

As officials sought to bring all members of the republics of Indians and Spaniards into the fold of a Christian commonwealth, sermons, chronicles, and spiritual parlays began to emphasize the spirituality of particularly devout men and women of color graced by Mary or Jesus. They promoted the idea of a comprehensive Christian dominion ruled by God over *all* colonial vassals, sovereign and subject. To promote the inclusiveness of their particular order, and to compete with other orders, Spanish friars exalted the virtues of devout indias and women of mixed parentage.[130] Local "saints" served the purpose of espousing Christian virtues of humility, charity, and poverty and inspiring young women to follow suit. Donadas therefore had many models of sanctity to draw on for inspiration and support. From priests and nuns, women heard about venerable blacks and exemplary saints like Benito Palermo, whose cult flourished in Lima after 1620.[131] But limeños had no shortage of their own local heroes. Many whispered tales of the miracles of the mulato donado Martín de Porres, who never closed his heart to anyone and whose beatification hearing concluded in the 1660s. As witnesses testified on his behalf, they repeated and embellished tales of his receptivity with animals, ability to cure the sick, and gift of prophecy.[132] Although less renowned, black visionaries like Úrsula de Jesús also gained a reputation for sanctity and the ability to save souls in purgatory.[133] Then there was the quiet presence of dozens of women of African and indigenous descent living exemplary lives of extreme penance and prayer in beaterios or recogimientos founded in the city throughout the seventeenth century.[134] Stories of lesser-known exemplary criadas and donadas—who, according to one chronicler, merited no lower a place than the nuns—circulated widely among limeños eager to exalt Lima as an epicenter of baroque spirituality.[135] Generally these women were characterized as exceptionally meek, reclusive, and even tolerant of discrimination. But occasionally a writer would record a minor sensation that had caused a stir in the city. The Franciscan chronicler Diego de Córdova y Salinas briefly referenced an unnamed indigenous donada who had committedly venerated the statue of Our Lady of the Miracles in the Franciscan convent. It was said that the Virgin had communicated directly to the dutiful donada, praising her devotion and promising to assist her in an "enviable" death.[136] Although often only comprising a few sentences or several paragraphs, these miniature vidas of the blessed servants of God were immortalized in the conventual chronicles of Diego de Córdova y Salinas (1651), Juan Meléndez (1681), and Francisco de Echave y Assu (1688), in the hope of inspiring young souls.[137] Such exemplary figures were representative of the hundreds of obscure pious men and women walking the dimly lit corridors of convents scattered throughout Spanish and Portuguese America.

Extolling the virtues of such men and women also served the didactic purpose of exemplum, and the various religious orders and convents competed to have the most illustrious, saintly nuns and servants. Although to a certain degree the women of color in Lima internalized the vision of the exceptional humble, penitent, and obsequious servant Marcela, this model did more than encourage mimesis and accentuate the inequality between the women and their Spanish superiors.[138] For donadas, the parameters of difference were clear in the tasks they were assigned and in the need to accrue capital or find a powerful matron. But their deeply felt experiences of Catholicism were not always shaped by church authorities, nor were they devout Catholics only because mimesis gave them power or prestige vis-à-vis the nuns. For receptive and observant girls who worked alongside pious women of color day after day, their elders served as models of sanctity in the flesh. For them, these "saints" did not need to become white to be venerable.[139] For instance, in 1673 María de Escobar, a fifty-year-old *quarterona de mestiza* (one-quarter mestizo) who had long been the companion of the blessed mulata donada María de Rojas, petitioned to receive the habit of donada because it was the wish of María de Rojas, "a great servant of God."[140] Occasionally the entrance petitions (autos de ingreso) mention particularly devout donadas such as the "virtuous" Inés de la Concepción, who served in the sacristy of Las Descalzas for two decades.[141] Shortly after the venerable Úrsula de Jesús (also called Úrsula de Christo) died in the Monasterio de Santa Clara, an aspirant named Francisca de la Cruz petitioned to enter the novitiate. The abbess claimed that "for over twenty years Francisca has served the convent with great virtue and perseverance. Following the example of the Mother, Úrsula de Christo, she has determined to take the habit of donada."[142]

Even if donadas were unable to share the full status as brides of Christ, their testimonies display a fervent desire to serve God and the Blessed Virgin. In many cases this motivation trumped other, more material concerns.[143] Moreover, they revered a God who saw them as equal to others. Although she was singular because of the support she gained among nuns and friars for her mystical abilities, the writings of the black mystic Úrsula de Jesús gave voice to the "insignificant and humble ones" of the convent who pleased God despite being outcasts among the religious community.[144] In several diary entries, she addressed the concern that donadas ought to define themselves primarily as spiritual beings, in spite of how others perceived them.[145] Although priests often limned the sentiment that God did not distinguish between servant and señora, and that all the bones of the dead were equal, the question is how women of color internalized or appropriated this discourse. Once, when Úrsula de Jesús lamented to God, "they say the profession of the donadas has no value," she received the following reply: "There is a difference because the nuns are white and of the Spanish nation, but with respect to the soul, all is one: Whoever does more is worth more."[146] Clearly, Úrsula de Jesús (and, I would add, her fellow donadas and servants) believed that all were equal before God. In their hearts donadas carried the cross of Christ, even if they could never hope to rest on a satin pillow to relieve their weariness.

Conclusions

As a close reading of the documents shows, women were drawn to become donadas by a variety of motivations—some material, others psychological or spiritual. Some women chose this path to ensure their freedom. The matriarchal intimacies of convent life and the positionality of donadas relative to others within the convents, as well as their ability to effectuate a spiritual life, also influenced their decisions and the opportunities presented to them. The sororial dialogues they maintained with their elders, their peers, and their spiritual models encouraged them to follow the spiritual path. Their decision to become a donada depended less on essentialized racial taxonomies than on whether they were free or enslaved, whether they had entered the convent as a donation or had been raised there from early childhood, whether they had been pressured by family members or nuns to take their vows, and how much power the matron supporting their candidacy wielded in the convent.[147] It also depended on the economic capital they could garner during their lifetime. Equally important, it also depended on how devoutly they ministered to God.

Clearly these supposedly subjugated women did not simply accept the world imposed on them, but neither did they always resist, negotiate their identities, or mimic their Spanish superiors. Nor were donadas marginalized and repressed servants "placated with unfulfilled promises."[148] If, as Martín has argued, donadas served as a "buffer between nuns and the hundreds of servants and slaves who inhabited the cloisters," what can the intimate politics of power relations tell us about the interstices of difference in colonial nonelite society?[149] Unveiling the matriarchal and restrictive relations between nuns and donadas also raises questions about the positionalities of self in relation to others and the "theatrics of dominance" taking place in other domestic spaces of colonial Lima.[150] More broadly, it argues that the *routes* taken and the *roots* established by generations of diasporic subjects involved different positionalities in relation to the rich variability of baroque Catholic expression. Donadas knew in their bodies and in their minds that the materiality of the sacred manifested not only in the altar cloths and thick candles they had fashioned but also in the sudsy water, stews and sauces, and brooms that grazed the floors.

Donadas, like others, had different convictions. Some did not believe that, facing the constraints they did and knowing that Spaniards considered them to be inferior, they must suffer like Christ to enjoy eternal glory. Others, however, subscribed to the viewpoint that suffering would purify the soul. They were not alone. Many Catholics, from America, Europe, and Africa, believed that "only he who perseveres until the end will be saved." Knowing they would work diligently until death, Afro-Peruvians might think to themselves, "We should not cease to carry our Cross in pursuit of Christ, because what other way is there? What good does it do us to have navigated our way favorably over a very long distance only to lose our way at the door?"[151] Ultimately, *everyone* carried the cross of Christ—in their hearts, on their shoulders, and in their obligations to others in their world.

MARÍA JACINTA MONTOYA, NICOLÁS DE AYLLÓN, AND THE UNMAKING OF AN INDIAN SAINT IN LATE SEVENTEENTH-CENTURY PERU

...

The year 1701 ended badly for María Jacinta Montoya, also known as María Jacinta de la Santíssima Trinidad. Prudently, she decided to denounce herself before Inquisition authorities and submit her conscience to scrutiny. Ecclesiastical authorities had been alarmed by her personal association with the beata Ángela de Carranza, condemned as a false mystic in 1694 (Ángela's life is discussed in chapter 3). Additionally, in several notebooks spanning more than two decades, María Jacinta had recorded the miracles of her husband and her own visions, dreams, sightings of demons, and mystical communications with God.[1] Although one of the spiritual confessors with whom she shared all of her writings told her she should not be concerned, she felt uneasy.[2] It turned out that her fears were not ungrounded. After questioning whether María Jacinta's flirtations with unorthodox practices verged on heresy, Inquisition authorities unanimously declared in early 1702 that she was "deluded and deceived," that her spirit was "not secure," and that "she was not following a righteous path."[3] To the various minor charges, she responded that all the fasting and penance must have affected her head and that she was nothing but a miserable, wretched woman.[4]

But María Jacinta was no ordinary, deluded mystic.[5] She was the widow of Nicolás de Ayllón (1632–77), an Indian (indio) tailor from the Chiclayo region of Peru, whose beatification process had been ongoing since 1684. Nicolás had lived most of his life in Lima and had developed a reputation over the years for his extreme charity in collecting alms for the poor and for souls in purgatory. Thanks to the efforts of his wife and others, public recognition of his virtues materialized immediately after his death in November 1677. Within seven years the authorities had initiated the ordinary diocesan process, the first stage toward beatification. By 1684 dozens of witnesses ranging from members of the Spanish and indigenous aristocracy to poor slaves had attested to his saintly qualities and heroic virtues.[6] During this initial critical phase, authorities were careful to follow the rules on non culto established by Pope Urban VIII in decrees made in 1625 and 1634 and overseen by the Sacred Congregation of Rites in Rome. These rules stated that until the papal decree of beatification arrived, limeños were to avoid any public displays of veneration, especially near the candidate's place of burial or in the chapels or churches he had frequented.[7]

Notwithstanding these mandates, María Jacinta was one of Nicolás's greatest publicists and advocates. For interested parties, she recopied and distributed excerpts from her notebook detailing his miracles; in 1684 she encouraged testimony on his behalf from people from far and wide, including members of the indigenous nobility from Nicolás's native Chiclayo and the highland provinces. She also raised money to pay for the costly beatification process.[8] She was not alone in her endeavors: a number of prominent ecclesiastical figures, including José de Buendía, a well-known Jesuit who had served as Nicolás's confessor, stood in the pulpit and extolled his virtues.[9] Key members of both the Mercedarian order and the Society of Jesus (Jesuits) eagerly promoted his candidacy. Commissioned by his fellow Spanish Jesuits, Bernardo Sartolo interviewed María Jacinta and then used notes she provided to write Nicolás's sacred biography, *Vida admirable y muerte prodigiosa de Nicolas de Ayllon* (1684).[10] The publication of a eulogistic life account was considered standard in cases of potential sanctity, and it showed that the Jesuits wished to claim Nicolás as one of their own.[11]

The arrival of Sartolo's book in Lima in late 1684 caused an immediate sensation.[12] Various copies, many soon dog-eared or full of comments, circulated among priests and nuns, who were eager to peruse the book. Following a standard hagiographic blueprint, it detailed Nicolás's virtues of mortification, penitence, patience, prophecy, and humility.[13] A chapter on the divine favors that Nicolás had received from God described the beata Ángela de Carranza's ecstatic vision of Nicolás holding his heart in his hand, an image of the Blessed Trinity impressed on it, offering it to the Immaculate Virgin.[14] This vision was considered a divine sign that mystical union with God had occurred and that Nicolás was indeed *bienaventurado*, or blessed. Although María Jacinta never named Ángela in her beatification hearing testimony in 1684, her confessors reportedly told Inquisition authorities that she had once shared with them Ángela's vision of Nicolás wearing a white alb and a crown of roses. The voice of Christ had said to Ángela, "This is how I reward those who love and serve me."[15]

In 1688 the Inquisition detained Ángela, and the amiable relations between her and Nicolás and María Jacinta led several Inquisition authorities to work behind the scenes to hinder Nicolás's beatification proceedings. Their fears that the three figures had confided in each other on spiritual matters (someone commented that Ángela visited the couple regularly on her way to Mass) deepened with the realization that all three had shared spiritual confessors, including don Ignacio de Híjar y Mendoza, the parish priest of San Marcelo, and Pedro de Ávila Tamayo. The latter would soon be targeted by the Inquisition for solicitation.[16]

Resistance in Lima to Nicolás's candidacy for beatification was far from unanimous. His candidacy was supported by select members of the Audiencia, the viceroy, the archbishop, and high-ranking members of distinct religious orders, including the Jesuits. In Europe both King Charles II and Pope Innocent XII thought Nicolás's canonization would bolster missionary endeavors in distant areas of the empire and promote a more inclusive Christianity. But slow transoceanic communication networks did not help matters. While on one side of the Atlantic the original beatification papers circulated among the members of the Rome tribunal, on the other an auto-da-fé was celebrated in 1694 in Lima to punish Ángela for false mysticism.[17] Two years later Sartolo's work was confiscated and its circulation prohibited, on charges that it had failed to comply with non culto regulations. Despite these setbacks, the Sacred Congregation in Rome signed the decree (*rótulo*) in 1699 certifying that the candidate's virtues qualified for beatification, that Nicolás's case should proceed, and that a stay of execution (*prórroga*) of three years (to gather new testimonies) should be granted.[18] In the long run, however, even with support among certain circles in Rome, Madrid, and Lima, the damning association with Ángela and the condemnation of Sartolo's biography weakened Nicolás's chances of beatification. Local interests prevailed.

The intriguing politics surrounding the unraveling of Nicolás's beatification proceso have been elaborated by several scholars. Some blame María Jacinta's machinations for the collapse, while others point to the complex and conflicting political agendas of the different parties involved.[19] This chapter focuses on how María Jacinta molded Nicolás's vida to fit within the Catholic baroque canon of the time as she navigated turbulent political waters and claimed authority as a renowned female spiritual leader. She understood quite well the politics of sanctity in colonial Lima, and over the decades she pursued several goals at once. She worked tirelessly to found a convent and to promote her husband's candidacy for sainthood, all the while serving as a mirror of his virtues.[20]

Most beatification proceedings involved collaborative labors to craft a historical fiction that resonated with orthodox Catholic narratives.[21] As Ronald Morgan has explained, these procesos were important for several reasons. They inspired readers (listeners) with accounts of miracles, saintly behavior, and attributes. They brought fame to a neighborhood or the affiliated institutions and religious orders involved. The beatification process could also convince skeptics that the candidate was worthy of veneration and that they should sponsor his or her cult once beatification was achieved.[22] At the same time as depositions provided evidence to support beatification and eventual sainthood, they enabled competing religious orders to promote their own marginal figures, whose histories were meant to edify, instruct, convert, and be accessible to all members of the Christian commonwealth.[23]

The ways in which these procesos were constituted and how popular notions of (and stories about) the potential saint evolved are also important to consider, however. After all, it was not unusual for authorities to script potential saints to fit a hagiographic model and to sweep negative aspects of their biographies under the proverbial rug. Nor was it unusual to disassociate candidates from followers deemed to be less than holy.[24] Like the more polished vidas or the fragmented petitions to become a donada (analyzed in the previous chapter), Nicolás's beatification hearings and Sartolo's vida of him were scripted. But, formulaic as they are, they also allow us to see agency and to gain innovative perspectives on how notions of sanctity altered.[25] Historians who have studied beatification hearings have considered how reports of miracles or assessments of the candidate's heroic virtues changed over time, and how political intrigue often shaped the ongoing discourse of these procesos.[26] Celia Cussen's important study of the diocesan (1660) and apostolic (1679–85) beatification hearings of Martín de Porres, for instance, emphasizes how testimonies about his miracles shifted over the course of twenty years and in response to legal restrictions, especially the non culto rules implemented by Pope Urban VIII. Following Michel de Certeau, Cussen also emphasizes how local contingencies in Lima played a major role in how the future saint would be fashioned.[27] The questions and answers about Porres responded to the concurrent processes of other candidates, especially that of Rosa de Lima, and to the way the regular orders in Lima actively promoted their own saints to the exclusion of those of other orders.[28] While the fierce competition helped some candidates to advance more rapidly, it also promoted Lima as a corpus mysticum with no shortage of saintly bienaventurado individuals. Like the hearings for Porres, the attempts to beatify Nicolás reflected collective and universalizing interests, but they also echoed the historicity of local sentiments and the intrigue of political machinations.

Seldom do historians get a chance to excavate the sedimentary layers that constitute a proceso like Nicolás's. And only rarely do we have an opportunity to see the sustained interventions of a woman toward that desired goal. María Jacinta actively and openly promoted her husband's cause through her writings and promotional efforts, and we find her voice in several documentary loci. She testified at Nicolás's beatification hearings in 1684 and again in October 1701, two months before her self-denunciation before the Inquisition. The self-denunciation, comprising sixty-four folios, contains excerpts from two of her notebooks in addition to interviews with her and a summation of charges against her by the Inquisition. In 1710, a year before her death, she testified once again at Nicolás's beatification hearing. Her mediated voice also appears in Sartolo's biography and in numerous letters she wrote to high-ranking Spanish and indigenous secular and ecclesiastical authorities and laypersons, some of whom had known Nicolás. We have access to fragments of an autobiographical account (*relación*) of her endeavors to found a convent, and a description of her death, housed in the archive of the Capuchin convent and edited by Rubén Vargas Ugarte. In addition, a posthumous account of the Spanish Capuchin nuns' transatlantic voyage to Lima to found the Monasterio de Jesús, María y José lauds María Jacinta as the savior of the institution.[29]

Through these different texts, we can detect and trace the circuits of knowledge constituting and undermining a saint in the making. María Jacinta revealed (sometimes inadvertently) how she fashioned Nicolás as someone already known, as a "saint" familiar to those who could project their own understandings of sanctity onto the humble tailor. With her deep understanding of late seventeenth-century piety and the politics of sanctity, she attempted to universalize him in a historically contingent manner by feeding information about his virtuous conduct and miracles to potential witnesses and others.[30] But to render the indigenous Nicolás into a saint, she had to convince others of her own authority. For more than thirty years, she cultivated a reputation in Lima as a powerful female spiritual leader. She was well known and well respected and considered by some to be an exemplary administrator of a prominent religious institution called the Beaterio de Jesús, María y José, which she and her husband had founded in 1671 as a more modest recogimiento.[31] Her letters reveal an articulate, well-educated, intelligent, tenacious, and somewhat authoritarian and ambitious individual. Excerpts from her notebooks contain her private dialogues with God and poetic expressions of her desires and frustrations. Testimonies from Nicolás's beatification hearing in 1684 describe her as a compassionate person in whom vulnerable, beleaguered women could confide. When juxtaposed, these different texts show a multifaceted individual difficult to pinpoint or characterize in a few words.

Gender analysis is also key to understanding how María Jacinta constructed the sacred biographies of Nicolás and herself. Because she was a woman speaking on behalf of her deceased husband, different audiences could comprehend Nicolás only through her gendered mediation. She had to follow accepted norms by portraying herself as his negative counterpart. She fashioned herself as Nicolás's holy wife and presented herself as a Magdalene figure converted by her humble, patient husband. She contrasted her own sexually wayward (*distraída*) past with Nicolás's sexual purity and ability to not only resist temptation but also conquer it. After his death in 1677, she promoted herself as a spiritual visionary destined to further her husband's dream of a unified Christian commonwealth. Her goal was to secure a fixed identity of sanctity for Nicolás and a blessed future for them both.

María Jacinta was keenly aware of the cultural milieu within which she was composing her and Nicolás's spiritual curricula. It was taken as a given that early modern women included the stories of others (whether mythic or historical) in their stories about themselves.[32] She operated within a nexus of social relations that included powerful ecclesiastical and secular authorities, both Spanish and indigenous. In their endeavors to craft the life of the indigenous tailor, she and various others drew on concurrent beatification processes and a well-entrenched bureaucracy established for that precise purpose.[33] Thus, María Jacinta's authorial autobiographical and biographical voices consisted of different configurations of voice that must be understood in relation to the political changes that occurred as her strategies backfired and Nicolás's beatification process slowly unraveled.

As the work of Elisa Sampson Vera Tudela has shown, María Jacinta, like many female religious in colonial Latin America, was actively involved in composing the religious history of the period.[34] Over the decades she established her authorial voice through distinct written and oral channels of communication.[35] She did this through the production and circulation of knowledge about Nicolás and what he represented in terms of his "Indian" nation. In her efforts to create a bienaventurado Indian saint, she emphasized his founding of a house for wayward women, his apostolic endeavors, his purity, and his virtues of charity and humility, as well as his miracles—all activities and characteristics that were key to sainthood.[36] As María Jacinta gathered and disseminated information, she became an archivist par excellence. In promoting her husband's candidacy for eventual canonization, she disseminated Nicolás's spiritual praesentia, or holy essence, in Lima and consciously aided in creating and maintaining a repository of texts and artifacts related to her husband's holy life. She did so, however, in a particularly fractious and competitive climate where women were taken seriously as religious leaders only under particular circumstances. It is no surprise that her every move was scrutinized by the authorities.

Indianness and Sanctity

When Nicolás died in 1677, causing a stir even in distant lands, "elites and plebeians, of all estates of persons," went to great efforts to see his corpse.[37] Only six years had passed since Rosa de Lima had been canonized, and only two since the Spanish friar Francisco Solano was beatified. Nicolás's saintly characteristics harmonized in several ways with different understandings of colonial baroque religious expression. Suffering extreme cruelty and discrimination certainly resonated with Christ's Passion, and both María Jacinta and others sought to highlight this aspect of Nicolás's character. Like Jesus the carpenter, Nicolás the tailor exhibited characteristics of charity by helping the poor and distributing alms on a daily basis. He also had the gift of prophecy: he predicted his own death as well as the beatification of Santa Rosa, whose portrait hung in the chapel of the recogimiento he had founded.[38] Some claimed that, like Martín de Porres, another local hero, Nicolás could be in two places at once.[39] He converted Indians by way of exemplum and, like the Augustinian friars who earlier in the century had worked as "slaves of the slaves," encouraged the Africans to attend Mass when they brought their mules laden with herbs to sell in the plazas, compensating their loss of income by giving them money and watching over their mules.[40]

Immediately following his death in November 1677, stories about the humble tailor began to circulate more widely throughout Lima and the highlands, as did venerated objects thought to contain his praesentia. As with other popular local saints, including the recently canonized Rosa de Lima, the beato Francisco Solano, Juan de Alloza, and Martín de Porres, Nicolás's likeness captured in engravings (estampas) was believed to have the power to cure illnesses or answer prayers. His corpse was also considered sacred. People came from far and wide to touch the body and be sanctified or converted. For three days the faithful filed past, taking bits of Nicolás's hair and nails or tearing off remnants of his garment to keep as talismans. Some reported instant miracles from these holy relics or from the copies of his estampas circulating among the local and provincial populace.[41] Fueled by this success, limeños flocked to offer testimonies in support of the beatification of this humble Indian "servant of God."[42] The indigenous elites of the Lima Valley were exuberant when they learned that Nicolás's candidacy for sainthood would be given serious consideration. In a letter to the Holy See on Nicolás's behalf, the caciques and other nobles noted he would be "the first [saint] of the Indies of his legitimate nation [and] with no other mixture."[43]

As María Jacinta collected and disseminated the written, oral, and physical word of her late husband, she helped foster a connection between spiritual ideas about him and the objects and places associated with his holiness.[44] Following Catholic understandings of the relationship between immateriality and materiality, she argued that the physical space of the beaterio where he had lived and prayed was a sacred site, not least because it was once the home of the Jesuit Juan de Alloza (1597–1666), whose diocesan process began in 1690, six years after Nicolás's. María Jacinta regularly received visitors at the parlor grille of the recogimiento-cum-beaterio, including "fathers on behalf of their children, Indian women for their husbands, and those with faith in [Nicolás], who does not deny [them]."[45] She reported that limeños clamored to appropriate Nicolás's praesentia in whatever way possible. Mothers placed moribund infants at the small altar in the beaterio for Nicolás to answer their supplications.[46] María Jacinta took note of any unusual or supernatural occurrence in her small notebook.

Although she continued to live in the beaterio after her husband's death, a cloistered existence did not hinder María Jacinta's creation of an epistolary network with the outside world. Even from her cell she was able to mediate transatlantic exchanges related to any progress on Nicolás's beatification process.[47] Months of oceanic travel time aside, she had no difficulties transmitting her messages to authorities in Lima, the provinces, and Europe. Through her correspondence, only a fraction of which is extant, she was regularly apprised of political changes in Madrid, Rome, and especially Lima.[48] Her contacts with commoners, caciques, and ecclesiastical authorities from different orders in Peru went a long way to promoting Nicolás's cult and creating an accessible sacred archive. Individuals corresponded regularly with her about how to obtain necessary documents to further the beatification and to promote the foundation of a monastery.[49] This paper trail enhanced her ability to track the dramatic permutations of Nicolás's proceso. It was also a discreet manifestation of power, because what she deemed to be collectable and how she inscribed materials with meaning helped to "create a cognitive universe that [could] be read and decoded."[50] She carefully stored originals and copies of correspondence and maintained up-to-date written accounts of the history of the letters.

Still, there were limits to how she much power she could exercise over the composition of Nicolás's sacred life. An authoritative religious woman could write letters and keep spiritual notebooks at the behest of her confessor, but she could not pen and then publish a hagiographic account of a blessed individual, much less her husband. But María Jacinta stretched gendered norms whenever possible. Her attempt to script a biography of Nicolás's life through different means paralleled a nearly century-long tradition in Lima of conventual chronicles penned by renowned male ecclesiastics, such as Diego de Córdova y Salinas, Antonio de la Calancha, and Juan de Meléndez, who relied on female informants for their accounts.[51] Meanwhile, handwritten life studies based on interviews with or informal writings by nuns remained closeted in convents and monasteries, taking up folios rather than volumes in the larger histories of a given order.[52] María Jacinta well understood the gendered limitations of female participation in a "lettered city" like Lima that privileged the written male word.[53]

María Jacinta may not have been authorized to pen a publishable work, but she could keep a running account of the expanding universe of Nicolás's spiritual power. Also, she could participate in the increasing circulation of that knowledge. To interested parties she disseminated accounts of Nicolás's miracles excerpted from a notebook called "De las misericordias" (Of the mercies). In her cell she kept a copy of the diocesan process of 1684, which gave her a distinct advantage in ensuring that the mythologization of Nicolás's actions and miracles remained consistent. As previously noted, she fed information about healings and other miraculous interventions to Sartolo so that his hagiographic account of Nicolás would be consonant with the hagiographic canon and would include episodes based on witnesses' depositions, adding local flavor to Nicolás's life story.[54] When Sartolo's biography of Nicolás arrived in Lima in 1684, María Jacinta made sure that prominent ecclesiastical authorities received copies. Later, following the book's confiscation in 1696, two local ecclesiastical figures requested María Jacinta's writings, deciding to take it on themselves to write sacred biographies of Nicolás.[55]

María Jacinta's careful acquisition and provenance of written and oral materials may have been standard operating procedure for male ecclesiastics in Lima at the time, but it was unusual for a woman. To frame the discourse on saintliness, however, she had to push the envelope in new directions. Although some creole and peninsular authorities believed that non-Spaniards could not achieve saintly equality with Spaniards because of their social marginality, lineage, or bodily characteristics, others, including María Jacinta, argued that in the eyes of God the poor and people of other nations were equal in virtue to all others. Within these two different positions there was ample room for interpretation. The unpublished diary of Nicolás's contemporary, the mystic Úrsula de Jesús, is exemplary in this regard. Some saw Úrsula's venerable qualities as transcending the stain of slavery and blackness, a motif echoed in the miniature biographies of other lesser-known exceptional figures who had also overcome extreme poverty, their lineage, or discrimination.[56] Other Spanish friars took a different tack in promoting non-Spanish mystics; they exalted the virtues of devout indias and women of mixed parentage to further the holiness, inclusiveness, and comprehensiveness of a particular order.[57] Also driving the agenda of ecclesiastics born in America was the need to demonstrate their spiritual equivalence to Europeans.[58] Devout non-Spanish figures were portrayed as charitable to an extreme, often working with the sickest in hospitals (where Nicolás may have contracted his fatal typhus), attending to the poor in manifold ways, and expressing extreme humility in the presence of Spaniards. The annual reports of the Jesuits stationed in Lima also included brief descriptions of pious indias ministering to migratory neophytes and bringing them into the fold. According to the Jesuits, Isabel Chinchero had taken it on herself to establish an informal beaterio where she provided refuge and protection to indigenous migrants just arriving in the city and taught them the rudiments of Christianity. She also preached in the villages encircling the viceregal capital.[59]

Following in the footsteps of the well-known Martín de Porres and the orphic Úrsula de Jesús, Nicolás with his meek tolerance of discrimination and cruelty, including having his hair cut off in public, fitted an emerging hagiographic canon for a potential baroque saint of color.[60] The rationale for Nicolás's sainthood was to promote the continued evangelization of indigenous peoples—parallel to monitoring the spiritual well-being of recently arrived Africans and their descendants, who congregated in large numbers in cities like Lima. For some secular and ecclesiastical authorities, the more Christianity expanded, the greater it would become. Indeed, at the heart of seventeenth-century baroque Catholicism was the idea of bringing all sinners into the fold.

By the 1660s ecclesiastical authorities had realized that the decades-long idolatry campaigns had been unproductive, leading them to search for more conciliatory ways to increase the Christian flock. By then, as Cussen has argued, stamping out idolatry and promoting local saints were seen as interrelated phenomena. Saintly individuals, regardless of their birthright or economic background, were "effective antidotes to idolatry."[61] As early as 1632, local secular authorities in Lima had stated that the indios of Peru would benefit greatly from the canonization of Rosa, "a person from their own land."[62] In that sense, the promotion of Nicolás's candidacy was no different. As María Jacinta argued, the recognition of his sanctity would form a connection to the "first fruits" of the conversion of the Indians that had taken place in the immediate postconquest period, and it would provide enormous spiritual benefit for contemporary Indians "of the same nation and *patria*," who might imitate his virtues.[63] Her logic echoed the truism repeated often in the testimonials in 1684 that Nicolás's sanctification would help convert those Indians still caught in the grips of superstitious beliefs. A simple Indian tailor could serve as a model of spiritual heroism for commoners and nobles alike, and "every stitch of his needle would be a mortal wound for the common enemy."[64] Not only was Nicolás a gifted visionary; he was also an Indian who could draw the two republics together in spiritual union. He could heal the wounds of conquest as all vassals of the crown knelt before the king as one. The clearest example of this harmony, as many witnesses liked to point out, was when Indians and Spaniards convened at Nicolás's funeral, honoring him equally and venerating the virtues of a man whose fame was celebrated.[65]

Certainly Lima—the immediate world of Nicolás, and a Catholic mecca—provided an exemplary model for provincial cities to follow. The *corregimiento* (political district) that included the viceregal capital maintained over three hundred priests, the rest of the archbishopric only two hundred.[66] Many of Lima's commoner (*indios del común*, comprising 8 percent of the total urban population) and elite coastal Andeans of the Lima river valleys invested heavily in confraternities, chaplaincies, and masses for the dead.[67] Translations of liturgical and other works into Quechua were integral to evangelical strategies throughout the Andes, and migrants brought these understandings with them to Lima.[68] For nearly two generations, the Colegio del Príncipe de Esquilache for caciques in Lima's indigenous district of El Cercado had been training the sons of the local and provincial indigenous elite to become Christian leaders.[69] Indigenous intellectuals actively invoked written, oral, and visual traditions to educate neophytes.[70] Limeños saw them, along with caciques and parish priests, as vital authority figures.[71]

María Jacinta's efforts to promote Nicolás as a tool for evangelization were consonant with the times in other ways. As the anti-idolatry campaigns were winding down, efforts to conquer the Indians in what had heretofore been considered peripheral or inaccessible areas were on the rise. In the 1680s and 1690s, Vatican authorities and members of the city council of Lima could agree that Nicolás's elevation to sainthood would do much to stamp out the evil thread of idolatry that persisted in uncharted areas of the Andes. Influenced by the foundation of the Sacred Congregation for the Propagation of the Faith by Pope Gregory XV in 1622, priests and friars began a global outreach program, aimed to adapt to local cultures and train local indigenous leaders. In line with this approach, dedicated members of the Society of Jesus, beginning in 1677, pushed to establish mission settlements in the Amazon and Orinoco River basins, and especially among the Mojos (whose territories extended from northern to southeastern Bolivia). María Jacinta was certainly aware of these activities; one of the missionaries eager to promote conversion efforts among the Mojos approached her and suggested that Nicolás's sacred history could serve as a missionizing tool. She gave him a copy of her notebook on Nicolás's virtues and miracles, and her blessing to preach to neophyte Christians about how God had rewarded Nicolás's virtuous conduct.[72]

Scripting an indio saint to fit late seventeenth-century hagiographic models still required a political balancing act, however. María Jacinta did not want Nicolás to appear too indio, which is why she emphasized in her testimony in 1684 how he had risen above his genus or nation. While some expressed admiration for Nicolás's extreme mortification practices—he whipped himself and "bathed the ground with his blood"—and for his vegetarianism, they also exclaimed that he could resist the laws of his genus. Although "Indian"—here a categorization associated with idolatry and non-Christian practices—Nicolás resisted falling prey to gluttony and excessive drink, vices usually thought to pass from one generation of Indians to the next.[73] As a young boy, María Jacinta asserted, he had had a gifted singing voice and preferred the company of a priest over that of a secular authority who might take him to the mines. His sense of discernment more secure as an adult, Nicolás attempted "to separate himself from the company [of Indians] and the indecent and foolish conversations generally had by the Indians because of their minimal capacity."[74]

María Jacinta knew firsthand that it would not be easy for some of Nicolás's close associates and clients, let alone strangers, to see an indio as a saintly man. She had seen him suffer discrimination and thus engage in what Jason Dyck has called the "discourse of nobility" to place himself above the fray of the plebeian indigenous or Spanish masses.[75] Not only did Nicolás convert idolatrous indios, but he made it easier for the members of Lima's aristocracy to see him in a different light. Several Spanish witnesses who expressed initial reticence at believing in the sanctity of an indio were swayed by Nicolás's kind and thoughtful comportment. Don Joseph de Medina, for instance, rationalized Nicolás's saintliness in his deposition in 1684 as an expression of God's exceptionalism, since "an Indian could not be [saintly] without God's favor and help."[76] Here was another kind of conversion, one that allowed the hierarchical scales to fall from the eyes of the elite; they could begin to see others lesser than themselves with God's compassionate eyes.[77] They could recognize that God disregarded all categories of distinction.

The greatest conversion story of them all, however, was the tale of the poor and humble long-suffering Indian tailor who transformed the recalcitrant María Jacinta−cum−Mary Magdalene.[78] It was a parable repeated in different archival inscriptions made by or about her, thus revealing how prevalent this truth narrative would become. As the story went, although María Jacinta married Nicolás at age eighteen, worldly diversions and walks about town (el paseo) lured her away from her pious husband, who tried to counsel her with spiritual teachings.[79] She was said to have an unsavory past, and marriage did little to stay her wandering eye. With Christlike patience Nicolás pleaded with her and tried to encourage the wayward Mary Magdalene.[80] His indigenous assistant at the recogimiento, Salvador de Jesús (originally from the highland town of Huaura, he had apprenticed with Nicolás since he was a boy), reported in 1684 that Nicolás always referred to María Jacinta with the utmost respect; he tolerated her "bad condition" with long-suffering and extreme patience, even when she treated him discourteously.[81]

Like other illegitimate girls from the highlands, María Jacinta had come to Lima at the tender age of four or five to reside in the household of her Spanish padrinos (godparents). Around the age of eight she entered the Monasterio de la Encarnación to work as a servant (criada).[82] Various storytellers, including María Jacinta herself, emphasized different details in their accounts of how her caretakers agreed that she should marry Nicolás, since he was a good man with a steady profession. The arranged union nearly backfired, however. After being pent up in a convent for so long, Sartolo explained, she was determined to enjoy her freedom.[83] Numerous witnesses described her fondness for costly clothes, fancy shoes, and gold adornments, a sign (as we saw in chapter 1) of spiritual contamination.[84]

Even a saintly Indian could lose his wife to the allure of the evil world. One Spaniard tried to warn Nicolás about the dangers of having a young, beautiful wife seated in the booth just outside his tailor's shop selling ribbons, silk, and paper. He remonstrated, "Indian, don't you realize the danger you are causing your wife—who is so young, and who by God's grace was blessed with beauty—by allowing her to sell wares in that booth?"[85] Nicolás's faith in God must have wavered momentarily, because he shut down the stall. On another occasion the meek tailor was beaten severely "like a black man" when he tried to follow his wife as she entered a private home unescorted.[86] Here we have the contrasting presentation of the pure and humble (and perhaps cuckolded) husband bearing the suffering of a morally lost (*perdida*) wife.

María Jacinta's (self-)scripting fit neatly into gendered ideas about conversion. Not only did she emphasize the oppositional Magdalene-Christ metaphor in her testimonies, she also played the role of the self-serving doubting Thomas to Nicolás's selfless and ever-abiding faith. She represented herself as too parsimonious to allow household funds to be donated to the poor, even though they always made ends meet; she selfishly discouraged him from taking in orphans because she craved the serenity of a small household, raising children of their own.[87] On more than one occasion, she noted that a little bread broken into smaller pieces staved off the hunger of invited guests, most of whom were poor.[88] (Here the analogy to Christ reproducing the loaves and the fishes was obvious.) Eventually, so the story went, by patience and good counsel, Nicolás persuaded his frugal wife to abandon her worldly, selfish interests.

By her own account, however, ever skeptical, she required a miracle to become a true believer. Once, after she had cut some flowers to adorn the altar too close to the root, Nicolás placed a little earth around the plant, and it not only survived but thrived. That miracle (recorded in her notebook) was the tipping point: it made her realize her husband was a "saint," and she truly began to love him as "his Wife." Still, remedying her ways took time, and only gradually did she begin to receive nourishment from the spiritual exercises and more frequent communion she began to take.[89] Then, according to different written accounts, she prostrated herself like Mary Magdalene at her husband's feet, asking for forgiveness.[90] She cut her hair and replaced her fine attire with a coarse hemp-cloth garment.[91] It was when the couple transferred to the neighborhood near the Iglesia de San Juan de Dios, some contended, that her spirit also "moved."[92] María Jacinta, too, considered as a turning point in her life her relocation to the house that would soon become a recogimiento for young mestiza, Spanish, and Indian girls. In her testimony in 1684 and her self-denunciation in 1701, she described her conversion similarly: "When I first converted I began to esteem him [Nicolás] greatly because of his great virtue, and because of the many tears, prayers and masses he had said on my behalf, asking His Divine Majesty for my perseverance."[93]

Now calling herself María Jacinta de la Santíssima Trinidad, she took vows of celibacy, living together with Nicolás like "tree trunks" in spiritual union. Opinions varied as to whether they continued to sleep in the same bed.[94] Moreover, María Jacinta abstained from the pleasure of eating fruit for seven years.[95] Living in conditions of near poverty, the couple spent part of each day collecting alms for their institution. María Jacinta expressed regret for the hardship she had caused her husband, reportedly telling Sartolo that "not only have I aggrieved Nicolás, but also God, who called to me through him [my husband]. I ignored so many callings. How many [demonstrations of his] virtues I have seen, but I have lived as a deaf woman, not to have heard his inspirations; and without eyes to stumble on my misdeeds. But [oh] Lord what you have given me [now] to see them, [you have] given me tears to cry about them."[96]

As Nicolás's fame grew, so too did María Jacinta's as a maternal, even spiritual, figure. Uncles began to entrust nieces to her care; abandoned wives sought her advice.[97] In several of the more heartfelt testimonies in 1684 about Nicolás's miracles and charitable gestures, María Jacinta appeared as a sympathetic, albeit background figure, who offered consolation to young women experiencing financial or marital difficulties; eventually she attracted a few to a life of rigorous seclusion in the beaterio.[98] Her own story appealed to wayward women who wanted to become "self-styled Magdalenes" willing to rely on divine providence for sustenance.[99] Juana de San Lorenso testified in 1684 that loneliness (her husband had been absent from Lima for fourteen years) had driven her to live in sin with another man while relying on her handwork to survive. But then she heard about a virtuous woman named María Jacinta, whose own willful experiences convinced Juana to became one of the sisters in the beaterio in true Magdalene fashion.[100]

The theme of conversion also played into María Jacinta's written and verbal portrayals of the couple's history in other ways. She utilized gender mirroring to portray her marriage to Nicolás as breaking down the barriers of *nación* (nation, status, type). Not only did the saintly tailor eventually succeed in attracting his Magdalene wife to a life of piety, but he convinced her of the good that would come from a "sacred union" of Indian and mestiza.[101] According to Sartolo, she was initially reticent to marry a man who was not her equal. He quoted her as saying, "[The fact that] my husband is an Indian, doesn't take away the fact that he was born well, and much less that he is affable, courteous, reserved, and virtuous. I did not marry a Nation, but a person, and it matters little that his Nation is not equal if the person is decidedly moral."[102] For her, it was far better to marry a kind and thoughtful Indian than a tyrannical Spaniard. Emphasizing Nicolás's exceptional and noble spirituality would have resonated with contemporary beliefs about creating a more inclusive Christianity.

María Jacinta highlighted Nicolás's ability to promote cultural and spiritual unity in other ways. Especially notable were his charitable efforts in providing an institutional space, called a *recogimiento*, where poor, humble, or beleaguered women could find spiritual and economic refuge.[103] She liked to tell others that divine encouragement had led Nicolás to give up his own home in 1671 to found the recogimiento. The Virgin had communicated to him in a vision that the couple would gain the license and protection of the Jesuits to become the Recogimiento de Jesús, María y José, with young Indian, Spanish, and mestiza women admitted in equal proportions.[104] Indeed, throughout the viceroyalties of New Spain and Peru, new beaterios and recogimientos were encouraging native American women (none was ever founded exclusively for women of African heritage) to profess informal vows.[105]

María Jacinta strongly endorsed Nicolás's vision of inclusivity in an institutional setting as one of his greatest strengths. She referred to the recogimiento that he founded as the most illustrative example of the union of what historian Juan Carlos Estenssoro Fuchs calls the "sacred family": a home where creoles, Spaniards, blacks, and Indians could live in spiritual harmony.[106] In her regular communications with local and international figures, she packaged the recogimiento-turned-beaterio (it was elevated to the higher status in 1678) as a microcosm of a unified Christian commonwealth. Others shared her viewpoint. Such was the support among Andean authorities for the beaterio that a cacique named Juan Arías traveled the great distance from the highlands to the coast to ask María Jacinta for a copy of the beaterio's regulations and daily regimen, which he hoped might serve as a template for a recogimiento he wished to found in the highland city of Huamanga.[107]

Not only did such institutions provide an inclusive space for the two republics, but they also served the purpose of converting wayward and fallen women, many of whom in reality were simply poor or lacked family connections.[108] Founding a recogimiento, as Nicolás had, was in line with the curriculum vitae of apostolic priests like Juan de Alloza, in whose home Nicolás had once lived, and José de Buendía and Francisco del Castillo, who had both served as Nicolás's spiritual confessors.[109] A number of witnesses at the hearing in 1684 attested to Nicolás's ability to persuade recalcitrant women, including prostitutes and adulterers, to relinquish their sinful lives.[110]

María Jacinta was well aware that even a model beaterio was considered to have less status and prestige than a convent. Knowing that the foundation of a Capuchin convent would help Nicolás's cause for beatification, María Jacinta tirelessly pursued her dream of obtaining a royal license to raise the beaterio to monastic status (it was established in 1713 as the Monasterio de Jesús, María y José). Her endeavor initially encountered roadblocks but eventually received wide support from the indigenous elite, the viceroy, and members of religious orders in Lima.[111] As early as 1688, Francisco de Echave y Assu's *La estrella de Lima convertida en sol* (meant to proclaim the virtues of Archbishop Toribio de Mogrovejo, who was said to have walked hundreds of miles to convert indigenous highlanders) claimed that "not women but angels" inhabited the beaterio that María Jacinta governed.[112] Such public-relations work certainly helped her cause, but she also found herself enmeshed in the quagmire of local ecclesiastical politics and struggling against those who resisted her efforts. To keep track of all the machinations, she meticulously maintained a paper trail of correspondence and kept a running account of who supported or opposed her goal.

During one anxious moment when local support for the institution had seriously ebbed, María Jacinta took up her quill and reached out to God. She asked him for a sign that all would be well and that men who opposed the institution would see the folly of their ways. She wanted the authorities to understand that women could be voices of God. A stanza of her poem read:

So that men can see
How the supreme and eternal King
works through women
Being of such a fragile sex.[113]

María Jacinta always insisted that the convent should be an inclusive institution, allowing indigenous and Spanish women (although not women of African heritage) to take their vows as nuns. In a letter to the king written in 1697, she argued that the republics of Indians and Spaniards would be united in the convent and that the daughters of the Indians would be "admitted in saintly equality with the king's other vassals."[114] Ecclesiastical authorities might see the foundation of a female convent for Indian nuns as a "symbol of the ultimate Christian conquest," but for many principal indigenous authorities, and for María Jacinta, it represented the highest plane of spiritual inclusion.[115]

Between a Rock and a Hard Place

To María Jacinta's joy, the royal license to found a convent arrived in 1698, and the official document (rótulo) from the papacy certifying that Nicolás's virtues were worthy of beatification arrived in 1699, giving ecclesiastical authorities in charge of the beatification proceedings three years to gather new witnesses. Bolstered by this international support, she redoubled her efforts to contact authorities in Lima and abroad to further her late husband's cause.[116] At the same time, a network of indigenous authorities throughout the province of Lima also endeavored to advance the beatification process quickly. In a letter to María Jacinta dated May 1701, the indigenous noble Nicolás de Mayta Escalante detailed how he had taken matters into his own hands. An active member of the confraternity dedicated to Our Lady of Copacabana in Lima (where a beaterio for indigenous women had recently been founded), Mayta Escalante explained how he had overseen the procession carrying the rótulo proclaiming Nicolás's eligibility for beatification throughout the city, an act that ensured that caciques outside of Lima would hear of it. He noted that in villages and towns throughout the highlands the news was celebrated—with masses in some cases, breaking the rules of non culto—when Nicolás's image was placed on the altars. Believing he had been cured of illness because of Nicolás's intervention, Mayta Escalante asked María Jacinta to procure a license for him to continue proselytizing in the highlands. He also requested additional printed portraits and asked her to obtain permission to commission a new painting of Nicolás, about eighteen inches in height, which he could carry with him as he journeyed the Andes by pack mule.[117]

But as the new century began, other events signaled to María Jacinta that not all was going according to plan. Just as the momentum among indigenous communities in Lima and elsewhere was building and the plenary beatification process got under way, Inquisition authorities intensified their efforts to undermine Nicolás's cause, spearheaded by the Franciscan Gregorio de Quesada y Sotomayor, a calificador (judge) of the Inquisition and inspector of books who was already familiar with the case. He had written the *calificaciones* (judgments/censures) against Ángela de Carranza and denounced Sartolo's biography of Nicolás for containing falsities. He had also blocked María Jacinta's efforts to procure local support to elevate the beaterio that she and Nicolás had founded into a convent.[118] Other ecclesiastical predilections played a part as well. According to Vargas Ugarte, in 1700 Dionisio Granado, the chaplain of Archbishop Melchor Liñán y Cisneros, was named a delegate on behalf of the Lima commission to collect information about Nicolás's miracles. Interestingly, he also served as a calificador of the Inquisition when it questioned María Jacinta in late 1701.[119]

Despite weak protests from some ecclesiastical quarters, the Inquisition managed to destabilize the proceso in several ways.[120] Normally, during the second round of questioning, testimonies emphasized the timeless heroic virtues of the potential saint.[121] Instead, the examiners spent their time scrutinizing and then undermining the witness testimonies of the ordinary process in 1684–85.[122] They also framed the set of questions for witnesses in the second round, which took place between 1701 and 1702, in an entirely different manner. Whereas the questions and answers in 1684 had sought to create a coherent, unified archive of Nicolás's heroic virtues, the second inquiry probed for discrepancies, contradictions, and falsities in miracles and visions attributed to Nicolás. Inquisition authorities compared information found in Sartolo's condemned biography to María Jacinta's notebooks, which had been confiscated by Archbishop Melchor Liñán y Cisneros the previous year, and to the depositions in 1684.[123] They looked for damning evidence of the couple's association with the condemned Ángela de Carranza.[124] It is no surprise that the depositions in 1701–2 were very different from the earlier ones. Gone were the lengthy explanations of Nicolás's charitable acts, or descriptions of the churches he had frequented, the altar cloths he had meticulously sewn, his devotion to the different saints, and wondrous healings. Gone, too, were references to Nicolás as a savior who could unite the colonial commonwealth or serve as a model for conversion efforts in the eastern Andes. No longer were there dozens of witnesses—neighbors, priests, and clients—eager to step forward to relay their experiences of Nicolás's benevolent gestures.[125] These latter sparse testimonies tended to portray Nicolás as more fallible.

Indeed, the questions for the hearing in 1701–2 were less about humanizing Nicolás and more about maligning María Jacinta's character and exposing her scheming. To get to the bottom of things, examiners pointedly asked deponents whether she had informed them of any of the supposed miracles, mortification practices, or other virtuous behaviors before they testified.[126]

They wanted to determine which miracles attributed to Nicolás, and previously referenced in María Jacinta's notebook but nowhere else, had been falsified or exaggerated. Thus, in her beatification deposition in 1701, she found it necessary to defend two of the specific miracles attributed to her husband.[127]

Two months later, as the second round of questioning of witnesses for the beatification proceeded, María Jacinta denounced herself before Granado, the head inquisitor, who then interrogated her. Because the self-denunciation and the witness depositions occurred simultaneously, inquisitors were able to compare Sartolo's book with both sets of depositions and material from María Jacinta's self-denunciation.[128] Among other discrepancies, they found one that was particularly troubling: none of Nicolás's confessors had directly reported his vision before Ayllón's death in 1677 that Rosa would be beatified in 1667.[129] They suspected that María Jacinta had given this information to Sartolo. They also wondered about a painting Nicolás had ordered of Rosa based on his beatific vision, which, once it became available for the public to view, only increased the fervor of devotion to Nicolás as a messenger of God. María Jacinta knew that publicizing Nicolás's vision would connect a venerated saint (Rosa was canonized in 1671) with him and help his cause.[130] Authorities never did get to the bottom of the reported miracle (or who had done the painting). But after María Jacinta was grilled about other visions and miracles, she confessed to having exaggerated some of them; for example, some of the female disciples of the recogimiento had placed incense near Nicolás's body so everyone would claim that it emitted the "fragrance of sanctity."[131]

Fueled by the Inquisition, many now blamed Nicolás's sullied beatification process on María Jacinta. Coached to answer formulaic questions containing the answer in them, witnesses testifying in 1701–2 deprecated María Jacinta's self-promotion and refused to trust her so-called saintly opinions. Several witnesses asked, "Why had she been so arrogant and self-serving in her attempts to turn a good man into a saint?" Those closely associated with Nicolás or the beaterio remained unconvinced that her Magdalene conversion had been successful. Juan Benítez, a Spaniard who had made it his life's pursuit to collect alms for the beaterio, observed, "María Jacinta did not behave in a sincere manner that a person of great credit who tries to live [a life of] perfection [does] because [these people] know when to be quiet which might cause [their] great opinion [held by others] to fall away. [But] she knows what to do to [increase] her great credit and esteem."[132] Cipriano Manrique, a witness who was a close associate of the couple, quoted one of Nicolás's confessors as having referred to María Jacinta as "an insect-eating little bird."[133]

María Jacinta had never claimed to be a model of sexual purity—quite the contrary—but the hearing in 1684 and Sartolo's biography had portrayed Nicolás as a paragon of sexual virtue. No one had ever emphasized *his* sexual conversion before his marriage to María Jacinta. Sartolo had portrayed Lima as a city where one could find concupiscence on every street corner and "where lasciviousness arms itself with ropes against chastity with the same ease as [those] dishonorable little women who sacrifice their bodies to lewdness."[134] As the story went, to resist temptation and hold in check his vulnerable flesh, Nicolás only intensified his charitable work with the poor and his mortification and prayer regimens.[135]

As it turned out, Nicolás was no stranger to illicit unions. Before meeting María Jacinta, he had fathered a child out of wedlock; one witness asserted that he sent the woman packing north to Trujillo to avoid embarrassing his wife. A slightly different version posited that the relationship ended when the child died.[136] In her self-denunciation in 1701, María Jacinta admitted that her assertion that Nicolás had lived "in fear and love of God his entire life" was false but that an unnamed priest had advised her not to mention the illegitimate union during the first beatification proceedings.[137] The deponents in 1701 were thus shocked when inquisitors showed them a passage in Sartolo's book stating that until his marriage to María Jacinta, Nicolás "had lived as a virgin and had never lost his baptismal grace." Ana María de Jesús, the governess of one of Lima's beaterios, then made the damning claim that Nicolás had once tried to seduce her at his tailor shop.[138]

Even if Nicolás's sexual conversion squared nicely with the résumés of other saints, Granado insisted on attacking his and María Jacinta's reputation as a model couple. After exposing Nicolás's indiscreet past, Granado asked María Jacinta pointedly about their vows of celibacy. How could a husband and wife who claimed to treat each other as brother and sister preserve their abstinence when they continued to sleep in the same bed?[139] But María Jacinta was not to be bullied on this point and stressed that the couple always slept in their clothes. It wasn't just that Granado doubted whether the assertion was true; he thought that María Jacinta's written claim that she had achieved a heightened spiritual state as a result of that celibacy was misguided. Only a few months after taking a vow of chastity at the age of twenty-four, she had recorded in her notebook, "God granted me the grace of Innocence."[140] "I felt no misgivings or any fear, but rather the benevolence and innocence of a two-year-old creature," she had written.[141] In other words, God had returned her to a pure state—a claim the inquisitor felt was going too far.

Next came several direct attacks against María Jacinta's character. Not only had Sartolo's book flagrantly eulogized a dead saint, Granado said, but it had also lauded the spiritual virtues of the *living* María Jacinta de la Santíssima Trinidad.[142] In addition to overstepping her authority by actively promoting Nicolás's cult, he argued, pride and vanity, two traits that had tempted many a female mystic who had eventually undergone inquisitorial scrutiny, were causing her to seek fame on her own accord.[143] According to her writings, after Nicolás's death she had begun to experience visions and to communicate directly with God (*en hablas interiores*), and her confessors obliged her to record her supernatural experiences. In one particularly troubling vision, she saw herself as a lowly worm placed in a little gold box and presented to the Lord: "[He] took it. As soon as it touched his hands it transformed into a very precious pearl and the Lord put it on his breast and showed it to all the Blessed Ones. . . . With deep love, His Majesty [then] said to me: 'My daughter, I assist you and enrich you with my goods, and you will be powerful to me and all the world will prostrate themselves at your feet and you will be the lord of all my things.'"[144] Another passage in her notebook noted that since limeños now saw her as the main link to the deceased Nicolás, they had begun to view her as a living saint. As she left Mass, throngs would gather, clamoring to kiss her hands as they would any person of stature and authority.[145] For Granado and others, the manner in which María Jacinta had noted her spiritual growth and desire for public attention was, indeed, a sign of false sanctity.

In addition to wishing to expose how María Jacinta had falsified or exaggerated Nicolás's miracles and promoted her own spiritual authority, Inquisition authorities attempted to undermine her authority as a writer and archivist and as governess of a religious institution. Writing, as many scholars have shown, was a double-edged sword for early modern European and Latin American female religious. But it is simplistic to argue that they were discouraged from writing when, in fact, confessors and other ecclesiastical authorities often ordered and encouraged them to keep notebooks of their interactions with the divine. María Jacinta was no exception. Over the decades her confessors had regularly reviewed her work. Having read Santa Teresa de Ávila's writings (and exhortations) carefully, she always cautioned that her written entries came from God.[146]

But now, Inquisition authorities scorned the contents of her writings; they were even more concerned with the wide circulation of copies of her manuscripts among indigenous, ecclesiastical, and other secular personages in Lima and various sites in the highlands—and in Madrid and Rome. Here was a female religious who had actively and strategically promoted the candidacy of her husband through writings, which, Granado proclaimed, were filled with errors and shortcomings. Thus confronted, María Jacinta begged for forgiveness and mercy before her superiors: "Although the notebook entitled 'De las misericordias' was not intended to leave the house [the beaterio], I did not comply, because it left for the Mojos and [to be taken to] Guamanga and Arequipa in the way I said it did and much of what I have written in the said notebook I realize shows my pride and vainglory."[147]

Finally, inquisitors questioned the overzealous manner in which María Jacinta administered her beaterio. What chroniclers like Echave y Assu had proclaimed as the paragon of spiritual excellence—that the beatas were involved in spiritual exercises for nearly eighteen hours a day and lived in exceptional poverty—was now levied as a criticism of María Jacinta's excesses in governance.[148] Inquisitors accused her of being too strict and of punishing beatas for the smallest infraction. Witnesses coached by inquisitors in the apostolic process in 1701 did the same. Manrique, a cleric who had collected alms for the institution for over twelve years, remonstrated against María Jacinta in his testimony in January 1701. The beatas, he stated, were "continually at war with her." She thought very highly of herself, he added, and believed "that she would return to God a saint."[149] He continued, "I took her to be a recogida woman, although she is the opposite of these things, not only in perfection, but in God's law, including [having] a lack of compassion toward others." When Manrique heard that others were calling her "an ecstatic woman," considered high praise in the Lima community, he approached María Jacinta's confessor, the friar Pedro Tovar, who demurred in his response: "This creature is governed by divine providence."[150]

Attacking María Jacinta's authority from every possible angle, Inquisition authorities used her archival repository to their advantage. By combing through the beatification depositions from 1684, Sartolo's book, and her self-denunciation, they had managed to characterize her as an arrogant and vain false visionary and a faulty administrator. After finding thirty-two dangerous and "useless, boastful, reckless, offensive to pious ears, seismic, dangerous, arrogant, stigmatizing, close to doctrinal error with a flavor of heresy and respective heresies," the Inquisition declared her on 1 February 1702 to be deluded.[151] As had often occurred with powerful female religious in the past, inquisitors prohibited her from henceforth recording any mystical occurrences or revelations received in prayer. She was also barred from writing or mentioning anything related to her self-denunciation, or distributing any notes she had taken or copies of papers or notebooks she had stored away. In other words, she could no longer keep and disseminate an archive.[152]

María Jacinta did not live to see her holy image reinstated or her citywide reputation as a visionary restored. She died on 25 December 1710. As the collection of witnesses for Nicolás's *proceso* continued, albeit at a snail's pace, the authorities decided to forward her self-denunciation to the Supreme Council in Madrid. Nicolás's beatification proceedings limped along for several more years before stalling completely after 1716. Neither María Jacinta nor Nicolás lived to see the beaterio become the Monasterio de Jesús, María y José in 1713, but the delay in the foundation was more due to exceptional international political circumstances than any attack on María Jacinta's intentions.[153]

One of the few convents to be founded in the eighteenth century, it partially fulfilled María Jacinta's dream by admitting twenty-two Spanish and eleven indigenous nobles as nuns of the black veil.[154] Capuchin nuns from Madrid were to serve as the foundresses. After a dangerous ocean crossing, the five nuns chosen by the bishop of Madrid in 1709 to found the new convent finally arrived at the port of Callao in February 1713. The lay brother (*hermano*) Juan Benítez, who had deprecated María Jacinta in his testimony in 1701, greeted them, looking "like Saint Francis of Padua."[155] Following protocol, the travel-weary nuns paid their respects to the nuns of the different convents of the city and met with the deceased viceroy's daughter, doña Josefa Portocarrero Laso de la Vega (the subject of chapter 6), whom they considered famous "both in Spain and throughout the Indies for the many trials she had to endure in order to become a nun."[156] For them, Lima was a city filled with spiritual heroines.

An account written in 1722 mythologized the nuns' epic journey as a spiritual odyssey and also vindicated María Jacinta.[157] It painted her as a visionary who had followed God's mandate to found the convent, prevailing despite blind and sometimes spiteful resistance from male ecclesiastics in Lima.[158] To capture the drama of their own Atlantic odyssey against great odds, the Capuchin nuns drew on María Jacinta's archive for material. Contrary to the inquisitors' orders in 1702, she had continued to write, albeit in a more circumscribed manner. We know this because three years after her death, an anonymous author, most likely a nun writing at the bequest of the vicar, compiled a history of the new convent by quoting extensively from notes tucked away among María Jacinta's papers.[159]

She who writes her own history is powerful. And she who can disseminate stories about herself and have others repeat them as truth is even more powerful. In the end, not everyone saw María Jacinta as a manipulative, arrogant woman who had ruined Nicolás's chances of beatification. For many of the sisters of the beaterio-cum-convent, she was bienaventurada, a visionary providentially blessed by God. An account housed in the monastery of how the religious community honored María Jacinta's still body is a particularly illustrative example of how the nuns believed her to be the embodiment of Christian heroic virtues. On the evening of her death, Madre Serafina, a nun who had shared a cell with María Jacinta for fourteen years, wrote an account (following the orders of the vicar) of the autopsy performed on the corpse. She and some of the other members of the religious community stood by while a doctor sliced open the thoracic cavity and noted that the heart had broken into two pieces, "as though it had been wounded with a Dart of fire."[160] Unable to find the pericardium, the doctor concluded that it had been consumed by the fire in María Jacinta's heart. A group of ecclesiastical experts later confirmed the organ's peculiar form and lack of corruptibility and deemed it a miracle. This was the ultimate sign of God's love, since the heart was where divinity resided. In the history of Christianity only a select few saints who had offered their entire self to God were rewarded with a divine piercing of that vital organ. No doubt Madre Serafina and the others present to witness the miracle called to mind the transverberation of Teresa de Ávila's heart—a popular subject in paintings, sermons, and other texts—when she expired in 1577. María Jacinta's heart, the seat of the soul, had also been thoroughly pierced. No direct association in writing was ever made to Nicolás, on whose heart Ángela de Carranza had once seen the Trinity imprinted. The implication, however, was that both husband and wife had achieved spiritual union with God and were now united in heaven. Despite the constraints they had faced in life and in death, María Jacinta and Nicolás were still local heroes, mirroring one another even in death.

AMPARADA DE MI LIBERTAD
Josefa Portocarrero Laso de la Vega
and the Meaning of Free Will

. . .

In the darkest hours of 9 October 1706, doña Josefa Portocarrero Laso de la Vega y Urrea (1681–1743) escaped the viceregal palace and sought refuge in the Monasterio de Santa Catalina. This dramatic move signaled the beginning of a protracted battle over Josefa's right to choose a religious vocation in the newly founded Monasterio de Santa Rosa in Lima (1708) and pitted her against her mother, doña Antonia Jiménez de Urrea, as well as, eventually, Archbishop Melchor Liñán y Cisneros and Philip V, king of Spain.

Historians familiar with this period of Peruvian history—a pivotal moment of transition from the Hapsburg to the Bourbon dynasty—most readily associate Josefa with her father, Melchor Portocarrero Laso de la Vega (1636–1705), the third Count of Monclova, who served as viceroy of Peru from August 1689 until his death on 22 September 1705. Biographers enthusiastically applaud Josefa's "heroic endeavors" to found the first female convent dedicated to Santa Rosa, Lima's patron saint. However, no scholar has explored in depth why Josefa was apparently desperate enough to leave the family home or why she spent years litigating to be *amparada de su libertad*: protected by her right to choose a monastic vocation.[1]

Integral to doña Josefa's struggle was a family squabble over inheritance rights. Because of the special affection the Count of Monclova had for her, his favorite among his six children and his constant companion, she was the first of the children to be named in his will and was awarded the spectacular amount of fifty thousand pesos.[2] However, after word reached Josefa's mother, the executrix of the estate, that Josefa had fled the viceregal palace to pursue a religious vocation, she decided to deny her daughter her rightful share of the inheritance. Claiming to the archbishop and other authorities that Josefa's escape to a convent was nothing but melodrama, doña Antonia insisted that her daughter return to Spain with her as promised.[3] The truth, as Josefa later said, was that she, the dutiful daughter, had promised her mother that she would return to Spain, but she had done so under extreme duress. Rather than succumb to her mother's violent will, however, she had silently kept her *true* vow to remain in Lima and become a nun in the Monasterio de Santa Rosa. She wrote that, "moved solely by the Desire to serve God and my Mother Santa Rosa more [fully]," she had decided to donate her still-awaited inheritance to the as-yet-to-be-established Monasterio de Santa Rosa.[4] This decision propelled the countess to file a legal complaint against her daughter before the ecclesiastical tribunal, claiming that the young woman's vows were illegal. Josefa's desire was to serve another madre. It seems that both mother and daughter had decided to dig in their heels.

What appears to be a straightforward story involving strong, willful women; a flagrant disregard for matriarchal authority; family honor; broken promises; and large sums of money is more complicated when we burrow below the surface. Once doña Antonia decided to question the legality of her daughter's decision to pursue her monastic vocation in Lima, an entire cast of illustrious and not-so-illustrious characters surfaced. Those who intervened directly or indirectly included the Spanish king Philip V; two archbishops, Melchor Liñán y Cisneros (archbishop, 1678–June 1708; interim viceroy, 1678–81) and Diego Ladrón de Guevara (archbishop and interim viceroy, September 1710 until 1716); and the members of the cathedral chapter, who held power during the vacancy of the holy office (sede vacante) from June 1708 until September 1710. In ecclesiastical circles the Mercedarians, Augustinians, and Jesuits, and especially Josefa's confessor, Alonso Messía Bedoya (1655–1732), also took sides in the conflict. In the secular government, the Count of Monclova's replacement, Manuel de Olms y de Santa Pau, the Marquis de Castell-dos-Rius (viceroy, July 1707–22 April 1710), and specific Audiencia members, including Miguel Nuñez de Sanabria (interim viceroy, September 1705–May 1707 and 22 April 1710–September 1710) and don Pablo Vázquez de Velasco, a prominent octogenarian judge and member of the Real Audiencia, were also deeply involved. Within the Portocarrero-Urrea family, the case involved Josefa, her brother, and her mother, as well as her grandmother, who was living in Spain. The protracted drama also deeply titillated the interest of limeños, who remained attentive to each labyrinthine twist and turn of the controversy.[5]

The knotty affair reflected larger issues as well. The sweeping changes and conflicts brought about in the transition from the Hapsburg to the Bourbon dynasty and the ongoing tensions over overlapping secular and ecclesiastical jurisdictions served as a spectacular backdrop to Josefa's struggles. Also at play were strong creole sentiments among Lima's populace, expressed in the particular zeal with which many supported Josefa's cause and the foundation of a convent dedicated to Santa Rosa, which came to fruition in early 1708 at the height of Josefa's dramatic affair.

A plethora of documentation, including individual correspondence, legal petitions, and even a juridical dissertation written in 1706, illustrates the complex machinations at play among some of the highest authorities of the Spanish Empire.[6] These documents also reveal the religious sensibilities of a well-educated, twenty-six-year-old aristocratic woman, who consulted with some of the leading theologians in Lima about her rights under canon law. Josefa's correspondence provides insights into her gendered interpretations of the canonical discourse associated with the concepts of freedom of will (*libertad, albedrío*) and freedom of conscience (*libertad de consciencia*) and what it meant to be protected (*amparada*) in her right to make choices that were seen as God given and based on natural law.[7] For Josefa, libertad was a legitimate and innate faculty based on reasoned choice (albedrío), to which Spanish male and female legal adults were entitled. *Libertad de estado* was their God-given prerogative, upheld by canon law, to choose the station (*estado*) of marriage or religion.[8] No one, not even her mother, the archbishop, or the king, could deny Josefa her rights. An elder could not exert force over or produce fearful reverence (*miedo reverencial*) in a child because of that elder's dependence on the child who was resisting the adult's will.[9] But Josefa was not a child, and although her mother made weak arguments about her irrationality as a woman, most of the protracted dispute centered around interpretations of Josefa's *vow*.

The case allows for a close inspection of mother-daughter relations as each attempted to control how Josefa's life story was being constructed and disseminated to others. While Josefa sought to define herself as a female adult who had chosen a path toward God and residence in the convent of her choosing, her mother emphasized family ties and obligations and the abstract idea of a self that was more than the sum of its parts. In both instances, the self was relational, but one interpretation aligned with divine will, and the other with family obligations.

Josefa's Story

While residing in the Monasterio de Santa Catalina in late 1706, Josefa wrote a lengthy account to the archbishop, responding point by point to a letter she had recently received from her mother (and perhaps copied to the archbishop). In what was more a testimonial than a rebuttal, doña Josefa reconstructed her life and the events leading up to her escape from the royal palace. She portrayed herself as having lived a typical life as the spoiled youngest daughter of an aristocratic family, with noble lineage on her mother's side dating back to the expulsion of the Moors and, on her father's side, with the bluest blood of saints, kings, and popes coursing through her veins. Of the six siblings, Josefa's two older sisters, Inés and María Felipa, had already left the household to become nuns of the black veil in Toledo in Spain. Life had not always been fair to Josefa. She was only eight years old when she was dealt a heavy blow: the death of her youngest brother, don Francisco Xavier Portocarrero, born in Lima in 1689 to "thunderous applause and commemoration."[10] Josefa maintained a stormy relationship with her eldest brother, Antonio José (1674–1736), who inherited the title of Count of Monclova on their father's death in 1705. She always felt the most affinity for her father, whose company she often sought.

As Josefa's adolescent years ended (she turned nineteen in 1700), her marriage became the topic du jour. Fawning suitors began to clamor for her attention. At that point in her life, Josefa's self-centered thoughts never strayed far from the "permissible entertainments" of the palace. Her autobiographical account described her great pleasure in being pampered with gifts and jewels from her affectionate parents and receiving attention from a retinue of obsequious servants who waited patiently for her every command.[11] Over the years she had the pleasure to learn to sing and to play various instruments, including the guitar, violin, harp, and organ; she was also trained to read music.[12]

But when her beloved father died at the age of seventy-four in September 1705, the twenty-four-year-old Josefa was plunged into a deep depression. As she gazed at her father lying in state, the habit of Saint Francis covering his corpse, her heart felt leaden. Her father had instilled in his children a deep piety and reverence for the sacred, and she prayed that he was now in God's care. To the end, the count had remained robust, although in the last few years of his reign he had tired of his post. In 1700 he had overseen the elaborate funerary exequies honoring the deceased Charles II, the last Hapsburg, who died without leaving a male heir.[13] But, as the first years of the new century progressed, he was increasingly impatient for the new viceroy to arrive (in fact, he did not reach Lima until 1707). To Josefa, it seemed that only several years, not nineteen, had passed since she had accompanied her father on his travels while he served as viceroy in New Spain (1686–88). Once he had been named viceroy of Peru, Josefa waited with him until the ship arrived that would carry them from Acapulco to Callao. She reminisced in her life story that sixteen years had passed since she and her father had gazed out the carriage window as the viceregal entourage entered Lima. She still recalled the faces of the expectant audience and the high-pitched sounds of pipes and trumpets that filled the air as the town crier announced the Count of Monclova's arrival at the four corners of the main plaza and proclaimed the viceroy's titles and merits.[14] Yet, compared to many of the entrances of heads of state, her father's had been subdued. The balconies draped with colorful banners still showed signs of devastation from the recent earthquake in 1687. As their carriage lurched over the uneven streets, Josefa and her father saw that much of the city had been razed (*por el suelo*) and, in the count's own words to the king, "the buildings so destroyed that the reports I read in Mexico did not adequately describe the ruination of the city."[15]

In the years that followed, Josefa had watched her father becoming increasingly burdened by news of pirate attacks, decreasing revenues, and grain shortages. Still, she had pleasant memories of their time together at family gatherings, investitures, and ceremonies, some of them extraordinary. Once, in December 1694, while she was still an adolescent, she had sat by his side in the Iglesia de Santo Domingo and witnessed the supremely "sacred" auto-da-fé of the legendary beata Ángela de Carranza.[16]

But now, as she viewed her departed father, she could only drink in the symbolic vestiges of his now-extinguished life. Over the habit of Saint Francis lay the habit of the Order of Santiago complete with all the insignia and accoutrements of the titles he had held as viceroy, captain general, and Grande de España. Not only had the count been a well-liked if not modest viceroy, but he had been a great military commander who had fought at key battles in Sicily, Portugal, Catalonia, and Flanders.[17] His troops had affectionately called him *brazo de plata* for the silver prosthesis that replaced the arm he had lost forty-seven years before his death. As Josefa listened to the funeral oration of the great Jesuit José de Buendía, recounting the count's heroic deeds, a lugubrious sensation crept into her soul. Her father, who had served two kings for sixteen years, one month, and seven days, was gone forever.

The loss struck her deeply, but the experience of melancholy that she described in her testimonial is reminiscent of the dark night of the soul faced by other spiritual devotees. In the months that followed, she entered a period of profound self-reflection in which, slowly, the scales fell from her eyes and she began to sense her true path:

> I recalled that I never felt healthy on the day I composed myself with excess. Later in my retirement, and while in a state of sadness, as I looked within I began to feel a very small light [flicker] within me. I wondered if, by throwing off my finery and splendor, I might regain my health. From this [self-realization] came a clarity within my soul so great that it seemed to me that the Crowns of the world were [nothing but] a filthy pigsty. With this recognition I felt happier, even happier than how I had felt when my Lord and Father governed.[18]

She felt drawn to take communion more often and began avoiding the company of her well-heeled peers. As she mused on how she had once craved applause, recognition, and flowers, she felt a deep sense of shame.

Such a profound change of heart left Josefa feeling confused and in need of guidance. She asked her mother's permission to speak with the Jesuit doctor of theology Alonso Messía Bedoya, who had consoled her father during the last solemn hours before his death. She timidly confided in Messía that she sensed an interior light growing within her. Perhaps, she pondered, if she shed her fripperies, she might find her path. Her new confessor advised against this sudden move (*repentina mundanza*) and instead urged her to devote herself to acts of charity, prayer, spiritual exercises, and regular communion. Like many new devotees eager to make dramatic changes, Josefa had become obsessed with mortifying her flesh, fasting, praying the rosary, walking the Stations of the Cross, and whispering her supplications to the Blessed Virgin. When her confessor disallowed her extreme practices, she faithfully acquiesced, although, as she pointed out, she was being denied her libertad (freedom of choice) to follow God's will.[19]

As Josefa's fevers ceased and her grief abated, her desire to devote herself completely to Santa Rosa quickened. She confessed her yearning to Father Messía, who counseled her to say a nine-day prayer (*novena*) to Lima's renowned saint. Father Messía also (wisely) urged her to seek the permission of her eldest brother, the fourth Count of Monclova. Josefa followed this council and prostrated herself before Antonio and her mother, pleading with them to allow her to follow her true vocation in Lima. She claimed that her brother and mother, who had not yet been filled with "strange impressions," both shed tears, were deeply moved, and offered their full support. At that moment the jubilant Josefa felt that she was "Queen of the World."[20]

However, the next day she awakened to another reality. Father Messía was no longer welcome in the family home, and Josefa's mother began to claim what would become her mantra over the next several years: that it was dishonorable for the *Spanish* Josefa to entertain thoughts of remaining in "one of the monasteries in the city." Josefa's "headstrong" nature, her mother scolded, had led God "'to seize her by His chain.'"[21]

To distract his sister and dissuade her from taking such a misguided path, Antonio whisked her off to two retreat areas for the wealthy in the Surco Valley and Lurín. There, in refreshing surroundings, the family offered her pleasant distractions. Josefa politely feigned happiness, all the while feeling pulled in a different direction. Each day she could not wait for the elaborate functions her brother had organized to end and the guests to depart so she could escape to a quiet place to whisper her prayers, finger her rosary beads, and take communion. Although forbidden to do so, she maintained a secret correspondence with Father Messía. When her brother realized that wooing her with gifts, lively company, and a peaceful ambience had failed, he switched tactics. One memorable afternoon, he exhorted her in a determined and extreme manner, threatening that if she did not relent, he would kill her or kill himself. In an act of deep passion, he struck his sister, causing her to bleed from the mouth. Alarmed by his actions, Josefa gave in to her brother and mother's wishes, swearing on a crucifix that she would return to Spain and there found a convent dedicated to Santa Rosa.

Within herself, however, Josefa silently communicated the truth to His Divine Majesty. Her true intention was to found a convent in the city where Rosa had performed her miracles, and she was deeply offended that her brother had behaved so violently toward her. The countess and count must have sensed Josefa's reticence because when the family returned to Lima from their sojourns, the doors throughout the palace were kept locked, hallways and corridors were blockaded, and the servants were punished if they failed to keep watch over her. It was then, as she reported in her testimonial, that she resolved to flee. On the night of 9 October 1706, the event that would become part of popular limeño lore occurred. In darkness, Josefa removed the balusters blocking her window, broke the glass, and scrambled down to the grounds of the palace, clutching a jeweled crucifix in one hand.[22] In her testimonial she defended her act, saying, "Even if I were a slave, as I am of my Mother and Lady, I could break the grilles to search for a Spiritual Director/ Protector (*Padrino*) who would acquire the [necessary] permission for me to enter a convent. Even a slave has the right to go out in search of *valedores* (protectors)."[23]

Once stories leave the mouths of their protagonists, they can quickly take on lives of their own, and Josefa's tale was no exception. Limeños hungry for gossip, intrigue, and evidence of the miraculous began spinning Josefa's escape in new ways. One hagiographic account reported that as she fled the viceregal palace she was struck with two ecstatic visions: one of the ecce homo and another of Our Lady of Sorrows, who encouraged her not to abandon her path. Father Messía was waiting to meet her once she had climbed down the wall, and he, along with her guardian angel, swept her away to the Monasterio de Santa Catalina, which would become her refuge for the next sixteen months. Sheltered in an austere cell throughout 1707, Josefa resolved to leave behind her vanity and the secular world forever. In a dramatic gesture she cut off her long tresses and donned the Dominican habit worn by her spiritual guide, Santa Rosa. In a reverie Josefa then had a vision of Santa Rosa placing a crown of roses on her head. She also saw vivid roses strewn about the floor, each flower a prescient symbol representing the nuns who would inhabit the future Monasterio de Santa Rosa.[24]

Josefa ended her impassioned testimonial: "Lastly, my dearly beloved Father and Lord died in this City; here I saw him on his throne, here I saw him in his worst misery, yes, here I saw him dead, and here I have to reconcile myself with the Lord who took him to heaven. . . . I am very confident that in the hands of His Excellency I will be protected in my liberty (*amparada en mi libertad*), and if God wants me to die, I will leave life where I left my hair, as a sign that I placed my soul in his hands."[25] Her beloved father gone, her home no longer a safe haven, Josefa felt that only His Excellency, God, could provide her with the paternal guidance and legal protection she now needed. Signing her name as Josefa de Santa Rosa, she dispatched the letter to the archbishop.

Furious with Josefa's "outrageous" behavior, the Countess of Monclova utilized all the political tools at her disposal to thwart her daughter's goal. Accustomed to getting her way, the countess wanted, first and foremost, for her daughter to be restituted to her control. From the comfort of the viceregal palace (she remained there until the new viceroy, Castell-dos-Rius, arrived in July 1707), doña Antonia began with a character assassination of her own flesh and blood. She referred to Josefa as a *niña* (child) and an "indignant creature," implying that she was incapable of making rational, adult decisions.[26] Josefa might be an adult and have free will (*libre albedrío*), but her character flaws induced her to make brazen, foolish choices. In her opinion, Josefa was ill prepared, inconstant, vain, and vulnerable. Her sheer determination to uphold her vow to found a convent to Santa Rosa in Lima was ample proof that she was "disillusioned by her vain pretensions."[27] The countess's biographical portrayal of her daughter drew from a repertoire of gendered stereotypes that characterized females as weak and feckless, unable to think rationally, and needing to remain under the *potestad* of their mothers.[28] This characterization echoed the sentiments of several male ecclesiastical authorities with whom the countess was closely aligned.

Early on in the drama, Archbishop Liñán y Cisneros gave his support to the countess, his cousin, and used the power of his office to dissuade Josefa from pursuing her course of action. He reasoned that they did not have to take Josefa seriously because she was so easily swayed by others and was especially susceptible to her confessor, Father Messía, whom the countess accused of misdirecting Josefa because of his desire to see the foundation of the Monasterio de Santa Rosa come to fruition. To that pointed accusation, Josefa responded that she had made up her mind even before she had sought Messía's counsel.

Others would argue that such characterizations were a "sort of artificial calculation to test doña Josefa's piety."[29] If the countess were to succeed in her intentions, she would need more substantive arguments. One strategy was to attack the nature of Josefa's vow. Aware that the Council of Trent (1545–63) mandated a probationary period of a year before a novice took formal monastic vows, the archbishop used that time to pressure Josefa.[30] During her novitiate year at Santa Catalina (1706–7), he ordered her to undergo several rigorous examinations to discern her true intentions. Two highly lettered, prudent, and esteemed doctors of theology scrutinized Josefa's conscience and spirit to determine whether the accusations made by her mother that she was nothing but a frivolous, irresponsible *woman* were true.[31] They found no evidence to support such an assertion.

There was still one other argument the countess and her team of advisors could make.[32] Josefa's vow to return to Spain and found a convent dedicated to Santa Rosa there, the countess reasoned, took precedence over her vow to serve God (and Santa Rosa) in Lima. Free will had nothing to do with it, nor did the fact that Josefa was a legal adult over twenty-six years of age, as Josefa explained in a letter to the king.[33] It did not matter that she had secretly made a very different vow to God, her true Father, and had promised to return to Spain only under duress. As her mother and executrix of the count's will, the countess could deny her daughter her fifty thousand–peso inheritance precisely because Josefa had broken a sacrosanct vow to her own flesh and blood.

Fortunately for Josefa, several high-level ecclesiastical officials offered interpretations of the vow that countered the position taken by the countess and the archbishop. Within weeks of Josefa's escape to the Monasterio de Santa Catalina, Diego Ladrón de Guevara, then bishop of Quito, was asked to give his opinion on the matter. The essence of the argument he made in his sixty-six-folio juridical, canonical, and moral dissertation was that any vow, but especially one related to marriage or the monastic state, had five requisites. It must be deliberated (*deliberada*), perfect (*perfecta*), and spontaneous (*espontanea*), and there must be an intention to commit oneself (*con intención de obligarse*) permanently, for life (*con permanencia*), knowing full well the responsibilities entailed in the commitment.[34] Even the intention of "transforming one's life into the condition (estado) of a male or female religious," he argued, carried the weight of a vow.[35] The Council of Trent decreed that a postulant must be over twelve years of age and that parents could not pressure (*irritar*) a daughter as she decided whether to take vows of chastity, enter a religious vocation, or make the more minor commitments of fasting, confession, and special types of prayer.[36] All involved free and spontaneous volition (*espontanea voluntad*). He concluded that because doña Josefa, of her own free will and natural right (*derecho natural*), willingly chose to become a nun of Santa Rosa, she was obligated to carry out her intention.

The bishop was willing to admit, however, that family obligations often carried more weight than the Council of Trent's dictum that an individual had the freedom (libertad) to choose the monastic state. In Lima the ecclesiastical court occasionally heard annulment suits initiated by men and women who argued that they had succumbed to family pressures to take monastic vows against their will because of the reverential fear (miedo reverencial) they felt toward their elders.[37] But this was not a case of forced monarchization per se. So, the vexing question remained: was doña Josefa compelled to follow through on her previously sworn promise (on a crucifix) to her mother to return to Spain, even though it had been forced on her and even though she had silently made an entirely different promise to God, as she explained in her letter? It seemed to Bishop Ladrón y Guevara that she should.[38] For from a "knotted promise" (*nuda promesa*) is born action, and that obligation must be fulfilled. Josefa, he thought, should follow through with her virtuous promise and exercise obedience to her mother.[39] Still, the desire, good intentions, and zeal to accelerate the process of taking her vows in the Monasterio de Santa Catalina were not, according to the bishop, a violation of the vow made before her mother.[40] On the contrary, he argued, the arduous Atlantic voyage should not impede or delay Josefa's desire to initiate the monastic life. Her mother did not have the right to question her daughter's right to take her vows *when* she wanted to take them, nor did maternal dominion hold sway over Josefa's right under God's law to choose her spiritual future.[41] *Where* she took her vows should not matter.[42]

Offspring who, by becoming religious, caused harm or were an economic detriment to their parents were another matter. This, in early modern law, referred to the economy of care. The countess insisted that she needed her only daughter (Josefa's two sisters were in Spain) to assist her in her "long peregrination [to Spain] and [because of her] grave illnesses." Continual bloodlettings were a testament to her weakened condition, and she claimed she would die of grief if she had to leave her daughter behind in Lima. (Josefa's older brothers were apparently unavailable to make the journey and had troubles of their own.)[43] Back in Spain, Josefa's grandmother, doña Antonia Jiménez de Urrea Clavero, the Countess of Aranda, echoed the arguments about family need when she sought theological council from her brother, the cardinal of Toledo, before directing a letter "bathed in tears" to King Philip. The countess contended in her letter that Josefa, still a girl (niña), had always been the daughter who tended to her mother's illnesses and that the Countess of Monclova would die of heartache if she had to leave Josefa behind. The fourth commandment, "Thou shalt obey thy mother and father," should take precedence over Josefa's monastic vow because of her mother's extreme need (*necesidad tan extrema*). To not obey this supreme precept would be paramount to committing a mortal sin.[44]

Ladrón de Guevara recognized the weaknesses inherent in the countess's argument about family necessity. To counter it, he recalled the story of Thomas Aquinas (1225–74), who also came from an aristocratic family. His mother, Theodora, was the Countess of Aquino in Naples and a descendant of the Hohenstaufen dynasty of Roman emperors. Landulf, Thomas's father, also a member of the high nobility, had a castle in Roccasecca in Naples. When Thomas announced his intention to become a mendicant of the Friars Preachers, it was considered an affront to the elite Aquinas family, not least because they had ties to the more prestigious Benedictine order. His distraught mother asked Emperor Frederick II (a relative) to intervene.[45] When this tactic failed, she plotted to have Thomas's brothers Landulf and Reynald abduct and imprison him in a castle two miles from the family residence. During nearly eighteen months of imprisonment, Thomas endured deprivation, hardship, and constant intimidation tactics from his father and brothers. The Friars Preachers appealed directly to Pope Innocent IV, who was infuriated at Thomas's unjust treatment. Under pressure, his mother allowed a member of the Dominican order to enter the prison to console him, but that was the limit of her willingness to compromise.[46] All ended well when Thomas eventually escaped through the window of the tower and took his vows as a Dominican friar at the age of seventeen.

The parallels with Josefa's story are apparent: pressure from well-heeled and well-connected family members, intimidation tactics, affiliation with the Dominican order, even the escape through a window—as well as the question of the degree to which family obligations should take precedence over the choice of a particular monastic order. No doubt Josefa was aware of the chapter in Thomas Aquinas's *Summa Theologica* entitled "Whether Duties toward Parents Are to Be Set Aside for the Sake of Religion" (derived from his own harrowing experiences), which stated that divine worship must prevail over filial duties.[47] The treatise did specify, however, that in principle children must ensure that their parents, and especially widows, were looked after before taking their vows. Only in cases of extreme economic necessity or illness were they to forgo their spiritual intentions. Out of respect and reverence, however, daughters and sons should ask their parents' permission before taking their vows.

Despite arguments from family members that the trip across the Atlantic was life threatening and that the countess's health was extremely delicate, most parties agreed that the health circumstances facing the countess could not be characterized as dire. Nor could they argue that economic necessity was a factor, because, like Thomas Aquinas's mother, the Countess of Monclova had more than enough to maintain her decently, and her son Antonio was at her beck and call.[48]

Josefa knew all this. As she explained in a letter to King Philip V, it was her mother's obligation to honor the law of God and respect her daughter's inviolable right to choose her own spiritual path. The countess's actions were far from exemplary, because they pitted mother against daughter, overstepped the bounds of ecclesiastical immunity (by trying to force her to leave a convent, where secular authorities were not permitted), and questioned the meaning of an individual's right to choose a religious vocation.[49] Although we are not privy to the inner workings of the mother-daughter relationship as it evolved over the years, Josefa insinuated that her mother's and grandmother's tears were not heartfelt and that they had their own interests, not hers, at heart. Despite the maternal pressure, Josefa was not willing to defer her vows "because of the veneration I owe my Mother, or [for] those who govern her . . . or for those who cry tears of blood to embarrass my vocation. They do not want me to follow Christ in order to accompany my mother, which I cannot carry out because I cannot turn my back on divine inspiration and [the] celestial voices that continually repeat in my heart, 'leave everything and follow God.'"[50]

Family obligations remained a constant leitmotiv of the litigation, but peninsular loyalties also ran deep. Both mother and grandmother genuinely feared permanently abandoning a family member of the Spanish aristocracy in remote imperial territory. By the time Josefa had repented of her "vain pretension," they argued, it would be too late, and their flesh and blood would remain forever stranded in a foreign convent in Lima.[51] Once Josefa had taken her formal vows, it would be nearly impossible to have them annulled. During a visit to see her daughter at the Monasterio de Santa Catalina, the countess had beseeched Josefa not to remain in such a forsaken place and to return to the family's ancestral lands.[52] The Countess of Aranda, Josefa's grandmother, iterated this point in her letter to Philip V. Not only was *her* daughter, the Countess of Monclova, grieving from her recent widowhood, but she now faced the nightmarish possibility of leaving behind "a girl [Josefa] of her social position (calidad) in such strange kingdoms."[53]

Here the peninsular versus creole sentiments of home and place were palpable. For a Spanish mother and grandmother, Lima was below their station; it was a forsaken culture. But, unfortunately for them, the count had died in Lima, and Josefa had shorn her locks in her monastic cell there—giving part of herself to the city that now harbored her father's bones. She had no desire to abandon her father, nor did she wish to abandon Santa Rosa, whose sacred remains formed an integral part of the mystical body (cuerpo místico) of Lima. The viceregal capital was Rosa's domain, and Josefa considered it her home as well. As she had stated in her autobiographical recounting of events, she wished to be a nun only in Lima and nowhere else.

Thus, creole sensibilities were integral to Josefa's case. For authorities, including Bishop Ladrón de Guevara, who had spent many years in the colonies, denying Josefa her wish was a symbolic affront to creole aspirations to found the Monasterio de Santa Rosa in Lima. Following Rosa's canonization in 1671, sentiment in support of founding a convent in her name had strengthened with each passing year. For supporters of a convent dedicated to Rosa in Lima, Josefa was a heroine, an aristocratic Spaniard who aspired to dedicate her life and inheritance funds to the worthiest cause in the universe, one that would enhance the glory and prestige of the viceregal capital.

As resistance from the countess and archbishop continued, rumors began circulating in the city that the archbishop was purposely delaying the foundation of the convent. Many limeños felt that this reticence threatened the heart and soul of Lima itself. In his dissertation the bishop pointed out that Josefa's decision not to donate her fifty thousand–peso inheritance to a convent in Spain was "pleasing to God" and that it was not a dignified Christian action on the part of the countess and her son Antonio to resist Josefa's efforts to apply those funds to a new convent in the viceregal capital. No one should take away the Monasterio de Santa Rosa from the city of Lima. The bishop concluded his treatise by stating that because Josefa, a legal adult, had sworn to God that she wanted to help found a convent to honor Santa Rosa in Lima, not in Spain, her inheritance should go to that effect.[54]

Power Politics, 1705–1713

Ladrón de Guevara's deliberations had no immediate effect, however. Quito was too far from Lima, the seat of power and the center of the maelstrom. The countess, with her considerable leverage, had already contacted the best lawyers and theologians and gained the support of two of the archbishop's intimate advisors (*domésticos*), don Juan Vázquez and don Dionisio Granado (who had deliberated in María Jacinta Montoya's and Ángela de Carranza's cases).[55] Together they conspired to build a case against Josefa.

To complicate matters, the Audiencia—infested by internecine rivalries that the countess could strategically maneuver—ruled between 1705 and 1707.[56] Its influence had begun to grow after 1700, as the Count of Monclova began losing his will to rule and the War of the Spanish Succession (pitting Austria and Portugal against France and Spain) limited communications with Spain. By 1705 Monclova was tired, disillusioned, and "anxious to avoid

[the] labyrinth" of the new Bourbon politics. Members of the high court were all too eager to fill the power vacuum.[57] A new faction in the high court insinuated itself into power, and several members slowly gained control over key economic and political decisions.[58] Josefa's case only exacerbated the factionalism as Audiencia members lined up to claim allegiance either to Josefa or to her mother.[59]

When the new viceroy, the Marquis of Castell-dos-Rius, assumed his post on 7 July 1707, he prudently refrained from intervening in Josefa's case, even though the countess mounted a campaign to convince him otherwise.[60] He may have been inclined to favor Josefa and felt tremendous public pressure to support her, but he was also reticent to lock horns with the archbishop and could guess the leanings of Philip V. By late 1707 relations between Josefa and her mother had become increasingly acrimonious. The countess had convinced the ailing Archbishop Liñán y Cisneros to nullify Josefa's initial vows (she was still in her novitiate year) and have them deferred to Spain. The archbishop issued a judicial decree that Josefa must leave the Monasterio de Santa Catalina immediately and accompany her mother back to Spain.[61] It is questionable whether he had the power of dispensation to remove doña Josefa from the Monasterio de Santa Catalina and transfer her vows to Spain on the grounds that she had made her vows in prejudice to her mother.[62] He may also have been overstepping the bounds of ecclesiastical immunity by disallowing Josefa's right to safe harbor in a place consecrated by God.[63]

Feeling threatened by the archbishop's overtures, Josefa appealed directly to the king for clemency.[64] In a letter written in December 1707, she argued that, according to the dictums of the Council of Trent, a twenty-six-year-old woman as a legal adult had the right to choose the estate she wished—whether to enter marriage or become a female religious—and the place where she wished to live.[65] She also iterated that she had the right to do with her inheritance as she wished. But Josefa was unaware, when she wrote her impassioned letters, that Philip V and the Council of the Indies had already sided with the archbishop and issued a decree supporting her removal from the Lima convent and the deferral of her vows to Spain. As the months went by and she received no response from the king, Josefa and her lawyer switched tactics. They now petitioned the viceroy and the royal court to consider her case, arguing that royal patronage (which ruled over secular and religious domains) granted crown authorities the authority to uphold the dictums of the Council of Trent. If the archbishop would not defend her rights, then the viceroy and royal court could help her to be amparada de su libertad.

In deciding to pursue this course, Josefa was wading into dangerous waters, especially given recent conflicts over ecclesiastical immunity in Lima and the fact that Liñán y Cisneros's career "was a notable example of the role played in that era by Spanish noblemen who were educated as clerics and rose to exalted positions in both the ecclesiastical and civil spheres."[66] In fact, the archbishop's championing of the rights of ecclesiastical privilege had put him seriously at loggerheads with the viceroy from 1681 to 1689, don Melchor de Navarra, the Duke of Palata, who felt he had similar prerogatives. Monclova's tenure as viceroy helped somewhat to mollify larger secular-religious tensions, but this peaceful interlude deteriorated with the ascendancy of the Audiencia in 1705 and the arrival of Castell-dos-Rius in 1707. By then, secular-religious squabbling and cronyism had infiltrated Josefa's case as different authorities took sides in the debacle.[67]

The inauguration of the new Monasterio de Santa Rosa on 2 February 1708, the Day of the Purification, brought some respite from the stalemate. It was a pivotal moment for the Count of Monclova's daughter and came as a relief to several authorities.[68] On that occasion, Josefa was once again reminded of her pious father, who would have been happy to hear the news, since the royal license to elevate the beaterio (founded in 1669) to a convent had been granted in January 1704 while he was still alive.[69] Why the process had been delayed by four years until February 1708 remains something of a mystery. The 400,000 pesos donated by the most illustrious members of Lima's aristocracy had certainly aided significantly in garnering the necessary license.[70] Some of the more skeptical limeños, including Josefa, believed that the archbishop and his associates had purposefully delayed the inauguration of the monastery to thwart Josefa's desires.[71]

All this was temporarily forgotten when the procession to inaugurate the newly established convent took place.[72] Following a long-established tradition of selecting nuns from an existing monastery to serve as foundresses of a new one, the feeble archbishop, the ministers of the ecclesiastical court, and other notable figures led four nuns in procession from the Monasterio de Santa Catalina to the cathedral.[73] Another procession originating at the Beaterio de Santa Rosa included nine ladies from Lima's most illustrious families, who accompanied the nine sisters (hermanas) from the beaterio in fine carriages.[74] The two processions united in the cathedral, and the nine beatas bowed reverentially to the nuns of Santa Catalina, then the two groups stood together to form the new community. Veils shrouding their faces, candles in their hands, they left the cathedral to walk the six main blocks of the city. (One nun followed in a carriage because of an injured foot.) In the main plaza stood silver and silk-laden litters with images of the Saints Domingo, Francisco, Augustine, and Pedro Nolasco, dressed in ornate, gold-threaded garments. The Archangel Michael led the procession, and at the vanguard were simulacra of Catherine of Siena and Rosa de Lima. As the nuns and beatas walked, bells tolled, musicians played, and choirs sang. To don Manuel Molina, the head notary of the archbishopric charged with describing the sacred event, it was as though Saint Catherine and Santa Rosa had descended from the tabernacles they occupied in eternal glory to don their earthly Dominican habits, now encrusted in pearls, emeralds, rubies, and diamonds.[75] Of course, the greatest platform (*andamio*) of the procession carried by the confraternity dedicated to Santa Rosa's cult and image was reserved for the Tuscan alabaster reliquary that held the saint's remains. Viceroy Castelldos-Rius, weary from an accident and afflicted by a bad heart, witnessed the spectacle from a colorfully decorated balcony. Well-wishers hovered in their balconies and tossed bouquets of spring flowers onto the street to honor their heavenly queen and patron saint Santa Rosa.[76] Once the nuns and beatas reached the new convent, the public gave them an obsequious farewell. The women then entered through two large wooden doors, which were ceremoniously bolted, excluding the secular world.[77]

Josefa did not attend the monumental event, although she described it in elaborate detail in a subsequent letter. Within two days, however, she had secretly transferred to the convent. For the beleaguered viceroy's daughter, this was a major victory. For sixteen long months she had been dependent on the charity of the abbess, nuns, and laywomen in Santa Catalina, because her mother had refused to offer any financial assistance. She had the abbess to thank for stoically resisting pressure from the archbishop to force her to leave Santa Catalina. Josefa had felt welcome and safe there, but it was a large institution with hundreds of nuns, girls, servants, and slaves. The more modest Monasterio de Santa Rosa, with only thirty-three nuns and a handful of slaves, offered a spiritual milieu more to her liking.[78]

Of course, the clandestine move to Santa Rosa infuriated the countess. After receiving the news, she immediately wrote to the viceroy.[79] Astonished that her daughter had blatantly disobeyed the archbishop's orders, she was even more incensed that the viceroy had consulted the Audiencia ministers about Josefa's case. The matter, the countess claimed, was outside his jurisdiction. She ended the missive with a veiled threat, letting Castell-dos-Rius know that she would await an explanation as to why he was paying close attention to Josefa's case. If she was not satisfied with his answer, she would use all her powers to "defend justice."[80]

Josefa was now safely ensconced in the monastery of her dreams, but her nightmare was not over. A decree from King Philip V to the viceroy dated 24 September 1707 finally arrived with the convoy in spring 1708. It roundly condemned Josefa's "repugnant" behavior for having entered Santa Catalina without her mother's consent. It also declared that it was within the archbishop's purview to dispense with Josefa's vows.[81] It warned that only in rare instances should the Audiencia intervene and interpret the mandates of the Council of Trent; Josefa's case was not a secular matter.[82] This now gave the countess considerable leverage in executing her will.

Bolstered by the king's response, the archbishop wrote a rare letter to Josefa, arguing even more forcefully that she must leave the convent and accompany her mother to Spain on the next available convoy.[83] The ecclesiastical judge (*provisor*), don Diego Montero de Aguila, even appeared in the visitors' parlor of Santa Rosa, exhorting Josefa to leave.[84] In the meantime the countess continued to assail the viceroy with letters, using both logic and emotion to convince him that he should desist in his efforts to deliberate the case.[85] By the end of May, the viceroy insinuated to the countess that he felt the case was outside his jurisdiction.[86] This was probably another stalling tactic, but the arrival of Philip V's letter had given Castell-dos-Rius pause for thought. Could he use his powers of royal patronage to protect the decrees of the Council of Trent without facing repercussions? He did not think so. The odds were no longer in Josefa's favor.

Be that as it may, Castell-dos-Rius was not particularly well disposed toward the countess, who had long had a reputation among limeños for being manipulative, surly, discourteous, and authoritarian.[87] She was so reviled that, according to historian Manuel Moreyra y Paz-Soldán, when she gave birth to a son in 1695, a theatrical production entitled "Worldly Hatred Indeed" was staged to commemorate the event.[88] By June 1708 it was becoming increasingly difficult for Castell-dos-Rius to maintain a neutral stance, even though the viceroy believed the archbishop had not followed proper juridical procedure.[89] In the back of his mind, he knew he could afford to wait a little longer. It was becoming glaringly apparent that the seventy-nine-year-old archbishop was no longer capable of governing his mitre. Rumors were now circulating on a daily basis that the disabling accident (perhaps a stroke) that Liñán y Cisneros had suffered only enhanced the power of several of his *domésticos*, who followed their own interests while pretending to govern on the archbishop's behalf. His frequent absences to a retreat outside of Lima merely confirmed suspicions that he was, indeed, not long for the world.[90] Couplets and *pasquines* (satirical posters) posted in key locations throughout the city criticized the corrupt ecclesiastical court, questioned the archbishop's sanity, and lamented Josefa's situation.

Although Philip V had made his position clear to the viceroy, the king resided on the other side of the Atlantic, and his decree was not a final arbitration in the matter. Castell-dos-Rius was the one who had to deal with the increasingly restless Lima community on a day-to-day basis.[91] Clearly Philip V, preoccupied with a major war and financial crisis, was out of touch with local politics that, as governmental authorities were left to their own devices, had for decades taken on a particularly creole cast. The viceroy sensed that if the countess accomplished her goal of extracting her daughter from the Monasterio de Santa Rosa, the city's inhabitants would riot.[92] Hundreds of miles to the north, the bishop of Quito, Ladrón de Guevara, felt the same way. As tensions mounted in June 1708, the viceroy wrote to Philip V stressing that Josefa's case was not a matter of an indignant creature behaving rashly, as family members had argued: it was an issue that affected all the pious inhabitants of America. The king's definitive resolution of Josefa's case, soon to arrive in the form of a *cédula* (decree), would have serious consequences for the entire kingdom.[93]

Serendipitously (some said Santa Rosa intervened), Archbishop Liñán y Cisneros died on 28 June 1708. Within several days the ecclesiastical council named a new ecclesiastical judge, Vicar General Gregorio de Loaysa. At 1 a.m. on 4 July, Josefa took her formal vows before him. Four doctors of theology and the prior of the Iglesia de San Agustín were present to witness the event.[94] Castell-dos-Rius received word later that morning that Loaysa had followed his better conscience in giving Josefa his benediction. Within hours, the news spread throughout the city. Church bells pealed continuously, and people openly celebrated in the streets and plazas, clamoring, "En hora Buena!"—"It's about time!" For too long they had impatiently hoped that Josefa would be freed from the "oppression [taken] against her free will, [and] the opposition against her intentions."[95] Josefa, limeños exclaimed, was now free to follow her spiritual path, a true limeña.

By the end of July 1708, the viceroy felt more comfortable openly extolling Josefa's constancy and heroic virtue in accomplishing her noble goal against such great odds. In an eighteen-folio letter summarizing the case, Castell-dos-Rius chastised the deceased archbishop, stating that he might have been more gracious and reserved. Josefa had proved beyond a shadow of a doubt that she was clear-sighted in her desire to uphold her natural right to choose her true vocation.[96] By October, King Philip V had been apprised that Josefa had formalized her vows, alleviating any necessity for him to intervene definitively in the matter.[97]

Knowing now that the chances of retrieving her daughter were severely diminished, the countess had to face other, messier realities. For over a year limeños had been accusing her of being more interested in the *hijuela* (plot) than the *hija* (daughter). The plot consisted of the fifty thousand pesos constituting Josefa's rightful inheritance. But an additional million pesos from the Count of Monclova's estate had also mysteriously disappeared. This information came to light in 1707 when King Philip V (following normal procedure) had ordered the oidor Juan de Peñalosa to send one million pesos from the Count of Monclova's estate to defray the costs of the viceroy's *residencia* (review of office). Somehow the funds had disappeared—some thought in an earlier shipment of the count's goods sent back to Spain.[98] When asked what had happened to the money, the countess replied that she had used it to pay for her husband's funeral and to support her household and children. A formal inspection of the residence revealed only objects of little value. Authorities found Josefa's desk empty of any contents, and a few yellowed garments in a chest.[99] Nervous servants and tenants averted their eyes, reluctant to provide additional information to inquisitive authorities.[100] Realizing that the Spanish government had to come up with the funds for the review, the once-sympathetic Council of the Indies and king now turned a cold shoulder to the countess.

By 1709 the countess was not the only one who felt ill at ease. Castell-dos-Rius had also acquired dangerous enemies in Lima. His accusers claimed he had turned a deaf ear to the customs and interests of the viceroyalty because of his Francophile leanings. Members of Lima's Consulado (the council charged with overseeing economic policies) abhorred his profiteering and corruption. In two years they had watched him amass a fortune and garner new revenue from mines to increase remittances to the royal treasury—greatly pleasing Philip V but alienating Lima's merchants. As tensions continued to mount and overtures were made to have him removed from office, on 22 April 1710 Castell-dos-Rius surprised everyone by dying.[101] For the second time in his career, Miguel Nuñez de Sanabria, an oidor of the Real Audiencia and a supporter of Josefa, took up the post of interim viceroy, from June until September 1710. Even more auspicious for Josefa, Bishop Ladrón de Guevara, who four years earlier had written the canonical dissertation in her defense, took up the post of bishop-viceroy in September 1710. He would remain in that post for five and a half years.

Still, the countess would not relinquish Josefa's inheritance.[102] In 1711, after four frustrating years, Sor Josefa once again took up her quill to compose two letters to King Philip V. In one, she detailed the extreme measures the countess had taken against her and expressed astonishment that after so much travail her mother still insisted that she return to her house and company and that she nullify her solemn vows as a cloistered nun.[103] Josefa wondered whether it was the devil, the common enemy, and not her mother, who was causing her spirit such agony. Even if the countess could no longer question Josefa's right to choose her vocation, she continued to deny her money for even basic necessities (*alimentos*) in the convent. She wanted her daughter to suffer indecency.[104] It had taken a written order from the viceroy Castell-dos-Rius for Josefa's mother and brother to provide a hundred pesos each month from her inheritance funds, and even then they complied only reluctantly (after a "war of pleadings [*guerra de ruegos*]").[105]

No one in Lima or Madrid could now accuse Sor Josefa of being a rebellious, shallow-thinking niña. As the prioress of one of the most beloved convents in Lima, she could tap into the king's religious sensibilities and "pious heart," and she could reference an even greater authority: Santa Rosa. The letters written to Philip V in 1711 show a mature, intelligent woman who now had the upper hand. The prioress could claim with authority that the denial of her lawful inheritance was a direct affront to the sacred (*lo sagrado*), "because [the inheritance] now belongs to God, and to this, [the king's] convent." The retrieval of the funds, to be used to complete the buildings, main temple, and chapels, was a matter of relevance for the king. "It is fitting that I should implore Your Majesty to favor my justifiable demand, because it is such a pious work. It is highly recommended, and proper of a deeply Christian Royal Sovereign." Josefa concluded by congratulating the king on his victory at Villaviciosa (in December 1710), which had ended the War of the Spanish Succession: "I have hope in God and in the intercession of my Mother Santa Rosa that the good dispatch will arrive during the celebration of new victories."[106] There was no doubt, she added, that if the king were to support the institution's efforts (and order the restitution of her inheritance), the blessings of Santa Rosa would be showered on him and the monarchy.[107]

Philip V may have finally heeded Josefa's supplications (we do not know for certain; he never responded directly to her letters); two years later, in 1713, the Council of the Indies ruled that her mother and brother had to pay the inheritance to the convent.[108] Before embarking for Peru, the newly appointed viceroy, Carmine Nicolao Caracciolo, the Prince of Santo Buono, was given orders not to allow the countess and Josefa's brother to leave for Spain until they had complied with the order.[109]

It is possible that the countess returned to Spain once or twice, but it is more likely that the high security risk posed by the enemy-infested waters deterred her.[110] Church historian Rubén Vargas Ugarte claims that she did return to Spain and that she had the count's remains exhumed from their resting place in the cathedral of Lima, but an archaeological dig found evidence of a silver prosthetic arm next to a cadaver in the cathedral's catacombs.[111] In the end, after her tireless efforts to leave the forsaken land of Peru with her daughter, the countess died in the viceregal capital on 1 January 1721 and was buried next to her husband in the cathedral.[112] Josefa's male siblings may also have had a change of heart. The brother closest in age to Josefa died in 1717, and his body was buried in Iglesia de San Francisco but his heart was buried in the Monasterio de Santa Rosa. When Sor Josefa's eldest brother, Antonio, with whom she had maintained a fractious relationship, died on 13 April 1736, his body was buried in Santa Rosa. After all the turmoil, it seemed that things had come full circle. The family was united in death on colonial soil.

Now protected by her free will and natural rights, Josefa lived a relatively calm life in the convent, serving several times as prioress until her death at the age of sixty-two. A semihagiographic account of Josefa's life written by a nun of Santa Rosa in 1912 stated that although part of her fortune was lost, the portion that was recovered served to build some of the interior chapels, choirs, and other necessary things.[113] Although the convent's wealth diminished over the course of the eighteenth century, the institution continued to attract young women from respectable families who wished to emulate Santa Rosa.[114] Fortunately, Josefa died three years before the catastrophic earthquake of 1746, which destroyed much of the convent her inheritance had helped to build.[115]

Conclusions

Josefa's escape from the viceregal palace in 1706 receives only a paragraph in Ricardo Palma's *Tradiciones peruanas*, a work that has immortalized the spicier side of Lima's history. To this day, however, she is considered one of Lima's heroines. Josefa is still beloved in the Monasterio de Santa Rosa, and her portrait, painted near the end of her life, hangs in one of its corridors. That a descendant of the purest Castilian lineage had fought the wishes of her aristocratic family and remained in Lima, close to Santa Rosa, was considered by many limeños to be an exemplary noble sacrifice that enhanced the city's spiritual grandeur.

Josefa's protracted efforts to choose a monastic vocation in a convent dedicated to Santa Rosa in Lima highlights different gendered interpretations of the innate faculty of freedom of will and freedom of conscience. At the core of the lawsuit initiated by Josefa's mother was what constituted an *adult* female, including what it meant to have the ability to reason and make respectable choices, how one should define weakness or fortitude of will, what it meant to make and keep a vow, and how the only female daughter in her mother's company could best meet family expectations. Of course, meddlesome political alliances played an important part as well. Were it not for Josefa's highborn lineage and her efforts to found a convent dedicated to the patron saint of Peru, Santa Rosa, her efforts to remain in Lima might have come to naught.

Josefa firmly believed that because of her deep, abiding faith in God, she had overcome great odds. Divine providence had prevailed. In the process, Josefa had become a local champion. Her fortitude and forbearance served as a model for other aristocratic women to follow; she exhibited the qualities of true heroic virtue in rejecting material wealth and choosing a spiritual vocation. She staunchly defended her natural, God-given rights in her confrontations with both church and state authorities. She even managed to stay the power of her mother, brother, and grandmother, all formidable foes. By exerting her will, she prevailed over the potestad of her mother, who used all the legal and extralegal means at her disposal to break her daughter's will. Such an expression of one's right to libertad may now seem antiquated, but at the beginning of the eighteenth century, it was considered a fundamental and sacrosanct right, especially by young, aristocratic women who felt they had received a higher calling.

Conclusion

The frisson caused by contact with holy hair, bone, and blood; beseeching words to an archbishop; stitching a gem on boldly colored cloth; stirring the daily stew: these were all ways women experienced and conveyed the command of the divine. In this quiet plurality, in this cacophony of form, substance, and phenomenality, gendered activities and experiences were taking place. Material interventions—so often discounted in documentary inscriptions by the historian's passing eye—are, in fact, key to comprehending early modern Catholic female spirituality. A mention of dressing a statue here, or arranging flowers there, might seem inconsequential when compared with the rich details of recorded dialogue or descriptions of momentous events. Because we yearn to know "what happened," we sometimes ignore the richness of the fleeting and the ordinary. We mistakenly contrast the so-called exteriorized nature of material objects with interior forms of (immaterial) spiritual expression. We distinguish self from object. But the logic and grammar of sacred objects, including how early modern people accessed, and, indeed, embodied, the immaterial and material properties of objects through the senses, must be investigated in tandem and more rigorously. Descriptions of trivial episodes—cheeks flushed with God's presence, the shearing of long locks, or the penning of a poem to God—are, in fact, evidence of what the apostle Matthew called the "salt and light" of spiritual praxis, whereby early modern women enhanced and enriched the flavors and the colors of God in the world (Matthew 5:13–14). These brief interludes are signs of the instantiation of the divine through that which was tangible.[1] They convey a sense of being in the body and in the world. They are evidence of the knower knowing and discerning, and then communicating that knowledge to others.[2] An exploration of the "words, things, sounds, silences, smells, sensations, gestures, powers, affects and effects" brings us closer to understanding how women lived the sacred and how the sacred lived through them.[3]

If the smallest of gestures, the briefest of interactions between a servant and her mistress, or descriptions of coarse cloth can tell the deepest of stories, how does identifying these ordinary practices advance our knowledge of female Catholic spirituality in the early modern world? How can such small moments help us grasp the spontaneity and the transitory moments that generally elude our grasp? Perhaps we can begin by reassessing our conceptualizations of religion. As the chapters in this volume demonstrate, it was not just a set of beliefs or theological precepts but involved calculated and spontaneous expressions of interiorized and exteriorized communion with the divine, whether in the most public of places or in the obscurity of a cell. "Religion," as Hent de Vries reminds us, is neither "linear nor cyclical but momentous, instantaneous, almost aleatory, subject to the least—and quite often unrelated—provocation."[4] Although it is difficult to discern spontaneity and momentariness in written sources such as vidas or beatification and Inquisition hearings, these and other sources provide glimpses of how women appropriated divine knowledge and engaged in their own expressions of theological literacy. From them we can glean, for example, that Rosa's disciples learned through their senses as they knelt beside her and dressed the "statue-person" of Catherine of Siena, their mother and confidante.[5]

Moreover, witness testimonials and other documents show that female bodies were not just sites of corruption or objectified by early modern men and women as a lesser "other." Ángela de Carranza's body, a reliquary fragmented into holy parts, held divine power and had multiple stories to tell to those who appropriated her virtus. Years before she was apprehended by the Inquisition, she was an *object* of veneration, not derision. By seeing, touching, tasting, or smelling her nail clippings, urine, or other parts of her self, the very materiality of her body became an active site of meaning making. The female body in ecstasy was also a readable text subject to both impulsive and scripted renderings. The body of the mystic Luisa Melgarejo was considered by her contemporaries to be a legitimate and acceptable text that could read/speak her own voice and the absent-but-present voice of the recently deceased Rosa, which was then recorded in writing. As Melgarejo spoke while in an ecstatic trance, her body served as a somatic vessel through which divine knowledge of the historic event of Rosa's ascension to heaven was transmitted and read by witnesses. It is true that the contents of this text—including its incorporation into Rosa's beatification hearing in 1617—were scripted because of expectations surrounding Rosa's eventual path toward sainthood, and that embedded in these passages are contemporary tropes related to sanctity and notions of the afterlife. Nevertheless, this recording of a mystic speaking while in an ecstatic trance is extremely valuable for comprehending how channels of communication and reception of the divine could occur through the body, whether scripted or not. The question is how scholars can access the spontaneous within the contrived and investigate how somatic literacy and orality were transformed into narrative biographical form.

A consideration of how women appropriated sacred materialities or how others accessed the divine in female bodies may answer some of the questions we have about the metaphysical aspects of Catholicism. But there are always caveats. As those of us who work on mysticism are painfully aware, linguistic narration and documentary inscriptions all too often muffle or flatten the poetic moments of exchange that are framed around "organizing discourses" about how mystical knowledge making occurred.[6] That is not to say, however, that the written word was not an important source of empowerment and communication for women. We know about such mystical events because women were witnesses to or participants in the kinds of knowledge exchanges that were taking place, exchanges that were later recorded, at times by women themselves. Josefa Portocarrero, Ángela de Carranza, and María Jacinta Montoya were active correspondents and spiritual autobiographers, and the written language gave them a command rarely afforded to pious women in colonial Lima. In writing they could actively represent their autobiographical selves to others. Sources such as letters, vidas, and the records of Inquisition and beatification hearings in combination with other material texts such as paintings, statues, and relics are useful for sharpening our exploration of the relationship between early modern understandings of immateriality and materiality and the ways women engaged with texts and rituals in composing biographical and autobiographical selves.

Michel de Certeau's investigations into the "arts of doing" were based on his premise that ordinary people use ordinary methods (he called them "tactics") to resist oppression and repression. Several of the women discussed in this volume responded to particular gender constraints by overstepping the bounds of prescribed authority. Ángela de Carranza assumed a power perhaps unprecedented in the history of Lima. Her body parts, she claimed, were sacred, and she made them available for purchase. She claimed a direct contact with multiple divine beings, and her original theological precepts and vociferous criticisms of ecclesiastical and secular authorities eventually raised eyebrows. María Jacinta Montoya gained authority as the governess of a recogimiento and beaterio, but her efforts to promote the candidacy for sainthood of her Indian tailor husband, Nicolás de Ayllón, through writing and the creation of an archive met with resistance from various quarters. Eventually she was derided for being arrogant and self-promotional and had to denounce herself to the Inquisition. To the Countess of Monclova, the weak, childish nature of her daughter, Josefa Portocarrero, had caused her to disregard family obligations in her choice to remain in Lima in the convent of her choosing. These are clear examples of how gendered interpretations of the bounds of female authority and legal rights affected the choices holy women made and others' interpretations of those choices. But does focusing on how women resisted patriarchal repression or internalized misogynist discourses tell the whole story? Was there such a thing as gender hegemony? I think not. My findings for seventeenth-century Lima echo the arguments made by Caroline Walker Bynum. In a seminal article first published in 1986, Bynum argued that medieval female religious generally paid little attention to notions that they were incomplete or fragile. Yes, women faced serious deterrents, but such obstacles did not always delineate the parameters of their spiritual expression or their relationship to their bodies as both spirit and matter.[7] Gendered notions were constituted socially and relationally based on internal notions of prescribed and perceived codes of conduct, norms, and constraints, and we see evidence of that throughout this volume. But there is more here than meets the gendered eye.[8] This book has attempted to move beyond the oppressor-oppressed paradigm and gender binary (weak women opposed to virile men) that has dominated women's religious history for so long. Gender analysis is useful for exploring some aspects of female religious expression, but women's attempts to engage in active and contemplative devotional practices were not always framed in spite of or because of patriarchal limitations.[9]

Another way to deepen our understanding of the parameters of female spirituality is to investigate what *relationality* meant in terms of the actualization of the sacred. As relational selves, women of the early modern period were part of an intimate and intricate connective web with living and deceased human and divine beings. The question "Who am I?" was foremost in the minds of many of the women discussed in this volume. Awareness of self was always relational, whether to their own personae, to God and divine beings, or to those in their immediate social circles. First and foremost, the positionality of self to other related most profoundly to the most powerful force of life: God. Women also related to mothers, brothers, archbishops, and husbands. María Jacinta Montoya expressed ideas of her self in a relational manner to her deceased husband, Nicolás de Ayllón, whom she hoped would be beatified. She utilized her personal connections with secular and religious officials and indigenous leaders, exerted her authority as the governess of a religious institution, and promoted her mystical experiences in her endeavors to fashion a male indigenous saint. More generally, María Jacinta's written interventions and efforts to collect and distribute information about her husband's miracles illustrate the nuanced and multifarious ways women could represent the self. Women like María Jacinta expressed themselves through their senses, in language, and in relation to multiple beings. Continuing to examine the mutually constitutive process of self-constitution and constitution by and with regard to others is fundamental to unraveling how spiritual autobiographies and biographies were crafted.

Self-transcendence or absorption of the divine into the body, or the union of the individual with God and into God, was integral to mystical experiences. The divine, as Luce Irigaray once wrote, would "in a silence, without any appearing" feel like a "kind of river that flows."[10] But what was the "it" that was being transcended? Transcendence did not involve only transcending one's gender or being concerned with spiritual maleness as a superior form of being.[11] The body, as we have learned, was more than flesh; it was composed of layers of the soul. Bodily practices might involve self-discipline and self-abnegation, as descriptions of Rosa's self-mortification rituals described in chapter 1 portrayed. But the body was also where communion with the divine and transcendence into the divine could occur. Those women who experienced ecstasy while still inhabiting a corporeal form were not just becoming some*thing* else but *being*, outside of space and time. Through their own bodily experiences, women like Ángela de Carranza, María Jacinta Montoya, and Josefa Portocarrero consciously created repositories of themselves as containers of divine will. Transcendence, therefore, was more than about becoming what was not-feminine. Moreover, the divine that enabled females to experience spiritual transcendence was accessible as imaginary, anthropomorphic figures, as energies, as bones, or as former living beings.

Finally, women served as spiritual models and teachers and guides to their protégées. Catholicism was not only profoundly relational but also profoundly imitative. Who better to emulate than the living and breathing holy women closest to you? María Jacinta Montoya gave council to wayward women and guided recogidas in their daily regimen, Rosa regularly exchanged knowledge with her disciples, and donadas communicated with their matrons or emulated pious elders in their midst. The impressionable young female students of Isabel de Porras Marmolejo, the governess of the Colegio de Santa Teresa, witnessed their beloved teacher's frequent raptures and levitations. From her example, they learned how to read and interpret divine signs manifested on Porras's body (text) and understand who they were in relation to God. Each conveyed to other women their comprehension of the path to inner perfection.

Interactive exchanges of knowledge did not occur only among living women; sororial dialogues took place on a daily basis with dead female mystics, some of whom had lived centuries before. In silent supplications girls communed with the medieval Italian Catherine of Siena or the Spanish Teresa de Ávila. They did so through material contact with objects associated with these saints—statues, cloth, or the word on the written page, which they listened to as it was spoken. Gerónima de San Francisco's unpublished vida, written in 1635, dialogued directly with Teresa de Ávila's writings, but Gerónima also embodied Teresa, by seeing and reading images (paintings and sculptures) and filling herself with God's spiritus projected through the influential saint's words. Such evidence of the imitatio morum and oral circuits of knowledge transmission among women requires further investigation in other Catholic sites.

Not all women who engaged with the sacred could rest their heads on satin pillows. Not all women had access to books or elite schools. Rosa de Lima's companion, María de Uzástegui, had enough wealth to acquire paintings, statues, and other religious objects to adorn the altar she maintained in her home. But someone like Rosa, from a humble background (her mother tutored the daughters of the wealthy), had to rely on the matronage of someone like Uzástegui, just as Estefanía de San Joseph, the daughter of a slave, relied on influential friars to loan her books. Their exemplary piety, however, gave them spiritual capital in the eyes of others. In convents, women of African, African-European, or indigenous descent were prohibited from becoming nuns. But their ability to engage with the materiality and immateriality of the sacred saw no bounds of color or status. They could walk the streets in tattered garments, begging for alms, or work their fingers to the bone sewing mattresses for hospitals. They could scrub floors in convents and feel that God cherished them. Convents and beaterios might afford a protective environment in which to commune quietly with the divine. Some women, however, fiercely resisted becoming donadas even if it meant gaining their freedom in ten or twenty years. They preferred a life of slavery outside the convent walls to one inside it. Others, like the orphaned mulata Josepha de la Concepción y Meneses, who stated in her entrance petition that she wanted to be the servant of the servants in the convent, would never have wished to rest her head on a satin pillow.[12] To be a truly spiritual being was to reject the superfluous and materialistic nature of the world. For some, even though they suffered discrimination and harsh work regimes in convents, God was the great equalizer. God's justice came for those who lived lives of *true* humility, including subservience to others. As Úrsula de Jesús expressed in her diary, "Whoever does more is worth more."[13]

By seeing the sacred in the everyday, by seeing holy materiality as alive and communicative, by critically examining the "I" voice in autobiographical and biographical writings, and by considering relationality as a part of how women defined and expressed themselves, we can move the discussion of female Catholic spirituality in new directions. More important, these approaches to the study of pious women in colonial Lima have implications for other colonial sites, and indeed for Spain itself. We know that post-Tridentine reforms and increasing inquisitorial surveillance affected women's choices, but these constraints need to be seen in tandem with the rich display of spiritual expression in the homes, churches, and streets of Lima and elsewhere. By continuing to explore how women adapted the complexities of Catholicism to their own notions of the divine, we can enhance our understanding that belief and praxis were ever evolving and alluring in multiple ways and in multiple contexts: whether in a whispered prayer, in inquisitorial chambers, or in the sensorial pulse of cloth touching skin.[14]

Notes

INTRODUCTION

1 "Cuerpo místico (mystical body) and "Christian Republic" come from Cobo, *Historia de la fundación*, 1:137. By "cuerpo místico," Cobo referred to what had originally been intended to represent the divine Christ in the Eucharist, and to the Church as the body politic with Christ as its head. The quote on "endless cycle" comes from Brading, *First America*, 322; Hayes, *Body and Sacred Place*, 95.

2 Iwasaki Cauti, "Vidas de santos."

3 Mujica Pinilla, "'Dime con quién andas,'" 200. The term *theatre state* comes from Clifford Geertz and was used by Edward Muir in his article "The Virgin on the Street Corner" (31). On the different kinds of spectacles that took place in Lima, see Osorio, *Inventing Lima*.

4 Barriga Calle, "Muerte en Lima," 96.

5 Cobo argued that Lima had reached a level of piety comparable to that of the great European cities. Cobo, *Historia de la fundación*, 1:137; Kantorowicz, *King's Two Bodies*, 196; Osorio, *Inventing Lima*, 81–102.

6 "Christ was simultaneously fully human and fully divine," and humans consumed the mystical body of Christ in the Eucharist. Hayes, *Body and Sacred Place*, xxi, 3; see also Sánchez-Concha Barrios, "La tradición política," 102–3. Augustine's *De civitate Dei: City of God* talks about humans (body-spirit) as inhabitants of earth and the heavens. Ernst Kantorowicz talks about the fusion of *corpus Christi* (the body of Christ) with *corpus mysticum* (the mystical body). He wrote, "The Pauline term [*corpus Christi*] originally designating the Christian Church now began to designate the consecrated host; contrariwise, the notion *corpus mysticum*, hitherto used to describe the host, was gradually transferred—after 1150—to the Church as the organized body of Christian society." Kantorowicz, *King's Two Bodies*, 196.

7 Sánchez-Concha Barrios, "La tradición política," 102–3, 113; Regalado de Hurtado, "Reflexión sobre el cuerpo." Muir has argued that towns "were themselves

mystical bodies, a corporation both in the legal sense and the literal one of a number of persons united in one body, nourished and protected by a civic patron saint." "Virgin," 26.

8 Braude, "Women's History"; Myers, *Neither Saints nor Sinners*, 3.

9 Lima maintained a strong character of *civitas* (the communal gathering of its inhabitants) by maintaining harmony between the two elements of piety and *policía*. Kagan, *Urban Images*, 11 (based on Covarrubias Orozco's dictionary, *Tesoro de la lengua castellana o española* [1611]), 126–28 (for Guaman Poma's definition of *policía*). Alexandre Coello de la Rosa quotes Bartolomé de las Casas's notion of policía (in the latter's *Apologética Historia Sumaria*). Coello de la Rosa, *Espacios de exclusión*, 48. On the various authors extolling the virtues of Lima, see Fray Buenaventura de Salinas y Córdova (his history of Lima, 1630), Antonio de la Calancha and Bernardo de Torres and Bernabé Cobo. The literature of the latter part of the seventeenth century follows this same trajectory; see the works of Diego Córdova y Salinas (*Crónica franciscana de las provincias del Perú*, 1651), Juan Meléndez (*Tesoros verdaderos de las Indias*, 1681), and Francisco de Echave y Assu (*La estrella de Lima . . .*, 1688).

10 Mills, "Naturalization of Andean Christianities."

11 Mills, "Religion."

12 For examples of vows of celibacy taken by young women, married couples, or widows, see Doña Baltasara de Bustamante, petition, Lima, 1633, Archivo Arzobispal de Lima (AAL), Celibato, no. 3. One witness said doña Baltasara took communion every day. See also Pedro Ruíz Vela and Juana Baptista de las Nabas, petition, Lima, 1606, AAL, Celibato, no. 1; Pedro Fernández de Peralta and doña María de Benavides, petition, Lima, 1620, Celibato, no. 2. For a discussion of the historical tradition of celibacy in marriage, see Elliott, *Spiritual Marriage*. For an example of a couple entering convents as religious servants (*donados*), see "Autos seguidos por Antonio de Cordova y Juana Maria Hurtado," Lima, 1665, AAL, Monasterio de la Encarnación, 11:86.

13 Bilinkoff, "Saint." Joanne Rappaport and Tom Cummins's *Beyond the Lettered City* reminds us that we need to consider how both Europeans and native Andean peoples understood literacy (reading and appropriation) of different kinds of visual, pictorial, and alphabetic texts.

14 D. Morgan, "Materialities of Sacred Economies."

15 Van Deusen, *Between the Sacred*, ch. 4; Premo, *Children of the Father King*; on slaves and disputes with masters over marriage choices or the right to cohabitate with one's spouse, see Wisnoski, "It Is Unjust"; McKinley, *Fractional Freedoms*.

16 The city-wide census of 1614 reports 820 female religious, equaling 16 percent of the total female Spanish population (4,359 + 820). The 1613 census (*padrón*) of all indigenous people in Lima counted 640 native Andean females. Of the five hundred adults, 30 percent were single, widowed, or divorced. Several of these women worked as servants in convents. Vergara Ormeño, "Migración y trabajo femenino," 136; Estenssoro Fuchs, "Construcción de un *más allá*," 415. By 1625 there were six convents; five of them included women of color, with over 130

women of color living and working as donadas. Van Deusen, *Between the Sacred*, 173–76.

17 See, for instance, the will of the Spanish Melchora de Ribera, a professed beata from the School of Carmen (AAL, Testamentos, 7, no. 10, 1618). She died in 1618, leaving fifty pesos for masses for the souls in purgatory and fifty masses for the "convent." Francisca de la Concepción, another beata affiliated with the Franciscans, lived in the neighborhood of San Lázaro (across the Rímac River from the core of the city) and in 1622 left money for 150 masses to be said in the Church of San Francisco and also to another beata, the widow Catalina de Jesús (AAL, Testamentos, 8, no. 10, 1622).

18 Van Deusen *Between the Sacred*; Meléndez, *Tesoros verdaderos*, 798–803; Martín, *Daughters of the Conquistadores*, 287–88.

19 Van Deusen, *Between the Sacred*, xv.

20 Cobo, *Historia de la fundación*.

21 Paul Charney's analysis of the *Padrón de Indios* of Lima (1613) concludes that 95 percent of the people designated as *indios* in that census (constituting 8 percent of Lima's total population) were migrants. Charney, "El indio urbano." Teresa Vergara Ormeño points out that only rarely did the census of 1613 specify the occupation of females beyond the generic designation "domestic servant." Vergara Ormeño, "Migración y trabajo femenino." Jane Mangan's *Trading Roles* effectively uses notarial records to find deeper evidence of females' contributions to the colonial economy.

22 Meléndez, *Tesoros verdaderos*, 3:746–67; on work, see 759; on her extreme poverty, see 760; on using *estampas* (printed images, in this instance of divine subjects) as her curtains, see 754. See also Vargas Ugarte, *Historia de la Iglesia*, 3:438–40.

23 An important work that views convents as centers of intellectual and economic exchange in colonial Peru is Kathryn Burns's *Colonial Habits*; Arenal and Schlau, "Leyendo yo y escribiendo ella." For a European perspective, see Diefendorf, "Rethinking the Catholic Reformation." On deeply religious women expressing their piety in uncloistered congregations or as individuals, see Rapley, *Dévotes*; and Delgado, *Troubling Devotion*.

24 Van Deusen, "Manifestaciones de la religiosidad femenina." It is hard to calculate the precise number of beatas or tertiaries in seventeenth-century Lima.

25 Some chroniclers emphasized how Rosa helped convert many lost and scandalous women. Meléndez, *Tesoros verdaderos*, 2:508–9, 3:795.

26 Jaffary, *False Mystics*, 5–11; van Deusen, "Circuits of Knowledge."

27 For a discussion of single women and their networks in eighteenth-century Mexico City, see Pescador, *De bautizados*; Boyer, *Lives of the Bigamists*, 167–217. For an example of networks in a French rural setting, see Cashmere, "Sisters Together."

28 Burns, *Colonial Habits*; van Deusen, *Between the Sacred*; O'Toole, "Danger in the Convent."

29 Ursula de Jesús, *Souls of Purgatory*, 32–37.

30 I argue that space and social location are gendered and that identities are constituted in part by the kind of space in which the individual *can* imagine herself. A
number of feminist geographers have explored this subject. See McDowell, *Gender, Identity and Place*; Massey, *Space, Place and Gender*, 264. Doreen B. Massey
conceptualizes space as "the simultaneous coexistence of social interrelations and
interactions at all spatial scales." Social relations, according to Massey, "always
have a spatial form and spatial content. They exist, necessarily both *in* space . . .
and *across* space" (168).

31 Anthony Giddens prefers the term *locale* to *place* in his discussion of social geog-
raphy, "for it carries something of the connotation of space used as a *setting* for
interaction" and communication. Giddens, *Social Theory*, 207.

32 Here I concur with Judith Butler, whose notion of performance is linked to the
idea that "gender is an identity tenuously constituted in time, instituted in an
exterior space through a *stylized repetition of acts*." Butler, *Gender Trouble*, 140.
See also Michel de Certeau, who considers identity to be a "spatial practice,"
which involves mapping and enunciating a theater of action. Certeau, *Practice of
Everyday Life*, 35, 98–100, 115–30.

33 Certeau, *Practice of Everyday Life*, 91–110. See Alejandra Osorio's detailed discussion of seventeenth-century descriptions of Lima. Osorio, *Inventing Lima*, 7–11.

34 Kelly, "Did Women Have a Renaissance?"

35 Herlihy, "Did Women Have a Renaissance?" See also Wiesner-Hanks, "Do
Women Need the Renaissance?"

36 De Groot and Morgan, "Beyond the 'Religious Turn'?," 397–98. On female
efforts to transform themselves through mystical conformity to God's will, see
Mack, *Visionary Women*. For the argument that mysticism was a transgressive
strategy to subvert male authority, see Finke, "Mystical Bodies."

37 Mack, "Religion, Feminism," 156–57.

38 Hollywood, *Sensible Ecstasy*, 113.

39 This point is made in the review essay by Leavitt-Alcántara, "Holy Women and
Hagiography."

40 For a consideration of gendered forms of religious expression, see Bilinkoff, "Navigating the Waves"; and Weber, "Gender."

41 In *Related Lives*, and "Confessors, Penitents," Jodi Bilinkoff demonstrates that while
some scholarship emphasizes the controlling nature of the confessor-penitent relationship, these confessor-confessee relations were complex, nuanced, and mutually influencing. In that vein, John Coakley has argued that male-female gendered
expressions of authority could coexist and build on one another. Coakley, *Spiritual Power*, 2–4; see also J. Hillman, "Soul Mates and Collaborators."

42 Iwasaki Cauti, "Mujeres al borde," 591. Fernando Iwasaki Cauti emphasizes the
dominant, censoring role of the confessor. Certainly, women reproduced and
adapted orthodox and popular spiritual knowledge learned from male clerics
and numerous confessors, but many had multiple confessors (Santa Rosa had
at least twelve), which indicates a varied influence and choice on the part of the
confessee.

43 Boydston, "Gender," 559.

44 Silverblatt, *Modern Inquisitions*. For a broader consideration of the early modern Inquisition, see Vose, "Beyond Spain."

45 Castañeda Delgado and Hernández Aparicio, *Inquisición en Lima*; Elliott, *Proving Woman*, 1–3; Giles, *Women in the Inquisition*; Holler, "Inquisition and Women," 124; Diefendorf, "Rethinking the Catholic Reformation," 46–47.

46 Scholars working with Inquisition records have long recognized the fluidity between orthodox and popular theological knowledge. Alberro, *Inquisición y sociedad*; Henningsen, "Evangelización negra"; Sánchez, "Mentalidad popular," 36; Mannarelli, *Hechiceras, beatas y expósitas*, 47. Women communicating "esoteric" ideas certainly did not always think in terms of orthodoxy versus heterodoxy. See Leonor de Verduga, deposition, Lima, 1621, Archivo Histórico Nacional de Madrid (AHNM), Inquisición, Lima, Leg. 1030, 251r–252r.

47 Luisa Melgarejo de Sotomayor, propositions, Lima, 1624, AHNM, Leg. 1647, no. 5, 16v.

48 The inquisitor Joan Gaytan cited an edict published in 1622 in Seville by the bishop of Cuenca, Andrés de Pacheco, which in effect considered anyone who possessed books related to revelations or ecstatic states or who wrote without official Church approval to be suspicious. This edict was read in the Cathedral of Lima on November 14, 1623 (Joan Gaytan, Theological Assessments [*Calificaciones*], Lima, 1624, AHNM, Inquisición, Leg. 4467). It served as the basis for prosecuting a number of beatas accused of *alumbrismo*, or illuminism and heresy.

49 Palma, *Inquisición de Lima*; Medina, *Tribunal de la Inquisición*; Millar, "Falsa santidad e Inquisición." Iwasaki Cauti considers the beatas' interest in religious matters to be an escape from domestic routines and conjugal patriarchy, Iwasaki Cauti, "Mujeres al borde," 584. A number of historians have unpacked the misogynist discourse behind the inquisitors' motives; see Guilhem, "La Inquisición."

50 Medieval scholar André Vauchez has discussed the "intermittent cycle" of lay piety that emerged in twelfth- and thirteenth-century Italy, and again at the end of the fourteenth century, when the feminization of lay spirituality occurred. Vauchez, "Lay People's Sanctity," 21, 24; Vauchez, *Sainthood*, 348–54, 369–86, 409; see also Weinstein and Bell, *Saints and Society*, 220–23; Bynum, *Holy Feast*, 16–30. A similar surge in lay feminine spirituality occurred in early seventeenth-century Lima.

51 For an important discussion of the diversity of mystical thought and mystics in early modern Spain, see Andrés Martín, "Pensamiento teológico"; and Andrés Martín, *Los místicos*. Until the 1620s the Jesuits, the preeminent religious society in Lima, openly advocated various types of divine contemplation and mental prayer. Diego Alvárez de la Paz (1549–1619) was a distinguished theologian, mystic, and influential teacher (he was prefect of advanced studies [*estudios mayores*] at the Colegio de San Pablo in 1609–17) who also served as the confessor of one of Lima's most well-known beatas, Luisa Melgarejo. Other Jesuits included Juan Sebastián Parra, Francisco de Contreras, Diego de Torres, and Diego Martínez. See Torres Saldamando, *Antiguos Jesuitas*, 349–53; Iwasaki Cauti, "Luisa Melgar-

ejo de Soto," 227. A Dominican, Pedro de Loayza (who had served as one of Santa Rosa's confessors), also supported the mystical practices of the beatas accused of heresy by the Inquisition in the 1620s.

52 Howells, "Early Modern Reformations," 119–23.

53 Van Deusen, "Circuits of Knowledge."

54 Ahlgren, "Negotiating Sanctity," 376; Kieckhefer, "Holiness"; Bynum, *Jesus as Mother*; Bynum, "'. . . And Woman His Humanity,'" 257–88; María de San José, *Wild Country*.

55 Mulder-Bakker, "Metamorphosis of Woman," 117.

56 Lynn Hankinson Nelson argues that "experience is inherently social, not individualistic," and that "what constitutes evidence for specific claims and theories includes the knowledge and standards constructed and adopted by epistemological communities. Based on our experiences, we can each contribute uniquely to what we know—but none of us knows what no one else could." "Epistemological Communities," 141.

57 "Relación de Causas," Lima, 1597, AHNM, Inquisición, Lima, Leg. 1028, 495v–497r. Doña Francisca Maldonado (from Seville), Luisa de Ocampo (Lima), Costança (Chuquisaca), Francisca de Espinosa (mestiza, Trujillo), Maria de Aguilar, Catalina de Mena, Mariana Clavez, and Francisca Ximenez were listed as the accused. Among other things, they taught one another invocations to Santa Martha, the stars, and the Holy Trinity to procure a man. See Osorio, *Inventing Lima*, ch. 4, who also questions this bifurcated paradigm.

58 Tausiet, *Urban Magic*, 1; Lamana, "What Makes a Story Amusing," 87–102.

59 "Calificación de unos papeles atribuídos a la Vicaria del Convento de las Descalças Reales," Lima, 1624, AHNM, Inquisición, Censuras, Leg. 4467, no. 11. African and European healers and barbers brought their own "magical-religious" healing practices into the convents where they worked. Tardieu, "Genio y semblanza," 566n32.

60 Doña Isabel de Angulo, deposition, Lima, 1592, AHNM, Inquisición, Lima, Leg. 1028, 262r–263v. She then recounted a specific ritual and prayer, which she had learned from nuns in Seville.

61 "Vida de Gerónima de San Francisco," Lima, 1635, Archivo Franciscano de Lima, Registro 17, no. 38, 477r.

62 Meléndez, *Tesoros verdaderos*, 2:433–34. She also carried an image of the baby Jesus, which she called "el Médico," (the doctor) and consulted it to determine the best medicine to cure an illness.

63 Fray Jerónimo Alonso de la Torre, testimony, Lima, 1633, AAL, Beatificaciones, Isabel de Porras Marmolejo, 32r–v. See the short vida of Isabel de Porras Marmolejo in Córdova y Salinas, *Crónica franciscana*, 938–48.

64 This important argument has been made by others. See Campos, "Mulher e universo magico"; Jaffary, "Virtue and Transgression," 9–28. Sara Scully says that women probably considered "witchcraft" (divination or sorcery) as "part of an economic strategy, which could also include marriage and prostitution," and that studies about their practices should form part of "family history" or "labor

studies" rather than "Inquisition studies." Scully, "Marriage or a Career?," 858. For Guatemala, see Few, "Women, Religion, and Power." For Peru, see Mannarelli, *Hechiceras, beatas y expósitas*; Osorio, "'*El callejón de la soledad.*'"

65 Weber, "Introduction."

66 Myers, *Neither Saints nor Sinners*, ix. As scholar Kathleen Myers explains, vidas draw on the complex traditions of confessional autobiographies and hagiographic biographies. See Velasco, "Teaching Spanish Women Mystics."

67 Ibsen, "Honor thy Father"; Myers, *Neither Saints nor Sinners*, vii–viii, 3–4.

68 Kristine Ibsen argues that although many vidas were ordered to be written with the colony's political interests in mind, they also offered women a narrative space for self-expression. Ibsen, *Women's Spiritual Autobiography*, 11, 13.

69 Like Mónica Díaz, I disagree with Certeau, who argues that hagiographies and biographies are completely different genres. Certeau, *Writing of History*, ch. 7 (esp. p. 277); M. Díaz, "Biografías y hagiografías," 540–41.

70 Meléndez, *Tesoros verdaderos*, 3:747. See also the request that Diego de Córdova y Salinas made to Juan de Tuesta to write a brief account of his confessee, Isabel de Cano. Córdova y Salinas, *Crónica franciscana*, 955–56. On the importance of conventual chronicles in seventeenth-century Lima, see Guibovich, "Hagiografía y política."

71 Bynum, *Holy Feast*; Greenspan, "Autohagiography"; Coon, *Sacred Fictions*; Kreiner, *Social Life of Hagiography*. For works that explore the gendered nature of hagiographies, see J. Smith, "Female Sanctity"; Mayeski, "New Voices"; Ashton, *Generation of Identity*. On the gendered male-female influences in the creation of spiritual autobiographies and other texts, see Coakley, *Spiritual Power*, 7–24.

72 Brewer-García, "Negro, pero blanco"; Brewer-García, "Imagined Transformations"; Rowe, "Her Face Turned White."

73 Ibsen, *Women's Spiritual Autobiography*, vii, 16–17; Certeau, *Writing of History*, 272–73; Kleinberg, *Prophets*.

74 Greenspan, "Autohagiography"; Sikorska, "Between Autohagiography and Confession," 87. For an important discussion of what constituted heroic virtues, see Myers, *Neither Saints nor Sinners*, 3–19.

75 For instance, Mariana Clavijo reported to the Inquisition that in Potosí women found out who knew a lot about cures and spells by word of mouth. Mariana Clavijo, deposition, Lima, 1597, AHNM, Inquisición, Lima, Leg. 1028, 508r.

76 Van Deusen, introduction to *Souls of Purgatory*, 40–44; Ibsen, *Women's Spiritual Autobiography*, 14–15.

77 See the short but useful essays about the importance of Teresa de Ávila in Weber, *Teaching Teresa of Ávila*.

78 Slade, *Saint Teresa of Avila*; Ibsen, *Women's Spiritual Autobiography*. Just as Teresa de Ávila's written works influenced women for centuries to come, works written by men about Rosa de Lima also influenced how other women scripted themselves. The vida of Mariana de Jesús (1618–45; she was beatified in 1850 and canonized in 1950) directly invoked Rosa de Lima. R. Morgan, "'Just Like Rosa.'"

79 Cussen, *Black Saint*, 138–39.

80 The term *rescripting* comes from Myers, *Neither Saints nor Sinners*, viii–ix.

81 Giles, *Women in the Inquisition*; Ahlgren, introduction to *Inquisition of Francisca*; Vollendorf, *Lives of Women*, 1–8; Jaffary, *False Mystics*, 5.

82 Schlau, *Gendered Crime and Punishment*, 15–18.

83 Schlau, *Gendered Crime and Punishment*, 15–18.

84 For an exploration of how different kinds of texts make up the autobiographical genre as expressed by distinct South Asian women, see Malhotra and Lambert-Hurley, *Speaking of the Self*, 4–7. See also van Deusen, "In So Celestial a Language."

85 Chartier, "Texts, Forms and Interpretations," 81.

86 White, "Value of Narrativity."

87 Cosslett, Lury, and Summerfield, *Feminism and Autobiography*.

88 Sidonie Smith and Julie Watson, *Reading Autobiography: A Guide for Interpretation of Life Narratives*.

89 Cosslett, introduction to *Feminism and Autobiography*.

90 Certeau, *Heterologies*, 81–83, 90.

91 Bynum, "Perspectives, Connections and Objects."

92 Often, as medievalist Claire Sponsler argues, when we consider artifacts, they become the "focal point of study rather than the 'process' of cultural creation and transmission." Her method, which has influenced the approach I take in this book, is to "find a way of accessing the shifting processes of appropriation that produced those results now apparently fixed in ink or paint or stone" (or paper). Sponsler, "In Transit," 19, 21.

93 Kopytoff, "Cultural Biography of Things," 67–68.

94 Bynum, *Christian Materiality*, 18.

95 Bynum, *Christian Materiality*, 30.

96 Mulder-Bakker, "Metamorphosis of Woman," 117. My methodology has been influenced by what Teresa de Lauretis calls "the epistemological priority which feminism has located in the personal, the subjective, the body, the symptomatic, the quotidian, as the very site of material inscription of the ideological; that is to say, the ground where socio-political determinations take hold and are real-ized." Lauretis, "Feminist Studies/Critical Studies," 11–12.

97 Whitehead, *Religious Statues and Personhood*, 5.

98 Saint Catherine is Santa Catalina in Spanish.

99 Woolf described a woman referring to her mother as a repository of memory in *A Room of One's Own* (101).

100 Bynum, "Why All the Fuss?"

101 For studies of Luisa Melgarejo, see Glave, *De Rosa y espinas*, 209–20; Iwasaki Cauti, "Luisa Melgarejo de Soto."

102 Bynum, *Christian Materiality*, 132.

103 Stanton, "Autogynography," 140.

104 Mary Mason points out that the relationship to divine beings was central to the self-conceptualizations of mystics. Mason, "Other Voice," 207–34.

105 Ursula de Jesús, *Souls of Purgatory*, 56.

106 Verboven, Carlier, and Dumolyn, "Art of Prosopography." Prosopography was and continues to be a useful method in classical studies, but Lawrence Stone's seminal essay "Prosopography" (1971) also popularized its usage for the early modern period.

107 S. Smith, *Poetics of Women's Autobiography*, 48.

108 Friedman, "Women's Autobiographical Selves."

109 See, for example, the edited volume by Daniella Kostroun and Lisa Vollendorf, *Women, Religion, and the Atlantic World (1600–1800)*.

CHAPTER 1: ROSA DE LIMA AND THE IMITATIO MORUM

1 Hansen, *Vida admirable, y muerte preciosa*. In works of art, hagiographies, and sermons, saintly individuals were sometimes placed in bucolic settings, considered to be places where one could easily sense the presence of God. Gardens were also symbols of the interior garden of one's own soul; see Mujica Pinilla, "El ancla," 69–71. The painting *Los árboles se inclinan ante Santa Rosa* (eighteenth century) was the eighth in a series. The artist, Laureano Dávila, was a painter of the Quito school. The painting is currently located in the Monasterio de Santa Rosa in Santiago, Chile, and is reproduced in Ramón Mujica Pinilla's "El ancla de Rosa de Lima." Juan de Lorenzana, one of Rosa's confessors, described how Rosa told him about her communications with the trees. Fray Juan de Lorenzana, O.P., testimony, 19 January 1618, transcribed in Jiménez Salas, *Proceso*, [259r], 337.

2 The legend on the above-cited painting says, "Sabiendo una matrona que Rosa convidava alas plantas, y arboles, a halabar de Dios, movida de curiosidad le pidio a Rosa, le entrase en su jardin, y al punto que entraron vio, q[ue] arboles y plantas se movian e inclinavan al suelo, en señal de reverencia de la qual, quedo muy admirada."

3 The building resembles a tower: could this be an allusion to Teresa de Ávila's inner castle? Or might it reference the Virgin as the tower from the Song of Songs—especially as the Virgin herself is a "garden enclosed"? On symbolic representations of the Immaculate Conception in art, see Stratton, *Immaculate Conception in Art*. I would like to thank Tanya Tiffany for this observation and reference.

4 Fray Pedro de Loayza, testimony, 19 January 1618, in Jiménez Salas, *Proceso*, [223r], 296–97; Fray Juan de Lorenzana, testimony, 29 January 1618, in Jiménez Salas, *Proceso*, [258v], 337. Celia Cussen says the cell's dimensions were about five feet by three feet. Cussen, "House of Miracles," 12.

5 Mulder-Bakker, "Metamorphosis of Woman," 117.

6 Mulder-Bakker, "Metamorphosis of Woman," 118.

7 Mulder-Bakker, "Metamorphosis of Woman," 117.

8 There are dozens of scholarly works about Rosa. A few important ones include Mujica Pinilla, *Rosa limensis*; chapter 1, "Redeemer of America: Rosa de Lima (1586–1617)—The Dynamics of Identity and Canonization," in Myers, *Neither*

Saints nor Sinners; Graziano, *Wounds of Love*; Hampe Martínez, *Santidad e identidad criolla*; and Millones, *Una partecita del cielo*.

9 Clerics emphasized how she helped convert many "lost and scandalous women." She also inspired the daughters of the wealthy, including the fifteen-year-old Lorenza de Eguia Otazu, whose severe mortification practices led to her death in 1618. Meléndez, *Tesoros verdaderos*, 2:508–9, 3:795–800.

10 Coakley, *Spiritual Power*, 175–76.

11 Fawtier and Canet, *Catherine Benincasa*, 68–69. On the distinctions between formal and informal vows, and cloistered and uncloistered communities, during Catherine of Siena's lifetime, see Luongo, *Saintly Politics*, 37–38.

12 Muessig, introduction to *Companion to Catherine of Siena*, 4. In chapter 4 of *The Saintly Politics of Catherine of Siena*, F. Thomas Luongo discusses some of the laymen who were her patrons.

13 Hansen, *Vida admirable de Santa Rosa*, 198.

14 See, for example, Fray Pedro de Loayza, testimony, in Jiménez Salas, *Proceso*, [215r], 286.

15 Bynum, *Christian Materiality*, 18.

16 Whitehead, *Religious Statues and Personhood*, 1–5.

17 Graziano, *Wounds of Love*, 61–62, 64–65; Mujica Pinilla, *Rosa limensis*, 90–91; Hampe Martínez, *Santidad e identidad criolla*; Jouve Martín, "En olor de santidad." The women who were placed on trial will be discussed further in chapter 2.

18 Catalina de Santa María, testimony, 7 February 1618, in Jiménez Salas, *Proceso*, [270v], 349.

19 Catalina de Santa María, testimony, 7 February 1618, in Jiménez Salas, *Proceso*, [270r], 348.

20 Fray Juan de Lorenzana, testimony, 29 January 1618, in Jiménez Salas, *Proceso*, [254r], 332.

21 Whitehead, *Religious Statues and Personhood*, 5 ("statue-persons").

22 Juan de Lorenzana, testimony, 29 January 1618, in Jiménez Salas, *Proceso*, [253r, 258r–v], 331, 336–37.

23 Pérez de Valdivia, *Aviso de gente recogida*, ch. 7; on his post-Tridentine recommendations for formalizing the process of taking vows as beatas, see pt. 3, chs. 1–2, and accompanying documents. On the emphasis on *recogimiento* as a moral virtue for women, see van Deusen, *Between the Sacred*, 1–15.

24 Gonzalo de la Maza, testimony, 16 September 1617, in Jiménez Salas, *Proceso*, [25v], 48; Vargas Ugarte, *Vida de Santa Rosa*. Luongo says that Catherine of Siena established her hermitage near where other female hermits lived. These women were well known to the inhabitants of Siena, who supported them with alms. Luongo, *Saintly Politics*, 28.

25 Nelson, "Epistemological Communities," 141–43; Simerka, "Feminist Epistemology."

26 Medieval Italian beatas, including Catherine of Siena, were public figures who experienced tensions with their confessors, who found it necessary to defend their public activities to higher ecclesiastical authorities; see Coakley, *Spiritual Power*,

175–77. On the need for beatas to mortify the flesh to defeat the enemy, see Pérez de Valdivia, *Aviso de gente recogida*, título (title) 7, chs. 1–2.

27 Luisa de Santa María, testimony, 4 December 1617, in Jiménez Salas, *Proceso*, [144v], 194. Luisa de Santa María also testified at the hearings in 1630–32.

28 Other testimonies are also framed in this way. I do not mean to imply that Rosa's modesty was feigned or disingenuous; she had once requested to God that her mortification practices not be seen by anyone. Mujica Pinilla, "El ancla," 64.

29 Meléndez, *Tesoros verdaderos*, 3:755.

30 Eakin, "Relational Selves, Relational Lives," 63.

31 Coakley, *Spiritual Power*, ch. 9.

32 Ricoeur, "World of the Text," 3:158.

33 As Bruno Latour argues, an object like a key can be an "active being" in the process of meaning making. Latour, "Berlin Key," 19.

34 Schneider, "Cloth and Clothing," 204.

35 Hughes, "Distinguishing Signs."

36 Estenssoro Fuchs, "Construcción de un *más allá*."

37 Around 1612 the thirty-four-year-old Luisa Melgarejo met Rosa at the home of María de Uzástegui, a mutual acquaintance. Melgarejo, Uzástegui, and Uzástegui's husband, Gonzalo de la Maza, maintained an exceptionally close relationship. Hansen, *Vida admirable de Santa Rosa*, 177; Vargas Ugarte, *Vida de Santa Rosa*, 39, 69.

38 Lucía de la Santíssima Trinidad, abadesa perpetua y fundadora de Santa Catalina (perpetual abbess and foundress of Santa Catalina), testimony, 2 April 1631, AAL, Beatificaciones, "Proceso de beatificación de Rosa de Santa María" (henceforth "Proceso de beatificación"), 220v–228r.

39 Luisa de Santa María (b. 1586) was the daughter of Juan Daza de Oliva and Juana de Valencia. She was thirty-one years old when she met Rosa through Pedro de Loazya, a confessor whom they shared. Luisa eventually became a nun in the Monasterio de Santa Catalina and in 1631 reported being a novice there. Luisa de Santa María, novicia del convento de Santa Catalina (novice in the convent of Santa Catalina), testimony, "Proceso de beatificación," 206v–215r.

40 Doña María de Bustamante, a nun in the Trinitarian convent, testimony, 5 September 1631, "Proceso de beatificación," 311–319v.

41 Doña María de Bustamante," a nun in the Trinitarian convent, testimony, 5 September 1631, "Proceso de beatificación," quote on 312r–v.

42 Catalina de Jesús, testimony, 6 September 1631, "Proceso de beatificación," "vanities of the world" quote on 320v. See her earlier testimony, Catalina de Jesús, a Trinitarian nun, testimony, 20 February 1618, in Jiménez Salas, *Proceso*, [309r–312r], 392–97. In 1618 Catalina said she had known Rosa for eight years, from the time she was twelve years old.

43 Doña Luisa Hurtado de Bustamante, testimony, 22 November 1631. "Proceso de beatificación," 543r–554v. Doña Luisa Hurtado de Bustamante, the thirty-year-old widow of the second lieutenant Bartolomé Alonso de Umbria, was the sister of doña Francisca Hurtado de Bustamante. Both had known Rosa from their

teenage years. Luisa reported that another sister, Joana de Jesús (544r), was a Franciscan beata and had developed a close friendship with Rosa and stayed with her in her cell.

44 Rosa's hermanas included Luisa de Santa María; Catalina, Lucía, Francisca, and Felipa de Montoya, all of whom, except Felipa (who later married), became nuns in the Monasterio de Santa Catalina; Bartola (Barbara?) López and Ana de los Reyes, daughters of Andrés López, the servant or squire (*escudero*) of Gonzalo de la Maza; María de Jesús, daughter of Simón de Sosa and María Flores; Leonor de Vitoria, a widow; and María Antonia, the widow of Juan Carrillo. Meléndez, *Tesoros verdaderos*, 2:401 (on the Montoya sisters); Vargas Ugarte, *Vida de Santa Rosa*, 77–78. Rubén Vargas Ugarte says that Catalina and Francisca entered the Monasterio de Santa Catalina when it was founded in 1624. Vargas Ugarte, *Vida de Santa Rosa*, 67.

45 Vargas Ugarte, *Vida de Santa Rosa*, 76–77.

46 Iwasaki Cauti, "Mujeres al borde," 606. On the slave girl Úrsula de Jesús observing Luisa Melgarejo and the women who surrounded Rosa, see Ursula de Jesús, *Souls of Purgatory*, 14–15.

47 Mariana de Oliva, testimony, 23 February 1618, in Jiménez Salas, *Proceso*, [316r–322r], 402–8.

48 Isabel Mejía, testimony, 1 March 1618, in Jiménez Salas, *Proceso*, [326r], 413. Intimate contact with servants, both young and old, fostered contacts with other women; for instance, the servant Mariana introduced Santa Rosa to a famous pious *cacica* (female indigenous governor), Catalina Huanca. Mujica Pinilla, "El ancla," 195; on the servant Mariana, see Vargas Ugarte, *Vida de Santa Rosa*, 57–58.

49 Gonzalo de la Maza was a Spanish hidalgo from Burgos, Spain; he was a member of the Order of the Caballero de Santiago and served as the Contador Mayor de la Tribunal de la Cruzada in Lima.

50 Vargas Ugarte, *Vida de Santa Rosa*, 39, 69.

51 Córdova y Salinas, *Crónica franciscana*, quote on 958.

52 See *Aparación del niño mientras Santa Rosa bordaba*, anonymous eighteenth-century painting, currently located in the Casa Lorca, Chosica, Lima, reproduced in Mujica Pinilla, "El ancla," 152; *Aparición del niño mientras la Santa bordaba*, anonymous Cuzqueño, eighteenth century, in José Flores Araoz, "Iconografía de Santa Rosa," 236; *Santa Rosa de Lima con el niño, bordando*, anonymous, eighteenth century, in José Flores Araoz, "Iconografía de Santa Rosa," 269. Juan de Lorenzana testified that the Christ child appeared to her several times while Santa Rosa did her embroidery. Juan de Lorenzana, testimony, 29 January 1618, in Jiménez Salas, *Proceso*, [253r–v], 331–32.

53 Luisa de Santa María, testimony, 4 December 1617, in Jiménez Salas, *Proceso*, [144v], 194.

54 Córdova y Salinas, *Crónica franciscana*, 954–55. The full biography is on pages 954–58.

55 On Isabel de Cano's activities as a sacristan, see Córdova y Salinas, *Crónica franciscana*, 955; on sewing mattresses and linens, 951, 956; on caring for the infirm in hospitals, 957.

56 The beata Catalina de Santa María reported staying with Rosa in her cell to help with the work that needed to be done to complete the floral arrangements for the "monument." Catalina de Santa María, testimony, 7 February 1618, in Jiménez Salas, *Proceso*, [270v], 349.

57 Meléndez, *Tesoros verdaderos*, 2:214.

58 Meléndez, *Tesoros verdaderos*, 2:214.

59 Doña Francisca Hurtado de Bustamante, wife of Gerónimo de Villalobos, 32 years old, testimony, 24 November 1631, "Proceso de beatificación," 555–563v; the phrase "pláticas eran celestiales" is found on f. 561r. Only later did writers recalibrate women's testimonies to fit the flowery baroque language of the time. See, for example, Hansen, *Vida admirable, y muerte preciosa*, 44–45.

60 Fray Pedro de Loayza, O.P., testimony, 19 January 1618, in Jiménez Salas, *Proceso*, [214r–v], 285. Catherine of Siena's biographer, Raymond of Capua, emphasized that even when Catherine was in others' company, she was there in body "but in soul she was totally present to her Spouse" and retreated to her cell whenever possible. Raymond of Capua, *Catherine of Siena*, pt. 2, ch. 1, no. 124, p. 119.

61 María de Uzástegui, testimony, 9 October 1617, in Jiménez Salas, *Proceso*, [79r], 111.

62 Luisa de Santa María, testimony, 4 December 1617, in Jiménez Salas, *Proceso*, [145v], 195.

63 C. Classen, *Deepest Sense*, 31.

64 Meléndez, *Tesoros verdaderos*, 3:796.

65 Hallett, *Senses in Religious Communities*, 98.

66 Schneider, "Cloth and Clothing," 204.

67 Van Whye, "Monastic Habit."

68 Agamben, *De la très haute pauvreté*, 25–26.

69 For example, see Roullet, "Le soin du vêtement"; Hallett, *Senses in Religious Communities*, 97–99. For eighteen years, the foundress of the Monasterio de Santa Catalina, Lucía de la Santíssima Trinidad, wore an interior tunic made of camel hair. Espinoza Ríos, "Finanzas del fervor," 45.

70 Meléndez, *Tesoros verdaderos*, 2:192.

71 Paresys, "Paraître et se vêtir," 25–26; Laspéras, "Quand l'habit"; Agamben, *De la très haute pauvreté*, 27–28, 30–31.

72 Agamben, *De la très haute pauvreté*, 28.

73 Córdova y Salinas, *Crónica franciscana*, 949; see also his description of Magdalene conversion more generally (954) and his description of Isabel de Cano's garments (955).

74 Warr, "Materiality and Immateriality."

75 She wore the white mantle even though she took only informal vows. Vargas Ugarte, *Vida de Santa Rosa*, 54–55. Catherine of Siena, Rosa's model, also took informal, not formal vows. Luongo, *Saintly Politics*, 39–42; Lehmijoki-Gardner, "Writing Religious Rules." Before she began wearing the Dominican habit, Rosa wore brown Franciscan robes.

76 Vargas Ugarte, *Vida de Santa Rosa*, 64.

77 Catalina de Santa María, testimony, 7 February 1618, in Jiménez Salas, *Proceso*, [273r], 352.

78 Castillo, *Segunda parte de la Historia general*; Meléndez, *Tesoros verdaderos*, 2:207. Some of the beatas tried by the Inquisition between 1623 and 1625 mentioned having read Raymond of Capua's biography of Saint Catherine of Siena, which means that a copy was circulating in Lima. Luisa de Santa María testified that after having read a biography of Saint Catherine of Siena she could see that Rosa "era un retrato de la dicha Santa Catherina de Siena" (was an exact likeness [literally, portrait] of Saint Catherine of Siena). Luisa de Santa María, testimony, 4 December 1617, in Jiménez Salas, *Proceso*, [146v], 196–97.

79 Warr, *Dressing for Heaven*, 165.

80 Catalina de Santa María, testimony, 7 February 1618, in Jiménez Salas, *Proceso*, [273r], 352; Luisa de Santa María, testimony, 4 December 1617, in Jiménez Salas, *Proceso*, [147v], 198; Raymond of Capua, *Catherine of Siena*, pt. 2, ch. 3, no. 135, pp. 130–31.

81 Raymond of Capua, *Catherine of Siena*, pt. 2, ch. 3, no. 137, p. 132.

82 Rosa also used *cilicios* (mortification devices) made of a metal chain with *piquillos* (small spikes) that she wrapped around her torso and arms. María de Uzástegui, testimony, 9 October 1617, in Jiménez Salas, *Proceso*, [69v], 101.

83 Luisa de Santa María, testimony, 4 December 1617, in Jiménez Salas, *Proceso*, [145r], 195.

84 Catalina de Jesús, testimony, 20 February 1618, in Jiménez Salas, *Proceso*, [310r], 394.

85 Mouchel, *Femmes de douleur*.

86 Hallett, *Senses in Religious Communities*, 97.

87 New Testament, Romans 8:13, "For if you live according to the flesh you will die, but if by the Spirit you put to death the deeds of the body you will live."

88 Cordelia Warr makes the connection between Catherine of Siena's shunning of frippery and her complete devotion to dressing the body of Christ in a local church. Warr, *Dressing for Heaven*, 165.

89 Kasl, "Delightful Adornments," 149.

90 Bynum, *Christian Materiality*, 52–53.

91 On María de Santo Domingo's vision while praying before the statue of Santa Inés at the altar of San Gerónimo, see María de Santo Domingo, deposition, Lima, 1624, AHNM, Inquisición, Lima, Leg. 1030, 313r. Doña María de Uzástegui testified at Rosa's beatification hearing that while Rosa was praying in Uzástegui's oratory, a painting of the Savior began to sweat. Fernández Fernández, *Santa Rosa de Lima*, 88–89.

92 Meléndez, *Tesoros verdaderos*, 3:761–62.

93 Whitehead, *Religious Statues and Personhood*, 5. Luisa de Santa María knew, for instance, that the Virgin Mary would awaken Rosa while she slept. Luisa de Santa María, testimony, 4 December 1617, in Jiménez Salas, *Proceso*, [145v], 196. The mystical marriage between Christ and Rosa occurred while she was kneeling before a statue of the Virgin of Rosario. Bertolini, *Rosa peruana*, ch. 20, pp. 175–86.

94 Meléndez, *Tesoros verdaderos*, 2:373.

95 Doña María Eufemia de Pareja, testimony, 30 October 1617, in Jiménez Salas, *Proceso*, [108v], 145. (Note that María Ufemia's name also appears as María Eufemia in other sources.)

96 Christian, "Images as Beings," 75 (for the term *hypercharged*), 78.

97 Coakley, *Spiritual Power*, 177–78.

98 Raymond of Capua, *Catherine of Siena*, pt. 2, ch. 6, no. 185, pp. 178–79.

99 Doña María Eufemia de Pareja, testimony, 10 December 1630, "Proceso de beatificación," 124v–125r.

100 Doña María Eufemia de Pareja, testimony, 30 October 1617, in Jiménez Salas, *Proceso*, [109r], 145; Christian, *Local Religion*; Christian, "Images as Beings." On the fluidity between the worlds of the living and the dead, see van Deusen, introduction to *Souls of Purgatory*, 37–49.

101 Llorca, "Statues habillées"; Silvestrini, Gri, and Pagnozzato, *Donne Madonne Dee.*

102 Webster, *Art and Ritual.*

103 Webster, "Shameless Beauty," 253–54; Silvestrini, "Abiti e simulacri," 17–26; Bray, *Sacred Made Real*; Doña María Eufemia de Pareja, testimony, 10 December 1630, "Proceso de beatificación," 128r.

104 Meléndez, *Tesoros verdaderos*, 2:374.

105 Hansen, *Vida admirable, y muerte preciosa*, 55.

106 Doña María Eufemia de Pareja, testimony, 10 December 1630, "Proceso de beatificación," 128r–v.

107 Luisa de Santa María also accompanied Rosa when she went to adorn the image of Our Lady of Loreto. Luisa de Santa María, testimony, 4 December 1617, in Jiménez Salas, *Proceso*, [145r], 195.

108 The original title reads, "Memoria para el vestido, que yo Rosa de Santa María, indigna esclava de la Reyna de los Ángeles, comienço a fabricar con el favor del Señor, a la Virgen Madre de Dios." Meléndez, *Tesoros verdaderos*, 2:355–56.

109 Meléndez, *Tesoros verdaderos*, 2:355–56. Another description of how to dress a statue of the Virgin written by Rosa comes from María de Uzástegui's testimony at the beatification hearing in 1617. A scribe also copied down the contents of a paper in Uzástegui's possession that had been written by Rosa on the Day of the Circumcision in 1616. It, too, describes the prayers to be said while dressing the Virgin. María de Uzástegui, testimony, 9 October 1617, in Jiménez Salas, *Proceso*, [97r], 132.

110 Felipa de Montoya, testimony, 17 March 1618, in Jiménez Salas, *Proceso*, [385v], 473; Bertolini, *Rosa peruana*, 191–92.

111 Lorea, *Santa Rosa*, 117–18.

112 María de Uzástegui, testimony, 9 October 1617, in Jiménez Salas, *Proceso*, [75r], 107.

113 María de Uzástegui, testimony, 9 October 1617, in Jiménez Salas, *Proceso*, [75r–v], 107. Doña Jusepa de Gúzman reported the same incident. Doña Jusepa de Gúzman, testimony, 24 November 1617, in Jiménez Salas, *Proceso*, [122v], 163. Even while bedridden and in declining health, Saint Clare of Assisi, the foundress

of the second Order of Poor Clares, continued to spin linen and make corporals (small white linen cloths on which the chalice and paten were placed on the altar during Mass) to be distributed to the churches near the town. Warr, *Dressing for Heaven*, 165, 167n50.

114 María de Uzástegui, testimony, 9 October 1617, in Jiménez Salas, *Proceso*, [99r], 134.

115 Luisa de Santa María named some of the people who were present at the de la Maza home when Rosa died. They included doña Luisa Melgarejo, doña Maria de Uzástegui and her two daughters, doña Ana Lopez and her sister, other daughters of Secretary Tineo and his wife, Tineo's wife's sister, Bartola (Barbara?) López and Ana de los Reyes (daughters of Andrés López), the servant of Gonzalo de la Maza, María Flores, and María Antonia. Luisa de Santa María, testimony, 29 March 1631, "Proceso de beatificación," 209r–v; María de Uzástegui, testimony, 9 October 1617, in Jiménez Salas, *Proceso*, [99v], 134.

116 Doña María Eufemia de Pareja, testimony, 10 December 1630, "Proceso de beatificación," 125r–v.

117 María Antonia, testimony, 9 December 1617, in Jiménez Salas, *Proceso*, [162v–163], 216–17; Luisa de Santa María, testimony, 4 December 1617, in Jiménez Salas, *Proceso*, [147v], 198; María de Uzástegui, testimony, 9 October 1617, in Jiménez Salas, *Proceso*, [99v], 134–35.

118 Luisa de Santa María, testimony, 29 March 1631, "Proceso de beatificación," 208r.

119 Luisa de Santa María, testimony, 29 March 1631, "Proceso de beatificación," 208v.

120 María Antonia, testimony, 9 December 1617, in Jiménez Salas, *Proceso*, [163v], 217.

121 María Antonia, testimony, 9 December 1617, in Jiménez Salas, *Proceso*, [162r], 215. Vargas Ugarte says that María de Uzástegui and two of the beatas washed and dressed her body for its final display. Vargas Ugarte, *Vida de Santa Rosa*, 157.

122 Vargas Ugarte, *Vida de Santa Rosa*, 157.

123 Coon, *Sacred Fictions*, 55.

124 Luisa de Santa María, testimony, 4 December 1617, in Jiménez Salas, *Proceso*, [148v], 199–200; Vargas Ugarte, *Vida de Santa Rosa*, 160.

125 Luisa de Santa María, testimony, 4 December 1617, in Jiménez Salas, *Proceso*, [149v], 201.

126 Catalina de Santa María, testimony, 7 February 1618, in Jiménez Salas, *Proceso*, [274v], 353.

127 Osorio, *Inventing Lima*, 121–43; Luisa de Santa María, testimony, 29 March 1631, "Proceso de beatificación," 213r–v; on requests for contact relics, see Gonzalo de la Maza, testimony, 16 September 1617, in Jiménez Salas, *Proceso*, [62r], 93.

128 Cussen, "House of Miracles."

129 Frank Graziano analyzes how the miracle story of Rosa walking in the garden with a small child, presumably Christ, changed and was aggrandized in the telling. Graziano, *Wounds of Love*, 41.

130 For instance, Juana Margarita de Jesús, a poor woman from the provincial area of Huaura, began wearing a Dominican tertiary habit after Rosa's death. Meléndez, *Tesoros verdaderos*, 3:796–98.

131 Luisa de Santa María, testimony, 29 March 1631, "Proceso de beatificación," 214v; Cussen, "House of Miracles," 13.

132 Vargas Machuca, *Rosa de el Perú*, 10–11.

133 Gonzalo de la Maza, testimony, 16 September 1617, in Jiménez Salas, *Proceso*, [62r], 93; Cussen, "House of Miracles."

134 Cussen, "House of Miracles," 13–14, 18. Cussen argues that efforts to establish a beaterio or convent of nuns on the property as well as a shrine where all residents of Lima might receive spiritual sustenance were incompatible because authorities argued that women needed to be enclosed and it would not be appropriate to live in a public sanctuary.

135 This occurred on several occasions, including when the papal bulls announced her beatification (1668) and at the foundation of the Beaterio de Santa Rosa (1669).

136 Meléndez, *Festiva pompa*, 17r–v.

137 Meléndez, *Festiva pompa*, 30v–31r.

138 Certeau, *Practice of Everyday Life*, 20.

CHAPTER 2: READING THE BODY

1 Certeau, *Mystic Fable*, 115.

2 Jones, "Power of Images," 28.

3 C. Classen, *Worlds of Sense*, 50–53.

4 "Vida de la Venerable Gerónima de San Francisco" (hereafter cited as "Vida . . . Gerónima"), Lima, 1635, Archivo Franciscano de Lima, Registro 17, no. 38, 449r.

5 "Vida . . . Gerónima," 456r–v.

6 Myers, *Neither Saints nor Sinners*, 9, 14; Ibsen, *Women's Spiritual Autobiography*, 15.

7 On reading religious objects in Spain, see Bouza, *Communication, Knowledge, and Memory*; on Lima, see van Deusen, "Circuits of Knowledge."

8 Certeau, *Practice of Everyday Life*, 174; Chartier, *Order of Books*, 2. Also see Chartier, *Order of Books*, 3–4.

9 Chartier, "Texts, Forms and Interpretations," 81.

10 Bouza, *Communication, Knowledge, and Memory*, 11.

11 Bouza, *Communication, Knowledge, and Memory*, 12, 15.

12 For a general discussion, see Chartier, "Reading Matter," 276–78. For Spain, see Frenk, *Entre la voz*, 16–20, 25. According to Fernando Bouza, scholars have interpreted the early modern period as moving toward new forms of literacy and, in doing so, have privileged the written (read: modern) over the spoken (read: recidivist) word. Such arguments assume an artificial divide between literate and nonliterate cultures and are based on deterministic notions of progress. Bouza, *Communication, Knowledge, and Memory*, 11.

13 Luis de Granada held to this tripartite notion. See Granada, *Símbolo de la fe*, 482.

14 Granada, *Símbolo de la fe*, 457. On the humors, which combined colors and other properties and served as receptors for the eyes, see Granada, *Símbolo de la fe*, 458.

15 Park, "Organic Soul," 466–69. The spiritus also carried heat to the heart, consid-

ered in Galenic thought to be "the instrument of life and of all actions." Temkin, *Galenism*, 142. See also Granada, *Símbolo de la fe*, 431.

16 The perceptual faculties of the common sense and the imagination then ensured that the impressions of absent sense objects (as a mental likeness or similitude of the object's essence) remained impressed within the sensitive soul. Granada, *Símbolo de la fe*, 451–52; Real Academia Española (RAE), *Diccionario de autoridades*, 5:83.

17 Rudy, *Mystical Language of Sensation*, 21; Granada, *Símbolo de la fe*, 482. Spanish mystics often used the word *sentir* (or the noun form, *sentimiento*) as spiritual perception rather than feeling. RAE, *Diccionario de autoridades*, 6:84. Mystics like John of the Cross, Teresa de Ávila, and Luis de Granada based their ideas about the spiritual senses on the thinking of the medieval theologian Origen as well as their own experiences. For a discussion of the "spiritual senses," see Canêvet, "Sens Spirituel," 14:599.

18 Granada, *Símbolo de la fe*, 483–84. Nonorganic functions occurred in the intellective soul. It included the three rational powers of intellect (both passive and active), memory (of concepts, as opposed to sense images), and will. Park, "Organic Soul," 467.

19 "Sermon de la Puríssima Consepción" (hereafter cited as "Sermón"), Archivo General de la Nación (AGNP), Sección Compañía de Jesús, Sermones, Leg. 61, Sermón 1, Chuquisaca, 1617, 1r–v.

20 Bynum, "Female Body," 186; Bynum, "Why All the Fuss?"

21 Maclean, *Renaissance Notion of Woman*, 44.

22 Maclean, *Renaissance Notion of Woman*, 35, 42. See the discussion of the gendered notion of the humoral body by Doctor Juan Huarte de San Juan (1529–88) in his important treatise *Examen de ingenios* (1575), explored in Huerga, *Historia de los alumbrados*, 2:359–60; also cited in Weber, *Teresa of Avila*, 140n14.

23 Weber, *Teresa of Avila*, 37.

24 Ricoeur, "World of the Text," 3:158.

25 On Spanish hagiographies (of which over 697 exist), see Sánchez Lora, *Mujeres*, 375. On Mexico, see María de San José, *Wild Country*, 260.

26 Haliczer, *Between Exaltation and Infamy*, 29.

27 "Sermón," 2r.

28 These include the lives of Saints Lutgarde (1182–1246), Gertrude the Great (1256–ca. 1302), Bridget of Sweden (1303–73), Angela of Foligno (1248–1309), Hildegarde of Bingen (1098–1179), Liduvina (1380–1433), Catherine of Siena (1347–80), and Catherine of Genoa (1447–1510). The works of Saint Gertrude, including *Oraciones y exercicios espirituales* (1604) and *Libro intitulado insinuación de la divina piedad* (1605), were available to Lima's female mystics, as were Raymond of Capua's biography of Catherine of Siena and a biography of Angela of Foligno translated into Spanish in 1618. See Iwasaki Cauti, "Luisa Melgarejo de Soto," 221.

29 Eighty percent of those works appeared after 1600. See Haliczer, *Between Exaltation and Infamy*, 30–31; J. Díaz, "Hagiografías"; Bilinkoff, *Related Lives*, 98.

30 Ibsen, *Women's Spiritual Autobiography.*

31 Guibovich, *Censura, libros e inquisición,* 206.

32 Frenk, *Entre la voz,* 21–26; Bouza, "Contextos materiales," 310.

33 For a general discussion, see Julia, "Reading and the Counter-Reformation," 239.

34 Lohmann Villena, "Un documento más"; Guibovich, "Libros para ser vendidos"; Hampe Martínez, "Libros profanos y sagrados."

35 Guibovich, *Censura, libros e inquisición,* 189. Book censorship in Lima came in three waves: in 1601–5, 1611–15, and 1621–25.

36 Guibovich, *Censura, libros e inquisición,* 93.

37 Guibovich, *Censura, libros e inquisición,* 65.

38 Bynum, "Female Body," 186.

39 For the more radical and misogynist perspective, see Huarte de San Juan's *Examen de ingenios,* in which he wrote, "Quedando la mujer en su disposición natural, todo género de letras y sabiduría es repugnante a su ingenio" (2: 375); quoted in Huerga, *Historia de los alumbrados,* 2: 360. On female readers in the Middle Ages, see Green, *Women Readers;* Boffey, "Women Authors," 159–82. On female reading in early modern Spain and Latin America, see Cruz and Hernández, *Women's Literacy.*

40 Guibovich, *Censura, libros e inquisición,* 205.

41 Vives, *Instrucción,* 13. See also the different opinions on female religious literacy in sixteenth-century Spain in Weber, *Teresa of Avila,* 20–22, 32–33.

42 Vives, *Instrucción,* 33. For a more elaborate discussion, see also chapters 4 and 5.

43 Iwasaki Cauti, "Santos y alumbrados"; Coakley, *Spiritual Power;* Dillon, "Holy Women"; Elliott, "Alternative Intimacies."

44 Myers, *Neither Saints nor Sinners,* 14.

45 Mujica Pinilla, "El ancla," 97. See also Vargas Ugarte, *Vida de Santa Rosa,* 102; Iwasaki Cauti, "Santos y alumbrados," 545–46.

46 They were María de Santo Domingo, Isabel de Ormaza (de Jesús), Ana María Pérez, Inés de Velasco, Luisa Melgarejo de Sotomayor, and Inés de Ubitarte. By the early seventeenth century, Inquisition authorities, and particularly calificadores, could draw on clearly established guidelines to determine and evaluate the veracity of visions and revelations. Juan de Horozco y Covarrubias's work *Tratado de la verdadera y falsa prophecia* (1588) was influential in this regard. The role of the spiritual advisor was also crucial in distinguishing false from true visions. Haliczer, *Between Exaltation and Infamy,* 129–30.

47 Inés de Velasco, deposition, 19 October 1623, AHNM, Inquisición, Lima, Leg. 1647, exp. 5, 12v.

48 Sánchez Lora, *Mujeres,* 375; Eguiguren, *Universidad de San Marcos,* 2:695–722; Inés de Velasco, deposition, 19 October 1623, AHNM, Inquisición, Lima, Leg. 1647, exp. 5, 12v; Doña Ana de Miranda, estate inventory, AGNP, Protocolos, Francisco de Acuña, no. 6, 19 June 1629, 240v–241; Pareja Ortíz, *Mujer sevillana,* 199.

49 Eguiguren, *Universidad de San Marcos,* 2:695–722; Haliczer, *Between Exaltation and Infamy,* 39–40; van Deusen, "Circuits of Knowledge," 146–47.

50 Loreto López, *Conventos femeninos*, 91; Ramos Medina, *Imagen de santidad*, 132; Ibsen, *Women's Spiritual Autobiography*, 9, 10, 62.

51 Muriel, "Lo que leían"; Bilinkoff, *Related Lives*, 100. On hagiographies, see Vitz, "From the Oral," 97.

52 Gonzalo de la Maza, testimony, 16 December 1617, in Jiménez Salas, *Proceso*, [30r], 54. Frenk argues that "lee, mira, oye, [and] escucha" were synonyms or equivalents. Frenk, *Entre la voz*, 47.

53 Coleman, *Public Reading*, 35.

54 Frenk, *Entre la voz*, 15–16; C. Classen, *Worlds of Sense*, 50; K. Zieman, "Reading, Singing and Understanding"; Hallett, *Senses in Religious Communities*, 69–85; Corbellini, *Cultures of Religious Reading*; Krug, *Reading Families*.

55 Evidence does not show a "progressive elimination, or marginalization, of orality in hagiography" in seventeenth-century Lima, as Evelyn Birge Vitz found for medieval Europe. Vitz, "From the Oral," 113. On the interactive relationship (in presentation, reception, and interpretation) between the reader and the audience, see Frenk, *Entre la voz*, 15–16; Green, *Women Readers*, 164.

56 Leonard, *Books of the Brave*, 268. For a detailed discussion of the various editions of the *Flos Sanctorum*, see Haliczer, *Between Exaltation and Infamy*, 29–32.

57 Coleman, *Public Reading*, 139.

58 Frenk, *Entre la voz*, 10; Camille, "Seeing and Reading."

59 Coleman, *Public Reading*, 2.

60 Vitz, "From the Oral," 113.

61 Inés de Velasco, deposition, 1623, AHNM, Inquisición, Lima, Leg. 1030, 257r; my emphasis.

62 Iwasaki Cauti, "Luisa Melgarejo de Soto," 221; Luisa Melgarejo, deposition, 1623, AHNM, Inquisición, Lima, Leg. 1647, exp. 5, 12v; Inés de Ubitarte, deposition, 8 August 1629, AHNM, Inquisición, Lima, Leg. 1030, 396v-397; Inés de Velasco, deposition, 1623, AHNM, Inquisición, Lima, Leg. 1030, 257v; Ibsen, *Women's Spiritual Autobiography*, 64.

63 Vives, *Instrucción*, 30.

64 Gerli, "*Castillo Interior.*" On the classic and medieval monastic practices of the craft of memory (as both storage and recollection), see Carruthers and Ziolkowski, "General Introduction," *Medieval Craft of Memory*, 1–31; Yates, *Art of Memory*.

65 Vives, *Instrucción*, 25.

66 Solterer, "Seeing, Hearing, Tasting Woman"; Kieckhefer, "Holiness."

67 Teresa de Ávila was particularly indebted to the works of Pedro de Alcántara and to Alonso de Madrid's *El arte para a servir a Dios* (Alcalá de Henares, 1526; Toledo, 1571); see Teresa de Ávila, *The Interior Castle*, ch. 4, pt. 3. See also Granada, *Obras completas*, vol. 1, *Libro de la oración*, chs. 4 and 5.

68 "Vida . . . Gerónima," 449v.

69 Luis de Granada and Ignatius de Loyola talked about the praxis of using the five senses of the interior imagination to render Christ present in one's life and in one's body. See also Teresa de Ávila, *Libro de la vida*, ch. 9.

70 For instance, Inés de Ubitarte, who confessed in 1629 that her arrobamientos had been feigned, claimed that the books of Saints Teresa, Catherine of Siena, Lutgarde, and Luis de Granada had influenced her. Inés de Ubitarte, deposition, 8 August 1629, Lima, AHNM, Inquisición, Lima, Leg. 1030, 396r–v; Iwasaki Cauti, "Santos y alumbrados," 564.

71 Solterer, "Seeing, Hearing, Tasting Woman," 142.

72 Teresa de Ávila, *Libro de la vida*, ch. 10. Teresa adapted the term *sentimiento* as a trope to discuss the reception of spiritual "matter" by the soul.

73 Teresa's *Libro de la vida*, ch. 4, no. 9, quoted in Ahlgren, *Teresa of Ávila*, 39.

74 Teresa de Ávila, *Libro de la vida*, ch. 26, no. 5, quoted in Myers, *Neither Saints nor Sinners*, 14, 210n22; Ahlgren, *Teresa of Ávila*, 40.

75 Ahlgren, *Teresa of Ávila*, 40.

76 Ursula de Jesús, *Souls of Purgatory*, 130; Teresa de Ávila, *Libro de la vida*, ch. 26, no. 5.

77 "Sermón," 3r.

78 Simons, "Reading a Saint's Body," 13.

79 Macola, "El 'no sé que,'" 36.

80 Ahlgren, *Teresa of Ávila*, 376; Kieckhefer, "Holiness"; Bynum, "'. . . And Woman His Humanity'"; Camille, "Image and the Self," 79.

81 Ahlgren, *Teresa of Ávila*, 106. On the practices and physiognomy of spiritual ecstasy, see Elliott, "Raptus/Rapture"; Dailey, "Body and Its Senses"; Elliott, "Physiology of Rapture"; Newman, "What Did It Mean"; Bynum, "Female Body"; Hollywood, *Sensible Ecstasy*.

82 In a certain sense, the soul "robs" (*roba*) the body of the use of its senses. RAE, *Diccionario de autoridades*, 1:416; Teresa de Ávila, *Camino de perfección*, in *Obras completas*, ch. 32.

83 Teresa de Ávila, *Libro de la vida*, ch. 20. The English translation comes from Cohen, *Life of Saint Teresa*, ch. 20. See also RAE, *Diccionario de autoridades*, 1:416.

84 Doctor Juan Huarte de San Juan (1529–88) wrote an important treatise, *Examen de ingenios* (1575), which explained the humoral reasons for the loss of the senses during ecstasy. Quoted in Huerga, *Historia de los alumbrados*, 361.

85 The English translation comes from Teresa de Ávila, *Interior Castle*, 101; my emphasis.

86 Teresa de Ávila, *Moradas*, ch. 3.

87 Ahlgren, *Entering Teresa of Avila's "Interior Castle,"* 86; Teresa de Ávila, *Moradas*, ch. 3.

88 Teresa de Ávila, *Libro de la vida*, ch. 27; Howells, *John of the Cross*, 110, 187n 90; Ahlgren, *Teresa of Avila's "Interior Castle,"* 79–109. Scholar Edward Howells explains that in the intellective soul, "the spiritual parallel of [ordinary] sensory perception occurs. In an analogous manner to the phantasms that pass from the ordinary senses to the interior of the soul, the soul receives 'purely spiritual apprehensions,' which in their 'substantial' form are already in the form of God through an immediate 'touch' with God's substance; they bring the soul into 'substantial

contact' with God, thus transforming the soul interiorly and finally achieving union." Howells, *John of the Cross*, 13. The phantasmata were new images created "with no counterpart in reality." Park, "Organic Soul," 471.

89 Inés de Velacso, deposition, 19 October 1623, AHNM, Inquisición, Lima, Leg. 1647, exp. 5, 10r; Doña Elvira de la Serna, deposition, 1623, AHNM, Inquisición, Lima, Leg. 1030, 249v.

90 Inés de Velasco, deposition, 19 October 1623, AHNM, Inquisición, Lima, Leg. 1647, exp. 5, 11v. On Melgarejo's mystical practices, see Schlau, "Flying in Formation."

91 Córdova y Salinas, *Crónica franciscana*, 970. He commented that the same would occur when he spoke with Isabel Porras Marmolejo (943).

92 Fernández Fernández, *Mujer*, 388; Córdova y Salinas, *Crónica franciscana*, 914.

93 Alison Weber includes a passage from Diego Pérez de Valdivia's *Aviso de gente recogida* (1585) describing the different physical effects of arrobamiento. Weber, "Between Ecstasy and Exorcism," 228.

94 Córdova y Salinas, *Crónica franciscana*, 947.

95 Weber, "Between Ecstasy and Exorcism," 222; Luisa de Santa María, deposition, 1622, AHNM, Inquisición, Lima, Leg. 1030, 325v.

96 Gonzalo de la Maza, testimony, 16 September 1617, in Jiménez Salas, *Proceso*, [33v], 58; Córdova y Salinas, *Crónica franciscana*, 865.

97 Inés de Velasco, deposition, 19 October 1623, AHNM, Inquisición, Lima, Leg. 1647, exp. 5, 10v, 20v; Doña Ana Gutíerrez, deposition, 1623, AHNM, Inquisición, Lima, Leg. 1030, 310v; Simons, "Reading a Saint's Body," 16.

98 Bynum, "Female Body"; Simons, "Reading a Saint's Body," 12–15; Butler, *Gender Trouble*, 140–41.

99 Córdova y Salinas, *Crónica franciscana*, 943.

100 Catalina de Santa María, testimony, 7 February 1618, in Jiménez Salas, *Proceso*, [271v], 350. See also Francisca de Montoya, testimony, 20 March 1618, in Jiménez Salas, *Proceso*, [380r], 478.

101 As Luis de Granada explained, fire was the purest of the four elements. Granada, *Símbolo de la fe*, 443. RAE, *Diccionario de autoridades*, 4:420.

102 "Vida y virtudes de la Venerable Isabel de Porras Marmolejo," AAL, Beatificaciones, Isabel de Porras Marmolejo, 1633, 2r–v (hereafter cited as "Vida y virtudes . . . Isabel de Porras Marmolejo").

103 María de los Angeles and Juana de Cea, testimonies, June 1633, "Vida y virtudes . . . Isabel de Porras Marmolejo," 45r, 47v–48v; Juana del Casar, testimony, 23 June 1633, "Vida y virtudes . . . Isabel de Porras Marmolejo," 51v; Doña Juana de la Cruz, testimony, 25 June 1633, "Vida y virtudes . . . Isabel de Porras Marmolejo," 57r; Doña Mariana de Molina, testimony, 26 June 1633, "Vida y virtudes . . . Isabel de Porras Marmolejo," 58v.

104 "Vida y virtudes . . . Isabel de Porras Marmolejo," 47v.

105 Certeau, *Practice of Everyday Life*, 81.

106 María de los Angeles and Juana de Cea, testimonies, 1633, "Vida y virtudes . . . Isabel de Porras Marmolejo," 45r, 48v.

107 Córdova y Salinas, *Crónica franciscana*, 944, 946. See also the testimony of friar Luis de Vera, Mercedarian, who stated that authorities made an impression (estampa) of her wound. Luis de Vera, testimony, 14 October 1633, "Vida y virtudes . . . Isabel de Porras Marmolejo," 30r.

108 Bouza, *Communication, Knowledge, and Memory*, 8, 23.

109 Córdova y Salinas, *Crónica franciscana*, 931.

110 For instance, the Franciscan Juan de la Cerda approved of doncellas reading but did not think they should learn to write because they might employ these skills to no good ends. Cerda, *Libro*, 12v.

111 Ahlgren, *Teresa of Avila*, 41–42. Teresa's confessor censored several versions of her *Vida*.

112 This idea comes from R. Menéndez Pidal, who is quoted in Torres-Alcalá, "Santa Teresa," 223. See also Certeau, *Practice of Everyday Life*, 141–42.

113 Certeau, *Practice of Everyday Life*, 188, 193.

114 Certeau, *Practice of Everyday Life*, 192; Frenk, *Entre la voz*, 13–14.

115 Mujica Pinilla, *Rosa limensis*, 172; Myers, *Neither Saints nor Sinners*, 7.

116 "Proposiciones, no. 4, De los raptos y su duración," AHNM, Inquisición, Lima, Leg. 1647, exp. 5, 6v.

117 Inés de Velasco, deposition, 1623, AHNM, Inquisición, Lima, Leg. 1030, 256v; Inés de Velasco, deposition, 19 October 1623, AHNM, Inquisición, Lima, Leg. 1647, exp. 5, 13r.

118 Vargas Ugarte, *Vida de Santa Rosa*, 41–42, quoted in Iwasaki Cauti, "Santos y alumbrados," 543.

119 Guibovich, *Censura, libros e inquisición*, 320; Mujica Pinilla, *Rosa limensis*, 78.

120 Inés de Velasco, deposition, 21 October 1623, AHNM, Inquisición, Lima, Leg. 1647, exp. 5, 12v.

121 Inés de Ubitarte, deposition, 8 August 1629, AHNM, Inquisición, Lima, Leg. 1030, 394v–406v; Guibovich, *Censura, libros e inquisición*, 179.

122 Fray Francisco de Madrid, deposition, 1623, AHNM, Inquisición, Lima, Leg. 1030, 247r. Madrid's testimony against Inés de Velasco was based, in part, on what he had read in her writings.

123 Inés de Velasco, deposition, 19 October 1623, AHNM, Inquisición, Lima, Leg. 1647, exp. 5, 13r; Inés de Hinojosa, deposition, 6 September 1623, AHNM, Inquisición, Lima, Leg. 1647, exp. 5, 16r.

124 "Calificación de unos papeles atribuídos ala Vicaria del Convento de las Descalças Reales," AHNM, Inquisición, Censuras, Leg. 4467, no. 11, 1624, n.p.

125 Bouza, *Communication, Knowledge, and Memory*, 52–53.

126 Chartier, foreword to *Communication, Knowledge, and Memory*, xiii.

127 Frenk, *Entre la voz*, 13.

128 Bouza, *Communication, Knowledge, and Memory*, 33, 36.

129 Teresa de Ávila, *Libro de la vida*, ch. 18; Haliczer, *Between Exaltation and Infamy*, 46; Ahlgren, *Entering Teresa of Avila's "Interior Castle,"* 38. Antonio Torres-Alcalá says that writing these experiences required a new "logic" because existing rules were insufficient. Torres-Alcalá, "Santa Teresa," 224.

130 Rudy, *Mystical Language of Sensation*, 6.

131 Teresa de Ávila, *Libro de la vida*, ch. 12; *The Interior Castle,* fourth mansion, ch. 2; Ziomek, "Percepciones sensoriales," 72. On mystical language and tropes (giving words new meanings), see Certeau, *Practice of Everyday Life*, 142–43. As Teresa de Ávila explained, at this level the self composed of flesh, mind, and spirit or soul is indistinguishable from God but still separate enough to read the experiences. Teresa de Ávila, *Libro de la vida*, ch. 18.

132 Juan del Castillo, testimony, 5 September 1617, in Jiménez Salas, *Proceso*, [14v], 34.

133 The medieval scholar Gordon Rudy makes the excellent point that it is difficult to separate language from experience because experience is a priori to language. Rudy, *Mystical Language of Sensation*, 10. The point here is not to debate which precedes the other but merely to explain how language informs mystical experience and the process by which experience is rendered into a sensorial language to be read by others.

134 Juan del Castillo, testimony, 5 September 1617, in Jiménez Salas, *Proceso*, [12r], 31; Mujica Pinilla, "El ancla," 92.

135 "Proposiciones, no. 4, De los raptos y su duración," AHNM, Inquisición, Lima, Leg. 1647, exp. 5, 5r.

136 "Proposiciones, no. 4, De los raptos y su duración," AHNM, Inquisición, Lima, Leg. 1647, exp. 5, 5r.

137 Teresa de Ávila, *Libro de la vida*, ch. 27.

138 Teresa de Ávila does claim, however, that the other senses are not suspended or put to sleep; they remain active, "which is not always the case in contemplation." *Vida*, ch. 27.

139 Teresa de Ávila, *Libro de la vida*, 27:2, 6, 8; Howells, *John of the Cross*, 175, n. 28.

140 Juan del Castillo, testimony, 5 September 1617, in Jiménez Salas, *Proceso*, [15r], 35.

141 Getino, *Santa Rosa de Lima*, 104; Mujica Pinilla, "El ancla," 97.

142 Mujica Pinilla, "El ancla," 102; Getino, *Santa Rosa de Lima*, 80.

143 Mujica Pinilla, "El ancla," 97–98.

144 Getino, *Santa Rosa de Lima*, 87.

145 Getino, *Santa Rosa de Lima*, 82, 127. The images Rosa drew, combining language and image, were considered a source of transmittable knowledge of the divine. Bouza, *Communication, Knowledge, and Memory*, 24.

146 Juan Costilla de Benavides, testimony, 1 March 1618, in Jiménez Salas, *Proceso*, [333v–334r], 423.

147 The visions of María Antonia, who also became "absorbed and in ecstasy" for about half an hour, were also recorded. Juan Costilla de Benavides, testimony, 1 March 1618, in Jiménez Salas, *Proceso*, [334v] 423; Bouza, *Communication, Knowledge, and Memory*, 37.

148 Gonzalo de la Maza, testimony, 16 September 1617, in Jiménez Salas, *Proceso*, [54v] 82.

149 Macola, "El 'no sé que,'" 42.

150 Certeau, *Practice of Everyday Life*, 190.

1 "Relación de doña Ángela Carranza, alias la Madre Ángela de Dios, 24/V/1696" (hereafter cited as "Relación"), AHNM, Inquisición, Lima, Leg. 1032, Libro 6, 345r; Hoyo, *Relacion completa*, 21r.

2 "Relación," 352r. Some sources claim that Ángela was born in 1634 or 1641. Historian Ana Sánchez claims she was thirty years old when she arrived in Lima. Sánchez, "Ángela Carranza," 279. Vargas Ugarte says she was nearly fifty. Vargas Ugarte, *Historia de la iglesia*, 3:317.

3 "Relación," 354r.

4 "Relación," 348v; Hoyo, *Relacion completa*, 37r–v.

5 "Relación," 336r; Hoyo, *Relacion completa*, 34r.

6 "Relación," 348r–v.

7 "Relación," 338r; Hoyo, *Relacion completa*, 17r–v, 27r.

8 "Relación," 314v–318v.

9 Like Claire Sponsler, I consider appropriation to be a *process*, not an end result. Sponsler, "In Transit," 19, 21.

10 "Relación," 361v.

11 Hoyo, *Relacion completa*, 32v.

12 Ángulo, "El Dr. Ignacio Híjar y Mendoza," 206.

13 "Relación," 349r.

14 Ángela's Augustinian confessors were eager to claim their own saint, and some scholars have argued that Inquisition authorities used Ángela as a scapegoat to punish them. Sánchez, "Ángela Carranza."

15 In notebook 275 she wrote that Friar Fernando Valdes, a Dominican, had warned her not to call herself the mother of priests. Gregorio Quesada y Sotomayor, "Dictamenes varios sobre diversos causas, de la mayor importancia que dio al santo tribunal de la ynquisicion de la ciudad de Lima," Biblioteca Nacional de Madrid, Mss. 4381, 18r (hereafter cited as Quesada y Sotomayor, "Dictamenes varios").

16 Diez de San Miguel y Solier, *Gran fee*, n.p.

17 Xaimes de Ribera, *Hazer de si mismo espejo*, 8r; Elso, "Sermon vespertino con ocasion de un gran terremoto que padecio la ciudad de Lima . . .," published posthumously in Elso, *Sermones varios*, n.p. Bernardo de Mispilivar's sermon *Sagrado arbitrio, commutacion de comedias de corpus* . . . predates the earthquake of 1687 but mentions praying to Santa Isabel as the patron saint of earthquakes to protect the fearful Lima populace (7r–v).

18 Diez de San Miguel y Solier, *Gran fee*, n.p.

19 Parts of Hoyo's work were later copied by Manuel de Odriozola in his *Colección de documentos literarios* (7:287–367) and served as a source for Ricardo Palma's *Tradiciones peruanas completas* and José Toribio Medina's *Historia del Tribunal de la Inquisición de Lima, 1569–1820*. Historian Alejandra Cebrelli has argued that nineteenth-century nationalist histories made use of costumbrista tales. Cebrelli, "Herencia conflictiva."

20 Mannarelli, "Fragmentos"; Sánchez, "Mentalidad popular."
21 Jouve Martín, "En olor de santidad"; Castañeda Delgado and Hernández Aparicio, *Inquisición en Lima*; Medina, *Tribunal de la Inquisición*.
22 Schlau, "Ángela de Carranza, Would-Be Theologian."; Schlau, "Ángela de Carranza: el género sexual."
23 "Relación," 355v.
24 "Relación," 355r, 362v.
25 Freedburg, *Power of Images*, 93–95.
26 Bynum and Gerson, "Body-Part Reliquaries," 3–4. On the body as both a performing and perceiving agent, see Belting, "Image, Medium, Body," 305–7.
27 P. Brown, *Cult of the Saints*, 88; Vauchez, *Sainthood*, 433–39.
28 "Relación," 312r, 346r.
29 Hoyo, *Relacion completa*, 43r, 303r; Quesada y Sotomayor, "Dictamenes varios," 64v.
30 Quesada y Sotomayor, "Dictamenes varios," 73v–74r.
31 "Relación," 300r, 302r–v.
32 Wright, "Inside My Body."
33 Bynum, "Female Body"; Bynum, "Why All the Fuss?"
34 Roa, *Antiguedad veneracion*, 148r.
35 Bouza Álvarez, *Religiosidad contrareformista*; Sánchez-Concha Barrios, *Santos y santidad*, 280; Boss, "Writing a Relic," 221; Christian, *Local Religion*, 126–46.
36 Meléndez, *Tesoros verdaderos*, 2:438.
37 Bynum and Gerson, "Body-Part Reliquaries," 3–4. By way of example: Archbishop Toribio de Mogrovejo's (1538–1606) heart was placed in the monstrance of the Monasterio de Santa Clara in Lima (1606). He was beatified in 1679.
38 Boss, "Writing a Relic," 214.
39 Mugaburu and Mugaburu, *Chronicle of Colonial Lima*, 27, 167.
40 Boss, "Writing a Relic," 212.
41 On 30 April 1669, as the beatification bull was read in the cathedral, the public viewed an image of Rosa holding the city of Lima on an anchor. Mujica Pinilla, "El ancla," 180–81.
42 Vauchez, *Sainthood*, 431.
43 Aquinas, *Summa Theologica*, 3.25, quoted in Vauchez, *Sainthood*, 429n7.
44 On Francisco Solano, see Oré, *Relación de la vida*, xix.
45 On Nicolás de Ayllón's corpse, see Sartolo, *Nicolas de Ayllon*, 215.
46 The items registered included the crosses Nicolás de Ayllón (and others) carried for self-mortification. Sartolo, *Nicolas de Ayllon*, 210.
47 We know that as early as the fourth century relics were necessary for the consecration of churches. Freedburg, *Power of Images*, 93. Reliquaries were relics made specifically to contain such relics and were also considered to be animated by divine presence and had the power to perform miracles.
48 John Chrysostom, quoted in Compañía de Jesús, *Tesoro de San Pedro*, 14.
49 Bynum and Gerson, "Body-Part Reliquaries," 4.
50 Brading, *First America*, 334.

51 Many limeños went to priests to request relics when all other remedies had failed. For an example, see Córdova y Salinas, *Vida, virtudes y milagros*.

52 Cummins, "Blessed Connections," 11–12. Cummins draws from Antonio de León Pinelo, *D. Toribio Alfonso Mogrovejo*, ch. 19.

53 Oré, *Relación de la vida*, xix.

54 Córdova y Salinas, *Crónica franciscana*, 539. Celia Cussen argues that Martín de Porres's miraculous qualities were magnified as witnesses were called to testify (in 1660 and again in 1679) and a hagiography was written about him. Over the decades, Porres evolved into a super-saint worthy of canonization. Cussen, "Fe en la historia."

55 Córdova y Salinas, *Vida, virtudes y milagros*, 390.

56 Porres, *Proceso de beatificación*, 1:354.

57 On Santa Rosa's curative powers, see Meléndez, *Tesoros verdaderos*, 2:420; on miracles associated with the transfer of her remains, see 2:436–37; on miracles associated with her relics, see 2:438–42; on miracles from the dirt surrounding her tomb, see 2:441–47.

58 Jouve Martín, "En olor de santidad," 187. The quotation "the presence of the absence" comes from Belting, "Image, Medium, Body," 312.

59 An official examination of the burial site of Isabel de Porras Marmolejo showed that she complied with the requisites of a *non culto*. "Autos e informaciones," AAL, Beatificaciones, Isabel de Porras Marmolejo, 1 August 1648, 9r. On the testimonies on behalf of the non culto of Martín de Porres, see Porres, *Proceso de beatificación*, 1:30–36. The summary process involved local ecclesiastical authorities collecting testimonies for review by the Holy See in Rome, which then determined whether to conduct a formal investigation (which the See oversaw) into the merits and virtues of the prospective saint. A number of years often passed between the diocesan or summary procedure and the apostolic one.

60 Sánchez-Concha Barrios, *Santos y santidad*.

61 Mugaburu and Mugaburu, *Chronicle of Colonial Lima*, 140.

62 Mugaburu and Mugaburu, *Chronicle of Colonial Lima*, 309; Porres, *Proceso de beatificación*, 10–11.

63 Vargas Ugarte, *Vida del siervo*, 89.

64 Hoyo, *Relacion completa*, 38r–v.

65 "Relación," 354r.

66 "Relación," 349v–350r.

67 Hoyo, *Relacion completa*, 43v. Martín de Porres encouraged a seriously ill friar to bathe in the convent's fountain. When he did, he was healed. Fray Andrés Martínez Ponce de León, testimony, Lima, 3 December 1664, in Porres, *Proceso de beatificación*, 360–61.

68 Cazelles, "Bodies on Stage," 57.

69 Cebrelli, "Herencia conflictiva," 9.

70 "Relación," 360v; Quesada y Sotomayor, "Dictamenes varios," 67v, 115r–v.

71 Quesada y Sotomayor, "Dictamenes varios," 134v.

72 Hoyo, *Relacion completa*, 36r, 338v.

73 "Relación," 359v. Ignacio de Híjar y Mendoza was tried by the Inquisition for believing that Ángela's visions were "divine mysteries." Quesada y Sotomayor, "Dictamenes varios," 218r. See also Ángulo, "El Dr. Ignacio Híjar y Mendoza"; Lastres, *Medicina peruana*, 2:165–68.

74 Hoyo, *Relacion completa*, 17v; Palma, *Inquisición de Lima*, 77.

75 This point is made by Boss, "Writing a Relic."

76 When Bartolomé de Ulloa, her first confessor, died, Francisco Barrena, one of Ángela's assistants (who also denounced her), kept copies of her papers. "Relación," 370r.

77 "Relación," 348v; Hoyo, *Relacion completa*, 42v.

78 Hoyo, *Relacion completa*, 42v.

79 Roa, *Antiguedad veneracion*, 9r.

80 Quesada y Sotomayor, "Dictamenes varios," 115r.

81 Reportedly, after Nicolás de Ayllón had a vision of Rosa's beatification, he contracted a painter to reproduce the vision as a relic. Apparently, the "painting was so lifelike, and full of grace and beauty that it was taken as a precious relic." Sartolo, *Nicolas de Ayllon*, 176.

82 "Relación," 282r.

83 Belting, *Likeness and Presence*, 183–84.

84 Mugaburu and Mugaburu, *Chronicle of Colonial Lima*, 204. Friar Antonio Gutiérrez testified that Martín de Porres regularly prayed on behalf of others in front of the painting of the Virgin and several saints, Porres, *Proceso de beatificación*, 292.

85 The first request to collect testimonies about Nicolás de Ayllón was made in 1679, but the archbishop did not open the inquiry into his life and virtues until 1689. Sartolo, *Nicolas de Ayllon*, 263–64; Vargas Ugarte, *Vida del siervo*, 89. Rome approved the opening of the apostolic process in 1699.

86 Hoyo, *Relacion completa*, n.p.

87 "Relación," 305v–306r, 308v–309r; Hoyo, *Relacion completa*, 19r–v.

88 Covarrubias Orozco, *Tesoro de la lengua castellana*, 46r: "gustar: llevar alguna cosa a la boca que la lengua y el sentido de gustar perciba el sabor." See also C. Classen, *Worlds of Sense*, 8.

89 Hoyo, *Relacion completa*, 19r, 28r.

90 C. Classen, "Odor of the Other"; C. Classen, *Worlds of Sense*, 79–105; C. Classen, "Breath of God," 376.

91 Hoyo, *Relacion completa*, 13v.

92 Fray Francisco de Oviedo, testimony, Lima, 3 December 1664, in Porres, *Proceso de beatificación*, 366. On the overpowering fragrance of Teresa de Ávila, see C. Classen, "Breath of God," 377.

93 Meléndez, *Tesoros verdaderos*, 2:431.

94 "Probanza de la sepultura, Isabel de Porras Marmolejo," 1642, AAL, Beatificaciones, Isabel de Porras Marmolejo, 9r–v. A shirt or tunic that had belonged to Martín de Porres healed an infirm woman of Lima's elite. Porres, *Proceso de beatificación*, 262.

95 Córdova y Salinas, *Vida, virtudes y milagros*, 346–47, 351, 364.

96 "Vida … Gerónima," 476v. On relics appearing out of nowhere, see Córdova y Salinas, *Vida, virtudes y milagros*, 351, 364.

97 See Luke 8:43–44.

98 "Relación," 302v, 312r; Hoyo, *Relacion completa*, 15r.

99 "Relación," 327r.

100 Mugaburu and Mugaburu, *Chronicle of Colonial Lima*, 314.

101 Ángela once saw blood spilling from Christ's side, and she claimed that it was *her* rosary that stopped the bleeding. Here the intermingling of fluid and relic brought about a healing exchange: a sign of her enormous powers.

102 "Relación," 311r.

103 Hoyo, *Relacion completa*, 17v.

104 Hoyo, *Relacion completa*, 17v.

105 Quesada y Sotomayor, "Dictamenes varios," 62r.

106 Quesada y Sotomayor, "Dictamenes varios," 63r.

107 Quesada y Sotomayor, "Dictamenes varios," 62v–63r.

108 Mugaburu and Mugaburu, *Chronicle of Colonial Lima*, 313. Juan B. Lastres says the outbreak began in 1687. Lastres, *Medicina peruana*, 2:180. Another smallpox epidemic struck Lima in 1692.

109 Laqueur, *Making Sex*, 117.

110 Quesada y Sotomayor, "Dictamenes varios," 67v (excerpted from Ángela's notebook 12).

111 Hoyo, *Relacion completa*, 15v.

112 "Relación," 350r–v.

113 "Relación," 321v.

114 Bynum, *Wonderful Blood*, 141.

115 Laqueur, *Making Sex*, 35.

116 "Relación," 276r, 312v, 348v; Lastres, *Medicina peruana*, 2:166.

117 Friar Tomás Martín, testimony, Lima, 2 December 1664, in Porres, *Proceso de beatificación*, 358.

118 Cazelles, "Bodies on Stage," 57.

119 "Relación," 304v; see also 301v.

120 "Relación," 300v.

121 Hoyo, *Relacion completa*, 50r.

122 Palma, *Inquisición de Lima*, 69.

123 Palma, *Inquisición de Lima*, 82.

124 Tribunal de la Inquisición, *Edicto*.

125 Hoyo, *Relacion completa*, 18v. For an analysis of how a list of relics can serve as a text to understand the lives of early modern female subjects, see van Deusen, "In So Celestial a Language."

126 Caviness, *Visualizing Women*, 131.

127 Alfred Lord Tennyson, "All Things Must Die," in *The Works of Alfred Lord Tennyson*, 3.

1 Aguilar, *Sermones varios*, 48v. Unless otherwise indicated, all archival references come from the AAL. The series have been abbreviated as follows: SC, Monasterio de Santa Clara; LC, Monasterio de la Concepción; LE, Monasterio de la Encarnación; LT, Monasterio de la Trinidad; and CN, Causas de Negros.

2 The First and Second Councils of Lima prohibited blacks and Indians (and, implicitly, the *castas*, or mixed-heritage groups) from becoming nuns. Tardieu, *Negros y la iglesia*, 1:385. The term *freila* was synonymous with *donada* or *hermana*. Covarrubias Orozco, *Tesoro de la lengua castellana*, 557; RAE, *Diccionario de autoridades*, 3:794.

3 RAE, *Diccionario de autoridades*, 3:334–35; RAE, *Diccionario de la lengua española*, 1:493.

4 Bowser, *African Slave*, 40–43, 72. Some convents, such as the Monasterio de la Encarnación, accepted more pardas and mulatas as donadas than other convents.

5 "Solicitud que presenta Antonía de Oviedo, mestiza de Huaylas," 1678, LC, 21:26; "Autos seguidos por Ana de Heredía, mulata de Panama," 1673, LC, 20:4; "Solicitud de Ventura Cortes, quarterona libre de Huaura," 1695, LC, 27:13; "Autos de profesion de Antonia María [de Leyba] y Juana Sacramento," 1681, SC, 17:42. Antonia María de Leyba and her sister were from the province of Guamalies, of unknown parents. See also "Autos de ingreso de la cuarterona Marcela de Alcozer para religiosa donada," 1698, SC, 21:46. Marcela was from Pisco and was a legitimate daughter.

6 The *padrón de indios* (census of Indians) of 1613 is filled with the "fragmented" and incomplete stories of young Indian girls (and boys), often orphaned, who looked for institutional support; see, for example, Contreras, *Padrón de los indios*, 453, 480–515. See also Vergara Ormeño, "Migración y trabajo feminino," 137; Estenssoro Fuchs, *Del paganismo*, 379. Some also attached themselves to households. Of the 140 girls between the ages of six and twelve listed in the census of 1613, 44 declared themselves to be orphans residing in the home of a master (*patrón*).

7 Martín, *Daughters of the Conquistadores*, 188; Tardieu, *Negros y la Iglesia*, 1:393, 397. Although ranked higher than the donadas, the nuns of the white veil were also sometimes viewed as servants. For examples, see "Autos . . . María Nuñez y Francisca de Guevara para monjas de velo blanco," 1632, SC, 4:25. See also "Autos . . . Francisca de la Cruz," 1666, SC, 4:32. See also Ruíz Valdés, "Recogidas, virtuosas y humildes."

8 Martín, *Daughters of the Conquistadores*, 185.

9 Ursula de Jesús, *Souls of Purgatory*, 121.

10 On accessing the voices of servants in India, see Banerjee, "Down Memory Lane," 682.

11 Burton, *Dwelling in the Archive*, 17.

12 Bhabha, *Location of Culture*, 88 ("tethered shadows"); Steedman, "Servants," 328.

13 Fra Molinero, "Ser mulato," 123.

14 Bennett, "Subject in the Plot," 122–24; Fernández Álvarez, *Casadas*, ch. 5; Fairchilds, *Domestic Enemies*, 102.

15 Davis, introduction to *Slavery and Beyond*, xiii, xvi; Bennett, *Africans*, ch. 6.

16 Thornton, "African Catholic Church," 147–48; Vanhee, "Central African Popular Christianity," 245, 257; Rey, "Kongolese Catholic Influences," 266; Bowser, *African Slave*, 40–41.

17 Gómez Acuña, "Cofradías de negros"; Graubart, "'So Color'"; Bowser, *African Slave*, 247–51. On confraternities in colonial Mexico, see Bristol, *Christians, Blasphemers and Witches*, 95–106; von Germeten, *Black Blood Brothers*.

18 Brewer-García, "Beyond Babel," 272 (for a discussion of the vidas of Martín de Porres, see 292–94).

19 Scholars who have questioned this model are Kenneth Mills, John Charles, and Claudia Brosseder.

20 Charney, "Sense of Belonging"; Ramos, *Death and Conversion*, 160–213.

21 Aguilar, *Sermones varios*.

22 Meléndez, *Tesoros verdaderos*, 2:169.

23 For the fifty-three entrance petitions to La Concepción that supplied age data, the breakdown is as follows: twenty entrants were between thirteen and sixteen years old, twenty were between seventeen and twenty years old, eleven were between twenty-one and thirty years old, and two were over thirty years old. For the forty-three petitions with data for Santa Clara, thirteen entrants were between thirteen and sixteen years old, eighteen were between seventeen and twenty years old, ten were between twenty-one and thirty years old, and two were over thirty years old. For an example of a couple taking vows of celibacy and becoming donados, see "Autos . . . Antonio de Cordova y Juana Maria Hurtado, esposos," 1665, LE, 11:86. Some older women entered the novitiate because the abbess found them useful; see "Expediente . . . Juana de Añazgo," 1687, LC, 25:7.

24 This total is based on all the extant autos de ingreso and autos de profesión documents for La Concepción (eighty-three), Santa Clara (eighty-six), and La Encarnación (sixty-eight). See also Tardieu, *Negros y la Iglesia*, 1:394. The Council of Trent stipulated that the applicant had to be free from bondage. See Tardieu, *Negros y la Iglesia*, 1:394; "Autos de profesión . . . Pascuala del Pulgar, negra donada," 1642, SC, 6:35; "Autos de profesion . . . Maria Rodriguez, cuarterona donada," 1642, SC, 6:37; "Autos de profesion . . . Gracia Maria de Jesus, negra," 1664, SC, 12:27.

25 Minh-ha, "Not You/Like You," 71.

26 Olaechea Labayen, *Mestizaje*, 292.

27 Boyer, "Respect and Identity," 492; Rappaport, *Disappearing Mestizo*, 4–5. Fifty-five of the 237 cases reported no data on physical characteristics.

28 The Council of Trent stipulated that the applicant had to be free from bondage, although the clarisas were more lax in promoting the candidacy of slaves who were subsequently freed. See Tardieu, *Negros y la Iglesia*, 1:394; "Autos de profesión . . . Pascuala del Pulgar, negra donada," 1642, SC, 6:35; "Autos de profesion . . . Maria Rodriguez, cuarterona donada," 1642, SC, 6:37; "Autos de profesion . . . Gracia Maria de Jesus, negra," 1664, SC, 12:27.

29 Fernández Fernández, *Mujer*, 190.

30 "Profesion de Beatriz del Arco," 1684, LC, 25:17.

31 "Solicitud . . . Maria de la Concepción," 1680, LC, 22:8. See also "Paula Maria de Albur," 1698, LC, 27:38.

32 "Autos . . . Antonio de Cordova y Juana Maria Hurtado," 1665, LE, 11:86; "Autos criminales . . . contra Jerónimo Alvaro," 1626–27, LT, 1:37.

33 The name of the newly professed donada was recorded in a *libro de profesiones*; for an example, see "Autos . . . doña Jeronima de Sejas," 1633–37, LC, 5:44. I have not been fortunate enough to find one of these libros de profesiones.

34 León Pinelo, *Velos antiguos*, ch. 8; Fernández Fernández, *Mujer*, 451.

35 "Solicitud . . . doña Florencia Barreto," 1622, LC, 2:14; also cited in Fernández Fernández, *Mujer*, 264.

36 "Solicitud . . . doña Andrea de Salas," 1623, LC, 3:6; Tardieu, *Negros y la Iglesia*, 1:393.

37 "Autos que sigue doña Luisa de Escobar," 1642, SC, 6:32.

38 "Causa de nulidad . . . Francisca de Valencia," 1626, LC, 3:16.

39 "Autos criminales seguidos contra Jerónimo Alvaro," 1626–27, LT, 1:37. In this case, see the fascinating testimonies of Francisca de Ayala, negra esclava (black slave), 43r–44r; Ana del Espíritu Santo, mestiza criada (mestiza servant), 44r; María del Castillo, donada, 46v–47r; and Ana del Castillo, donada, 47r–48r.

40 "Auto," 1630/31, Papeles Importantes, 24:8; Tardieu, *Negros y la Iglesia*, 1:400; Fernández Fernández, *Mujer*, 141.

41 *Constituciones generales*, 101. The papal bull of Gregory VIII (1583) stated that the convent should have no more than one criada for every ten nuns. On the excessive comings and goings of servants and slaves, which pushed the archbishop to restrict the numbers of servants and slaves in convents, see "Auto arzobispal por Fernando Arias de Ugarte," 1636, LT, 3:10; "Auto dado por el arzobispo de Lima, Villagómez," 1664, LE, 11:30. On the expulsion of servants and slaves in 1664, see "Relacion de las criadas," 1664, LC, 16:30. On the concern over children in convents, see "Auto seguido," Monasterio de Santa Catalina de Sena, 1695, 8:87; and "Testimonios dados," 1695, SC, 21:10.

42 *Constituciones generales*, 145; "Autos . . . María Micaela de Jesús Nazareno," 1688, Monasterio de Santa Catalina de Sena, 8:4.

43 *Constituciones generales*, 145; Fernández Fernández, *Mujer*, 451.

44 Aguilar, *Sermones varios*, 257r–270v.

45 Elso, "Sermon de la Presentación de Nuestra Señora en un convento de religiosas; de el título de la Encarnación, Fiesta que hazen las Sirvientas Seglares de dicho Convento," in Elso, *Sermones varios*, 233–55.

46 "Solicitud . . . Josefa de la Concepcion y Meneses," 1664, LC, 16:49.

47 Dickey, "Mutual Exclusions," 52–53; Minh-ha, "Not You/Like You," 71.

48 "Solicitud . . . doña Juana de Melendez," 1685, SC, 18:41.

49 "Profesión de Ursula de la Concepcion," 1687, LC, 25:33; "Oficios . . . 1688," 1687, LC, 25:35. For a description of tasks in Puebla, Mexico's convents, see Loreto López, *Conventos femeninos*, 125–33.

50 Fernández Fernández, *Mujer*, 315; "Expediente . . . Mariana de Jesus," 1687, LC, 25:13; "Oficios . . . 1697," 1696, LC, 27:45.

51 "Solicitud . . . Maria de Escobar," 1673, LC, 20:3.

52 Loreto López, "Prácticas alimenticias," 493.

53 "Autos . . . doña Maria de Ventura y Jesús," 1668, SC, 12:171.

54 Ursula de Jesús, *Souls of Purgatory*, 52–53.

55 Fernández Fernández, *Mujer*, 361.

56 "Autos . . . doña Jerónima de Sejas," 1633/37, LC, V: 44, 3r; Ursula de Jesús, *Souls of Purgatory*, 30–31.

57 Loreto López, "Prácticas alimenticias," 493; "Autos . . . doña Jerónima de Sejas," 1633/37, LC, V: 44, 3r; Ursula de Jesús, *Souls of Purgatory*, 30–31.

58 Martín, *Daughters of the Conquistadores*, 191; Fernández Fernández, *Mujer*; Burns, *Colonial Habits*, 130.

59 "Sobre los oficios . . . La Encarnación," 1630/31, Papeles Importantes, 24:8; "Cuaderno de Autos," doc. 7; and "Oficio . . . para cubrir los oficios," 1682, SC, 17:47.

60 See "Autos . . . doña Ana de Zarate," 1636, SC, V: 42; "Autos . . . Juan Gómez, labrador," 1638, LE, V: 26; "Autos . . . Juana de Aguilar," 1639, CN, 7:37; "Autos . . . Antonia María y Juana de Leiba," 1693, SC, 20:66; "Autos . . . doña Jerónima de Sejas," 1633–37, LC, V: 44; "Autos . . . doña Melchora de los Reyes," 1628–29, LE, 3:8A.

61 "Autos . . . doña Jerónima de Sejas," 1633/37, LC, V: 44; "Solicitud de la abadesa," 1630, LE, 3:22; "Autos . . . Juan Gómez, labrador," 1638, LE, V: 26; "Carta de libertad de Ursula, negra criolla," 1646, LC, 9:29; "Expediente de Ines de Guevara," 1655, CN, 12:4; "Autos . . . doña Ana de Zarate," 1636, SC, V: 42; "Autos de la demanda," 1647, CN, 10:11.

62 AGNP, Protocolos, Joseph de Aguirre Urbina, 69 (1644–45), 2–3v. Cells could be small and spare, or they could be the size of an ample apartment complete with separate rooms, including sleeping quarters for family members and servants, a kitchen, and a garden.

63 *Constituciones generales*, 99v, 144.

64 Fernández Fernández, *Mujer*, 316; Ursula de Jesús, *Souls of Purgatory*, 25–30.

65 "Oficios. . . . 1679," 1678, LC, 21:43; "Oficios . . . 1680," 1679, LC, 21:77. See also "Autos . . . Josefa Maria de Larraga," 1679–1722, SC, 12:99; Fernández Fernández, *Mujer*, 214; RAE, *Diccionario de autoridades*, 5:581; "Oficios," SC, 20:73.

66 "Autos . . . Lorenza de Mesa, mulata," 1677, LE, 13:87. See also "Autos . . . María de San José," LT, 3:3; and "Autos . . . Lorenza de la Madre de Dios de la Soledad," 1666, SC, 12:112.

67 For a fascinating study of female solidarity in convents in Mexico, see Kirk, *Convent Life*.

68 Of all of the known donadas (237 in total), 96 stated that they had been raised in the convent, 124 had no data, and 18 had not been raised there. Based on the 114 cases where data are available (96 + 18), 85 percent were raised in the convent.

69 María de San Cristóbal to Catalina de San Joseph, donation, 7 February 1648, AGNP, Francisco de Acuña (hereafter FA), 29 (1648), 80r–v.

70 "Solicitud . . . María de Escobar (50 años)," 1673, LC, 20:3.

71 Because the numbers of servants vary throughout the seventeenth century, I calculated an overall average of 130 for La Encarnación and 150 for Santa Clara and La Concepción before 1670. After 1670 the numbers of servants increased dramatically. One can assume that, in the last third of the seventeenth century, the percentage of donadas selected from the overall number of servants raised in the convent decreased significantly.

72 *Constituciones generales*, 9; "Autos . . . María de Mancilla," 1673, EN, 13:6; "Autos . . . Catalina de San Antonio," 1674, EN, 13:10.

73 van Deusen, *Between the Sacred*, 173–74.

74 See Martín, *Daughters of the Conquistadores*, 192–200, in particular his discussion of the Garabito-Illescas "clan" in the Monasterio de la Encarnación; see also Fernández Fernández, *Mujer*, 444–45. For Cuzco, see Burns, *Colonial Habits*.

75 RAE, *Diccionario de autoridades*, 2:657.

76 Premo, *Children of the Father King*.

77 See Jane Mangan's *Transatlantic Obligations* for a discussion of how Spanish-indigenous households were maintained culturally and economically in the sixteenth century.

78 "Autos . . . Ursula, mulata esclava," SC, 19:81; "Expediente . . . Ana de la Santíssima Trinidad," LC, 24:10; "Autos . . . doña Antonia Clavijo," LE, 2:5; "Autos . . . Ursula, mulata esclava," SC, 19:81; "Autos . . . la esclava de la abadessa," SC, 21:28.

79 RAE, *Diccionario de autoridades*, 2:657.

80 "Solicitud de María Marchan," 1681, LC, 22:51. Curiously, another (or the same?) María Marchan appears in the records in 1697 soliciting a license to enter the novitiate. "Solicitud de María Marchan," 1697, LC, 17:55.

81 "Autos . . . doña Ana de Pineda," 1630, EN, 3:17.

82 "Relación de las sirvientas," n.d., LT, 1:38 s/f. These "nations," as scholars Rachel O'Toole, Sherwin Bryant, and others have shown, may have had little reference to African territorialities and ethnic groupings but still acquired meanings as distinguishing forms of identification in the colonial context in Lima. See Bryant, *Rivers of Gold*, and O'Toole, "From the Rivers of Guinea."

83 "Autos . . . Ana de Heredía, mulata de Panama," 1673, LC, 20:4; "Profesión . . . Beatriz del Arco," 1687, LC, 25:17.

84 "Expediente . . . Ana Casilda, de Pisco," 1683, LC, 23:23; "Autos . . . Ursula de la Concepcion," 1687, LC, 25:33; "Expediente . . . Margarita de Jesus," 1685, LC, 24:14; "Bernarda de San Joseph," 1692, LC, 26:60; "Autos . . . Maria de Cristo," 1664, LE, 11:59; "Autos . . . doña Luisa Ordoñes de Pineda," 1666, LE, 11:103; "Autos . . . doña Maria Josefa de Jesús," 1666, LE, 11:106.

85 "Testimonios dados por algunas religiosas," 1694, SC, 21:10; Lorensa de la Encarnación, testament, AGNP, Protocolos, Gregorio de Urtazo, 1103 (1709), 671–69v.

86 "Donación," 7 October 1645, AGNP, Protocolos, Joseph de Aguirre Urbina, 69 (1644–45), 2–3v.

87 Of the forty nuns listed as having cells in La Trinidad, seven lived with donadas. LT, 1:38, n.d., cited in Fernández Fernández, *Mujer*, 335–36. On the importance of cells to convent culture, see Burns, *Colonial Habits*; Evangelisti, "Rooms to Share."

88 Codicil, 12 July 1670, AGNP, Protocolos, Marcelo Antonio de Figueroa, 665, 1670-B, 1419r–1421r, quote on 1420v.

89 Hallett, *Senses in Religious Communities.*

90 Burns, *Colonial Habits.*

91 María de San Cristóbal, donation, 7 February 1648, AGNP, Protocolos, FA, 29 (1648), 80–80v; "Will . . . doña Francisca Vásquez," 21 April 1653, Protocolos, FA, 34 (1653); "Autos . . . Isabel de Ulloa," 1665, SC, 12:74; "Autos . . . Josefa de Herrera," 1665, SC, 12:58.

92 "Autos . . . Ana Maria de los Santos, mulata esclava," 1665, LE, 11:88; "Autos . . . Andrea de Solorzano," 1685, SC, 18:38; "Autos . . . Andrea de Solorzano," 1688, SC, 19:37; "Solicitación . . . don Martín Riquelme," 1631, LC, V:8.

93 "Autos . . . Lorenza Agustina del Carmen," 1665, SC, 12:42; Martín, *Daughters of the Conquistadors,* 186.

94 "Autos . . . Catalina de San Antonio," 1674, LE, 13:10.

95 "Autos . . . Ventura de la Fuente," 1687, SC, 18:91.

96 Bernalda de la Palma, testament, 13 June 1652, AGNP, Protocolos, FA, 33 (1652), 294–296; McKinley, *Fractional Freedoms,* 176–202; "Till Death," 382–85.

97 Van Deusen, introduction to *Souls of Purgatory,* 32–37.

98 "Causa . . . Luis de Alvarado Bracamonte," 1617-25, LC, 2:6; Premo, *Father King,* 220–21.

99 I have borrowed this term from Cope, *Limits of Racial Domination,* 93. See "Expediente . . . Fernando de Sotomayor," CN, 6:25.

100 Premo, *Children of the Father King,* 84, 86–88.

101 RAE, *Diccionario de autoridades,* 3:334–35. On conditional freedom, see "Solicitud . . . doña Juana de Tello," 1688, LC, 25:60; Isabel de Espinoza, testament, 25 June 1652, AGNP, Protocolos, FA, 33 (1652), 315–316v; Doña Antonia de San Francisco Coello, letter of freedom, 21 May 1654, AGNP, Protocolos, FA, 35 (1654), 281–282. Doña Juana de Contreras donated a three-year-old *mulatilla* (little girl of African heritage) named María Pascuala, the daughter of Doña Juana's slave, to serve in the sacristy of the Monasterio de las Descalzas de San José, and, specifically, an individual nun named Paula de San Ignacio until the nun's death, at which time María Pascuala would be freed *only* if she became a donada. Doña Juana de Contreras, donation, 27 June 1648, AGNP, Protocolos, FA, 29 (1648), 400v–401v.

102 "Autos que sigue Ana de Mora, negra libre," SC, 12:120, 12r–15v.

103 See also Doña Juana de Contreras, testament, 27 June 1648, AGNP, Protocolos, FA, 29 (1648), 400v–401v; and "Solicitud . . . Maria Pascuala, mulata," AAL, Monasterio de Las Descalzas, 4:79.

104 "Autos que sigue Ana de Mora, negra libre," 1667, SC, 12:120, 19r, 34r–v.

105 "Autos que sigue Ana de Mora, negra libre," 1667, SC, 12:120, 34v.

106 See J. Brown, *Invalidating Effects,* 35–38; Premo, "Maidens," 291. I discuss the legal relationship between "reverential fear" and free will in chapter 6 of this volume.

107 "Causa de nulidad . . . Maria de San Francisco," 1632, LC, V: 27.

108 "Autos . . . Leonor de San Nicolás," 1656, Monasterio de Las Descalzas, 2:50; "Autos . . . Juana de Santa Rosa," 1672, LC, 19:64.

109 "Autos . . . María de Carbajal Galindo, Petronila de Oviedo San José, mulata, y Nicolasa de Aguilar, mulata libre," 1667, LT, 6:70.

110 "Expediente . . . de Lucia Bravo," 1638, LC, 7:22; "Expediente . . . Margarita de Jesús," 1685, LC, 24:14; "Autos . . . Magdalena de Espinoza, 'una hija legítima,'" 1679, SC, 16:47; Fernández Fernández, *Mujer*, 336; "Autos . . . doña Jerónima de Sejas," 1633–37, LC, V: 44.

111 "Expediente . . . María Magdalena y Francisca de Jesús de Lima, 15 y 11," 1691, LC, 26:28; "Autos . . . Magdalena y Francisca de Lomba," 1700, LC, 28:11; "Autos . . . Francisca Rebollo, india, Bartola y Francisca Rebollo, pardas," 1674, LE, 13:29.

112 "Autos . . . Isabel de San José," 1646, Monasterio de Las Descalzas, 2:49; "Autos . . . Josefa Duarte," 1657, LT, 5:69; "Autos . . . Maria de Cristo," 1664, LE, 11:59. On mothers working, see "Expediente . . . Juana de Añazgo," 1687, LC, 25:7; "Expediente . . . Petronila de la Visitación," 1689, LC, 25:74; "Autos . . . Francisca de la Concepcion," 1678, SC, 16:15; "Autos . . . doña Beatriz de Herrera," 1665, SC, 12:64.

113 "Autos . . . de doña Nicolasa del Puerto," 1675, SC, 14:72.

114 Isabel de Atocha, testament, 1 December 1657, AGNP, Protocolos, FA, 38 (1657), 650v–652v; van Deusen, *Between the Sacred*, chs. 4 and 6.

115 Martín, *Daughters of the Conquistadores*, 188; "Solicitud . . . María de los Reyes," 1609, LE, 1:7.

116 "Cuentas presentadas," Cofradías, 31:2. On the numerous confraternities founded by and operated by people of African descent, see Bowser, *African Slave*, 247–51, 261; Graubart, "'So Color,'" 43–64; Charney, "Sense of Belonging."

117 Francisca Terranova, testament, 4 April 1651, AGNP, Protocolos, FA, 32 (1651), 253r–v; Joana Quispe, sister (*hermana*) of the Cofradía de Nuestra Señora de Loreto, testament, 23 May 1651, AGNP, Protocolos, FA, 32 (1651), 350v–351r; Teresa de la Cruz, hermana of the Cofradía of Nuestra Señora de Loreto, testament, 14 June 1651, AGNP, Protocolos, FA, 32 (1651), 431v–432v; Ana de Tierra Folupa, free morena, confraternity member of the Folupos (in the Iglesia de San Francisco), testament, 13 September 1653, FA, 34 (1653), 510–511; Francisca de Vallalba, free morena from the land of the Brans, confraternity member of the Confraternity of the Bañones (Cofradía de los Bañones), testament, 29 August 1660, FA, 40 (1660), 347v–349v; Gómez Acuña, "Cofradías de negros," 36.

118 Martín, *Daughters of the Conquistadores*, 184; "Autos . . . María de los Reyes," 1609, LE, 1:7; Fernández Fernández, *Mujer*, 184; Tardieu, *Negros y la Iglesia*, 1:399.

119 "Solicitud de Petrona Roldán," 1689, LC, 25:83.

120 "Solicitud . . . Agustina de los Rios," 1688, LC, 25:66. See also Agustín de Mora speaking on behalf of his daughter, in "Autos . . . Maria de Mora," 1699, SC, 21:66.

121 "Doña Manuela de Billaruela y Mendosa," 1668, SC, 12:157.

122 "Autos . . . Magdalena de San Jose, mulata," 1665, LE, 11:68; "Solicitud . . . Lucia Bravo de Laguan y Catalina de la Madre de Dios," 1683, LC, 23:18.

123 "Solicitud . . . María de la Cueva," 1678, LC, 21:24; "Solicitud . . . Petrona de Avendaño," 1680, LC, 22:4; "Solicitud . . . Josefa de la Concepcion," 1664, LC, 16:49.

124 "Autos . . . Jerónima Clavijo, Luisa Rebata y Beatríz Rodríguez," 1674, LE, 13:28.

125 Aguilar, *Sermones varios*, "De la Presentación."

126 "Autos . . . Bartolomé Delgado . . . against the goods of (*bienes de*) [the deceased donada] Melchora de los Reyes," 1628–29, LE, 3:8A. For another example of a nun investing in an altar in a convent, see "Traslado . . . doña Magdalena Carrillo," 1656–57, LE, 9:39.

127 "Will of Magdalena Choque, professed india donada in the Monasterio de la Encarnación (Lima)," 1664, Capellanías, 36:2.

128 Josefa del Espíritu Santo, testament, 24 June 1652, AGNP, Protocolos, FA, 32 (1651), 471–472v.

129 Aguilar, *Sermones varios*, 257r–270v.

130 Brewer-García, "Beyond Babel," 274.

131 "Relación de la fundación," Biblioteca Nacional del Perú, Ms. B 124, 50r; Morabito, "San Benedetto," 241–43; Busto Duthurburu, *San Martín*, 57n20; Rowe, "Her Face Turned White," 737–40.

132 See Celia Cussen's important recent study, *Black Saint of the Americas*.

133 Bristol, *Christians, Blasphemers and Witches*, 23–62; Ursula de Jesús, *Souls of Purgatory*; van Deusen, "Ursula de Jesús."

134 Van Deusen, *Between the Sacred*, ch. 6; van Deusen, "Circuits of Knowledge," 142–43.

135 Echave y Assu, *Estrella de Lima*, 232, 228–29; "Autos . . . María Josepha de Todos los Santos y Juana Maria de la Resurrección," 1668, Monasterio de Las Descalzas, 4:32; Fernández Fernández, *Mujer*, 243–44; "Solicitud . . . Maria de la O," 1643, LE, 6:21; "Memoria de los oficios . . . 1657," 1656, LC, 12:14.

136 Córdova y Salinas, *Crónica franciscana*, 535.

137 Calancha, *Crónica moralizada*; Córdova y Salinas, *Crónica franciscana*; Echave y Assu, *La estrella de Lima*; Meléndez, *Tesoros verdaderos*, 2:72; Montalvo, *Sol del Nuevo Mundo;* Vázquez de Espinoza, *Compendio*. The pages of these and other *crónicas conventuales* are filled with exemplary donadas and criadas, whose spiritual gifts served as a model for others in the religious community.

138 Bhabha, *Location of Culture*, 127; RAE, *Diccionario de autoridades*, 2:657; "Autos . . . María de Carbajal Galindo, Petronila de Oviedo San José, mulata, y Nicolasa de Aguilar," 1667, LT, 6:70, 1r.

139 Úrsula de Jesús's biographer, an anonymous Franciscan, emphasized Úrsula's whiteness, in terms of the purity of her soul. "Vida de la Venerable Úrsula de Jesús," Archivo Franciscano del Perú, Registro 17, no. 45, n.d. See also Brewer-García, "Beyond Babel."

140 "Solicitud . . . Maria de Escobar," 1673, LC, 20:3.

141 "Solicitud . . . abadesa Juana del Niño Jesus," n.d., Monasterio de las Descalzas, 4:86.

142 "Autos . . . Francisca de la Cruz, parda," 1666, SC, 12:96.

143 "Expediente de ingreso . . . Juana de San José," LC, 1665, 17:15.

144 Ursula de Jesús, *Souls of Purgatory*, 56, 93–94.

145 Ursula de Jesús, *Souls of Purgatory*, 30.

146 Ursula de Jesús, *Souls of Purgatory*, 121; Granada, *Guía de peccadores*, 375.

147 Tardieu, *Negros y la Iglesia*, 1:394–95.

148 Fernández Álvarez, *Casadas*, 197.

149 Martín, *Daughters of the Conquistadores*, 185.

150 Boyer, "Respect and Identity," 492; Adams and Dickey, *Home and Hegemony*.

151 Granada, *Guía de peccadores*, 375.

CHAPTER 5: MARÍA JACINTA MONTOYA, NICOLÁS DE AYLLÓN, AND THE UNMAKING OF AN INDIAN SAINT IN LATE SEVENTEENTH-CENTURY PERU

1 "Proceso de doña María Jacinta Montoya" (henceforth "Proceso"), AHNM, Inquisición, Lima, 1649, no. 51, 1701, 1r, 10v–13v, 27r–v, 30r–31r, 35v–36r. One of the notebooks was described as containing 189 folios covered in vellum and written in María Jacinta's hand, beginning with "En el nombre de la Santíssima Trinidad"; the second one contained 55 unbound folios and began, "La Gloria sea para Dios," and ended with "mereser gozarle en la eternal vida amen." The third notebook, covered in vellum and written in her hand, was 33 folios, with 3 separate folios attached at the end.

2 "Proceso," 9v–10r.

3 "Referencia al espíritu de María Jacinta, por Martín de los Reyes y Rocha," n.d., Beatificaciones, Nicolás de Ayllón, AAL.

4 To the charges against her, María Jacinta said, "Que estava ilusa y engañada en mis revelaciones, sueños, y hablas interiores y escritos." "Proceso," 11r; see also 13r ("miserable muger") and 15v ("de los ayunos y penitensias que yo hasia en aquellos tiempos, tendría la cavesa desvanesida").

5 An important work about deviant orthodoxy is Nora E. Jaffary's *False Mystics*.

6 Gathering testimonies from a cross section of Lima society was also central to Rosa's ordinary and diocesan processes, since it was claimed that she was to be the first *American* saint. Hampe Martínez, *Santidad e identidad criolla*; Mujica Pinilla, *Rosa limensis*, 56–58.

7 On the need for a non culto (the lack of public recognition of the candidate as a saint) to exist, see Estenssoro Fuchs, *Del paganismo*, 481; R. Morgan, *Spanish American Saints*, 29. The non culto, established by Pope Urban VIII, prohibited public displays of ex-votos, recognition of miracles and divine favors, and access to the tomb until the canonization process was complete. Bernardo Sartolo's "protesta" at the beginning of his book claimed to be "obedient to the precepts of Urban VIII." Sartolo, *Nicolas de Ayllon*. In the proceso in 1684, one ecclesiastic was careful to point out that he saw no candles or other items placed near Ayllón's tomb. Fernando de Peñalosa, testimony, May 1684, in "Processus [Nicolás de Ayllón]" (henceforth "Processus"), Archivio Segreto Vaticano, Congregazione Riti Processus, 1309, 283r.

8 José R. Jouve Martín mentions one of Ángela de Carranza's visions that criticized the excessive costs of beatification. Jouve Martín, "En olor de santidad," 188.

9 On Ayllón's affiliations with the members of various religious orders and Buendía's sermon, see Benito Álfaro, testimony, January 1701, AAL, Beatificaciones,
Nicolás de Ayllón, vol. 5, 30r; Estenssoro Fuchs, *Del paganismo*, 477.

10 By no means was Montoya solely responsible for feeding information to Sartolo.
According to Sartolo, two of Ayllón's ardent supporters were don Pedro García
de Ovalle, oidor of the Real Chancillería of Lima, and Juan Alonso de Zerecedes,
a Jesuit from the Colegio de San Martín, who encouraged the publication of the
vida by Sartolo. Sartolo, *Nicolas de Ayllon*, 3–4, 491. Rubén Vargas Ugarte (*Vida
del siervo de Dios*) states that García de Ovalle was commissioned to oversee the
collection of materials to be used for Ayllón's spiritual biography, but Juan Carlos
Estenssoro Fuchs believes that Buendía, Ayllón's spiritual confessor, may have
prepared the text for Sartolo. Estenssoro Fuchs, *Del paganismo*, 486–87. Sartolo
cites Montoya several times, which supports the assertion that she had shared
with him a copy of the notebook "De las misericordias," filled with details of
Ayllón's virtues and miracles.

11 On the Jesuit influence and Sartolo's authority in Spain, see Espinoza Rúa, "A
las puertas," n.p. The Jesuits were also in the process of promoting Juan de Alloza and Francisco del Castillo. Coello de la Rosa, "Agencías políticas," 628. On
writing of hagiographies as a stage in the beatification process, see Coello de la
Rosa, "Era Sanctorum." An example of Dominican support for Martín de Porres
can be seen in Bernardo de Medina's *Vida prodigiosa del venerable siervo de Dios
Fray Martín de Porras*, written sometime between 1660 and 1662 and published
in Madrid in 1675. It was also published as part of Juan Meléndez's *Tesoros verdaderos de las Indias* in Rome in 1681. Porres's apostolic process overlapped with
Ayllón's diocesan hearing.

12 Duplicate of letter written by members of the Inquisition Tribunal, 31 August
1696, in "Proceso." Circulation of the book was prohibited by an edict of 1696;
for a transcribed copy of the edict of 1696 prohibiting the book's circulation, see
Vargas Ugarte, *Vida del siervo*, 96–97.

13 RAE, *Diccionario de autoridades*, 6:496. Supernatural virtues (prophecy, etc.) include the ability to act over nature. Theological virtues would originate with those
who have God as their principal motive and are based on faith, hope, and charity.

14 Sartolo, *Nicolas de Ayllon*, 265–67. Sartolo reported that when Carranza (who
remained unnamed in the book) related the vision to her confessor, he told her,
"Juzgò este no se debia callar este testimonio porque confirmaba la opinión de
todos" (267). Sartolo mentioned a vision by another unnamed "sierva de Dios"
who had seen Ayllón with Christ (269). A number of witnesses referred to
Ángela de Carranza; see Benito Álfaro, testimony, AAL, Beatificaciones,
Segunda información, vol. 5, 271; "Notable #8," in "Proceso," 38v. During her
self-denunciation, Montoya declared that she was deeply afraid when the Inquisition condemned Carranza in a public auto-da-fé in 1694. When she asked her
confessor, Juan Yañez, whether she should burn her notebook, he assured her
that she had nothing to fear. "Proceso," 9v–10. Only her confessor saw the second
notebook, which dealt with her "interior visions."

15 María Jacinta Montoya, testimony, 17 May 1684, in "Processus," 238r.

16 Vargas Ugarte, *Historia de la Iglesia*, 3:319.

17 Hoyo, *Relacion completa*.

18 On the dangers of hagiographic works containing suspect material, see the chapter "La China Poblana" in Myers, *Neither Saints nor Sinners*, ch. 2. On the timing of the book's confiscation and concurrent consideration of Ayllón's beatification in Rome, see Estenssoro Fuchs, *Del paganismo*, 486–87. On the arrival of the rótulo, see Fray Joseph Ordanza y Závala, Mercedarian Order, testimony, 6 May 1702, AAL, Beatificaciones, Nicolás de Ayllón, Segunda información, vol. 5, n.p.

19 Vargas Ugarte, *Vida del siervo*, 91; Estenssoro Fuchs, *Del paganismo*. See also the thesis of Celes Alonso Espinoza Rúa, "A las puertas de cielo," and his article, "Un indio camino a los altares."

20 Sartolo, *Nicolas de Ayllon*, 67.

21 Jouve Martín, "En olor de santidad," 182. By *historical fiction* I mean inventions and truths that are used as evidence to fit into a credible narrative about saintliness. Authors who have considered this method include Cussen, "Fe en la historia"; Rubial García, *Santidad controvertida*, 41–42, 83–84.

22 R. Morgan, *Spanish American Saints*, 24–25.

23 For examples, see Gunnasdóttir, *Mexican Karismata*; Salvador, "Steadfast Saints." On the cult of saints as a particularly useful didactic tool for the conversion of Indians, see Cussen, "Search for Idols"; Estenssoro Fuchs, *Del paganismo*. On the politics of controversial candidates, see Rubial García, *Santidad controvertida*, 77–83. On saints of color, see the chapter "La China Poblana" in Myers, *Neither Saints nor Sinners*; Greer, *Mohawk Saint*; Bristol, "'Although I Am Black.'"

24 Myers, *Neither Saints nor Sinners*, 33 and the rest of the chapter "Redeemer of America."

25 Coon, *Sacred Fictions*; Ashton, *Generation of Identity*.

26 Rubial García, *Santidad controvertida*, 144–52, 203–50.

27 Certeau, *Writing of History*, 272–73; Cussen, *Black Saint*.

28 Rodrigo, *Manual para instruir*; Hampe Martínez, *Santidad e identidad criolla*; Coello de la Rosa, "Agencias políticas"; Rubial García, *Santidad controvertida*.

29 Vargas Ugarte, *Relaciones de viajes*. Vargas Ugarte also cites documents and letters written by Montoya in *Historia de la Iglesia*, 4:38–39. See also María Rosa, *Journey*.

30 One of Ayllón's confessors, don Ignacio Híjar y Mendoza (who had also served as Ángela de Carranza's confessor), claimed that he learned from Montoya about Ayllón's prediction that the recogimiento would become a convent. Don Ignacio Yjar [Híjar] y Mendoza, testimony, 11 May 1684, in "Processus," 197v.

31 The recently arrived viceroy, Melchor Liñán y Cisneros, gave his support for the beaterio in 1678, the same year he approved opening Ayllón's diocesan process. AHNM, Inquisición, Leg. 1649, exp. 51, 8r–v.

32 Cosslett, Lury, and Summerfield, eds., "Introduction," *Feminism and Autobiography*, 2–3.

33 Canonizations included those of Rosa de Lima (1671), Francisco Solano (1675),

and Toribio de Mogrovejo (1679). A miracle attributed to Juan Masías (who would be canonized in the nineteenth century) occurred in 1678, and Juan Meléndez included his biography in volume 3 of his *Tesoros verdaderos*. Proceedings to beatify the Spanish Mercedarian Pedro Urraca García (1583–1657) began the year of his death. Jouve Martín, in "En olor de santidad," says that the paperwork for Toribio de Mogrovejo's canonization traveled by ship with that for Ayllón's ordinary proceso. Because ecclesiastical authorities served as judges or witnesses on multiple tribunals, they already knew how to craft their depositions. For instance, Ayllón's confessor, don Ignacio de Híjar y Mendoza, who testified on Ayllón's behalf in 1684, had overseen the beatification hearing for Martín de Porres; see don Ignacio de Yjar [Híjar] y Mendoza, testimony, 11 May 1684, in "Processus," 193r.

34 Vera Tudela, *Colonial Angels*.

35 Greenspan, "Autohagiography"; A. Classen, *Woman's Voice*, 1–6.

36 On the criteria used in determining a seventeenth-century saint, see Burke, "How to Be."

37 The members of the confraternity of "Ingas, Caciques and the eight parishes of Cuzco" attested to this some twenty-four years after the fact. Vargas Ugarte, *Vida del siervo*, 106.

38 María Jacinta de la Santíssima Trinidad, testimony, 13 May 1684, in "Processus," 204r–v.

39 Sartolo, *Nicolas de Ayllon*, 344.

40 Sartolo, *Nicolas de Ayllon*, 339–42.

41 A pastry maker testified that he had had a scrofulous tumor on his neck. After consulting with a slave who tried to cure him, he went with his mother to see Ayllón's corpse lying in repose. His mother got down on her knees, took the hand of the dead man, and placed it on her son's neck. The next day the tumor was gone. Juan de Gamboa, testimony, 1701, AAL, Beatificaciones, Nicolás de Ayllón, vol. 5, 34v. On his portrait, see Estenssoro Fuchs, *Del paganismo*. Both Spanish and Andean traditions involved the belief that it was possible to harness unseen powers to achieve various aims, for good or for evil. Mills, *Idolatry*, especially ch. 4.

42 Following Ayllón's death, coastal caciques immediately requested that testimonies be gathered. Estenssoro Fuchs reports that over eighty witnesses testified in 1684. Estenssoro Fuchs, *Del paganismo*, 486.

43 Petition presented by don Joseph Mexia de Estela, General Legal Representative of the Indians, and signed by thirty-two high ranking indigenous nobles and others in the presence of the Archbishop don Pedro de Villagomez, 27 May 1679, in "Processus," 1v; Vargas Ugarte, *Vida del siervo*, 89. See also Letter from the Twenty-Four Incas from Cuzco to King, 30 October 1706, AGI, Lima, 536.

44 Boss, "Writing a Relic."

45 Sartolo, *Nicolas de Ayllon*, 264. By looking at the portrait of Ayllón, an india named Lucia saved her unborn child. Sartolo, *Nicolas de Ayllon*, 263. See also Vargas Ugarte, *Vida del siervo*, 79–80.

46 Sartolo, *Nicolas de Ayllon*, 253.

47 Vera Tudela talks about the spiritual journeys—traveling to purgatory or bilocating to remote deserts or to heaven—that visionary nuns took from the so-called confines of their cells. *Colonial Angels*, 4–6.

48 For a broader discussion of lettered female communication networks, see the anthology *Early Modern Women and Transnational Communities of Letters*, edited by Julie D. Campbell and Anne R. Larson.

49 Espinoza Rúa, "Un indio camino a los altares," 62.

50 Mbembe, "Power of the Archive," 20.

51 I am not aware of any conventual chronicle written by a nun in Lima; however, they did exist in Italy. See Lowe, *Nuns' Chronicles*.

52 R. Morgan, *Spanish American Saints*, 21–22.

53 Rama, *Ciudad letrada*.

54 "Proceso," 18v; Sartolo, *Nicolas de Ayllon*, 251–52; Cussen, "Fe en la historia," 287.

55 In her self-denunciation Montoya mentioned that Reverend Maestro Lisperguer had approached her, saying he wanted to write another biography and requesting access to Montoya's writings and the proceso of 1684. "Proceso," 18v. Another biography still in manuscript form, written by Francisco Azedo y Porres (1679), is housed in the Monasterio de Jesús, María y José.

56 Ursula de Jesús, *Souls of Purgatory*; Dyck, "Sacred Historian's Task," 205–6; Bristol, "'Although I Am Black.'"

57 Brewer-García, "Beyond Babel," 274.

58 Dyck, "Sacred Historian's Task," 212; Cañizares-Esguerra, "Creole Identity."

59 Estenssoro Fuchs, *Del paganismo*, 463–64.

60 Celia Cussen's monograph on Martín de Porres discusses how his tolerance of racism from his superiors only lent further credibility to his characteristic of extreme humility and suffering. Cussen, *Black Saint*. Kenneth Mills investigates the Andeanness of the cult of saints in "The Naturalization of Andean Christianities." The diary of the Afro-Peruvian mystic Úrsula de Jesús is filled with her experiences of discrimination and her dilemma about how to be an obedient and faithful servant to the nuns and to God. Ursula de Jesús, *Souls of Purgatory*.

61 Cussen, "Search for Idols," 448; see also 418–19, 421, and, on Ayllón as an effective antidote, 446; Estenssoro Fuchs, *Del paganismo*, 484–85, 488; Vargas Ugarte, *Vida del siervo*, 89–92.

62 R. Morgan, *Spanish American Saints*, 85. He says that Leonardo Hansen's biography of Rosa talks about her weeping over the ongoing idolatry and the need to send out additional priests to increase conversion efforts.

63 Petition from María Jacinta Montoya to king, 1697, AGI, Lima, 336. The Protector de los Naturales (royal authority charged with protecting the legal rights of indigenous people), Francisco de Roxas y Azevedo, encouraged the canonization process to proceed in an expeditious manner. Beatificaciones, Nicolás de Ayllón, 1701, AAL. On Montoya's vision that Ayllón would serve as a model among the Mojos, in what is now southwest Bolivia, and on conversion efforts in Arequipa and Huamanga, see "Proceso," 24r.

64 Estenssoro Fuchs, *Del paganismo*, 476. The quote comes from Pedro de Soto,

prior and provincial vicar, Augustinian order, to the king, 12 November 1690, in Vargas Ugarte, *Manuscritos peruanos*, 5:9–10.

65 Sartolo, *Nicolas de Ayllon*, 225.

66 Lima had four parishes and two vice-parishes (San Lázaro and Niños Huérfanos). To attract Indians who resided on agricultural plots outside the city (they were included in the parish of the cathedral), they added the Indians from Cienegilla and all those who lived far away from El Cercado into the *doctrina* (ecclesiastical district) of Pachacamac. Vargas Ugarte, *Historia de la Iglesia*, 3:17.

67 Paul Charney argues that Christianity, and particularly confraternities (as mutual-aid societies), promoted communal organization and a sense of a corporate identity. Charney, *Indian Society*, 93, and ch. 4. Just how Catholic they were is not something I wish to debate here. On this topic, see Ramos, *Death and Conversion*.

68 Durston, *Pastoral Quechua*.

69 Flores Galindo, *Buscando un inca*, 92, 100, appendix 2; Alaperrine-Bouyet, *Educación*.

70 See Ramos and Yannakakis, introduction to *Indigenous Intellectuals*; Ramos, "Indigenous Intellectuals"; and Charles, "Trained by Jesuits." On visual literacy as a tool of empowerment and education, see Rappaport and Cummins, *Beyond the Lettered City*.

71 Charney found that a number of coastal Indians considered a good priest one who punished Indians for not attending Mass, was devoted to his flock, and faithfully administered the sacraments without demanding immediate payment. Charney, *Indian*, 108n53.

72 "Proceso," 171, 53v. On 13 January 1702 don Joseph de Acuña was called in to clarify some of the information regarding Ayllón. He had testified in 1684 and was called in again in 1702 to say that Ayllón's beatification and canonization would serve as a means of conversion for the people living in the mountains near the Marañon River. Joseph de Acuña, testimony, 14 February 1702, Beatificaciones, Nicolás de Ayllón, Segunda Información, AAL, vol. 3, n.p. The bishop of Arequipa also asked for a copy of Montoya's notebook, purportedly for the same reasons. On the efforts to convert the Mojos, see Livi Bacci, *El Dorado*, ch. 4.

73 Sartolo, *Nicolas de Ayllon*, 460, 464.

74 María Jacinta de la Santíssima Trinidad, testimony, 13 May 1684, in "Processus," 229v–230r; Don Joseph de Medina, testimony, 19 July 1684, in "Processus," 446v.

75 Dyck, "Sacred Historian's Task," 247–48.

76 Don Joseph de Medina, testimony, 19 July 1684, in "Processus," 434v.

77 See, for example, the testimony of the friar Pedro de Ávila, 16 December 1686, in "Processus," 594r.

78 Vargas Ugarte, *Vida del siervo*, 38–39, 43.

79 Don Bartolomé Vivas, testimony, 3 December 1700, AAL, Beatificaciones, Nicolás de Ayllón, 8r, 9v.

80 Benito Álfaro, testimony, AAL, Beatificaciones, Nicolás de Ayllón, 30v; Sartolo, *Nicolas de Ayllon*, 69.

81 Salvador de Jesús, testimony, 24 May 1684, in "Processus," 243r, 248v (for the phrase "mala condición").

82 She was from the village of Pausa in the province of Parinacochas, the illegitimate daughter of don Antonio de Montoya y Espinosa and Juana del Rosario. Her padrinos were Capítan Francisco de Arteaga and Cathalina de Carvajal. "Proceso," 4v–5r.

83 Sartolo, *Nicolas de Ayllon*, 69.

84 Don Bartolomé Vivas, testimony, 3 December 1700, AAL, Beatificaciones, Nicolás de Ayllón, 8r, 9v.

85 Don Bartolomé Vivas, testimony, 3 December 1700, AAL, Beatificaciones, Nicolás de Ayllón, 9r.

86 Salvador de Jesús, testimony, 25 May 1684, in "Processus," ASV, 256r–v.

87 "Proceso," 6r.

88 María Jacinta de la Santíssima Trinidad, testimony, 13 May 1684, in "Processus," 218r.

89 Sartolo, *Nicolas de Ayllon*, 76–77, 98–99; Juan Benites (or Benítez), testimony, 1700, AAL, Beatificaciones, Nicolás de Ayllón, 4r.

90 Sartolo, *Nicolas de Ayllon*, 102.

91 Juan de Gamboa, testimony, 1700, Beatificaciones, Nicolás de Ayllón, AAL, 39r.

92 Salvador de Jesús, testimony, 20 May 1684, ASV, "Processus," 249r.

93 "Proceso," 5v.

94 "Proceso," 14r.

95 "Proceso," 9r.

96 Quoted in Sartolo, *Nicolas de Ayllon*, 101.

97 Agustín Mexia, testimony, 10 July 1684, in "Processus," 401v.

98 Doña Nicolasa de Toledo was deeply afflicted by her alcoholic husband's behavior. After he had driven them into poverty, she sought Montoya's advice, who counseled her that God would rectify everything and that "she should count on Nicolás who would attain health for her husband." Doña Nicolasa de Toledo, testimony, 7 July 1685, in "Processus," 522r.

99 For a discussion of Antonia Lucía del Espíritu Santo, a contemporary of Montoya's, see Arenal and Schlau, *Untold Sisters*, 305. Throughout the years Montoya frequently referred to her beaterio as having survived owing to divine providence. María Jacinta de la Santíssima Trinidad, testimony, 13 May 1684, in "Processus," 201v; Vargas Ugarte, *Relaciones de viajes*, 217–21.

100 Juana de San Lorenso, testimony, 5 July 1684, in "Processus," 338r. She also testified in 1701; 1 December 1701, AAL, Beatificaciones, Nicolás de Ayllón, 17r.

101 Estenssoro Fuchs, *Del paganismo*, 478.

102 Quoted in Sartolo, *Nicolas de Ayllon*, 64–65.

103 Van Deusen, *Between the Sacred*, ch. 6.

104 "Expediente que trata de la fundación de un combento de monjas en Lima," 1697, AGI, Lima, 336.

105 Asunción Lavrin says that the Monastery of Corpus Christi for Indian women was not established until 1724. Lavrin, "Indian Brides of Christ," 225; see also

M. Díaz, *Indigenous Writings*. On the discourse of inclusivity, see Vera Tudela, "Fashioning a Cacique Nun," 171–72. In Lima the Beaterio de Nuestra Señora de Copacabana (founded in 1691) was begun by doña Francisca Ignacia Manchipura de Carabajal, a descendant of the caciques of the village of Maranga in the neighboring district of Magdalena. She donated a large sum to provide a sacred space for noble indigenous women to profess formal vows. AAL, Cofradías, Copacabana, Leg. 10-C D, n.p.; Appendix 3, "Heirs of Curacas of Maranga," Charney, *Indian Society*, 178. The members of the confraternity of Copacabana also supplied funds for mestizas of noble Andean descent to take their vows in the Lima convent of their choice. AAL, Cofradías, Copacabana, 1714, Leg. 42, exp. 9, 2r.

106 Estenssoro Fuchs, *Del paganismo*, 478.

107 María Jacinta recalled that he later returned them. "Proceso," 17r.

108 María Mina, testimony, 27 July 1685, in "Processus," 548r.

109 Estenssoro Fuchs, *Del paganismo*, 477. Francisco del Castillo (1615–73), one of Ayllón's confessors, was known for his saintly activities in Lima, particularly with regard to wayward women. His own beatification proceso was initiated in 1677, with 138 witnesses, among them 3 bishops and 53 members of distinct orders. See also Nieto Vélez, *Francisco del Castillo*. Castillo founded the Recogimiento de las Amparadas, an institution designed to save wayward and so-called fallen women. Van Deusen, *Between the Sacred*, ch. 6.

110 Van Deusen, *Between the Sacred*, 142.

111 For the correspondence associated with these efforts, see "Carta del Conde de la Monclova," 14 September 1690, AGI, Audiencia de Lima, 88, no. 20; "Carta del Arzobispo de Lima," 28 November 1690, AGI, Audiencia de Lima, 88, no. 20. By 1697 twenty-three beatas were reported to be living off the charity of limeños. The lawyer in charge of Ayllón's case in Rome encouraged Montoya to pursue the goal of converting the beaterio into a convent. "Expediente que trata de la fundación de un combento de monjas en Lima," 1697, AGI, Lima, 336; Espinoza Rúa, "A las puertas de cielo," 61–62; Vargas Ugarte, *Relaciones de viajes*, 211–55.

112 Echave y Assu, *Estrella de Lima*, 225.

113 Para que vean los hombres / Rey soberano y eterno / Lo que obra en las mujeres / Siendo de tan frágil sexo.

114 "Expediente que trata de la fundación de un combento de monjas en Lima," 1697, AGI, Lima, 336; Vargas Ugarte, *Manuscritos peruanos*, 5:158–59. Members of the indigenous nobility in Cuzco iterated this argument as late as 1706. "Letter from the Indian nobility of Cuzco to king, 1706," in Vargas Ugarte, *Vida del siervo*, 105.

115 The quote comes from Lavrin, "Indian Brides of Christ," 242, in reference to the rationale for founding the Monastery of Corpus Christi in Mexico.

116 Sartolo, *Nicolas de Ayllon*, 254–55.

117 Nicolás de Mayta Escalante to María Jacinta de la Santíssima Trinidad, letter, AAL, Beatificaciones, Nicolás de Ayllón, 1701, s.p. Estenssoro Fuchs speculates that the Inquisition may have ordered the confiscation of images of Ayllón soon thereafter. Estenssoro Fuchs, *Del paganismo*, 488.

118 Vargas Ugarte, *Relaciones de viajes*, 223–25.

119 Vargas Ugarte, *Historia de la Iglesia*, 3:317–18; Vargas Ugarte, *Vida del siervo*, 90. This overlap between beatification and Inquisition hearings, in terms of personnel and methods of proof, was not uncommon. See Elliott, *Proving Woman*, 119–79.

120 Espinoza Rúa, "A las puertas."

121 Cussen, "Fe en la historia," 289.

122 By 1701 Granado had requested that the ordinary beatification process be remitted to him to determine if there was something that merited censure, 17 December 1701, "Proceso," 25v.

123 The exact opposite happened in the second beatification hearing of Martín de Porres, when a unified and more glorified Porres emerged. Cussen, "Fe en la historia," 288.

124 In her deposition in 1684, María Jacinta demurred by stating that she did not have the license to name the person but that she had told her confessors Carranza's vision of Ayllón wearing a white alb and a crown of roses with Christ saying to her, "This is how I reward those who love and serve me." María Jacinta Montoya, testimony, 17 May 1684, in "Processus," 238r. During her self-denunciation she also claimed not to know who had scratched out one of the "supposed" revelations that had come from Carranza in Montoya's notebooks. "Proceso," 19v. When interrogated in 1702, Fernando de Peñalosa admitted that the person who had seen a vision of the Trinity imprinted on Ayllón's heart was Ángela de Carranza. Fernando de Peñalosa, testimony, 13 February 1702, AAL, Beatificaciones, Nicolás de Ayllón, n.p.

125 Witnesses who testified in 1710, the year Montoya died, and again in 1716 were also in short supply. Vargas Ugarte, *Vida del siervo*; "Proceso," 61v. Proponents of the cause were relieved that the new viceroy, Diego Ladrón de Guevara (1710–16), supported Ayllón's case, even when members of the ecclesiastical community did not. Estenssoro Fuchs, *Del paganismo*, 489.

126 Bachiller don Joseph de Acuña, testimony, 3 January 1702, AAL, Beatificaciones, Nicolás de Ayllón, 60v.

127 María Jacinta de la Santíssima Trinidad, testimony, 29 October 1701, AAL, Beatificaciones, Nicolás de Ayllón, 58r–59v.

128 For instance, Cipriano Manrique testified that he did not know where the story came from that the *recogidas* in the house were distraught when Ayllón was gone from the house, although Sartolo quotes Montoya directly and the members of the beatification tribunal pointed out the pages in the biography. Cipriano Manrique, testimony, 7 January 1701, AAL, Beatificaciones, Nicolás de Ayllón, 13r; Sartolo, *Nicolas de Ayllon*, 161–62.

129 "Proceso," 40r–v; Sartolo, *Nicolas de Ayllon*, 169–81. The Mercedarian Fernando de Peñalosa testified in 1684 that José de Buendía (Ayllón's confessor) had told him that Ayllón had confided to him that he had been transported to the canonization festivities of Rosa de Lima in Rome while in a state of mystical ecstasy. Fernando de Peñalosa, testimony, 19 June 1684, in "Processus," 283v.

130 Sartolo, *Nicolas de Ayllon*, 177.

131 "Proceso," 23r.

132 Juan Benítez, testimony, 3 December 1700, AAL, Beatificaciones, Nicolás de Ayllón, 5v.

133 Cipriano Manrique, testimony, 7 January 1701, AAL, Beatificaciones, Nicolás de Ayllón, 16r.

134 Sartolo, *Nicolas de Ayllon*, 50.

135 It had been reported to Sartolo that some Indians followed Ayllón's example and became monogamous after years of succumbing to their lascivious appetites. Sartolo, *Nicolas de Ayllon*, 235.

136 Madre Ana María de Jesús, testimony, 4 September 1711, AAL, Beatificaciones, Nicolás de Ayllón, n.p.

137 During her self-denunciation, Montoya revealed that Ayllón had been "amancebabo" with another woman before marrying Montoya and that he had a daughter with her. "Proceso," 22v, 41v–42r. When questioned again years later, she brushed it off as "a thing of the young" (por aver sido *cosa de moços*). María Jacinta de la Santíssima Trinidad, testimony, 23 December 1710, AAL, Beatificaciones, Nicolás de Ayllón, n.p.

138 Ana María de Jesús, testimony, 12 February 1716, AAL, Beatificaciones, Nicolás de Ayllón, n.p.

139 Sartolo, *Nicolas de Ayllon*, 113.

140 "Proposicion no. 7," in "Proceso," 32r.

141 "Proposicion no. 7," in "Proceso," 32r–v.

142 "Proceso," 2v.

143 "Proceso," 2v; Espinoza Rúa, "A las puertas," 64.

144 "Proposición no. 29," in "Proceso," 35v.

145 "Proceso," 40r.

146 For example, Montoya wrote, "Postrada en tierra y pegado mi rostro con el suelo pedia a Dios que no permitiese que yo escribiese cossa que fuese para daño mio sino para gloria suya y entendi que me desia el Señor no temas que yo lo dispongo assi, y lo que escribiera es mio y de todo sere servido." "Proceso," 31v.

147 "Proceso," 24r.

148 Echave y Assu, *Estrella de Lima*, 235.

149 Cipriano Manrique, testimony, 7 January 1701, AAL, Beatificaciones, Nicolás de Ayllón, 13r.

150 Cipriano Manrique, testimony, 7 January 1701, AAL, Beatificaciones, Nicolás de Ayllón, 13r–v.

151 "Proceso," 31r.

152 "Proceso," 63r.

153 Although the founders of the convent received the license in 1698, the actual inauguration did not occur until 1713, nearly three years after Montoya's death. Some blame the delay on a change in succession (from Charles II to Philip V) and to a new dynasty (from the Hapsburgs to the Bourbons), which culminated in a protracted war of succession that caused several years of instability in Europe and at sea. Vargas Ugarte, *Relaciones de viajes*; María Rosa, *Journey*.

154 Estenssoro Fuchs, *Del paganismo*, 477.

155 María Rosa, *Journey*, 176.

156 María Rosa, *Journey*, 185.

157 María Rosa, *Journey*.

158 Later religious histories would paint her as "as virtuous as her husband." García y Sanz, *Apuntes*, 383, 387.

159 Vargas Ugarte, *Relaciones de viajes*, 211–255, contains the transcribed document, titled, "En que se contiene la relación del origen y fundación de el Beaterio de Jesús, María y José de esta ciudad de Lima y de la vida y virtudes de la Madre María Jacinta de la Santíssima Trinidad, su fundadora." It is dated 29 December 1713 and the anonymous nun signed it by writing, "This paper I have written because of the orders of the head Canon, don Manuel Antonio Gómez de Silva, legal representative of this [religious] house of Jesús, María and José" ("Este papel he escrito por orden del Señor Canónigo Don Manuel Antonio Gómez de Silva, Provisor de esta Casa de Jesús, María y José"). Although the nun wrote at the bequest of the provisor, she based the account on some notes left among Montoya's papers. Vargas Ugarte's biography of Nicolás de Ayllón also relied heavily on this account.

160 Vargas Ugarte, *Relaciones de viajes*, 254.

CHAPTER 6: *AMPARADA DE MI LIBERTAD*

1 Olms y de Santa Pau, *Relación*, 89r; Mendiburu, *Diccionario histórico-biográfico*, 9:230–32; Palma, *Tradiciones peruanas*, 247–48; Eguiguren, *Leyendas y curiosidades*, 313. For a brief account of Josefa's life, see García y Sanz, *Apuntes*, 393–94. Josefa's name is also spelled Josepha in the documents.

2 "Poder para testar," in Moreyra y Paz-Soldán, *Virreinato peruano*, vol. 3, appendix A, 313.

3 Moreyra y Paz-Soldán, *Virreinato peruano*, vol. 3, appendix A, 312, 313.

4 Quoted in Ladrón de Guevara, *Dissertación jurídica*, 60r.

5 Moreyra y Paz-Soldán, *Virreinato peruano*, 3:xiv. See also doña Josepha Portocarrero Laso de la Vega to King Philip V, letter, 16 December 1707, AGI, Lima, 1586, 2r. In that letter she describes how the provisor had accused her in an *auto* of being a "rebel, in having alarmed the City."

6 These include, among other documents, two letters to Philip V from Josefa in December 1707 (one is dated "December," the other "16 December" with an addendum dated 24 December) and another letter from her to the queen, which is undated but probably written in December 1707. These letters can be found in AGI, Lima, 1586. They were received by the Council of the Indies one year later (3 December 1708). An entire *legajo* (a document bundle divided into two *cuadernos* [notebooks]), cataloged as "Professión de Josefa Portocarrero en las Dominicas de Lima," AGI, Lima, 554, 1707–10, contains copies of correspondence among the different parties, petitions, and decrees.

7 Natural law or *jus naturae* referred to God's moral principles as well as the ca-

pacity of humans to observe and understand these principles and the true nature of the world. The work of the Jesuit legal scholar Francisco Suárez (1548–1617), among others, provides an important synthesis of previous scholastic moral-legal theory, including Aristotelian and Catholic theological interpretations and understandings of natural law and humans' capacity to discern God's moral principles. For Suárez and others, discerning natural law was a moral imperative. Haakonsson, "Divine/Natural Law Theories in Ethics," 1318–24; Premo, *Enlightenment on Trial,* 70–71. On the relationship among agency, submission to God's will, and freedom of choice among eighteenth-century Quaker women, see Mack, "Religion, Feminism," 156–57.

8 RAE, *Diccionario de autoridades,* 4:396; Covarrubias Orozco, *Tesoro de la lengua castellana,* 42v–43r, 91r.

9 Ladrón de Guevara, *Dissertación jurídica,* 12r–17r; J. Brown, *Invalidating Effects,* 35–38; Premo, "Maidens," 291.

10 Olms y de Santa Pau, *Relación,* 89r; Mendiburu, *Diccionario histórico-biográfico,* 9:220.

11 Josefa de Portocarrero to Archbishop Liñán y Cisneros, letter, 4 December 1706, AGI, Lima, 1561.

12 Josefa de Portocarrero to Archbishop Liñán y Cisneros, letter, 4 December 1706, AGI, Lima, 1561. Ismael Portal paints a slightly different picture, claiming that Josefa felt a calling to become a nun from an early age. Portal, *Lima religiosa,* 76.

13 Buendía, *Parentación real.*

14 Moreyra y Paz-Soldán, *Virreinato peruano,* 3:x, 316; Bromley, "Recibimientos de virreyes."

15 Quoted in Moreyra y Paz-Soldán, *Virreinato peruano,* 3:ix.

16 Hoyo, *Relación completa,* 1r.

17 Lorente, *Historia del Perú,* 9; Olms y de Santa Pau, *Relación;* Moreyra y Paz-Soldán, *Virreinato peruano,* 3:vi.

18 Josefa de Portocarrero to Archbishop Liñán y Cisneros, letter, 4 December 1706, AGI, Lima, 1561.

19 Josefa de Portocarrero to Archbishop Liñán y Cisneros, letter, 4 December 1706, AGI, Lima, 1561.

20 Josefa de Portocarrero to Archbishop Liñán y Cisneros, letter, 4 December 1706, AGI, Lima, 1561.

21 Josefa de Portocarrero to Archbishop Liñán y Cisneros, letter, 4 December 1706, AGI, Lima, 1561.

22 Josepha de Santa Rosa, abbess, to King Philip V, letter, Lima, 23 October 1711, AGI, Lima, 536, 2r (describing the crucifix).

23 Josefa de Portocarrero to Archbishop Liñán y Cisneros, letter, 4 December 1706, AGI, Lima, 1561.

24 Accounts written centuries later report that a prescient Josefa knew eighteen years before the count's death that she would flee her home. Madre Toribia de Santa Rosa, "Breve relación de la vida de Sor Josefa de Santa Rosa," March 1912, Monasterio de Santa Rosa, Lima.

25 Josefa de Portocarrero to Archbishop Liñán y Cisneros, letter, 4 December 1706, AGI, Lima, 1561.

26 Countess to the archbishop, copy of petition, Lima, 20 December 1708, AGI, Lima, 554, n.p.

27 Countess to the archbishop, copy of petition, Lima, 20 December 1708, AGI, Lima, 554, n.p.

28 Given the preponderance of women in Lima, some of them single mothers or widows who were raising their or others' children, ecclesiastical judges reviewing annulment suits (for marriage and religious vocations) sometimes interpreted *patria potestad* to include maternal rights. Premo, "Maidens," 284–87.

29 Ladrón de Guevara, *Dissertación jurídica*, 51r.

30 Twenty-Fifth Session, On Regulars and Nuns, Chapter 15, Council of Trent, http://www.documentacatholicaomnia.eu/o3d/1545-1545,_Concilium _Tridentinum,_Canons_And_Decrees,_EN.pdf.

31 Doña Josepha Portocarrero Laso de la Vega to King Philip V, letter, Lima, December 1707, AGI, Lima, 1586, 2v. They were Dr. Don Juan de Soto Cornexo, canon of the cathedral, and Dr. Don Martín de los Reies, prebendary (*racionero)* of the cathedral.

32 The Council of Trent mandated that a woman not be compelled to take monastic vows and that no one should prevent her from doing so if she wished, *except in cases permitted by law*. Twenty-Fifth Session, On Regulars and Nuns, Chapters 17 and 18, Council of Trent, http://www.documentacatholicaomnia .eu/o3d/1545-1545,_Concilium_Tridentinum,_Canons_And_Decrees,_EN .pdf

33 Doña Josepha Portocarrero Laso de la Vega to King Philip V, letter, Lima, December 1707, AGI, Lima, 1586, 2r.

34 Ladrón de Guevara, *Dissertación jurídica*, 3r. He was not the only one to write a treatise on the matter, according to Luis de Eguiguren. Eguiguren quoted historian Enrique Torres Saldamando, who said that the Jesuit José Mudarra also wrote a manuscript on the legality of the religious vows taken by doña Josefa. Torres Saldamando, *Antiguos jesuitas*, 325; Eguiguren, *Universidad de San Marcos*, 856. Mudarra (1651–1739) was rector of the Colegio de San Pablo from 1709 to 1712.

35 Ladrón de Guevara, *Dissertación jurídica*, 4r.

36 Twenty-Fifth Session, On Regulars and Nuns, Chapters 17 and 18, Council of Trent, http://www.documentacatholicaomnia.eu/o3d/1545-1545,_Concilium _Tridentinum,_Canons_And_Decrees,_EN.pdf

37 Premo, "Maidens." On donadas attempting to nullify their vows, see van Deusen, "God Lives," 146–48.

38 Ladrón de Guevara, *Dissertación jurídica*, 17v.

39 Ladrón de Guevara, *Dissertación jurídica*, 19r–v.

40 Ladrón de Guevara, *Dissertación jurídica*, 29v.

41 Ladrón de Guevara, *Dissertación jurídica*, 33r.

42 Ladrón de Guevara, *Dissertación jurídica*, 43r.

43 In the same year that Josefa decided to seek refuge in the Monasterio de Santa

Catalina, Antonio had a son out of wedlock. "Relación," 88v; Moreyra y Paz-Soldán, *Virreinato peruano*, 3:xiv. In a letter to Castell-dos-Rius, the countess details her visit to Santa Catalina to plead with her daughter and express her maternal love. Countess to the viceroy, Marques de Casteldosrrius, letter, Lima, 16 May 1708, AGI, Lima, 554, n.p.

44 Countess of Aranda to Philip V, letter, n.p., AGI, Lima, 1561, IV.

45 Bishop Ladrón de Guevara failed to mention in this account that Thomas was destined for a religious life. As a member of the Italian nobility, he was supposed to follow in the footsteps of his uncle, an abbot, and join the Benedictines, a more prestigious order than the mendicant friars.

46 Ladrón de Guevara, *Dissertación jurídica*, 45r.

47 Aquinas, *Summa Theologica*, 1.69.4.

48 Ladrón de Guevara, *Dissertación jurídica*, 45v, 47r.

49 Doña Josepha Portocarrero Laso de la Vega to King Philip V, letter, Lima, December 1707, AGI, Lima, 1586.

50 Josefa de Portocarrero to Archbishop Liñán y Cisneros, letter, 4 December 1706, AGI, Lima, 1561.

51 Countess of Aranda to Philip V, letter, [1707], AGI, Lima, 1561, 1r.

52 Countess of Monclova to Virrey Castel-dos-rius, letter, 16 May 1709, AGI, Lima, 554, n.p.

53 Countess of Aranda to Philip V, letter, [1707], AGI, Lima, 1561, 1r.

54 Ladrón de Guevara, *Dissertación jurídica*, 51r–52r.

55 Doña Josepha Portocarrero Laso de la Vega to King Philip V, letter, Lima, 16 December 1707, AGI, Lima, 1586, IV.

56 Moreyra y Paz Soldán, *Virreinato peruano*, 1:xii.

57 Moreyra y Paz-Soldán, *Virreinato peruano*, 1:xii.

58 The three most powerful members were Juan de Peñalosa, don Pablo Vázquez de Velasco, and Miguel Nuñez de Sanabria; see Moreyra y Paz-Soldán, *Virreinato peruano*, 3:xi.

59 Lorente, *Historia del Perú*, 9, 14. Castell-dos-Rius had the honor of presenting to Louis XIV the will of Charles II, which designated Philip V as his heir.

60 Vargas Ugarte, *Historia del Perú*, 3:51.

61 King Philip V supported the archbishop's decision in a royal decree. Copy of royal decree, 24 September 1707, AGI, Lima, 554, n.p. Josefa thought that the archbishop's coldness toward her could be attributed to the kinship ties he had with her mother, the countess. Doña Josepha Portocarrero Laso de la Vega to King Philip V, letter, Lima, 16 December 1707, AGI, Lima, 1586.

62 On 16 May 1708 the countess mentions the auto of July 1707 in a letter to the Marquis of Castell-dos-Rius. Countess to the viceroy, Marques de Casteldosrrius, letter, Lima, 16 May 1708, AGI, Lima, 554, n.p.

63 Ladrón de Guevara, *Dissertación jurídica*, 38r–v.

64 Doña Josepha Portocarrero Laso de la Vega to King Philip V, letter, Lima, 16 December 1707, AGI, Lima, 1586; Olms y de Santa Pau, *Relación*; Moreyra y Paz-Soldán, *Virreinato peruano*, 3:vi.

65　Doña Josepha Portocarrero Laso de la Vega to King Philip V, letter, Lima, December 1707, AGI, Lima, 1586, 2r.

66　Crahan, "Clerical Immunity," 178.

67　Moreyra y Paz-Soldán, *Virreinato peruano*, 1:xxiv.

68　Other documents say September 2, 1708. See Mendiburu, *Diccionario histórico-biográfico*, 9:231; "Relación de la fundación del Real Monasterio de Santa Rosa de Santa María ... 2 de febrero de 1708" (hereafter cited as "Relación"), in Ángulo, *Santa Rosa de Santa María*, 61–67.

69　Mendiburu, *Diccionario histórico-biográfico*, 9:230–32. See a letter encouraging this decision from the confessor of King Philip V to Philip V, Madrid, 4 December 1703, AGI, Lima, 1561.

70　Doña Elena Rodríguez de Corte Real had also donated a large sum to that effect several decades before and served as the first prioress. Vargas Ugarte, *Historia del Perú*, 3:51. As early as 1695, over 246,000 pesos "de principal situados en diferentes y seguras fincas que han contribuido de limosnas" were available for the foundation, including the building, valued at 16,000 pesos. Count of Monclova to Charles II, letter, 13 August 1695, AGI, Lima, 537. On successful efforts to evict the beatas and recogidas living in the Casa de las Amparadas de la Puríssima Concepción and use the building for the new monastery, see van Deusen, *Between the Sacred*, ch. 6.

71　"Don Pedro de Loayza Coco, petition," 20 June 1708, AGI, Lima, 554, n.p.

72　On the centrality of religious processions to Lima's culture, see Osorio, *Inventing Lima*, ch. 5.

73　"Don Pedro de Loayza Coco, petition," 20 June 1708, AGI, Lima, 554, n.p.

74　"Relación," in Ángulo, *Santa Rosa de Santa María*, 62.

75　"Relación," in Ángulo, *Santa Rosa de Santa María*, 63. As discussed in chapter 1, early modern subjects believed that the image of the saint "made the saint physically present" yet supernatural at the same time. Belting, *Likeness and Presence*, 299.

76　"Relación," in Ángulo, *Santa Rosa de Santa María*, 66.

77　The return of two of these nuns to the Monasterio de Santa Catalina produced a small crisis in Lima. Portal, *Lima religiosa*, 76.

78　Sor Josefa de Santa Rosa to King Philip V, letter, Lima, December 1707, AGI, Lima, 1586. On the history of the Monasterio de Santa Catalina, see Espinoza, "De Guerras y de Dagas."

79　Castell-dos-rius to Philip V, report, 31 July 1708, Lima 554, n.p.

80　Countess of Monclova to the viceroy, letter, 6 February 1708, AGI, Lima, 554, n.p. In an undated petition to the viceroy, the countess requested further information on the matter pending before the Real Audiencia. Countess of Monclova to Viceroy Marques Castell-dos-Rius, petition, AGI, Lima, 554, n.p.

81　Confessor of King Philip V to the king, cover letter, 29 June 1707, AGI, Lima, 1561.

82　King to Viceroy Marques Castell-dos-Rius, copy of royal decree, Madrid, 24 September 1707, AGI, Lima, 554, n.p.

83 Liñán y Cisneros to Josefa Portocarrero, letter, 12 April 1708, AGI, Lima, 1561. He also sent a letter on 22 April to the viceroy ordering him to comply with the king's mandate. Castell-dos-rius to Philip V, letter, Lima, 31 June 1708, AGI, Lima, 554, n.p.

84 Copy of the auto from Archbishop Liñán y Cisneros to remove Josefa de Porto-carrero from the Monasterio de Santa Catalina, Lima, 15 December 1707, AGI, Lima, 554, n.p.

85 Castell-dos-Rius refers to a letter sent to him by the countess on 23 April. Castell-dos-Rius to Philip V, letter, Lima, 31 July 1708, AGI, Lima, 554, n.p.

86 Castell-dos-Rius to the Countess of Monclova, letter, 25 May 1708, AGI, Lima, 554, n.p.

87 According to Vargas Ugarte, the countess once directed a letter to the city council that was so discourteous and written in such denigrating terms that the council members decided to return the letter to her. Vargas Ugarte, *Historia del Perú*, 3:19n8. While her husband, the viceroy, was still alive, her infamous "agrio y violentísimo natural" manifested itself in her vehement opposition to one candidate for the position of the Franciscan provincial, much to her husband's chagrin. Moreyra y Paz Soldán, *Virreinato peruano*, 2:xxxiv; Vargas Ugarte, *Historia del Perú*, 3:10–11.

88 Moreyra y Paz Soldán, *Virreinato peruano*, 3:xiii–xiv (the title of the play is found on xiii).

89 Viceroy Marques de Castel-dos-rius to Philip V, report, 31 July 1708, AGI, Lima, 554, n.p.

90 "Don Pedro de Loayza Coco, petition," 20 June 1708, AGI, Lima, 554, n.p. Josefa references the dire condition of the archbishop in an addendum dated 24 December 1707. Doña Josepha Portocarrero Laso de la Vega to King Philip V, addendum to 16 December 1707 letter, Lima, dated 24 December 1707, AGI, Lima, 1586, 2r.

91 Castell-dos-rius to Philip V, letter, Lima, 31 July 1708, AGI, Lima, 554, n.p.

92 Castell-dos-rius to Philip V, letter, Lima, 31 July 1708, AGI, Lima, 554, n.p.

93 "Bishop of Quito, Ladrón de Guevara to king Philip V, report," Quito, 10 June 1708, AGI, Lima, 408.

94 Castell-dos-rius to Philip V, letter, Lima, 31 July 1708, AGI, Lima, 554, 19r; Vargas Ugarte, *Historia del Perú*, 3:16–17.

95 Vargas Ugarte, *Historia del Perú*, 3:51; Mendiburu, *Diccionario histórico-biográfico*, 9:231; Castell-dos-rius to Philip V, letter, Lima, 31 July 1708, AGI, Lima, 554, n.p.

96 Castell-dos-rius to Philip V, letter, Lima, 31 July 1708, AGI, Lima, 554, 33r–v. According to Ladrón de Guevara, when it came to judging human fragility in making decisions, he had determined that doña Josefa was one of the most "erudite, cautious and conscientious" religious candidates he had known, and her vocation "a marked calling selected by God." "Bishop of Quito, Ladrón de Guevara to king Philip V, report," Quito, 10 June 1708, AGI, Lima, 408.

97 The king responded to the letter written by Ladrón de Guevara in June 1708, acknowledging that he was aware that she had already taken her formal vows.

Philip V to the bishop of Quito, Madrid, 21 October 1709, AGI, Quito, 210, Leg. 6, 43r–v.

98 Suspecting that Peñalosa was involved in the scandal (he had been the supervisory judge of the Casa de Moneda and was closely allied with the countess), Castell-dos-Rius urged the king to consider choosing a more disinterested minister such as don Pablo Vázquez de Velasco to investigate the matter. Lohmann Villena, *Ministros de la Audiencia*, 98.

99 Don Juan de Peñalosa to King Philip, report, 1 September 1707, AGI, Lima, 409, 10r–v.

100 Castell-dos-Rius to the king, report, Lima, 6 January 1710, AGI, Lima, 409, 2r. This report was received by the Council of the Indies in February 1712 and reviewed in June. Vargas Ugarte, *Historia del Perú*, 3:17. The mystery of Josefa's inheritance was never resolved, but most likely parts of it were included in the allotment sent back to Spain.

101 Lorente, *Historia del Perú*, 18.

102 "Fragmento de los autos . . . Condessa de la Monclova sobre la recepción del hábito y professión de doña Josefa Portocarrero," Lima, 21 March 1709, AAL, Monasterio de Santa Rosa, Leg. 1:21, 1709.

103 Sor Josepha de Santa Rosa to King Philip V, letter, Lima, 23 October 1711, AGI, Lima, 536, 1r–v.

104 Doña Josepha Portocarrero Laso de la Vega to the queen, letter, 1707, AGI, Lima, 1586, 3r–v; Sor Josefa de Santa Rosa to King Philip V, letter, Lima, 23 October 1711, AGI, Lima, 536.

105 Don Ramón de Auñon, fiscal officer for the Monasterio de Santa Rosa, reported that all efforts to gain the paternal inheritance and other personal items (jewels, etc.) "had been in vain and that nothing had been found." Don Ramón de Auñon to King Philip V, memorandum, Lima, 12 September 1712, AGI, Lima, 536, 1r, 2r. See also Sor Josepha de Santa Rosa, Abadessa, to King Philip V, letter, 23 October 1711, AGI, Lima, 536, 2r.

106 The location may have been poignant for other reasons as well; her father had been wounded at a battle at Villaviciosa in 1665. Mendiburu, *Diccionario histórico-biográfico*, 9:221. Sor Josepha de Santa Rosa to King Philip V, letter, Monasterio de Santa Rosa, Lima, 23 October 1711, AGI, Lima, 536, 2r. Josefa had adopted this tone, appealing to the religious sensibilities of the queen and king, in an earlier letter in 1707. Doña Josepha Portocarrero Laso de la Vega to the queen, letter, 1707, AGI, Lima, 1586, 1r–2v, 4r–v.

107 Sor Josepha de Santa Rosa, Abadesa, to Philip V, letter, Monasterio de Santa Rosa, Lima, 23 October 1711, AGI, Lima, 536, 2v–3r.

108 The lawyer had made this recommendation to the king on 12 September 1712, but the Council of the Indies did not make its ruling until 30 March 1713. See also the petition from don Ramón de Auñon, the fiscal officer for the Monasterio de las Rosas, to King Philip V on 12 September 1712, stating that the monastery had still not received the inheritance funds. AGI, Lima, 536.

109 Vargas Ugarte, *Historia del Perú*, 3:17.

110 Vargas Ugarte, *Historia del Perú*, 3:17.

111 Vargas Ugarte, *Historia del Perú*, 3:16; Aufderheide, *Scientific Study of Mummies*, 130.

112 Olms y de Santa Pau, *Relación*, 88v.

113 Madre Toribia de Santa Rosa, "Breve relación de la vida de Sor Josefa de Santa Rosa," March 1912, n.p., Monasterio de Santa Rosa, Lima.

114 An example of the declining revenue can be seen in a letter written to the Council of the Indies in 1732, requesting that the four scholarships established in 1707 for daughters of ministers or other "deserving citizens" (*vezinos beneméritos*) be rescinded and that all entering nuns pay the 3,159 peso dowry to maintain themselves with the "corresponding decency." See "Council of the Indies Review of a Petition from the Prioress of Santa Rosa," 9 August 1732, AGI, Lima, 539. On the economic decline of monastic institutions in Lima in the eighteenth century, see Walker, *Shaky Colonialism*.

115 The income of the convent was severely diminished as a result of the earthquake of 1746. See Archbishop Pedro de Barroeta Ángel to King Ferdinand VI, letter, 31 December 1754, Lima, AGI, Lima, 523. See also Lozano, "Relación del Terremoto," 38–39.

CONCLUSION

1 Meyer and Houtman, "Introduction," 5.

2 Anderson, "Epistemological-Ethical Approach," 92.

3 Vries, "Introduction," 10, also 4.

4 Vries, "Introduction," 1.

5 Hollywood, "Practice," 74–79.

6 Certeau, *Practice of Everyday Life*, 48, 77–78.

7 Bynum, ". . . And Woman His Humanity," was first published in 1986 in *Gender and Religion*.

8 Haslanger, "Gender and Race," 34.

9 Diefendorf, "Rethinking the Catholic Reformation," 43–44.

10 Irigaray, *Prières quotidiennes*, quoted in Howie and Jobling, "Introduction," 1.

11 Bynum, ". . . And Woman His Humanity," 119.

12 AAL, LC, XVI: 49, "Solicitud . . . Josefa de la Concepcion y Meneses."

13 Ursula de Jesús, *Souls of Purgatory*, 121.

14 Mills, "Naturalization of Andean Christianities," 505–6.

Bibliography

MANUSCRIPT COLLECTIONS
Archivo Arzobispal de Lima (AAL)

Beatificaciones
    Isabel de Porras Marmolejo, 1648.
    Nicolás de Ayllón, 1700–1716.
    Rosa de Santa María, 1630–32.
Capellanías (Indios), Leg. 36:2 (1664).
Causas de Negros (CN), 5:27 (1627); 6:25 (1633); 7:37 (1639); 10:11 (1647); 12:4 (1655).
Celibato, nos. 1, 2, 3.
Cofradías, 31:2 (1608).
    Copacabana, Leg. 10-C D.
    Copacabana, 1714, Leg. 42, exp. 9, 2r.
Monasterio de La Concepción (LC), Leg. 2:6 (1617–25); 2:14 (1622); 3:6 (1623); 3:16 (1626); 5:8 (1631); 5:27 (1632); 5:44 (1633–37); 7:22 (1638); 9:29 (1646); 12:14 (1656); 16:30 (1664); 16:49 (1664); 17:15 (1665); 17:55 (1697); 19:64 (1672); 20:3 (1673); 20:4 (1673); 21:24 (1678); 21:26 (1678); 21:43 (1678); 21:77 (1679); 22:4 (1680); 22:8 (1680); 22:26 (1680); 22:51 (1681); 23:18 (1683); 23:23 (1683); 24:1 (1685); 24:10 (1685); 24:14 (1685); 25:7 (1687); 25:12 (1687); 25:13 (1687); 25:17 (1687); 25:33 (1687); 25:35 (1687); 25:60 (1688); 25:66 (1688); 25:74 (1689); 25:83 (1689); 26:28 (1691); 26:60 (1692); 27:13 (1695); 27:29 (1696); 27:38 (1696); 27:45 (1696); 28:11 (1700).
Monasterio de La Encarnación (LE), Leg. 1:6 (1607); 1:7 (1609); 2:5 (1626); 3:8A (1628–29); 3:22 (1630); 5:26 (1638); 6:21 (1643); 9:39 (1656–57); 11:30 (1664); 11:57 (1664); 11:59 (1664); 11:59 (1664); 11:68 (1665); 11:86 (1665); 11:88 (1665); 11:103 (1666); 11:106 (1666); 12:14 (1656); 13:6 (1673); 13:10 (1674); 13:28 (1674); 13:29 (1674); 13:87 (1677); 17:70 (1690).
Monasterio de La Trinidad (LT), Leg. 1:37 (1626–27); 1:38 (n.d.); 3:3 (1636); 3:10 (1636); 5:69 (1657); 6:70 (1667).

Monasterio de Las Descalzas, Leg. 2:49 (1646); 2:50 (1646); 4:15 (1665); 4:32 (1668); 4:79 (1672); 4:86 (n.d.).

Monasterio de Santa Catalina de Sena, Leg. 3:32 (1653); 8:4 (1688); 8:4 (1688); 8:87 (1695).

Monasterio de Santa Clara (SC), Leg. 4:25 (1632); 4:32 (1632); 4:42 (1633); 5:42 (1636); 6:35 (1642); 6:37 (1642); 12:27 (1664); 12:42 (1665); 12:58 (1665); 12:64 (1665); 12:74 (1665); 12:99 (1666); 12:112 (1666); 12:117 (1668); 12:120 (1667); 12:131 (1667); 12:157 (1668); 12:171 (1678); 13:55 (1670); 13:88 (1671); 14:72 (1675); 16:15 (1678); 16:47 (1679); 17:42 (1681); 17:47 (1682); 18:7 (1684); 18:38 (1685); 18:41 (1685); 18:91 (1687); 19:37 (1688); 19:38 (1688); 19:81 (1689); 20:66 (1693); 20:73 (1693); 21:10 (1695); 21:28 (1697); 21:46 (1698); 21:66 (1699).

Monasterio de Santa Rosa, Leg. 1:21.

Papeles Importantes, Leg. 24:8 (1630–31).

Archivo San Francisco de Lima

Registro 17, no. 38. "Vida de Gerónima de San Francisco," Lima, 1635.

Registro 17, no. 43. Vida de Estephania de San Joseph.

Registro 17, no. 45. "Vida de la Venerable Ursula de Jesús," 585r–607v.

Archivo General de Indias (AGI)

Lima 88, 336, 408, 409, 523, 536, 537, 539, 554, 1561, 1586

Quito 210

Archivo General de la Nación (AGNP)

Protocolos

Francisco de Acuña (FA) no. 6 (1629); 29 (1648); 30 (1649); 31 (1650); 32 (1651); 33 (1652); 34 (1653); 35 (1654); 37 (1656); 38 (1657); 40 (1660).

Joseph de Aguirre Urbina 69 (1644–45).

Marcelo Antonio de Figueroa, 665 (1670-B).

Gregorio de Urtázo, 1103 (1709).

Sección Compañía de Jesús, Sermones. Leg. 61, Sermon 1, Chuquisaca, 1617, "Sermón de la Puríssima Concepción de la S. S. Virgen María."

Testamentos, 7, no. 10; 8, no. 10.

Archivo Histórico Nacional de Madrid (AHNM)

Inquisición, Lima, Leg. 1028, 1029, 1030, 1032, 1647, expediente 5; 1649, expediente 51.

Inquisición, Censuras, Leg. 4467, no. 11.

Archivio Segreto Vaticano (Vatican City, Rome)

Congregazione Riti Processus, 1309, Processus [Nicolás de Ayllón].

Biblioteca Nacional del Perú

Ms. B 124, Diego Córdova y Salinas, "Relación de la fundación de la Santa Provincia de los Doce Apóstoles."

Biblioteca Nacional de Madrid

Ms. 4381, Gregorio Quesada y Sotomayor, "Dictamenes varios sobre diversos causas, de la mayor importancia que dio al santo tribunal de la ynquisicion de la ciudad de Lima."

Monasterio de Santa Rosa (Lima)

Madre Toribia de Santa Rosa, "Breve relación de la vida de Sor Josefa de Santa Rosa." March 1912.

PRIMARY AND SECONDARY SOURCES

Adams, Kathleen M., and Sara Dickey. *Home and Hegemony: Domestic Service and Identity Politics in South and Southeast Asia.* Ann Arbor: University of Michigan Press, 2000.

Agamben, Giorgio. *De la très haute pauvreté.* Translated by Joël Gayraud. Paris: Payot et Rivages, 2011.

Aguilar, Joseph [José] de. *Sermones varios.* Brussels: Mercador de Libros, 1684.

Ahlgren, Gillian T. W. *Entering Teresa of Avila's "Interior Castle": A Reader's Companion.* New York: Paulist Press, 2005.

———. Introduction to *The Inquisition of Francisca: A Sixteenth-Century Visionary on Trial*, edited by Gillian T. W. Ahlgren, 1–40. Chicago: University of Chicago Press, 2005.

———. "Negotiating Sanctity: Holy Women in Sixteenth-Century Spain." *Church History* 64, no. 3 (1995): 373–90.

———. *Teresa of Avila and the Politics of Sanctity.* Ithaca, NY: Cornell University Press, 1996.

Alaperrine-Bouyet, Monique. *La educación de las élites indígenas en el Perú colonial.* Lima: Institut Français d'Études Andines and Instituto de Estudios Peruanos, 2007.

Alberro, Solange. *Inquisición y sociedad en México, 1571–1700.* Mexico City: Fondo de Cultura Económica, 1988.

Anderson, Pamela Sue. "An Epistemological-Ethical Approach to Philosophy of Religion: Learning to Listen." In *Feminist Philosophy of Religion: Critical Readings*, edited by Pamela Sue Anderson and Beverley Clack, 87–102. London: Routledge, 2004.

Andrés Martín, Melquiades, ed. *Los místicos de la edad de oro en España y América: Antología*. Madrid: Biblioteca de Autores Cristianos, 1996.

———. "Pensamiento teológico y vivencia religiosa en la reforma española, 1400–1600." In *Historia de la Iglesia en España*, edited by Ricardo García Villoslada, 3.2: 269–301. Madrid: Edica, 1979.

Angela of Foligno. *Vida de la bienaventurada Santa Angela de Fulgino*. Translated from Latin to Spanish by Doña Francisca de los Rios. Madrid: Juan de la Cuesta, 1618.

Ángulo, Domingo. "El Dr. Ignacio Híjar y Mendoza y la Santa Inquisición." *Revista Histórica* 3, no. 2 (1906): 205–46.

———. *Santa Rosa de Santa María: Estudio bibliográfico*. Lima: n.p., 1917.

Arenal, Electa, and Stacey Schlau. "'Leyendo yo y escribiendo ella': The Convent as Intellectual Community." *Journal of Hispanic Philology* 13, no. 3 (1989): 214–29.

———, eds. *Untold Sisters: Hispanic Nuns in Their Own Works*. Translated by Amanda Powell. Albuquerque: University of New Mexico Press, 1989.

Ashton, Gail. *The Generation of Identity in Late Medieval Hagiography: Speaking the Saint*. London: Routledge, 2000.

Aufderheide, Arthur C. *The Scientific Study of Mummies*. Cambridge: Cambridge University Press, 2003.

Augustine, Saint. *De civitate Dei = City of God. Books VI & VII*. Edited and with an introduction, translation, and commentary by P. G. Walsh. Warminster: Aris & Phillips, 2009.

Banerjee, Swapna M. "Down Memory Lane: Representations of Domestic Workers in Middle Class Personal Narratives of Colonial Bengal." *Journal of Social History* 37, no. 3 (2004): 681–708.

Barriga Calle, Irma. "La experiencia de la muerte en Lima: Siglo XVII." *Apuntes* 31, no. 2 (1992): 81–102.

Belting, Hans. "Image, Medium, Body: A New Approach to Iconology." *Critical Inquiry* 31, no. 2 (2005): 302–19.

———. *Likeness and Presence: A History of the Image before the Era of Art*. Translated by Edmund Jephcott. Chicago: University of Chicago Press, 1994.

Bennett, Herman L. *Africans in Colonial Mexico: Absolutism, Christianity, and Afro-Creole Consciousness, 1570–1640*. Bloomington: Indiana University Press, 2009.

———. "The Subject in the Plot: National Boundaries and the 'History' of the Black Atlantic." *African Studies Review* 43, no. 1 (2000): 101–24.

Bertolini, F. Serafino. *La Rosa peruana overo vita della sposa di Christo, Suor Rosa di Santa Maria, native della città di Lima nel Regno del Perù, del Terz'Ordine di S. Domenico*. Rome: Gio Battista Pasquati, 1669.

Bhabha, Homi K. *The Location of Culture*. London: Routledge, 1994.

Bilinkoff, Jodi. "Confessors, Penitents, and the Construction of Identities in Early Modern Avila." In *Culture and Identity in Early Modern Europe (1500–1800): Essays in Honor of Natalie Zemon Davis*, edited by Barbara B. Diefendorf and Carla Hesse, 83–100. Ann Arbor: University of Michigan Press, 1993.

———. "Navigating the Waves (of Devotion): Toward a Gendered Analysis of Early Modern Catholicism." In *Crossing Boundaries: Attending to Early Modern Women*, edited by Jane Donawerth and Adele Seeff, 161–72. Newark: University of Delaware Press, 2000.

———. *Related Lives: Confessors, Female Penitents, and Catholic Culture, 1450–1750.* Ithaca, NY: Cornell University Press, 2005.

———. "Saint." In *Lexikon of the Hispanic Baroque: Transatlantic Exchange and Transformation*, edited by Evonne Levy and Kenneth Mills, 287–95. Austin: University of Texas Press, 2013.

Boffey, Julia. "Women Authors and Women's Literacy in Fourteenth- and Fifteenth-Century England." In *Women and Literature in Britain, 1150–1500*, edited by Carol M. Meale, 152–82. Cambridge: Cambridge University Press, 1996.

Boss, Julia. "Writing a Relic: The Uses of Hagiography in New France." In *Colonial Saints: Discovering the Holy in the Americas, 1500–1800*, edited by Allan Greer and Jodi Bilinkoff, 211–34. New York: Routledge, 2003.

Bouza, Fernando. *Communication, Knowledge, and Memory in Early Modern Spain.* Translated by Sonia López and Michael Agnew. Philadelphia: University of Pennsylvania Press, 2004.

———. "Los contextos materiales de la producción cultural." In *España en tiempos del Quijote*, edited by Antonio Feros Carrasco and Juan Eloy Gelabert González, 309–44. Madrid: Santillana Ediciones Generales, 2004.

Bouza Álvarez, José Luis. *Religiosidad contrarreformista y cultura simbólica del barroco.* Madrid: Consejo Superior de Investigaciones Científicas, 1990.

Bowser, Frederick P. *The African Slave in Colonial Peru, 1524–1650.* Stanford: Stanford University Press, 1974.

Boydston, Jeanne. "Gender as a Question of Historical Analysis." *Gender and History* 20, no. 3 (2008): 558–83.

Boyer, Richard. *Lives of the Bigamists: Marriage, Family, and Community in Colonial Mexico.* Albuquerque: University of New Mexico Press, 1995.

———. "Respect and Identity: Horizontal and Vertical Reference Points in Speech Acts." *Americas: A Quarterly Review of Inter-American Cultural History* 54, no. 4 (1998): 491–509.

Brading, David A. *The First America: The Spanish Monarchy, Creole Patriots, and the Liberal State, 1492–1867.* New York: Cambridge University Press, 1991.

Braude, Ann. "Women's History *Is* American Religious History." In *Retelling U.S. Religious History*, edited by Thomas A. Tweed, 87–107. Berkeley: University of California Press, 1997.

Bray, Xavier. *The Sacred Made Real: Spanish Painting and Sculpture, 1600–1700.* London: National Gallery, 2009.

Brewer-García, Larissa. "Beyond Babel: Translations of Blackness in Colonial Peru and New Granada." PhD diss., University of Pennsylvania, 2013.

———. "Imagined Transformations: Color, Beauty, and Black Christian Conversion in Seventeenth-Century Spanish America." In *Envisioning Others: Representations of "Race" in the Iberian and Ibero-American World*, edited by Pamela A. Patton, 111–41. Leiden: Brill, 2015.

———. "Negro, pero blanco de alma: La ambivalencia de la negrura en la *Vida prodigiosa* de Fray Martín de Porras (1663)." *Cuadernos del CILHA* 13, no. 2 (2012): 113–46.

Bristol, Joan Cameron. "'Although I Am Black I Am Beautiful': Juana Esperanza de San Alberto, Black Carmelite of Puebla." In *Gender, Race and Religion in the Colonization of the Americas*, edited by Nora E. Jaffary, 67–80. Burlington, VT: Ashgate, 2007.

———. *Christians, Blasphemers and Witches: Afro-Mexican Ritual Practice in the Seventeenth Century*. Albuquerque: University of New Mexico Press, 2007.

Bromley, Juan. "Recibimientos de virreyes en Lima." *Revista Histórica* 20 (1953): 5–108.

Brown, James Victor. *The Invalidating Effects of Force, Fear, and Fraud upon the Canonical Novitiate*. Washington, DC: Catholic University of America Press, 1951.

Brown, Peter. *The Cult of the Saints: Its Rise and Function in Latin Christianity*. Chicago: University of Chicago Press, 1981.

Bryant, Sherwin. *Rivers of Gold, Lives of Bondage: Governing through Slavery in Colonial Quito*. Chapel Hill: University of North Carolina Press, 2014.

Buendía, Joseph de. *Parentación real al Soberano nombre e immortal memoria del católico rey de las Españas y Emperador de las Indias, el Sereníssimo Señor, Don Carlos II*. Lima: Joseph de Contreras, 1701.

Burke, Peter. "How to Be a Counter-Reformation Saint." In *Religion and Society in Early Modern Europe, 1500–1800*, edited by Kaspar von Greyerz, 45–55. London: George Allen and Unwin, 1984.

Burns, Kathryn. *Colonial Habits: Convents and the Spiritual Economy of Cuzco, Peru*. Durham, NC: Duke University Press, 1999.

Burton, Antoinette M. *Dwelling in the Archive: Women Writing House, Home, and History in Late Colonial India*. New York: Oxford University Press, 2003.

Busto Duthurburu, José Antonio del. *San Martín de Porras (Martín de Porras Velásquez)*. Lima: Pontificia Universidad Católica del Perú, Fondo Editorial, 2001.

Butler, Judith. *Gender Trouble*. London: Routledge, 1990.

Bynum, Caroline Walker. "'. . . And Woman His Humanity': Female Imagery in the Religious Writing of the Later Middle Ages." In *Gender and Religion: On the Complexity of Symbols*, edited by Caroline Walker Bynum, Stevan Harrell, and Paula Richman, 257–88. Boston: Beacon Press, 1986.

———. "'. . . And Woman His Humanity': Female Imagery in the Religious Writing of the Later Middle Ages." In *Women and Religion: Critical Concepts in Religious Studies*, edited by Pamela Klassen with Shari Bolberg and Danielle Lefebvre, 1:107–31. London: Routledge, 2009.

———. *Christian Materiality: An Essay on Religion in Late Medieval Europe*. New York: Zone Books, 2011.

———. "The Female Body and Religious Practice in the Latter Middle Ages." In *Fragments for a History of the Human Body*, edited by Michel Feher, Ramona Naddaff, and Nadia Tazi, 160–219. New York: Cambridge University Press, 1989.

———. *Holy Feast and Holy Fast: The Religious Significance of Food to Medieval Women*. Berkeley: University of California Press, 1987.

————. *Jesus as Mother: Studies in the Spirituality of the High Middle Ages.* Berkeley: University of California Press, 1982.

————. "Perspectives, Connections and Objects: What's Happening in History Now?" *Daedalus* 138, no. 1 (winter 2009): 1–16.

————. "Why All the Fuss about the Body? A Medievalist's Perspective." *Critical Inquiry* 22, no. 1 (1995): 1–33.

————. *Wonderful Blood: Theology and Practice in Late Medieval Northern Germany and Beyond.* Philadelphia: University of Pennsylvania Press, 2007.

Bynum, Caroline Walker, and Paula Gerson. "Body-Part Reliquaries and Body Parts in the Middle Ages." *Gesta* 36 (1997): 3–7.

Calancha, Antonio de la. *Crónica moralizada de Antonio de la Calancha.* Edited by Ignacio Prado Pastor. 6 vols. Lima: Universidad Nacional Mayor de San Marcos, 1974–81.

Calancha, Antonio de la, and Bernardo de Torres. *Crónicas augustinianas del Perú.* 1639. Madrid: Consejo Superior de Investigaciones Científicas, 1972.

Camille, Michael. "The Image and the Self: Unwriting Late Medieval Bodies." In *Framing Medieval Bodies,* edited by Sarah Kay and Miri Rubin, 62–99. Manchester: Manchester University Press, 1994.

————. "Seeing and Reading: Some Visual Implications of Medieval Literacy and Illiteracy." *Art History* 8, no. 1 (1985): 26–49.

Campbell, Julie D., and Anne R. Larson. *Early Modern Women and Transnational Communities of Letters.* Burlington, VT: Ashgate, 2009.

Campos, Alzira. "Mulher e universo magico: Beatas e curandeiras." *História* 12 (1993): 29–47.

Canêvet, Mariette. "Sens spirituel." In *Dictionnaire de spiritualité ascétique et mystique, doctrine et histoire,* edited by Marcel Viller, 14:599–617. Paris: Beauchesne, 1990.

Cañizares-Esguerra, Jorge. "Racial, Religious, and Civic Creole Identity in Colonial Spanish America." *American Literary History* 17, no. 3 (2005): 420–37.

Carruthers, Mary J., and Jan M. Ziolkowski, eds. *The Medieval Craft of Memory: An Anthology of Texts and Pictures.* Philadelphia: University of Pennsylvania Press, 2002.

Cashmere, John. "Sisters Together: Women without Men in Seventeenth-Century French Village Culture." *Journal of Family History* 21, no. 1 (1996): 44–62.

Castañeda Delgado, Paulino, and Pilar Hernández Aparicio. *La Inquisición de Lima, 1570–1820.* 3 vols. Madrid: Deimos, 1989–95.

Castillo, Fray Hernando de. *Segunda parte de la Historia general de Santo Domingo y de su Orden.* Valladolid: n.p., 1612–13. https://books.google.ca/books?id=jd cwvQmUNQgC&dq=Hernando+del+Castillo+Historia+de+Santo+Domingo ,+v.+2&source=gbs_navlinks_s.

Caviness, Madeline H. *Visualizing Women in the Middle Ages: Sight, Spectacle, and Scopic Economy.* Philadelphia: University of Pennsylvania Press, 2001.

Cazelles, Brigitte. "Bodies on Stage and the Production of Meaning." In *Corps Mystique, Corps Sacré: Textual Transfigurations of the Body from the Middle Ages to the Seventeenth Century,* edited by Françoise Jaouën and Benjamin Semple, 56–74. New Haven, CT: Yale University Press, 1994.

Cebrelli, Alejandra. "Una herencia conflictiva: El imaginario religioso colonial y la construcción de identidades nacionales." *Andes: Revista de Antropología e Historia* 11 (2000): 1–41.

Cerda, Juan de la. *Libro intitulado vida política de todos los estados de mujeres.* Álcala de Henares: Juan Gracián, 1599.

Certeau, Michel de. *Heterologies: Discourse on the Other.* Translated by Brian Massumi. Minneapolis: University of Minnesota Press, 1986.

——. *The Mystic Fable: The Sixteenth and Seventeenth Centuries.* Translated by Michael B. Smith. Chicago: University of Chicago Press, 1992.

——. *The Practice of Everyday Life.* Translated by Steven F. Rendall. Berkeley: University of California Press, 1984.

——. *The Writing of History.* Translated by Tom Conley. New York: Columbia University Press, 1988.

Charles, John. "Trained by Jesuits: Indigenous Letrados in Seventeenth-Century Peru." In *Indigenous Intellectuals: Knowledge, Power, and Colonial Culture in Mexico and the Andes*, edited by Gabriela Ramos and Yanna Yannakakis, 60–78. Durham, NC: Duke University Press, 2014.

Charney, Paul. *Indian Society in the Valley of Lima, Peru, 1532–1824.* Lanham, MD: University Press of America, 2001.

——. "El indio urbano: Un analisis económico y social de la población india de Lima en 1613." *Histórica* 12, no. 1 (1988): 5–33.

——. "A Sense of Belonging: Colonial Indian *Cofradías* and Ethnicity in the Valley of Lima." *The Americas* 54, no. 3 (1998): 379–407.

Chartier, Roger. Foreword to *Communication, Knowledge, and Memory in Early Modern Spain*, by Fernando Bouza, translated by Sonia López and Michael Agnew, ix–xvi. Philadelphia: University of Pennsylvania Press, 2004.

——. *The Order of Books: Readers, Authors, and Libraries in Europe between the Fourteenth and Eighteenth Centuries.* Stanford, CA: Stanford University Press, 1994.

——. "Reading Matter and 'Popular' Reading." In *A History of Reading in the West*, edited by Guglielmo Cavallo and Roger Chartier, translated by Lydia G. Cochrane, 269–83. Cambridge: Polity, 1999.

——. "Texts, Forms and Interpretations." In *On the Edge of the Cliff: History, Language, Practices*, edited by Robert Chartier, translated by Lydia G. Cochrane, 81–89. Baltimore: Johns Hopkins University Press, 1997.

Christian, William A., Jr. "Images as Beings in Early Modern Spain." In *Sacred Spain: Art and Belief in the Spanish World*, edited by Ronda Kasl, 75–100. Indianapolis: Indianapolis Museum of Art; New Haven, CT: Yale University Press, 2009.

——. *Local Religion in Sixteenth-Century Spain.* Princeton, NJ: Princeton University Press, 1981.

Classen, Albrecht. *The Power of a Woman's Voice in Medieval and Early Modern Literatures: New Approaches to German and European Women Writers and to Violence against Women in Premodern Times.* Berlin: Walter de Gruyter, 2007.

Classen, Constance. "The Breath of God: Sacred Histories of Scent." In *The Smell Culture Reader*, edited by Jim Drobnick, 375–90. Oxford: Berg, 2006.

————. *The Deepest Sense: A Cultural History of Touch.* Urbana: University of Illinois Press, 2012.

————. "The Odor of the Other: Olfactory Symbolism and Cultural Categories." *Ethos* 20, no. 2 (June 1992): 133–66.

————. *Worlds of Sense: Exploring the Senses in History and across Cultures.* New York: Routledge, 1993.

Coakley, John. *Women, Men, and Spiritual Power: Female Saints and Their Male Collaborators.* New York: Columbia University Press, 2006.

Cobo, Bernabé. *Historia de la fundación de Lima.* Monografías históricas sobre la ciudad de Lima, vol. 2. Lima: Gil, 1935.

Coello de la Rosa, Alexandre. "Agencias políticas y políticas de la santidad en la beatificación del padre Juan de Alloza, S.J. (1597–1666)." *Hispania Sacra* 57, no. 116 (2005): 627–49.

————. "Era Sanctorum: La beatificación inconclusa del padre Diego Martínez (1627–1634)." *Hispania Sacra* 61, no. 123 (2009): 191–225.

————. *Espacios de exclusión, espacios de poder: El Cercado de Lima colonial (1568–1606).* Lima: Pontificia Universidad Católica del Perú and Instituto de Estudios Peruanos, 2006.

Coleman, Joyce. *Public Reading and the Reading Public in Late Medieval England and France.* Cambridge: Cambridge University Press, 1996.

Compañía de Jesús. *El tesoro de San Pedro: Colección de cuerpos y reliquias de santos y mártires.* Lima: San Martí, 1907.

Constituciones generales para todas las monjas, y religiosas, sujetas a la obediencia de la Órden de nuestro Padre San Francisco, en toda la familia cismontana. Madrid: Imprenta Real, 1748.

Contreras, Miguel de. *Padrón de los indios de Lima en 1613.* Edited by Noble David Cook. Lima: Universidad Nacional Mayor de San Marcos, 1968.

Coon, Lynda. *Sacred Fictions: Holy Women and Hagiography in Late Antiquity.* Philadelphia: University of Pennsylvania Press, 1997.

Cope, R. Douglas. *The Limits of Racial Domination: Plebeian Society in Colonial Mexico City, 1660–1720.* Madison: University of Wisconsin Press, 1994.

Corbellini, Sabrina, ed. *Cultures of Religious Reading in the Late Middle Ages: Instructing the Soul, Feeding the Spirit and Awakening the Passion.* Turnhout: Brepols, 2013.

Córdova y Salinas, Diego de. *Crónica franciscana de las provincias del Perú.* 1651. Facsimile ed. Edited by Lino G. Canedo. Washington, DC: Academy of American Franciscan History, 1957.

————. *Vida, virtudes y milagros del apóstal del Perú: B.P. Fr. Francisco Solano.* Madrid: Imprenta Real, 1676.

Cosslett, Tess. Introduction to *Feminism and Autobiography: Texts, Theories, Methods,* edited by Tess Cosslett, Celia Lury, and Penny Summerfield, 1–22. London: Routledge, 2000.

Cosslett, Tess, Celia Lury, and Penny Summerfield, eds. *Feminism and Autobiography: Texts, Theories, Methods.* London: Routledge, 2000.

Covarrubias Orozco, Sebastián de. *Tesoro de la lengua castellana o española.* Madrid:

Luis Sánchez, 1611. https://books.google.ca/books?id=K1oMJdL7pGIC&prin
tsec=frontcover&dq=covarrubias+orozco+diccionario&hl=en&sa=X&ved=o
ahUKEwjO-_eooZvLAhXmu4MKHboABR4Q6AEIHDAA#v=onepage&q&f
=false.

Crahan, Margaret E. "Clerical Immunity in the Viceroyalty of Peru, 1684–1692: A
Study of Civil-Ecclesiastical Relations." PhD diss., Columbia University, 1967.

Cruz, Anne J., and Rosilie Hernández, eds. *Women's Literacy in Early Modern Spain
and the New World.* Burlington, VT: Ashgate, 2011.

Cummins, Victoria. "Blessed Connections: Sociological Aspects of Sainthood in Colonial Mexico and Peru." *Colonial Latin American Historical Review* 3, no. 1 (1994):
1–18.

Cussen, Celia. *Black Saint of the Americas: The Life and Afterlife of Martín de Porres.*
Cambridge: Cambridge University Press, 2014.

———. "La fe en la historia: Las vidas de Martín de Porras." In *Historia, memoria y
ficción,* edited by Moisés Lemlij and Luis Millones, 281–301. Lima: Seminario Interdisciplinario de Estudios Andinos, 1996.

———. "A House of Miracles: Origins of the Sanctuary of Saint Rosa in Late Seventeenth-Century Lima." *Colonial Latin American Historical Review* 14, no. 1 (2005):
1–23.

———. "The Search for Idols and Saints in Colonial Peru: Linking Extirpation and
Beatification." *Hispanic American Historical Review* 85, no. 3 (2005): 417–48.

Dailey, Patricia. "The Body and Its Senses." In *Cambridge Companion to Christian
Mysticism,* edited by Amy Hollywood and Patricia Z. Beckman, 264–76. Cambridge: Cambridge University Press, 2012.

Davis, Darién J., ed. *Slavery and Beyond: The African Impact on Latin America and the
Caribbean.* Wilmington, DE: SR Books, 1995.

de Groot, Joanna, and Sue Morgan. "Beyond the 'Religious Turn'? Past, Present
and Future Perspectives in Gender History." *Gender and History* 25, no. 3 (2013):
395–422.

Delgado, Jessica. *Troubling Devotion: Laywomen and the Church in Colonial Mexico,
1630–1770.* Forthcoming.

Díaz, José Simón. "Hagiografías individuales publicadas en español de 1480 á 1700."
Hispania Sacra 30 (1977): 421–82.

Díaz, Mónica. "Biografías y hagiografías: La diferente perspectiva de los géneros." In
*Actas del XV Congreso de la Asociación Internacional de Hispanistas, "Las Dos Oril-
las," Monterrey, México, del 19 al 24 de julio de 2004,* edited by Beatríz Mariscal and
María Teresa Miaja de la Peña, 535–46. Mexico City: Fondo de Cultura Económica,
2007.

———. *Indigenous Writings from the Convent: Negotiating Ethnic Autonomy in Colonial Mexico.* Tucson: University of Arizona Press, 2010.

Dickey, Sara. "Mutual Exclusions: Domestic Workers and Employers on Labor, Class,
and Character in South India." In *Home and Hegemony: Domestic Service and
Identity Politics in South and Southeast Asia,* edited by Kathleen A. Adams and Sara
Dickey, 31–62. Ann Arbor: University of Michigan Press, 2000.

Diefendorf, Barbara B. "Rethinking the Catholic Reformation: The Role of Women." In *Women, Religion and the Atlantic World (1600–1800)*, edited by Daniella Kostroun and Lisa Vollendorf, 31–59. Toronto: University of Toronto Press, 2009.

Diez de San Miguel y Solier, Nicolás Antonio. *La gran fee del centurion español: Sermon moral que en la capilla del Santo Oficio de la Inquisicion desta ciudad de los Reyes, el primer jueues de Quaresma / predico el Doct. D. Nicolas Antonio Diez de San Miguel, y Solier.* Lima: Joseph de Contreras y Alvarado, 1695.

Dillon, Janette. "Holy Women and Their Confessors or Confessors and Their Holy Women? Margery Kempe and Continental Tradition." In *Prophets Abroad: The Reception of Continental Holy Women in Late Medieval England*, edited by R. Voaden, 115–40. Cambridge: Cambridge University Press, 1996.

Durston, Alan. *Pastoral Quechua: The History of Christian Translation in Colonial Peru, 1550–1650.* Notre Dame, IN: University of Notre Dame Press, 2007.

Dyck, Jason. "The Sacred Historian's Task: Francisco de Florencia and Creole Identity in Seventeenth-Century New Spain." PhD diss., University of Toronto, 2012.

Eakin, John Paul. "Relational Selves, Relational Lives: The Story of the Story." In *True Relations: Essays on Autobiography and the Postmodern*, edited by G. Thomas Couser and Joseph Fichtelberg, 63–82. Westport, CT: Greenwood, 1998.

Echave y Assu, Francisco de. *La estrella de Lima convertida en sol sobre svs tres coronas el B. Toribio Alfonso Mogrobexo, sv segvndo arzobispo: celebrado con epitalamios sacros, y solemnes cultos.* Antwerp: J. B. Verdussen, 1688.

Eguiguren, Luis Antonio. *Diccionario histórico cronológico de la real y pontificia Universidad de San Marcos y sus colegios: Crónica é investigación.* 2 vols. Lima: Torres Aguirre, 1940.

———. *Leyendas y curiosidades de la historia nacional.* Lima: n.p., 1945.

Elliott, Dyan. "Alternative Intimacies: Men, Women and Spiritual Direction in the Twelfth Century." In *Christina of Markyate: A Twelfth-Century Holy Woman*, edited by Samuel Fanous and Henrietta Leyser, 160–83. London: Oxford University Press, 2005.

———. "The Physiology of Rapture and Female Spirituality." In *Medieval Theology and the Natural Body*, edited by Peter Biller and Alastair Minnis, 141–73. Woodbridge, UK: York Medieval Press, 1997.

———. *Proving Woman: Female Spirituality and Inquisitional Culture in the Later Middle Ages.* Princeton, NJ: Princeton University Press, 2004.

———. "Raptus/Rapture." In *Cambridge Companion to Christian Mysticism*, edited by Amy Hollywood and Patricia Z. Beckman, 189–99. Cambridge: Cambridge University Press, 2012.

———. *Spiritual Marriage: Sexual Abstinence in Medieval Wedlock.* Princeton, NJ: Princeton University Press, 1993.

Elso, Gerónimo de. *Sermones varios, obra posthuma del Padre Gerónimo de Elso, de la Compañía de Jesús, en la Provincia de Lima, Reyno del Perú, que da á luz su fiel amigo D. Diego Portales y Meneses.* Madrid: Imprenta Real, 1731.

Espinoza [Ríos], [Javier] Augusto. "De Guerras y de Dagas: Crédito y parentesco en una familia limeña del siglo XVII." *Histórica* 37, no. 1 (2013): 7–56.

Espinoza Ríos, Javier Augusto. "Las finanzas del fervor: Las prácticas económicas en el Monasterio de Santa Catalina de Lima (1621–1682)." Licentiate thesis, Pontificia Universidad Católica del Perú, 2012.

Espinoza Rúa, Celes Alonso. "A las puertas de cielo: Santidad e influencia inquisitorial en el caso del 'siervo de Dios' Nicolás de Ayllón." Licentiate thesis, Pontificia Universidad Católica del Perú, 2009.

———. "Un indio camino a los altares: Santidad e influencia inquisitorial en el caso del 'siervo de Dios' Nicolás de Ayllón." *Histórica* 36, no. 1 (2012): 135–80.

Estenssoro Fuchs, Juan Carlos. "La construcción de un *más allá* colonial: Hechiceros en Lima 1630–1710." In *Entre dos mundos: Fronteras culturales y agentes mediadores*, edited by Berta Ares Queija and Serge Gruzinski, 415–39. Seville: Escuela de Estudios Hispano-Americanos, 1997.

———. *Del paganismo a la santidad: La incorporación de los indios del Perú al catolicismo, 1532–1750*. Translated by Gabriela Ramos. Lima: Instituto Francés de Estudios Andinos and Pontificia Universidad Católica del Perú, Instituto Riva-Agüero, 2003.

Evangelisti, Silvia. "Rooms to Share: Convent Cells and Social Relations in Early Modern Italy." *Past and Present*, supplement 1 (2006): 55–71.

Fairchilds, Cissie. *Domestic Enemies: Servants and Their Masters in Old Regime France*. Baltimore: Johns Hopkins University Press, 1984.

Fawtier, Robert, and Louis Canet. *La double expérience de Catherine Benincasa (Sainte Catherine de Sienne)*. Paris: Gallimard, 1948.

Fernández Álvarez, Manuel. *Casadas, monjas, rameras y brujas: La olvidada historia de la mujer española en el renacimiento*. Madrid: Espasa Calpe, 2002.

Fernández Fernández, Amaya, Margarita Guerra Martiniére, Lourdes Leiva, and Lidia Martínez. *La mujer en la conquista y la evangelización en el Perú (Lima 1550–1650)*. Lima: Pontificia Universidad Católica del Perú, 1997.

———. *Santa Rosa de Lima*. Lima: Brasa, 1995.

Few, Martha. "Women, Religion, and Power: Gender and Resistance in Daily Life in Late-Seventeenth-Century Santiago de Guatemala." *Ethnohistory* 42, no. 4 (1995): 627–37.

Finke, Laurie A. "Mystical Bodies and the Dialogics of Vision." In *Women, Autobiography, Theory: A Reader*, edited by Sidonie Smith and Julia Watson, 402–14. Madison: University of Wisconsin Press, 1998.

Flores Araoz, José. "Iconografía de Santa Rosa." In *Santa Rosa de Lima y su tiempo*, edited by José Flores Araoz, 216–302. Lima: Banco de Crédito del Perú, 1995.

Flores Galindo, Alberto. *Buscando un inca: Identidad y utopía en los Andes*. Mexico City: Grijalbo, 1993.

Fra Molinero, Baltasar. "Ser mulato en España y América: Discursos legales y otros discursos literarios." In *Negros, mulatos, zambaigos: Derroteros africanos en los mundos ibéricos*, edited by Berta Ares Queija and Alessandro Stella, 123–47. Seville: Consejo Superior de Investigaciones Científicas, Escuela de Estudios Hispano-Americanos, 2000.

Freedburg, David. *The Power of Images: Studies in the History and Theory of Response*. Chicago: University of Chicago Press, 1989.

Frenk, Margit. *Entre la voz y el silencio (la lectura en tiempos de Cervantes).* Alcalá de Henares, Spain: Centro de Estudios Cervantinos, 1997.

Friedman, Susan Stanford. "Women's Autobiographical Selves: Theory and Practice." In *The Private Self: Theory and Practice of Women's Autobiographical Writings,* edited by Shari Benstock, 34–62. Chapel Hill: University of North Carolina Press, 1988.

García y Sanz, Pedro. *Apuntes para la historia eclesiástica del Perú, segunda parte.* Lima: Tipografía "La Sociedad," 1876.

Gerli, E. Michael. "El *Castillo Interior* y el *Arte de la memoria.*" In *Santa Teresa y la literatura mística hispánica,* edited by Manuel Criado de Val, 331–37. Madrid: EDI-6, 1984.

Gertrude the Great, Saint. *Libro intítulado insinuación de la divina piedad.* Translated by Leandro Granada y Mendoza. Salamanca: Antonia Ramírez viuda, 1605.

———. *Oraciones y exercicios espirituales, con la práctica de los quales Sancta Gertrudis subio a la alteza de la Gloria: que possee oy enlos Cielos.* Salamanca: Antonia Ramírez viuda, 1604.

Getino, Luis G. Alonso. *Santa Rosa de Lima, patrona de America, su retrato corporal y su talla intelectual según los nuevos documentos.* Madrid: M. Aguilar, 1942.

Giddens, Anthony. *Central Problems in Social Theory.* Berkeley: University of California Press, 1979.

Giles, Mary, ed. *Women in the Inquisition: Spain and the New World.* Baltimore: Johns Hopkins University Press, 1998.

Glave, Luis Miguel. *De Rosa y espinas: Economía, sociedad y mentalidades andinas, siglo XVII.* Lima: Banco Central de Reserva del Perú, Fondo Editorial, 1998.

Gómez Acuña, Luis. "Las cofradías de negros en Lima (siglo XVII): Estado de la cuestión y análisis de caso." *Páginas* 129 (1994): 28–39.

González, Antonio. *Rosa mística, vida y muerte de Santa Rosa de Santa María, virgen de la tercera Orden de Santo Domingo.* Rome: Nicolás Angel Tinassio, 1671.

Granada, Luis de. *Guía de peccadores.* Edited by José María Balcells. Barcelona: Planeta, 1986.

———. *Introducción del símbolo de la fe.* Edited by José Maria Balcells. Madrid: Cátedra, 1989.

———. *Obras completas.* Vol. 1, *Libro de la oración y meditación.* Edited by Álvaro Huerga. Madrid: Fundación Universitaria Española and Dominicos de Andalucia, 1994.

Graubart, Karen. "'So Color de una Cofradía': Catholic Confraternities and the Development of Afro-Peruvian Ethnicities in Early Colonial Peru." *Slavery and Abolition* 33, no. 1 (2012): 43–64.

Graziano, Frank. *Wounds of Love: The Mystical Marriage of Saint Rose of Lima.* New York: Oxford University Press, 2004.

Green, Dennis H. *Women Readers in the Middle Ages.* Cambridge: Cambridge University Press, 2007.

Greenspan, Kate. "Autohagiography and Medieval Women's Spiritual Autobiography." In *Gender and Text in the Later Middle Ages,* edited by Jane Chance, 216–36. Gainesville: University of Florida Press, 1996.

Greer, Allan. *Mohawk Saint: Catherine Tekakwitha and the Jesuits.* New York: Oxford University Press, 2005.

Guibovich, Pedro. *Censura, libros e inquisición en el Perú colonial, 1570–1754.* Seville: Consejo Superior de Investigaciones Científicas, Escuela de Estudios Hispano-Americanos; Universidad de Sevilla and Diputación de Sevilla, 2003.

———. "Hagiografía y política: Las crónicas conventuales en el virreinato peruano." In *Máscaras, tretas y rodeos del discurso colonial en los Andes,* edited by Bernard Lavallé, 75–83. Lima: Instituto Francés de Estudios Andinos, Instituto Riva-Agüero, 2005.

———. "Libros para ser vendidos en el Virreinato del Perú a fines del siglo XVI." *Boletín del Instituto Riva-Agüero* 13 (1987): 85–114.

Guilhem, Claire. "La Inquisición y el verbo femenino." In *Inquisición española: Poder político y control social,* edited by Bartolomé Bennassar, 171–207. Barcelona: Editorial Crítica, 1981.

Gunnasdóttir, Ellen. *Mexican Karismata: The Baroque Vocation of Francisca de los Angeles, 1674–1744.* Lincoln: University of Nebraska Press, 2004.

Haakonssen, Knud. "Divine/ Natural Law Theories in Ethics." In *The Cambridge History of Seventeenth-Century Philosophy,* vol. 2, edited by Daniel Garber and Michael Ayers, 1317–57. New York: Cambridge University Press, 2003.

Haliczer, Stephen. *Between Exaltation and Infamy: Female Mystics in the Golden Age of Spain.* Oxford: Oxford University Press, 2002.

Hallett, Nicky. *The Senses in Religious Communities, 1600–1800.* Farnham: Ashgate, 2013.

Hampe Martínez, Teodoro. "Libros profanos y sagrados en la biblioteca del Tesorero Antonio Dávalos (1583)." *Revista de Indias* 46, no. 178 (1986): 385–402.

———. *Santidad e identidad criolla: Estudio del proceso de canonización de Santa Rosa.* Cuzco: Centro de Estudios Regionales Andinos Bartolomé de las Casas, 1998.

Hansen, Leonard. *Vida admirable de Santa Rosa de Lima, patrona del nuevo mundo.* Vergara, Spain: Editorial El Santísimo Rosario, 1929.

———. *Vida admirable, y muerte preciosa, de la venerable Madre Soror Rosa de Santa Maria.* Translated from Latin by Tomás de Rocaberti. Valencia: Gerónimo Vilagrafa, 1665.

Haslanger, Sally. "Gender and Race: (What) Are They? (What) Do We Want Them to Be?" *Noûs* 34, no. 1 (2000): 31–55.

Hayes, Dawn Marie. *Body and Sacred Place in Medieval Europe, 1100–1389.* New York: Routledge, 2003.

Henningsen, Gustav. "La evangelización negra: Difusión de la magia europea por la América colonial." *Revista de la Inquisición* 3 (1994): 9–27.

Herlihy, David. "Did Women Have a Renaissance? A Reconsideration." In *Women, Family and Society in Medieval Europe: Historical Essays, 1978–1991,* 33–56. Providence, RI: Berghahn Books, 1995.

Hillman, Jennifer. "Soul Mates and Collaborators: Spiritual Direction in Late Medieval and Early Modern Europe." *History Compass* 13, no. 9 (2015): 476–84.

Holler, Jacqueline. "The Holy Office of the Inquisition and Women." In *Religion and Society in Latin America: Interpretive Essays from Conquest to Present,* edited by Lee M. Penyak and Walter Petry. Online ed. Maryknoll, NY: Orbis Books 2009.

Hollywood, Amy. "Practice, Belief, and Feminist Philosophy of Religion." In *Women and Religion: Critical Concepts in Religious Studies*, vol. 3, *Texts, Rituals and Authoritative Knowledge*, edited by Pamela Klassen with Shari Golberg and Danielle Lefebvre, 64–83. London: Routledge, 2009.

———. *Sensible Ecstasy: Mysticism, Sexual Difference, and the Demands of History*. Chicago: University of Chicago Press, 2002.

Horozco y Covarrubias, Juan de. *Tratado de la verdadera y falsa prophecia*. Segovia: Juan de la Cuesta, 1588.

Howells, Edward. "Early Modern Reformations." In *The Cambridge Companion to Christian Mysticism*, edited by Amy Hollywood and Patricia Z. Beckman, 114–34. Cambridge: Cambridge University Press, 2012.

———. *John of the Cross and Teresa of Ávila: Mystical Knowing and Selfhood*. New York: Crossroad, 2002.

Howie, Gillian, and J'annine Jobling. "Introduction." In *Women and the Divine: Touching Transcendence*, edited by Gillian Howie and J'annine Jobling, 1–12. New York: Palgrave Macmillan, 2009.

Hoyo, Joseph del. *Relacion completa, y exacta del auto publico de fe que se celebró en esta ciudad de Lima a 20 de diziembre de 1694*. Lima: Joseph de Contreras, 1695.

Huarte de San Juan, Juan. *Examen de ingenios para las sciencias*. 2nd ed. Baeza: Juan Baptista Montoya, 1594.

Huerga, Álvaro. *Historia de los alumbrados (1570–1630)*. Vol. 2, *Los alumbrados de La Alta Andalucía, 1575–1590*. Madrid: Fundación Universitaria Española, 1978.

Hughes, Diane Owen. "Distinguishing Signs: Ear-Rings, Jews and Franciscan Rhetoric in the Italian Renaissance City." *Past and Present* 112 (1986): 3–59.

Ibsen, Kristine. "Honor Thy Father: Women's Autobiographical Writing as Confessional Discourse in Colonial Spanish America." *a/b: Auto/Biography Studies* 13, no. 2 (1998): 182–98.

———. *Women's Spiritual Autobiography in Colonial Spanish America*. Gainesville: University Press of Florida, 1999.

Index librorum prohibitorum, 1559. Cambridge, MA: Harvard University Press, 1980.

Iwasaki Cauti, Fernando. "Luisa Melgarejo de Soto y la alegría de ser tu testigo, señor." *Histórica* 19, no. 2 (1995): 219–51.

———. "Mujeres al borde de la perfección: Rosa de Santa María y las alumbradas de Lima." *Hispanic American Historical Review* 73, no. 4 (1993): 581–613.

———. "Santos y alumbrados: Santa Rosa y el imaginario limeño del siglo XVII." In *Actas del III Congreso Internacional sobre los Dominicos y el Nuevo Mundo*, edited by Paulino Castañeda Delgado, 531–76. Madrid: Deimos, 1991.

———. "Vidas de santos y santas vidas: Hagiografías reales e imaginarias en Lima colonial." *Anuario de Estudios Americanos* 51, no. 1 (1994): 47–64.

Jaffary, Nora E. *False Mystics: Deviant Orthodoxy in Colonial Mexico*. Lincoln: University of Nebraska Press, 2004.

———. "Virtue and Transgression: The Certification of Authentic Mysticism in the

Mexican Inquisition." *Catholic Southwest: A Journal of History and Culture* 10 (1999): 9–28.

Jiménez Salas, Hernán, ed. *Primer proceso ordinario para la canonización de Santa Rosa de Lima.* Lima: Monasterio de Santa Rosa de Santa María de Lima, 2002.

Jones, Pamela M. "The Power of Images: Paintings and Viewers in Caravaggio's Italy." In *Saints and Sinners: Caravaggio and the Baroque Image*, edited by Franco Mormando, 28–48. Boston: McMullen Museum of Art, Boston College, 1999.

Jouve Martín, José R. "En olor de santidad: Hagiografía, cultos locales y escritura religiosa en Lima, siglo XVII." *Colonial Latin American Review* 13, no. 2 (2004): 181–98.

Julia, Dominique. "Reading and the Counter-Reformation." In *A History of Reading in the West*, edited by Guglielmo Cavallo and Roger Chartier, translated by Lydia G. Cochrane, 238–68. Cambridge: Polity, 1999.

Kagan, Richard. *Urban Images of the Hispanic World, 1493–1793.* New Haven, CT: Yale University Press, 2000.

Kantorowicz, Ernst H. *The King's Two Bodies: A Study in Mediaeval Political Theology.* Princeton, NJ: Princeton University Press, 1957.

Kasl, Ronda. "Delightful Adornments and Pious Recreation: Living with Images in the Seventeenth Century." In *Sacred Spain: Art and Belief in the Spanish World*, edited by Ronda Kasl, 147–63. Indianapolis: Indianapolis Museum of Art; New Haven, CT: Yale University Press, 2009.

Kelly, Joan. "Did Women Have a Renaissance?" In *Women, History and Theory: The Essays of Joan Kelly*, edited by Joan Kelly, 19–50. Chicago: University of Chicago Press, 1984.

Kieckhefer, Richard. "Holiness and the Culture of Devotion: Remarks on Some Late Medieval Male Saints." In *Images of Sainthood in Medieval Europe*, edited by Renate Blumenfeld-Kosinski and Timea Szell, 288–305. Ithaca, NY: Cornell University Press, 1991.

Kirk, Stephanie L. *Convent Life in Colonial Mexico: A Tale of Two Communities.* Gainesville: University of Florida, 2007.

Kleinberg, Aviad M. *Prophets in Their Own Country: Living Saints and the Making of Sainthood in the Later Middle Ages.* Chicago: University of Chicago Press, 1992.

Kopytoff, Igor. "The Cultural Biography of Things: Commoditization as Process." In *The Social Life of Things: Commodities in Cultural Perspective*, edited by Arjun Appadurai, 64–91. Cambridge: Cambridge University Press, 1986.

Kostroun, Daniella, and Lisa Vollendorf, eds. *Women, Religion, and the Atlantic World (1600–1800).* Toronto: University of Toronto Press, 2009.

Kreiner, Jamie. *The Social Life of Hagiography in the Merovingian Kingdom.* Cambridge: Cambridge University Press, 2014.

Krug, Rebecca. *Reading Families: Women's Literate Practice in Late Medieval England.* Ithaca, NY: Cornell University Press, 2002.

Ladrón de Guevara, Diego. *Dissertación jurídica, canónica y moral de voto.* Quito, 1706. Madrid: Casa de Diego Martínez Abad, 1712.

Lamana, Gonzalo. "What Makes a Story Amusing: Magic, Occidentalism and Overfetishization in a Colonial Setting." *Journal of Latin American Cultural Studies* 19, no. 1 (2010): 87–102.

Laqueur, Thomas. *Making Sex: Body and Gender from the Greeks to Freud.* Cambridge, MA: Harvard University Press, 1990.

Laspéras, Jean-Michel. "Quand l'habit faisait le péché: Mode et morale en Espagne au Siècle d'Or." In *Paraître et se Vêtir au XVIe siècle: Actes du XIIIe Colloque du Puy-en-Velay,* edited by Marie Viallon, 159–71. Saint-Étienne: Publications de l'Université de Saint-Étienne, 2006.

Lastres, Juan B. *Historia de la medicina peruana.* 5 vols. Lima: Santa María, 1951.

Latour, Bruno. "The Berlin Key or How to Do Words with Things." In *Matter, Materiality and Modern Culture,* edited by Paul M. Graves-Brown, 10–21. London: Routledge, 2000.

Lauretis, Teresa de. "Feminist Studies/Critical Studies: Issues, Terms, and Contexts." In *Feminist Studies/Critical Studies,* edited by Teresa de Lauretis, 1–19. Bloomington: Indiana University Press, 1986.

Lavrin, Asunción. "Indian Brides of Christ: Creating New Spaces for Indigenous Women in New Spain." *Mexican Studies/Estudios Mexicanos* 15, no. 2 (1999): 225–60.

Leavitt-Alcántara, Brianna. "Holy Women and Hagiography in Colonial Spanish America." *History Compass* 12, no. 9 (2014): 717–28.

Lehmijoki-Gardner, Maiju. "Writing Religious Rules as an Interactive Process—Dominican Penitent Women and the Making of Their *Regula.*" *Speculum* 79, no. 3 (2004): 660–87.

Leonard, Irving A. *Books of the Brave.* Berkeley: University of California Press, 1992.

León Pinelo, Antonio de. *Velos antiguos i modernos en los rostros de las mugeres.* Santiago de Chile: Centro de Investigación de la Historia de América, 1966.

———. *Vida del illustríssimo i reverendíssimo D. Toribio Alfonso Mogrovejo.* Madrid: n.p., 1653.

Livi Bacci, Massimo. *El Dorado in the Marshes: Gold, Slaves and Souls between the Andes and the Amazon.* Cambridge: Polity, 2010.

Llorca, Marlène Albert. "Les statues habillées dans le catholicisme: Entre histoire de l'art, histoire religieuse et anthropologie." *Archives de Sciences Sociales des Religions* 58, no. 164 (2013): 11–23.

Lohmann Villena, Guillermo. "Un documento más sobre un libro limeño esquivo." *Revista del Archivo General de la Nación* 25 (2005): 401–5.

———. *Los ministros de la Audiencia de Lima en el reinado de los Borbones, 1700–1821.* Seville: Consejo Superior de Investigaciones Científicas, Escuela de Estudios Hispano-Americanos, 1974.

Lorea, Antonio de. *Santa Rosa, religiosa de la tercera orden de S. Domingo.* Madrid: Por Francisco Nieto, 1677.

Lorente, Sebastián. *Historia del Perú bajo los Borbones, 1700–1821.* Lima: Librería de Gil y Aubert, 1871.

Loreto López, Rosalva. *Los conventos femeninos y el mundo urbano de la Puebla de los Ángeles del siglo XVIII.* Mexico City: El Colegio de México, 2000.

———. "Prácticas alimenticias en los conventos de mujeres en la Puebla del siglo xviii." In *Conquista y comida: Consecuencias del encuentro de dos mundos*, edited by Janet Long, 481–504. Mexico City: Universidad Nacional Autónoma de México, 1996.

Lowe, Kate J. P. *Nuns' Chronicles and Convent Culture in Renaissance and Counter-Reformation Italy*. Cambridge: Cambridge University Press, 2003.

Lozano, Pedro. "Relación del Terremoto que arruinó a Lima e inundó al Callao el 28 de Octobre de 1746." In *Terremotos: Colección de las relaciones de los más notables que ha sufrido esta capital*, edited by Manuel de Odriozola, 36–47. Lima: Tipografía de Aurelio Alfaro, 1863.

Luongo, F. Thomas. *The Saintly Politics of Catherine of Siena*. Ithaca, NY: Cornell University Press, 2006.

Mack, Phyllis. "Religion, Feminism, and the Problem of Agency." *Signs* 29, no. 1 (2003): 149–77.

———. *Visionary Women: Ecstatic Prophecy in Seventeenth-Century England*. Berkeley: University of California Press, 1992.

Maclean, Ian. *The Renaissance Notion of Woman*. Cambridge: Cambridge University Press, 1980.

Macola, Erminia. "El 'no sé que,' como percepción de lo divino." In *Santa Teresa y la literatura mística hispánica*, edited by Manuel Criado de Val, 33–43. Madrid: EDI-6, 1984.

Madrid, Alonso de. *El arte para servir a Dios*. Alcalá de Henares: Miguel de Eguía, 1526.

Malhotra, Anshu, and Siobhan Lambert-Hurley. *Speaking of the Self: Gender, Performance, and Autobiography in South Asia*. Durham, NC: Duke University Press, 2015.

Mangan, Jane. *Trading Roles: Gender, Ethnicity, and the Urban Economy in Colonial Potosí*. Durham, NC: Duke University Press, 2005.

———. *Transatlantic Obligations: Creating the Bonds of Family in Conquest-Era Spain and Peru*. Oxford: Oxford University Press, 2015.

Mannarelli, María Emma. "Fragmentos para una historia posible: Escritura/crítica/cuerpo en una beata del siglo XVII." In *Historia, memoria, y ficción*, edited by Moisés Lemlij and Luis Millones, 266–80. Lima: Biblioteca Peruana de Psicoanálisis and Seminario Interdisciplinario de Estudios Andinos, 1996.

———. *Hechiceras, beatas y expósitas: Mujeres y poder inquisitorial en Lima*. Lima: Ediciones del Congreso del Perú, 1998.

María de San José. *A Wild Country Out in the Garden: The Spiritual Journals of a Colonial Mexican Nun*. Edited by Kathleen Myers and Amanda Powell. Bloomington: Indiana University Press, 1999.

María Rosa, Madre. *Journey of Five Capuchin Nuns*. Edited by Sarah Owens. Toronto: Center for Reformation and Renaissance Studies, 2009.

Martín, Luis. *Daughters of the Conquistadores: Women of the Viceroyalty of Peru*. Dallas: Southern Methodist University, 1989.

Mason, Mary G. "The Other Voice: Autobiographies of Women Writers." In *Autobiography: Essays, Theoretical and Critical*, edited by James Olney, 207–34. Princeton, NJ: Princeton University Press, 1980.

Massey, Doreen B. *Space, Place and Gender*. Minneapolis: University of Minnesota Press, 1994.

Mayeski, Marie Ann. "New Voices in the Tradition: Medieval Hagiography Revisited." *Theological Studies* 63, no. 4 (2002): 690–710.

Mbembe, Achille. "The Power of the Archive and Its Limits." In *Refiguring the Archive*, edited by Carolyn Hamilton, Verne Harris, and Graeme Reid, 19–26. Dordrecht: Kluwer Academic, 2002.

McDowell, Linda. *Gender, Identity and Place: Understanding Feminist Geographies*. Minneapolis: University of Minnesota Press, 1999.

McKinley, Michelle. *Fractional Freedoms: Slavery, Intimacy, and Legal Mobilization in Colonial Lima, 1600–1700*. New York: Cambridge University Press, 2016.

———. "Till Death Do Us Part: Testamentary Manumission in Seventeenth-Century Lima." *Slavery and Abolition: A Journal of Slave and Post Slave Studies* 33, no. 3 (2012): 381–401.

Medina, Bernardo. *Vida prodigiosa del venerable siervo de Dios Fray Martín de Porras*. Madrid: Domingo García Morràs, 1675.

Medina, José Toribio. *Historia del Tribunal de la Inquisición de Lima, 1569–1820*. 2 vols. Santiago de Chile: Fondo Histórico y Bibliográfico, 1956.

Meléndez, Juan. *Festiva pompa, culto religioso, veneracion reverente, fiesta, aclamacion, y aplauso a la beatificación de la bienaventurada virgin Rosa de S. María*. Lima: n.p., 1671.

———. *Tesoros verdaderos de las Indias: Historia de la Provincia de S[an] Juan Baptista del Perú, del Órden de Predicadores*. 3 vols. Rome: Nicolás Tinassio, 1681.

Mendiburu, Manuel de. *Diccionario histórico-biográfico*. 11 vols. Lima: Enrique Palacios, 1931–34.

Meyer, Birgit, and Dick Houtman. "Introduction: Material Religion—How Things Matter." In *Things: Religion and the Question of Materiality*, edited by Dick Houtman and Birgit Meyer, 1–27. New York: Fordham University Press, 2012.

Millar Carvacho, René. "Falsa santidad e Inquisición: Los procesos a las visionarias limeñas." *Boletín de la Academia Chilena de la Historia* 108–9 (2000): 277–305.

Millones, Luis. *Una partecita del cielo: La vida de Santa Rosa de Lima narrada por D[o]n Gonzalo de la Maza a quien ella llamaba padre*. Lima: Horizonte, 1993.

Mills, Kenneth. *Idolatry and Its Enemies: Colonial Andean Religion and Extirpation, 1640–1750*. Princeton, NJ: Princeton University Press, 1997.

———. "The Naturalization of Andean Christianities." In *The Cambridge History of Christianity: Reform and Expansion, 1500–1660*, edited by R. Po-chia Hsia, 504–35. New York: Cambridge University Press, 2008.

———. "Religion in the Atlantic World." In *Oxford Handbook of the Atlantic World*, edited by Nicholas Canny and Philip Morgan, 434–48. Oxford: Oxford University Press, 2013.

Minh-ha, Trinh T. "Not You/Like You: Post-colonial Women and the Interlocking Questions of Identity and Difference." *Inscriptions* 3–4 (1988): 71–77.

Mispilivar, Bernardo de. *Sagrado arbitrio, commutacion de comedias de corpus* . . . Lima: Luis de Lyra, 1679.

Montalvo, Francisco Antonio. *El sol del Nuevo Mundo, ideado y compuesto en las esclarecidas operaciones del bienaventurado Toribio Arçobispo de Lima.* Rome: Angel Bernavò, 1683.

Morabito, Vittorio. "San Benedetto il Moro, da Palermo, prottetore degli africani di Siviglia, della penisola iberica e d'America latina." In *Negros, mulatos, zambaigos: Derroteros africanos en los mundos ibéricos,* edited by Berta Ares Queija and Alessandro Stella, 223–73. Seville: Consejo Superior de Investigaciones Científicas, Escuela de Estudios Hispano-Americanos, 2000.

Moreyra y Paz-Soldán, Manuel. *Virreinato peruano, documentos para su historia: Colección de cartas de Virreyes, Conde de la Monclova.* Vol. 3, *1699–1705.* Lima: Instituto Histórico del Perú 1955.

Morgan, David. "Materialities of Sacred Economies." *Material Religion* 11, no. 3 (2015): 387–91.

Morgan, Ronald J. "'Just Like Rosa': History and Metaphor in the 'Life' of a Seventeenth-Century Saint." *Biography* 21, no. 3 (1998): 275–310.

———. *Spanish American Saints and the Rhetoric of Identity, 1600–1810.* Tucson: University of Arizona Press, 2002.

Mouchel, Christian. *Les femmes de douleur: Maladie et sainteté dans l'Italie de la Contre-Réforme.* Besançon: Presse Université de Franche-Comté, 2007.

Muessig, Caroline. Introduction to *A Companion to Catherine of Siena,* edited by Caroline Muessig, George Ferzoco, and Beverly Mayne Kienzle, 1–22. Leiden: Brill, 2012.

Mugaburu, Josephe de, and Francisco de Mugaburu. *Chronicle of Colonial Lima: The Diary of Josephe and Francisco Mugaburu, 1640–1697.* Norman: University of Oklahoma Press, 1975.

Muir, Edward. "The Virgin on the Street Corner: The Place of the Sacred in Italian Cities." In *Religion and Culture in the Renaissance and Reformation,* edited by Steven Ozment, 25–40. Kirksville: Northeast Missouri State University, 1989.

Mujica Pinilla, Ramón. "El ancla de Rosa de Lima: Mística y política en torno a la patrona de América." In *Santa Rosa de Lima y su tiempo,* edited by José Flores Araoz, 53–211. Lima: Banco de Crédito del Perú, 1995.

———. "'Dime con quién andas y te diré quién eres': La cultura clásica en una procesión sanmarquina de 1656." In *La tradición clásica en el Perú virreinal,* compiled by Teodoro Hampe Martínez, 191–219. Lima: Sociedad Peruana de Estudios Clásicos and Universidad Nacional Mayor de San Marcos, 1999.

———. *Rosa limensis: Mística, política e iconografía en torno a la patrona de América.* Lima: Instituto Francés de Estudios Andinos, Fondo de Cultura Económica, Banco Central de Reserva del Perú, 2001.

Mulder-Bakker, Anneke B. "The Metamorphosis of Woman: Transmission of Knowledge and the Problems of Gender." In *Gendering the Middle Ages,* edited by Pauline Stafford and Anneke B. Mulder-Bakker, 112–34. Malden, MA: Blackwell, 2001.

Muriel, Josefina. "Lo que leían las mujeres de la Nueva España." In *La Literatura novohispana: Revisión crítica y propuestas metodológicas,* edited by José Pascual Buxó and Arnulfo Herrera, 159–73. Mexico City: Universidad Nacional Autónoma de México, 1994.

Myers, Kathleen Ann. *Neither Saints nor Sinners: Writing the Lives of Women in Spanish America*. Oxford: Oxford University Press, 2003.

Nelson, Lynn Hankinson. "Epistemological Communities." In *Feminist Epistemologies*, edited by Linda Alcoff and Elizabeth Potter, 121–59. New York: Routledge, 1993.

Newman, Barbara. "What Did It Mean to Say 'I Saw'? The Clash between Theory and Practice in Medieval Visionary Culture." *Speculum* 80, no. 1 (2005): 6–41.

Nieto Vélez, Armando. *Francisco del Castillo, Apóstal de Lima*. Lima: Pontificia Universidad Católica del Perú, 1992.

Odriozola, Manuel de. *Colección de documentos literarios del Perú*. 11 vols. Lima: Aurelio Alfaro, 1864–76.

Olaechea Labayen, Juan Bautista. *El mestizaje como gesta*. Madrid: Mapfre, 1992.

Olms y de Santa Pau, Manuel de. *Relación que la Real Audiencia y Chancillería de los Reyes hizo de su gobierno en vacante*. Lima: n.p., 1707.

Oré, Gerónimo de. *Relación de la vida y milagros de San Francisco de Solano*. Edited by Noble David Cook. Lima: Pontificia Universidad Católica del Perú, 1998.

Osorio, Alejandra. "*El callejón de la soledad:* Vectors of Cultural Hybridity in Seventeenth-Century Lima." In *Spiritual Encounters: Interactions between Christianity and Native Religions in Colonial America*, edited by Nicholas Griffiths and Fernando Cervantes, 198–229. Lincoln: University of Nebraska Press, 1999.

———. *Inventing Lima: Baroque Modernity in Peru's South Sea Metropolis*. New York: Palgrave Macmillan, 2008.

O'Toole, Rachel Sarah. "Danger in the Convent: Colonial Demons, Idolatrous *Indias*, and Bewitching *Negras* in Santa Clara (Trujillo del Perú)." *Journal of Colonialism and Colonial History* 7, no. 1 (2006). http://muse.jhu.edu/article/196746.

———. "From the Rivers of Guinea to the Valleys of Peru: Becoming a Bran Diaspora within Spanish Slavery." *Social Text* 25, no. 3.92 (Fall 2007): 19–36.

Palma, Ricardo. *Anales de la Inquisición de Lima*. Madrid: Ediciones del Congreso de la República, 1957.

———. *Tradiciones peruanas completas*. Madrid: Aguilar, 1953.

Pareja Ortíz, María del Carmen. *Presencia de la mujer sevillana en Indias: Vida cotidiana*. Seville: Diputación Provincial de Sevilla, 1994.

Paresys, Isabelle. "Paraître et se vêtir au XVIe siècle: Morales vestimentaires." In *Paraître et se Vêtir au XVIe siècle: Actes du XIIIe Colloque du Puy-en-Velay*, edited by Marie Viallon, 11–36. Saint-Étienne: Publications de l'Université de Saint-Étienne, 2006.

Park, Katherine. "The Organic Soul." In *The Cambridge History of Renaissance Philosophy*, edited by Charles B. Schmitt, 464–85. Cambridge: Cambridge University Press, 1988.

Pedro de Alcántara. *Tratado de la oración, y meditación*. Seville: Lucas Martín de Hermosilla, 1689.

Pérez de Valdivia, Diego. *Aviso de gente recogida*. 1585. Madrid: Universidad Pontificia de Salamanca, Fundación Universitaria Española, 1977.

———. *Aviso de gente recogida*. Barcelona: Hieronymo Genoves, 1585. https://books

.google.ca/books?id=Fog1roTbhFYC&printsec=frontcover&source=gbs_ge
_summary_r&cad=0#v=onepage&q=ropa&f=false.

Pescador, Juan Javier. *De bautizados a fieles difuntos: Familia y mentalidades en una parroquia urbana, Santa Catarina de México, 1568–1820*. Mexico City: Colegio de México, 1992.

Portal, Ismael. *Lima religiosa*. Lima: Gil, 1924.

Premo, Bianca. *Children of the Father King: Youth, Authority and Legal Minority in Colonial Lima*. Chapel Hill: University of North Carolina Press, 2005.

———. *The Enlightenment on Trial: Ordinary Litigants and Colonialism in the Spanish Empire*. New York: Oxford University Press, 2017.

———. "The Maidens, the Monks, and Their Mothers: Patriarchal Authority and Holy Vows in Colonial Lima, 1650–1715." In *Women, Religion, and the Atlantic World (1600–1800)*, edited by Daniella Kostroun and Lisa Vollendorf, 275–301. Toronto: University of Toronto Press, 2009.

Proceso de beatificación de fray Martín de Porres. Vol. 1, *Proceso diocesano, años, 1660, 1664, 1671*. Palencia, Spain: Secretariado "Martín de Porres," 1960.

Rama, Ángel. *La ciudad letrada*. Hanover, NH: Ediciones del Norte, 1984.

Ramos, Gabriela. *Death and Conversion in the Andes*. Notre Dame, IN: University of Notre Dame Press, 2010.

———. "Indigenous Intellectuals in Andean Colonial Cities." In *Indigenous Intellectuals: Knowledge, Power, and Colonial Culture in Mexico and the Andes*, edited by Gabriela Ramos and Yanna Yannakakis, 21–38. Durham, NC: Duke University Press, 2014.

Ramos, Gabriela, and Yanna Yannakakis. Introduction to *Indigenous Intellectuals: Knowledge, Power, and Colonial Culture in Mexico and the Andes*, edited by Gabriela Ramos and Yanna Yannakakis, 1–17. Durham, NC: Duke University Press, 2014.

Ramos Medina, Manuel. *Imagen de santidad en un mundo profano*. Mexico City: Universidad Iberoamericana, 1990.

Rapley, Elizabeth. *The Dévotes: Women and Church in Seventeenth-Century France*. Montreal: McGill-Queen's University Press, 1990.

Rappaport, Joanne. *The Disappearing Mestizo: Configuring Difference in the Colonial New Kingdom of Granada*. Durham, NC: Duke University Press, 2014.

Rappaport, Joanne, and Thomas Cummins. *Beyond the Lettered City: Indigenous Literacies in the Andes*. Durham, NC: Duke University Press, 2012.

Raymond of Capua. *The Life of Catherine of Siena*. Translated by Conleth Kearns, O.P. Wilmington, DE: Michael Glazier, 1980.

Real Academia Española (RAE). *Diccionario de autoridades*. Vols. 1–6. Facsimile. Madrid: Gredos, 1963.

———. *Diccionario de la lengua española*. Vols. 1–2. Decimanovena ed. Madrid: Espasa Calpe, 1970.

Regalado de Hurtado, Liliana. "Reflexión sobre el cuerpo en el virreinato del Perú." *Colonial Latin American Review* 11, no. 2 (2002): 305–15.

Rey, Terry. "Kongolese Catholic Influences on Haitian Popular Catholicism: A Sociohistorical Exploration." In *Central Africans and Cultural Transformations in the*

American Diaspora, edited by Linda M. Heywood, 265–85. Cambridge: Cambridge University Press, 2002.

Ricoeur, Paul. "The World of the Text and the World of the Reader." In *Time and Narrative*, by Paul Ricoeur, translated by Kathleen McLaughlin and David Pellauer, 3:157–79. Chicago: University of Chicago Press, 1988.

Roa, Martín de. *Antiguedad veneracion i fruto de las sagradas imagenes, i reliquias: Historias i exenplos a este proposito*. Seville: Gabriel Ramos Vejarano, 1623.

Rodrigo, Romualdo. *Manual para instruir los procesos de canonización*. Salamanca: Universidad Pontificia de Salamanca, 1988.

Rodríguez de León Pinelo, Juan. *Vida del illustríssimo i reverendíssimo D. Toribio Alfonso Mogrovejo*. Madrid: n.p., 1653.

Roullet, Antoine. "Le soin du vêtement au couvent, entre uniforme et distinction: Les carmélites déchaussées espagnoles, années 1560–1630." *Revue d'Histoire Moderne et Contemporaine* 62, no. 1 (2015): 104–26.

Rowe, Erin Kathleen. "After Death, Her Face Turned White: Blackness, Whiteness and Sanctity in the Early Modern Hispanic World." *American Historical Review* 121, no. 3 (2016): 727–54.

Rubial García, Antonio. *La santidad controvertida*. Mexico City: Universidad Nacional Autónoma de México, Fondo de Cultura Económica, 1999.

Rudy, Gordon. *Mystical Language of Sensation in the Later Middle Ages*. New York: Routledge, 2002.

Ruíz Valdés, Javiera. "Recogidas, virtuosas y humildes: Representaciones de las donadas en el Monasterio de la Encarnación de Lima, siglo XVII." In *América colonial: Denominaciones, clasificaciones e identidades*, edited by Alejandra Araya Espinoza and Jaime Valenzuela Márquez, 235–55. Santiago de Chile: RIL Editores, 2010.

Salinas y Córdova, Buenaventura de. *Memorial de las historias del Nuevo Mundo*. Lima: Gerónymo de Contreras, 1630.

Salvador, Ryan. "Steadfast Saints or Malleable Models? Seventeenth-Century Irish Hagiography Revisited." *Catholic Historical Review* 91, no. 2 (2005): 251–77.

Sánchez, Ana. "Angela Carranza, alias Angela de Dios. Santidad y poder en la sociedad virreinal peruana (s. XVII)." In *Catolicismo y extirpación de idolatrías. Siglos XVI–XVIII*, edited by Gabriela Ramos and Henrique Urbano, 236–92. Cuzco: Centro Bartolomé de Las Casas, 1993.

———. "Mentalidad popular frente a ideología oficial: El Santo Oficio en Lima y los casos de hechicería (siglo XVII)." In *Poder y violencia en los Andes*, edited by Henrique Urbano and Mirko Lauer, 33–52. Cuzco: Centro de Estudios Regionales Andinos Bartolomé de las Casas, 1991.

Sánchez-Concha Barrios, Rafael. *Santos y santidad en el Perú virreinal*. Lima: Vida y Espiritualidad, 2003.

———. "La tradición política y el concepto de 'cuerpo de república' en el Virreinato." In *La tradición clásica en el Perú virreinal*, compiled by Teodoro Hampe Martínez, 101–14. Lima: Sociedad Peruana de Estudios Clásicos and Universidad Nacional Mayor de San Marcos, 1999.

Sánchez Lora, José L. *Mujeres, conventos y formas de la religiosidad barroca.* Madrid: Fundación Universitaria Española, 1988.

Sartolo, Bernardo. *Vida admirable y muerte prodigiosa de Nicolas de Ayllon, y con renombre mas glorioso Nicolas de Dios, natural de Chiclayo en las Indias del Peru.* Madrid: Por Juan Garcia Infançon, 1684.

Schlau, Stacey. "Ángela de Carranza: El género sexual, la comercialización religiosa, y la subversión de la jerarquía eclesiástica en el Perú colonial." In *Nictimene ... sacrílega: Estudios coloniales en homenaje a Georgina Sabat-Rivers,* edited by Mabel Moraña and Yolanda Martínez-San Miguel, 111–33. Mexico City: Universidad del Claustro de Sor Juana, 2003.

———. "Ángela de Carranza, Would-Be Theologian." In *The Catholic Church and Unruly Women Writers,* edited by Jeanna DelRosso, Leigh Eicke, and Ana Kothe, 69–85. New York: Palgrave Macmillan, 2007.

———. "Flying in Formation: Subjectivity and Collectivity in Luisa Melgarejo de Soto's Mystical Practices." In *Devout Laywomen in the Early Modern World,* edited by Alison Weber, 133–51. New York: Routledge, 2016.

———. *Gendered Crime and Punishment: Women and/in the Hispanic Inquisitions.* Leiden: Brill, 2013.

Schneider, Jane. "Cloth and Clothing." In *Handbook of Material Culture,* edited by Chris Tilley, Webb Keane, and Susanne Kuechler, 203–20. London: Sage, 2006.

Scully, Sally. "Marriage or a Career? Witchcraft as an Alternative in Seventeenth-Century Venice." *Journal of Social History* 28, no. 4 (1995): 857–76.

Sikorska, Liliana. "Between Autohagiography and Confession: Generic Concerns and the Question of Female Self-Representation in Anna Maria Marchocka's *Mystical Autobiography.*" *Florilegium* 23, no. 1 (2006): 85–96.

Silverblatt, Irene. *Modern Inquisitions: Peru and the Origins of the Civilized World.* Durham, NC: Duke University Press, 2004.

Silvestrini, Elisabetta. "Abiti e simulacri: Itinerario attraverso mitologie, narrazioni e riti." In *Donne Madonne Dee: Abito sacro e riti di vestizione, gioiello votivo, "vestitrici": Un itinerario antropológico in area lagunare veneta,* edited by Elisabetta Silvestrini, Giampaolo Gri, and Riccarda Pagnozzato, 17–65. Padua: Il Poligrafo, 2003.

Silvestrini, Elisabetta, Giampaolo Gri, and Riccarda Pagnozzato. *Donne Madonne Dee: Abito sacro e riti di vestizione, gioiello votivo, "vestitrici." Un itinerario antropológico in area lagunare veneta.* Padua: Il Poligrafo, 2003.

Simerka, Barbara. "Feminist Epistemology and Pedagogy in Teresa de Avila." In *Approaches to Teaching Teresa of Ávila and the Spanish Mystics,* edited by Alison Weber, 107–13. New York: Modern Language Association, 2008.

Simons, Walter. "Reading a Saint's Body: Rapture and Bodily Movement in the *Vitae* of Thirteenth-Century Beguines." In *Framing Medieval Bodies,* edited by Sarah Kay and Miri Ruben, 10–23. Manchester: Manchester University Press, 1994.

Slade, Carolyn. *Saint Teresa of Avila: Author of a Heroic Life.* Berkeley: University of California Press, 1995.

Smith, Julia M. H. "The Problem of Female Sanctity in Carolingian Europe c. 780–920." *Past and Present* 146 (1995): 3–37.

Smith, Sidonie. *A Poetics of Women's Autobiography: Marginality and the Fictions of Self-Representation*. Bloomington: Indiana University Press, 1987.

Smith, Sidonie, and Julia Watson, eds. *Women, Autobiography, Theory: A Reader*. Madison: University of Wisconsin Press, 1998.

Solterer, Helen. "Seeing, Hearing, Tasting Woman: Medieval Senses of Reading." *Comparative Literature* 46, no. 2 (1994): 129–45.

Sponsler, Claire. "In Transit: Theorizing Cultural Appropriation in Medieval Europe." *Journal of Medieval and Early Modern Studies* 32, no. 1 (2002): 17–39.

Stanton, Domna C. "Autogynography: Is the Subject Different?" In *Women, Autobiography, Theory: A Reader*, edited by Sidonie Smith and Julia Watson, 131–44. Madison: University of Wisconsin Press, 1998.

Steedman, Carolyn. "Servants and Their Relationship to the Unconscious." *Journal of British Studies* 42 (2003): 316–50.

Stone, Lawrence. "Prosopography." *Daedalus* 100, no. 1 (1971): 46–79.

Stratton, Suzanne L. *The Immaculate Conception in Art*. Cambridge: Cambridge University Press, 1994.

Tardieu, Jean Pierre. "Genio y semblanza del santo varón limeño de origen africano (fray Martín de Porras)." *Hispania Sacra* 15 (1993): 555–74.

———. *Los negros y la Iglesia en el Perú, siglos XVI–XVII*. 2 vols. Quito: Centro Cultural Afroecuatoriano, 1997.

Tausiet, María. *Urban Magic in Early Modern Spain: Abracadabra Omnipotens*. Translated by Susannah Howe. London: Palgrave Macmillan, 2014.

Temkin, Owsei. *Galenism: Rise and Decline of a Medical Philosophy*. Ithaca, NY: Cornell University Press, 1973.

Tennyson, Alfred Lord. *The Works of Alfred Lord Tennyson*. London: Macmillan and Company, 1886.

Teresa de Ávila. *The Interior Castle*. Edited and translated by E. Allison Peers. New York: Doubleday Books, 1961.

———. *Las Moradas*. 2nd ed. Buenos Aires: Espasa-Calpe, 1942.

———. *Libro de la vida*. Barcelona: Penguin Random House, 2015.

———. *The Life of Saint Teresa of Ávila by Herself*. Edited and translated by J. M. Cohen. Harmondsworth: Penguin Books, 1957.

———. *Obras completas*. Edited by Luis Santullano. Madrid: Aguilar, 1957.

Thornton, John. "The Development of an African Catholic Church in the Kingdom of Kongo, 1491–1750." *Journal of African History* 25, no. 2 (1984): 147–67.

Torres-Alcalá, Antonio. "Santa Teresa: Más allá de la palabra." In *Santa Teresa y la literatura mística hispánica*, edited by Manuel Criado del Val, 223–27. Madrid: EDI-6, 1984.

Torres Saldamando, Enrique. *Los antiguos Jesuitas del Perú: Biografías y apuntes para su historia*. Lima: Imprenta Liberal, 1882.

Tribunal de la Inquisición. *Edicto para recoger los cuadernos, retrato, cuentas . . .* Lima: n.p., 1694.

Ursula de Jesús. *The Souls of Purgatory: The Spiritual Diary of a Seventeenth-Century Afro-Peruvian Mystic, Ursula de Jesús*. Edited and translated by Nancy E. van Deusen. Albuquerque: University of New Mexico Press, 2004.

van Deusen, Nancy E. *Between the Sacred and the Worldly: The Institutional and Cultural Practice of Recogimiento in Colonial Lima.* Stanford, CA: Stanford University Press, 2001.

———. "Circuits of Knowledge among Lay and Religious Women in Early Seventeenth-Century Peru." In *Gender, Race and Religion in the Colonization of the Americas,* edited by Nora E. Jaffary, 137–51. Burlington, VT: Ashgate, 2007.

———. "'In So Celestial a Language': Text as Body, Relics as Text." In *Women's Negotiations and Textual Agency in Latin America, 1500–1799,* edited by Mónica Díaz and Rocío Quispe-Agnoli, 62–81. New York: Routledge, 2017.

———. Introduction to *The Souls of Purgatory: The Spiritual Diary of a Seventeenth-Century Afro-Peruvian Mystic, Ursula de Jesús.* Edited and translated by Nancy E. van Deusen, 1–77. Albuquerque: University of New Mexico Press, 2004.

———. "'The Lord Walks among the Pots and Pans': Religious Servants of Colonial Lima." In *Africans to Spanish America: Expanding the Diaspora,* edited by Sherwin Bryant, Rachel O'Toole, and Ben Vinson III, 136–60. Urbana: University of Illinois Press, 2012.

———. "Manifestaciones de la religiosidad femenina del siglo XVII: Las beatas de Lima." *Histórica* 33, no. 1 (1999): 47–78.

———. "Ursula de Jesús: A Seventeenth-Century Afro-Peruvian Mystic." In *Human Tradition in Colonial Latin America,* edited by Kenneth J. Andrien, 88–103. Wilmington, DE: Scholarly Resources, 2002.

Vanhee, Hein. "Central African Popular Christianity and the Making of Haitian Vodou Religion." In *Central Africans and Cultural Transformations in the American Diaspora,* edited by Linda M. Heywood, 243–64. Cambridge: Cambridge University Press, 2002.

Van Whye, Cordula Hildegard. "The Making and Meaning of the Monastic Habit in Spanish Habsburg Courts." In *Early Modern Habsburg Women: Transnational Contexts, Cultural Conflicts, Dynastic Continuities,* edited by Anne J. Cruz and Maria Galli Stampino, 243–75. Farnham: Ashgate, 2013.

Vargas Machuca, Juan de. *La Rosa de el Perú: Soror Isabel de Santa María.* Seville: Juan Gómez de Blas, 1659.

Vargas Ugarte, Rubén. *Historia de la Iglesia en el Perú, 1511–1900.* 5 vols. Lima: Burgos, 1953–62.

———. *Historia del Perú: Virreinato (siglo xviii), 1700–1790.* Lima: n.p., 1956.

———, ed. *Manuscritos peruanos en las bibliotecas y archivos de Europa y América.* Vol. 5. Buenos Aires, n.p., 1947.

———, ed. *Relaciones de viajes (siglos XVI, XVII y XVIII).* Biblioteca Histórica Peruana 5. Lima: Compañía de Impresiones y Publicidad, 1947.

———. *Vida del siervo de Dios, Nicolás Ayllón o por otro nombre Nicolás de Dios, natural de Chiclayo.* Buenos Aires: López, 1960.

———. *Vida de Santa Rosa de Santa María.* 2nd ed. Lima: n.p., 1951.

Vauchez, André. "Lay People's Sanctity in Western Europe: Evolution of a Pattern (Twelfth and Thirteenth Centuries)." In *Images of Sainthood in Medieval Europe,* edited by Renate Blumenfeld-Kosinski and Timea Szell, 21–32. Ithaca, NY: Cornell University Press, 1991.

———. *Sainthood in the Later Middle Ages.* Translated by Jean Birrell. New York: Cambridge University Press, 1997.

Vázquez de Espinosa, Antonio. *Compendio y descripción de las Indias occidentales.* 1630. Washington, DC: Smithsonian Institution, 1948.

Velasco, Sherry. "Teaching Spanish Women Mystics with Theories of Autobiography." In *Approaches to Teaching Teresa of Ávila and the Spanish Mystics,* edited by Alison Weber, 102–6. New York: Modern Language Association of America, 2009.

Vera Tudela, Elisa Sampson. *Colonial Angels: Narratives of Gender and Spirituality in Mexico, 1580–1750.* Austin: University of Texas Press, 2000.

———. "Fashioning a Cacique Nun." *Gender and History* 9, no. 2 (1997): 171–200.

Verboven, Koenraad, Myriam Carlier, and Jan Dumolyn. "A Short Manual to the Art of Prosopography." Department of Modern History at Oxford University. http://prosopography.modhist.ox.ac.uk/images/01%20Verboven%20pdf.pdf. Last accessed on April 14, 2017.

Vergara Ormeño, Teresa. "Migración y trabajo femenino a principios del siglo XVII: El caso de las indias en Lima." *Histórica* 21, no. 1 (1997): 135–57.

Vitz, Evelyn Birge. "From the Oral to the Written in Medieval and Renaissance Saints' Lives." In *Images of Sainthood in Medieval Europe,* edited by Renate Blumenfeld-Kosinski and Timea Szell, 97–114. Ithaca, NY: Cornell University Press, 1991.

Vives, Juan Luis. *Instrucción de la mujer cristiana.* 4th ed. Buenos Aires: Espasa-Calpe, 1948.

Vollendorf, Lisa. *The Lives of Women: A New History of Inquisitional Spain.* Nashville, TN: Vanderbilt University Press, 2005.

von Germeten, Nicole. *Black Blood Brothers: Confraternities and Social Mobility for Afro-Mexicans.* Gainesville: University Press of Florida, 2006.

Vose, Robin. "Beyond Spain: Inquisition History in a Global Context." *History Compass* 11, no. 4 (2013): 316–29.

Vries, Hent de. "Introduction: Why Still Religion?" In *Religion: Beyond a Concept,* edited by Hent de Vries, 1–100. New York: Fordham University Press, 2008.

Walker, Charles. *Shaky Colonialism: The 1746 Earthquake-Tsunami and Its Long Aftermath.* Durham, NC: Duke University Press, 2009.

Warr, Cordelia. *Dressing for Heaven: Religious Clothing in Italy, 1215–1545.* Manchester: Manchester University Press, 2010.

———. "Materiality and Immateriality." *Material Religion* 6, no. 3 (2010): 372–73.

Weber, Alison, ed. *Approaches to Teaching Teresa of Ávila and the Spanish Mystics.* New York: Modern Language Association of America, 2009.

———. "Between Ecstasy and Exorcism: Religious Negotiation in Sixteenth-Century Spain." *Journal of Medieval and Renaissance Studies* 23, no. 2 (1993): 221–34.

———. "Gender." In *The Cambridge Companion to Christian Mysticism,* edited by Amy Hollywood and Patricia Z. Beckman, 315–27. New York: Cambridge University Press, 2012.

———. "Introduction, Devout Laywomen in the Early Modern Catholic World: The

Historiographic Challenge." In *Devout Laywomen in the Early Modern World*, edited by Alison Weber, 1–28. Abingdon, Oxon: Routledge, 2016.

———. *Teresa of Avila and the Rhetoric of Femininity*. Princeton, NJ: Princeton University Press, 1990.

Webster, Susan Verdi. *Art and Ritual in Golden Age Spain: Sevillian Confraternities and the Processional Sculpture of Holy Week*. Princeton, NJ: Princeton University Press, 1998.

———. "Shameless Beauty and Worldly Splendor: On the Spanish Practice of Adorning the Virgin." In *The Miraculous Image in the Late Middle Ages and Renaissance*, edited by Erik Thunø and Gerhard Wolf, 249–72. Rome: L'Erma di Bretschneider, 2004.

Weinstein, Donald, and Rudolph Bell. *Saints and Society: The Two Worlds of Western Christendom, 1000–1700*. Chicago: University of Chicago Press, 1982.

Wiesner-Hanks, Merry E. "Do Women Need the Renaissance?" *Gender and History* 20, no. 3 (2008): 539–57.

White, Hayden. "The Value of Narrativity in the Representation of Reality." *Critical Inquiry* 7, no. 1 (1980): 5–27.

Whitehead, Amy. *Religious Statues and Personhood: Testing the Role of Materiality*. London: Bloomsbury, 2013.

Wisnoski, Alexander, III. "It Is Unjust for the Law of Marriage to Be Broken by the Law of Slavery: Married Slaves and Their Masters in Early Colonial Lima." *Slavery and Abolition* 35, no. 2 (2014): 234–52.

Woolf, Virginia. *A Room of One's Own*. New York: Harcourt Brace Jovanovich, 1957.

Wright, Wendy M. "Inside My Body Is the Body of God: Margaret Mary Alacoque and the Tradition of Embodied Mysticism." In *The Mystical Gesture: Essays on Medieval and Early Modern Spiritual Culture*, edited by Robert Boenig, 185–92. Aldershot, UK: Ashgate, 2000.

Xaimes de Ribera, Juan. *Hazer de si mismo espejo*. Lima: Manuel de los Olivos, 1689.

Yates, Frances A. *The Art of Memory*. New Haven, CT: Yale University Press, 1966.

Zieman, K. "Reading, Singing and Understanding: Constructions of the Literacy of Women Religious in Late Medieval England." In *Learning and Literacy in Medieval England and Abroad*, edited by Sarah Rees Jones, 97–120. Turnhout, Belgium: Brepols Press, 2003.

Ziomek, Henryk. "El uso de las percepciones sensoriales en la obra de Santa Teresa." In *Santa Teresa y la literatura mística hispánica*, edited by Manuel Criado de Val, 67–73. Madrid: EDI-6, 1984.

Index

asceticism, 9, 25

Audiencia, 4, 86, 119, 145, 156–59

Augustine, Saint, 83, 159, 175n6

Augustinians, 5, 17, 61, 71, 73, 75, 123, 144, 199n14; Ángela de Carranza and, 82

Auñon, Don Ramón de, 228n105, 228n108

autobiography, autobiographies, 11–12, 14, 65, 169, 171, 173; of Doña Josefa Portocarrero Laso de la Vega y Urrea, 146, 148, 150, 169; of María Jacinto de Montoya, 121; of Santa Rosa, 64–65

autos, 98, 222n5, 225n62

autos-da-fé, 52, 213n14; of Ángela de Carranza, 74, 90–91, 119, 147

autos de ingreso (entrance petitions), 14, 98, 101, 103, 112, 114

autos de profesión (profession documents), 97

Ávila Tamayo, Pedro de, 119

Ayllón, Nicolás de, 80, 202n85, 215n33, 220n128, 221n137; beatification of, 3, 19, 118–20, 140, 213n11, 214n31, 219n111, 220n128; confessors of, 118, 133, 136, 214n30, 219n109, 220n129; death and funeral of, 123, 127, 212n7, 215n42; images of, 84, 134, 219n117; María Jacinta de Montoya and, 117, 170, 218n98, 220n124; marriage of, 129–30; miracles of, 117, 125–26, 130, 135–36, 215n41, 215n45; mortification practices of, 128, 200n46; relics of, 124; sexuality of, 122, 137, 221n135; supporters of, 213n10, 220n125; *vida* of, 216n63, 222n159; visions of, 127, 132, 136, 202n81, 213n14, 220n124, 220n129

Barreto, Doña Isabel, 85–86

beatas (lay pious women), 5, 37, 71, 97, 177n17, 179n49, 179n51, 180n51, 184n26, 187n56, 190n121, 219n111; Council of Trent and, 5; Dominican, 29, 43; Franciscan, 31, 186n43; habits of, 34–35; Inquisition and, 9, 55, 58, 179n48, 188n78; in Lima, 2, 177n24; mestizas as, 33; Santa Rosa and, 27, 42–43; writing of, 81. *See also specific names of beatas*

Beaterio de Jesús, María y José, 122

Beaterio de las Mercedarias, 91

Beaterio de Nuestra Señora de Copacabana, 219n105

Beaterio de Santa Rosa, 158, 191n135. *See also* Monasterio de Santa Rosa

beaterios (lay pious houses for women), 3, 4, 90, 113, 131–32, 139, 172, 191n134, 214n31, 218n99, 219n111; for indigenous women, 134; in Lima, 219n105

beatification: conventions of, 12; expense of, 118; of Isabel de Porras Marmolejo, 62; of Martín de Porres, 215n33, 220n123; of Nicola de Ayllón, 3, 19, 118–20, 140, 213n11, 214n31, 217n72, 219n111, 220n128; of Pedro Urraca García, 215n33; process of, 13, 120, 219n109, 220n119, 220n122; Rome and, 2, 191n135, 200n41; of Santa Rosa, 16, 26–27, 43, 45, 68. *See also* apostolic process of beatification; diocesan process of beatification

Benedictines, 154, 225n45

Benítez, Juan, 136, 140

Benito de Palermo, Saint, 113

Bible: Genesis, 47; Gospel of Saint Matthew, 167; Song of Songs, 183n3; vernacular, 58

Bilinkoff, Jodi, 8, 178n41

biography, biographies, 11–12, 173, 181n66, 181n69, 192n28, 216n55, 216n62; of Nicolás de Ayllón, 220n128, 222n159; re-creation of, 14; spiritual, 63, 68, 171. *See also* autobiography, autobiographies; hagiography, hagiographies; *vidas*

bishops, 179n48, 217n72. *See also* archbishops of Lima

blacks, 97, 110, 113, 115, 204n2. *See also* Africans and Afro-Peruvians

body, bodies, 50, 59, 194n69, 195n82, 198n131; of Ángela de Carranza, 75–76, 168; of female mystics, 48, 69, 75–76; functions of, 88–89; as living books, 58–62; materiality of, 73; reading of, 47–69, 64; as texts, 16–17, 69; of women, 51, 62–63

Bolivia, 4, 52, 128, 216n63

books, 49, 52–53, 55; bodies as living, 58–62. *See also* texts; *vidas*

God, 17, 23, 27–28, 49–50, 74, 76, 77, 111, 115, 165, 195–96n88, 198n131, 213n13, 218n98, 222–23n7; communication with, 50–51, 56–58, 65, 69, 117, 138; *donadas* and, 102, 112, 114; Grace of, 62; knowledge of, 60; mystics and, 3–4, 12; presence of, 58, 61, 83; union with, 2, 33, 59, 66, 119, 171; will of, 10, 148; the Word and, 47, 50, 103. *See also* divine

Granada, Luis de, 26, 50, 57, 192n17, 194n69, 195n70, 196n101; writings of, 31, 53–54, 56, 58

Granado, Dionisio, 135, 137–39, 156

Gregory XV, Pope, 128

Guamanga, 139

habits and veils, 32, 34–35, 41, 102

hagiography, hagiographies, 2, 14, 53, 55, 56, 57, 181n66, 181n69, 194n55, 201n54; conventions of, 119–20, 126; of Santa Rosa, 29, 43. *See also* biography, biographies; *vidas*

hair shirts and sackcloth, 35, 36, 41–42, 187n69. *See also* mortification practices

Hansen, Leonardo, 26, 39, 216n62

Hapsburg Dynasty, 143, 147, 221n153

healing, healers, 5, 33, 180n59, 181n75; Ángela de Carranza and, 72, 86; miracles of, 11, 40–41, 201n67, 202n94, 215n41; relics and, 10, 79, 85–86, 201n51, 203n101

heresy, 9, 13–14, 90, 117, 179n48, 180n51

hermanas (sisters), 111, 204n2; of Santa Rosa, 26, 186n44

Híjar y Mendoza, Don Ignacio de, 82, 89, 119, 202n73, 214n30, 215n33

hijas espirituales (spiritual daughters), of Santa Rosa, 16, 30

Holy Ghost, Holy Spirit, 48, 67, 76, 78, 82, 87

holy matter. *See* sacred materialities

Holy See, 124, 201n59

Holy Trinity, 86, 119, 141, 180n57, 220n124

holy water, 81, 89

hospitals, 5, 7, 10, 30, 33, 44, 60, 107, 126, 172

Hoyo, José (Joseph) del, 74–75, 91, 199n19

Huamanga, 132

Huaura, 96, 129

Huaylas, 96

humility, 34, 35

hysteria (Freudian), 9

idolatry, 128

Ignatius de Loyola, Saint, 87, 194n69

images, 2, 14, 134, 180n62, 198n145; of devil, 27, 29; Inquisition and, 219n117; of saints, 3, 31, 83–84, 159, 200n41, 226n75. *See also* paintings; statues

imagination, 49–50, 192n16, 194n69

imitatio morum (imitation of ways), 10, 16, 26, 30, 39, 172; Santa Rosa and, 25, 27, 41–43, 44

Immaculate Conception, 39, 60, 102

immateriality, materiality and, 20, 27, 36, 48, 52, 72, 124, 169, 172

incantations, 11

Index Librorum Prohibitorum, 53, 58

indias, 11, 176–77n16, 186n48, 215n45, 218n105, 219n115; as *donadas*, 96, 102, 113–14; limitations on religious life of, 4–5, 204n2; Santa Rosa and, 31–32

indigenous people, Indians, 1, 118, 204n6, 216n63, 217n66, 217n71, 219n114; Christianity and, 99; conversion of, 127; elite, 118, 124, 128; evangelization of, 127; sanctity and, 123–34

Innocent IV, Pope, 154

Innocent XII, Pope, 119

Inquisition, 4, 7–8, 11, 61, 74, 76, 180n57, 181n64, 181n75, 193n46, 213n14, 220n119; Ángela de Carranza and, 71, 73, 75, 82–83, 90, 117, 119, 168, 202n73, 213n14; Augustinians and, 199n14; *beatas* and, 6, 58, 180n51, 188n78; censorship by, 53–55, 66; false mystics and, 52, 55; Inquisitors, 137, 179n48; Isabel de Porras Marmolejo and, 62; María Jacinta de Montoya and, 19, 117–18, 121, 138–39, 170; Nicolás de Ayllón, and, 134–35, 219n117; records of, 9–10, 169, 179n46, 180n60; Santa Rosa and, 27, 55, 65

interioridad (deep internal spiritual contemplation), 10, 48

Irigaray, Luce, 171
Isabel María (slave), 110
Italy, 179n50, 184n26, 216n51, 225n45
Iwasaki Cauti, Fernando, 178n42, 179n49

Jerome, Saint, 87
Jesuits (Society of Jesus), 5, 9, 52, 65, 83,
    124, 128, 132, 144, 148, 213n10, 223n7,
    224n34; in Lima, 53, 126, 179n51;
    Nicolás de Ayllón and, 118–19
Jesús, Ana María, 137
Jesús, Catalina de, 31, 36–37, 177n17, 185n42
Jesús, Felíciana de, 5, 29, 37
Jesús, Juana de, 31
Jesús, Salvador de, 129
Jesús, Úrsula de, 105, 11–14, 211n139; as
    black donada mystic, 52, 59, 97, 115,
    216n60; spiritual diary of, 18, 98, 104,
    115, 126, 173
Jesus Christ, 10, 32, 56–57, 76, 86–87, 89,
    102–3, 175n6, 213n14; as baby and child,
    31, 32, 88, 180n62, 186n52, 190n129; in
    Catholic theology, 50–51; Cross of, 78,
    95–96, 111, 115–16, 149–50, 200n46;
    Crucifixion of, 63; Eucharist and, 1, 84,
    175n1, 175n6; as the Incarnation, 50;
    presence of, 69, 194n69; Santa Rosa and,
    67, 188n93; as Savior, 188n91; suffering
    and Passion of, 9, 36, 58, 76–77, 123;
    visions of, 36, 59, 119, 203n101, 220n124
Jiménez de Urrea Clavero, Doña Antonia
    (mother of Doña Josefa Portocarrero
    Laso de la Vega y Urrea). See Monclova,
    Antonia Jiménez de Urrea, Countess of
John, Saint, 87
John Chrysostom, Saint, 77
John of the Cross, Saint, 50–51, 192n17;
    writings of, 65–66
Joseph, Saint, 87
Jouve Martín, José R., 212n8, 215n33
Julius II, Pope, 102
jus naturae (natural law), 145, 222–23n7

Kelly, Joan, 7
kinship, 5, 107, 108, 111–12
knowledge exchange, 14, 25–26, 45, 169, 172

Ladrón de Guevara, Diego, 144, 152–53,
    156, 162, 220n125, 225n45, 227nn96–97
language, 47–48, 50, 68, 198n138; of God,
    65, 67, 69; of mystical narratives, 62–69,
    198n133
levitation, 62, 68, 171
libertad (freedom of will), 145, 165
libertad de conciencia (freedom of con-
    science), 145
libre albedrío (free will), 143–65
Lima, 54, 118, 127, 158, 179n50, 188n78,
    212n6, 219n109; Ángela de Carranza
    and, 74, 91; beatas and beaterios in, 5,
    177n24, 218–19n105; Cathedral of, 78,
    80, 91, 164, 179n48, 224n31; churches
    in, 37, 42; city council of, 128, 227n87;
    Consulado of, 162; conventual culture
    of, 18; creole sentiment in, 145, 155–56;
    donadas in, 95–116; earthquakes in, 74,
    83, 112, 147, 164, 199n17, 229n115; econ-
    omy of, 74; elites of, 83, 158, 202n94;
    First Council of, 204n2; hagiography
    in, 192n28, 194n55; as holy site, 80;
    hospitals in, 5, 7, 10, 30, 33, 44, 60, 107,
    126, 172; indigenous people of, 96, 99,
    127; Inquisition in, 9, 58, 71, 74, 75, 76;
    Jesuits in, 53, 126, 179n51; as lettered
    city, 125; local heroes of, 141, 164; main
    plaza of, 147, 158–59; migration to, 5,
    107; Monasterio de Santa Rosa and, 156;
    as mystical body of Christian republic,
    1, 89; mystics in, 51–52, 53, 64; neigh-
    borhoods and parishes of, 5, 177n17,
    217n66, 219n105; Nicolás de Ayllón
    and, 118–19, 121, 124, 126; Padrón
    de Indios of, 177n21; piety in, 173,
    175n5, 176n9; population figures of,
    176–77n16, 177n21; printing press in,
    49, 53; prostitutes in, 137; reading habits
    in, 49, 52–58; Real Chancillería of,
    213n10; relics in, 77–79; religious orders
    in, 33, 133; schools in, 62; Second Coun-
    cil of, 204n2; slaves in, 102; spiritual
    conventicles in, 60; statues in, 37; Valley
    of, 124; as viceregal capital, 1–2, 4, 74,
    77; women in, 4, 224n28

Portocarrero Laso de la Vega y Urrea, Doña Inés (Josefa's sister), 146, 153

Portocarrero Laso de la Vega y Urrea, Doña Josefa (Josepha), 140, 171, 222nn5–6, 223n24, 225n61; autobiographical writings of, 146, 148, 150, 169; brothers of, 153, 164; calling of, 223n12, 227n96; death of, 164; father and, 146–48, 158, 228n106; free will and, 143–65; inheritance of, 144, 162, 228n100; as local hero, 164; Monasterio de Santa Catalina and, 224–25n43; Monasterio de Santa Rosa and, 156, 164; mother and, 153, 170; Philip V and, 157, 162–63; Santa Rosa and, 19; visions of, 150; vows of, 161, 224n34, 227n97

Portocarrero Laso de la Vega y Urrea, Doña María Felipa (Josefa's sister), 146, 153

Portocarrero Laso de la Vega y Urrea, Don Francisco Xavier (Josefa's brother), 146

Portocarrero-Urrea family, 144–46

positionality: of *donadas*, 103, 106–7, 112, 115; of self, 170–71

potentia (power), 76, 77

Potosí, 4, 96, 181n75

poverty, 28, 34; vows of, 35, 102, 112

Prado, Joseph de, 82

praesentia (God's presence), 76, 83; of Nicolás de Ayllón, 123–24

prayer, prayers, 26, 61, 66, 148–49, 189n109; books of, 48, 53–55; Hail Mary and Our Father, 39; Santa Rosa's regimen and, 26, 29, 38

priests, 127, 217n71. *See also* confessors

processions, 7, 88; cross carried in, 105; at inauguration of Monasterio de Santa Rosa, 158–59; statues in, 16, 30, 37–41, 44, 159

prophecy, prophets, 5, 123, 213n13

prosopography, 14, 183n106; of *donadas*, 18, 97, 100

public spaces, women in, 7, 29

purgatory, 26, 61, 72, 118, 177n17, 216n47

Quechua, translations of church texts into, 128

Quesada y Sotomayor, Gregorio de, 75, 134–35

Quito, 152, 156

race: racism and, 216n60; taxonomies of, 115

Rappaport, Joanne, 176n13

rapture, raptures, 9–10, 60–61, 64–67; of Isabel de Porras Marmolejo, 62–64, 171

Raymond of Capua, 187n60, 188n78, 192n28

reading, 49, 51, 56; as actualization, 63; in Lima, 52–58; scriptures, 61

Real Audiencia, 145, 162, 226n80

Real Chancillería of Lima, 213n10

Recogimiento de Jesús, María y José, 132

Recogimiento de las Amparadas, 219n109

recogimientos (female institutions of enclosure and education), 4, 113, 123, 131–32, 214n30

relationality, 19, 98, 170–71, 173; definition of, 17–18; of *donadas'* status, 100–101

relics, 3, 14, 17, 26, 77, 79; Ángela de Carranza and, 76–77, 82, 84, 86, 91; consecration of churches and, 200n47; contact, 14, 17, 30, 43, 77–78; corporeal, 77; healing and, 201n51, 203n101; of Nicolás de Ayllón, 124; organs as, 200n37; paintings as, 202n81; in Lima, 77–78; of Santa Rosa, 80; as texts, 169. *See also* reliquaries

religion: reconceptualization of, 168; supernatural and, 10–11

religious orders, 5, 100–101, 120

reliquaries, 17, 79, 80, 200n47; Ángela de Carranza as, 71–92, 168; of Santa Rosa, 159

Retes, María de, 110

Reyes, Ana de los, 186n44, 190n115

Reyes, Melchora de los, 112–13

Ricoeur, Paul, 51

Rímac River, 177n17

Rios, Augustina de los, 112

Rios, Pablo de, 112

Roa, Martín de, 83

Roch, Saint, 88

Rojas, María de, 114

Rome, 78, 220n129; beatification and, 2, 13; Sacred Congregation of Rites in, 80, 118–19

Rosa de Lima (Santa), 5, 17, 35, 66, 78, 81, 121, 127, 172, 181n78, 186n48; acquaintances of, 185–86n43, 185n37, 185n39; adorns images, 189n107, 189n109, 198n138; autobiography of, 55, 64–65, 67; beatification of, 26–27, 32, 61–62, 80, 168, 188n91, 189n109, 191n135, 202n81; canonization of, 19, 52, 123, 156, 214n33, 220n129; Catherine of Siena and, 36, 38, 187n75, 188n78; cell of, 30, 33, 43, 183n4, 186n43, 187n56; confessors of, 35, 41, 64, 178n42, 180n51, 183n1, 185n39; converted "lost" women, 177n25, 184n9; death of, 41–42, 190n115, 190n121, 190n130; disciples of, 16, 25, 28, 30–32, 37–38, 44, 96–97, 168, 171, 186n44; Doña Josefa Portocarrero Laso de la Vega y Urrea and, 148–49, 163; hagiographies of, 26, 39, 43, 216n62; images of, 44, 124, 159, 200n41; *imitatio morum* and, 23–45; Jesus Christ and, 186n52, 188n93; Lima and, 144, 212n6; miracles of, 11, 43, 190n129; mortification practices of, 32, 35–37, 40–42, 171, 185n28, 188n82; Nicolás de Ayllón and, 136; paintings of, 23–25, 183n1; relics and reliquaries of, 79–80, 85, 159; as role model, 5–6, 43, 55, 164; as saint, 30, 144, 165; Teresa de Ávila and, 64–65; as text, 48; visions of, 62, 67

Rosary, 57, 60, 148, 149, 203n101; rosary beads and, 72, 86–87

Ruíz, Juan, 63

sacred: feminine knowledge of, 10; senses and, 167–68, 173

Sacred Congregation for the Propagation of the Faith, 128

sacred materialities and objects, 3, 14, 20, 26

sacred spaces, 4, 7, 112, 124

sacred texts, 25–26

saints, 12, 13, 29, 43, 53, 64, 78, 113, 123, 176n7, 199n14, 199n17, 201n59, 212nn6–7; days of, 87; emulation of, 52–53, 56; images and statues of, 3, 28, 37–41, 83–84, 124, 159, 226n75; miracles and, 11, 13. *See also* relics; *vidas; and names of individual saints*

San Cristóbal, María de, 106

sanctity, 68, 121–22, 138; fragrance of, 85, 136; Indianness and, 123–34; models of, 113–14

San Francisco, Gerónima de, 11, 17, 52, 57–58, 60, 64, 65; Teresa de Ávila and, 48–50; *vida* of, 13, 85–86, 172

San Francisco, María de, 101–2, 110

San Joseph, Catalina de, 106

San Joseph (José), Estefanía de, 33, 35, 172

San Joseph, María de, 107

San Lázaro parish, 5, 177n17, 217n66

San Lorenso, Juana de, 131

San Marcelo parish, 82, 119

Santa María, Catalina de, 29, 35–36, 42; Santa Rosa and, 27, 29, 61–62, 187n56

Santa María, Luisa de, 185n27; Santa Rosa and, 33, 41, 185n39, 186n44, 189n107, 190n115

Santa Rosa. *See* Rosa de Lima

Santíssima Trinidad, Lucía de la, 31, 65, 187n69

Santíssima Trinidad, María Jacinta de la. *See* Montoya, María Jacinta de

Santo Buono, Carmine Nicolao Caracciolo, Prince of, 163

Sartolo, Bernardo, 130–32, 136–37, 212n7, 213n14, 221n135; *vida* of Nicolás de Ayllón by, 118–21, 125–26, 135, 138, 213n10, 213n12, 220n128

Schlau, Stacey, 14

Schneider, Jane, 30

scriptures, 61. *See also* Bible

Sejas, Juana de, 105

senses, 49; Ángela de Carranza and, 72–73; discovering divinity through, 41, 47–48; divine worship and, 28–29; ecstasy and, 195n84; intellective soul and, 195n88; internal, 49, 59; learning process and,

Valera, Francisco, 75–76
Vargas Ugarte, Rubén, 31–32, 121, 135,
    164, 186n44, 190n121, 199n2, 222n159,
    227n87
Vatican, 13, 128
Vázquez, Don Juan, 156
Vázquez de Velasco, Don Pablo, 145, 156,
    225n58, 228n98
Velasco, Inés de, 55, 56, 64, 65, 193n46,
    197n122
Velásquez, Catalina, 110
Vera Tudela, Elisa Sampson, 123
viceroys of Peru, 19, 73, 119, 132, 214n31,
    220n125, 226n80, 227n83, 227n87; arch-
    bishops vs., 158; interim, 144–45, 162;
    Count of Monclova, 143, 147; Marquis
    de Castell-dos-Rius, 145, 151, 157–59;
    Prince Santo Buono, 163; *residencia* of,
    162
vidas (life writings), 8, 29, 38, 53, 58, 59,
    181n66, 181n68, 181n78, 213n11; con-
    ventions of, 12–13; as genre, 11–12; of
    Gerónima de San Francisco, 13, 48; of
    Nicolás de Ayllón, 118–19, 125–26, 126,
    213n10; of Santa Rosa, 39, 45; as sources,
    169
Vincent Ferrer, Saint, 77
Virgin Mary, 58, 103; Ángela de Carranza
    and, 76, 82, 86–87; appeals to, 10; Com-
    munion and, 87; as divine book, 50, 59;
    donadas and, 114; in *donadas'* vows, 102;
    Josefa and, 148; life of, 57; paintings
    of, 202n84; Santa Rosa and, 39; statues
    of, 28, 30, 189n109; symbols of, 183n3;
    visions of, 119, 132. *See also* "Our Lady
    of" entries

virtues, 12, 13, 213n13
virtus (divine energy), 42, 44, 76, 168; in
    cloth, 27, 30, 40
visionaries, 64–66, 71, 113, 122, 127, 140;
    female, 48, 60–61; Inquisition and, 52,
    62
visions, 9, 58, 60–61, 66–67, 97, 138, 150,
    193n46, 198n147, 213n14, 216n47; of
    Ángela de Carranza, 72–73, 76, 82, 86,
    88, 90, 119, 141, 202n73, 212n8, 220n124;
    of Nicolás de Ayllón, 132, 136, 202n81
Viveros, Doña Aldonsa de, 102
Vives, Juan Luis, 54, 57
vocation, religious, 143, 155
vows (*votos*), 35, 151–56, 165, 187n75,
    224n32, 224n34; of *donadas*, 95, 101–2,
    110, 112; of Doña Josefa Portocarrero
    Laso de la Vega y Urrea, 145, 161,
    227n97; nullification of, 157, 160
Vries, Hent de, 168

War of the Spanish Succession, 156, 163,
    221n153
Whitehead, Amy, 16
women: bodies of, 62–63; of color, 14,
    31, 33, 115, 186n48, 218n105; economic
    strategies of, 4, 6, 28, 180n64; education
    of, 4, 11, 62; elite, 6, 11, 62, 74, 106–7,
    145, 165, 184n9; fallen, 177n25, 219n109;
    in Lima, 4, 5, 7, 224n28; as mystics, 2,
    3–4, 133; orthodoxy and, 9, 179n46;
    reading and writing and, 54, 138, 181n68,
    181n78, 197n110; religion and, 2, 8, 170,
    176–77n16; Santa Rosa and, 30–31;
    Spanish, 4, 31; spirituality of, 3, 51, 171,
    167, 178n42, 179n50